Making Strategy Count in the Health and Human Services Sector

Michael Mortell, MS, is director of the Strategy Counts Initiative at the Alliance for Children and Families. This $5.3 million grant to the Alliance by The Kresge Foundation is a multiyear project with 20 pilot sites that serves as a learning lab for accelerating the transformation of the nonprofit human services sector toward greater impact by elevating the role of strategy. Mortell came to the Alliance after directing a $5.1 million Workforce Innovation in Regional Economic Development (WIRED) grant for the Greater Milwaukee Committee, where he designed and launched the Innovation Fund to provide seed funding for regional partnerships and projects to enhance southeastern Wisconsin's economic competitiveness. For 10 years prior to this role, he oversaw operations across the multiple locations of a 12-agency human services partnership. As a senior member of the American Society for Quality, he has served as an examiner with a state-level Baldrige-based process promoting performance excellence. Mortell earned a master's degree in industrial organizational psychology and has additional training in Lean Six Sigma, organizational culture, and real-time strategic change.

Tine Hansen-Turton, MGA, JD, is the chief strategy officer of Public Health Management Corporation, one of the largest health and human services nonprofit organizations in Pennsylvania, where she oversees and leads corporate strategy, business development, mergers and acquisitions, and operations for a national leading public health institute and its public health foundation, generating annual revenues in excess of $300 million. She has direct oversight over 70% of the organization. Hansen-Turton also serves as the founding executive director for the Convenient Care Association (CCA), the national trade association of over 1,450 private-sector retail clinics, serving 20 million people with basic health care services across the country. Additionally, she serves as CEO of the National Nursing Centers Consortium (NNCC), a nonprofit organization supporting the growth and development of over 500 nurse-managed health centers serving more than 2.5 million vulnerable people across the country in urban and rural locations. Hansen-Turton is known as a serial social entrepreneur who has started several national social and public innovations in the health and human services sector. For the past two decades she has also been instrumental in positioning nurse practitioners as primary health care providers globally. Hansen-Turton received her BA from Slippery Rock University, her master's in government/public administration from the University of Pennsylvania Fels Institute, and her JD from the Temple University Beasley School of Law.

Making Strategy Count in the Health and Human Services Sector

Lessons Learned From 20 Organizations and Chief Strategy Officers

Michael Mortell
Tine Hansen-Turton
Editors

ALLIANCE™
for Children & Families

SPRINGER PUBLISHING COMPANY
NEW YORK

Springer Publishing Company, LLC
11 West 42nd Street
New York, NY 10036
www.springerpub.com

Acquisitions Editor: Stephanie Drew
Production Editor: Shelby Peak
Composition: Amnet

ISBN: 978-0-8261-2975-8
e-book ISBN: 978-0-8261-2982-6

13 14 15 16 / 5 4 3 2 1

The author and the publisher of this Work have made every effort to use sources believed to be reliable to provide information that is accurate and compatible with the standards generally accepted at the time of publication. The author and publisher shall not be liable for any special, consequential, or exemplary damages resulting, in whole or in part, from the readers' use of, or reliance on, the information contained in this book. The publisher has no responsibility for the persistence or accuracy of URLs for external or third-party Internet websites referred to in this publication and does not guarantee that any content on such websites is, or will remain, accurate or appropriate.

Library of Congress Cataloging-in-Publication Data

Making strategy count in the health and human services sector / Michael Mortell & Tine Hansen-Turton, editors.
   p. ; cm.
Includes bibliographical references and index.
ISBN 978-0-8261-2975-8 (print : alk. paper) — ISBN 978-0-8261-2982-6 (e-book)
I. Mortell, Michael, editor of compilation. II. Hansen-Turton, Tine, editor of compilation.
[DNLM: 1. Health Services—United States. 2. Organizations, Nonprofit—United States. 3. Health Care Sector—United States. 4. Health Planning—United States. 5. Health Planning Organizations—United States. 6. Pilot Projects—United States. W 84 AA1]
RA445
362.10973—dc23

2013032538

Printed in the United States of America by McNaughton & Gunn.

This book is dedicated in memory of Peter B. Goldberg. The Strategy Counts initiative was conceived by Peter while he served as president and CEO of the Alliance for Children and Families, because he saw the tremendous potential for the human services sector to achieve even more impact through strategy.

Strategy Counts was one of many contributions Peter made to the nonprofit field. He saw it begin to take shape with support from The Kresge Foundation, and was actively engaged in the initial planning until his unexpected passing on August 12, 2011. This book, and the fruits of this endeavor, stem from the insight and passion that Peter had for the entire nonprofit human services sector.

Contents

Contributors

Francine Axler, MPH
Senior Research Associate
Public Health Management Corporation
Philadelphia, Pennsylvania

Michael Bedrosian, BSE
Managing Director, Information Systems
Public Health Management Corporation
Philadelphia, Pennsylvania

Joseph Benamati, EdD, MSW
Senior Faculty
Sanctuary Institute, ANDRUS
Yonkers, New York

Richard Benoit, LEED, AP
Workplace Consultant, Advanced Solutions Team
Steelcase
Philadelphia, Pennsylvania

Jim Bettendorf, BS
Chief Strategy Officer
Volunteers of America of Minnesota
Minneapolis, Minnesota

Sandra L. Bloom, MD
Associate Professor
Drexel University
Philadelphia, Pennsylvania

Archana Bodas LaPollo, MPH
Senior Research Associate
Public Health Management Corporation
Philadelphia, Pennsylvania

David Bonbright, BA, JD
Chief Executive
Keystone Accountability
London, UK

Nancy Bradberry, BA
Co-owner
Bradberry & Kheradi
Wayne, Pennsylvania

Anne Callan, MPH, CPH
Senior Strategy Manager
Public Health Management Corporation
Philadelphia, Pennsylvania

Elizabeth Carey, BASW, MSW
Executive Vice President and Chief Strategy and Administrative Services Officer
Starr Commonwealth
Albion, Michigan

Rose Chapman, MSW, LCSW
Chief Executive Officer
Jewish Family and Children's Service of Sarasota-Manatee, Inc.
Sarasota, Florida

Richard Cohen, PhD
President and CEO
Public Health Management Corporation
Philadelphia, Pennsylvania

Maria Cristalli, MPH
Chief Strategy and Quality Officer
Hillside Family of Agencies
Rochester, New York

Amanda Dahlquist, MA
Research Associate
Alliance for Children and Families
Milwaukee, Wisconsin

Daniel L. Daly, MA, PhD
Executive Vice President and Director Youth Care
Father Flanagan's Boys' Home
Boys Town, Nebraska

Susan Dreyfus, BS
President and CEO
Families International
Milwaukee, Wisconsin

Nina Esaki, PhD, MBA, MSW
Director of Research
Sanctuary Institute, ANDRUS
Yonkers, New York

Amy Friedlander, MBA
CEO
Council for Relationships
Philadelphia, Pennsylvania

Richard Graziano, BS, MA
President/CEO
The Village Network
Smithville, Ohio

Christina Gullo, BA, MSW, MBA
Chief Executive Officer
Villa of Hope
Rochester, New York

Tine Hansen-Turton, MGA, JD
Chief Strategy Officer
Public Health Management Corporation
Philadelphia, Pennsylvania

Guillermina Hernandez-Gallegos, BS, MPA, PhD
Program Director
The Kresge Foundation
Troy, Michigan

Vincent Hillyer, MSW
President
Great Circle
Saint Louis, Missouri

John Hollingsworth, BA, MBA
Director of Communications
Starr Commonwealth
Albion, Michigan

Laura M. Hopson, PhD, MSSW
Assistant Professor
University of Alabama
Tuscaloosa, Alabama

Victoria L. Hummer, LCSW
Director of Trauma Services
Crisis Center of Tampa Bay
Tampa Bay, Florida

John Jeanetta, MBA, MSW
President and CEO
Heartland Family Service
Omaha, Nebraska

Timothy Johnstone, BS, MBA
Chief Strategy Officer
Hopelink
Redmond, Washington

Ellen Katz, MA, MBA
President and CEO
The Children's Home of Cincinnati
Cincinnati, Ohio

Jennifer Keith, MPH, CPH
Research Associate
Public Health Management Corporation
Philadelphia, Pennsylvania

Lisa R. Kleiner, BS, MSS, JD
Senior Research Associate
Public Health Management Corporation
Philadelphia, Pennsylvania

Lynne Kotranski, PhD
Managing Director
Public Health Management Corporation
Philadelphia, Pennsylvania

Elizabeth Kunde, BA
Communications Specialist
Alliance for Children and Families
Milwaukee, Wisconsin

Donald Layden Jr., JD
Attorney
Quarles & Brady
Milwaukee, Wisconsin

Alex Lehr O'Connell, MPH, CPH
Director, Technical Assistance and Consultation
Public Health Management Corporation
Philadelphia, Pennsylvania

Marilyn Mason-Plunkett, MS, MBA, JD
CEO
Hopelink
Redmond, Washington

Jennifer S. Middleton, PhD, LCSW
Assistant Professor
University of Maine
Orono, Maine

Michael Mortell, MS
Director, Strategy Counts
Alliance for Children and Families
Milwaukee, Wisconsin

Kathleen O'Brien, BS, MSW
Chief Strategy Officer
Great Circle
Saint Louis, Missouri

Dave Paxton, MA, MSM
Chief Strategy Officer
The Village Network
Smithville, Ohio

Laura T. Pinsoneault, MS
Director, Evaluation and Research Services
Alliance for Children and Families
Milwaukee, Wisconsin

Alex Reed, BEE
Chief Strategy Officer
Eckerd
Clearwater, Florida

Denise Roberts, BA
Consultant
Jewish Family and Children's Service of Sarasota-Manatee, Inc.
Sarasota, Florida

Rebecca M. Robuck, MPA, MSW
Senior Associate
ChildFocus, Inc.
Washington, DC

Greg Ryan, MS, MA
Chief Strategy Officer
Heartland Family Service
Omaha, Nebraska

Shannon Starkey-Taylor, BA, MSW, MEd
Vice President of Strategic Development
The Children's Home of Cincinnati
Cincinnati, Ohio

Barbara Vollmer, BA, MA
Vice President of Strategy and Youth Care Administration
Father Flanagan's Boys' Home
Boys Town, Nebraska

Glenn Wilson, MS, MEd
Chief Strategy and Innovation Officer
Holy Family Institute
Pittsburgh, Pennsylvania

Patricia Winsten, BA, MS
President
Miller Winsten Communications
Bonita Springs, Florida

Sarah Yanosy, LCSW
Director
Sanctuary Institute, ANDRUS
Yonkers, New York

Foreword

Susan Dreyfus, BS

President and CEO
Families International
Milwaukee, Wisconsin

Every day across America, nonprofit human services organizations carry on some of our society's most important work—equipping people with the tools to improve their lives. In the aftermath of the Great Recession that started in 2007, these organizations are challenged to work not just harder, but also *smarter*. With client rolls swollen and finances sliced, nonprofits need to transcend old patterns of doing business to pioneer program innovations, secure new sources of funding, and leverage new partnerships. But in today's "do more with less" environment, where can they find the time, support, and intellectual capital necessary to engineer these essential strategic breakthroughs?

Enter Strategy Counts, an initiative to elevate the role of strategy across the sector. Funded by a generous investment from The Kresge Foundation and conceived and implemented by the Alliance for Children and Families, Strategy Counts engaged a cohort of 20 pilot agencies as pathfinders in hardwiring strategy into their operations. Today, after 18 months of intensive connectivity and shared leadership among these organizations, we are proud to publish *Making Strategy Count in the Health and Human Services Sector* to present the early lessons of this groundbreaking initiative.

We extend our sincere thanks to The Kresge Foundation for being an engaged partner on Strategy Counts, as well as to project director Michael Mortell of the Alliance for his leadership of the program.

Strategy Counts is just one example of how the Alliance for Children and Families acts as an essential "radar" for the sector, anticipating local agencies' emerging needs from its vantage point as a national network of more than 500 human services and community development organizations. Our mission is not just to detect the trends of the future, but also to equip our members—and, by sharing widely, the entire sector—with bona fide answers to their most pressing challenges and opportunities.

America's nonprofit human-serving organizations are social and economic engines and a critical part of the fabric of vibrant and productive communities. America can realize its fullest potential only if these organizations continue to develop their capacities as high-impact organizations. We are proud to be part of a movement that is shaping our future as a nation.

Foreword

Guillermina Hernandez-Gallegos, BS, MPA, PhD

Program Director
The Kresge Foundation
Troy, Michigan

At The Kresge Foundation, we work to expand opportunities for low-income people in America's cities. Our human services program advances that goal through efforts to strengthen organizations that are committed to improving the quality of life and economic security of vulnerable people. None of these are small tasks.

But as stewards of a philanthropic organization created by a man who aspired to "promote human progress," we have developed strategies for deploying resources where we believe they will be most effective. Membership organizations such as the Alliance for Families and Children are, we believe, among those places.

These organizations know their members and are well positioned to propose actions that can help human services agencies help individuals and families lead self-sufficient, self-determined, and productive lives.

In 2011, we made a 4-year, $5 million–plus commitment to an Alliance plan to enhance human services agencies' ability to adapt and refine their own strategies.

Among the goals are producing human services organizations that can better serve families and better manage through challenging economic times, as well as giving rise to a new understanding of what approaches and changes are most likely to improve such agencies' effectiveness.

We're pleased to pause and examine some results near midpoint.

In *Making Strategy Count in the Health and Human Services Sector*, the Alliance for Children and Families and its Strategy Counts initiative pilot sites deepen our understanding of how human services organizations—from different parts of the country and with varying histories, cultures, and missions—respond during times of transition.

Here, contributors share real stories from a bottom-up perspective about hiring and integrating chief strategy officers and implementing transformational projects. They describe practical responses to shrinking resources, increasing demands for services and accountability, changing demographics, and the growing need to heed constituents' voices.

The book connects fundamental organizational abilities and strategy, including the role of data in driving change. Strategy, it is clear, must be diffused throughout an organization. Strategy is about making choices, about learning and then sharing that learning within the organization as well as with partners.

Too often, we human services professionals have relied on traditional approaches that "fix" situations for people rather than partnering with clients to develop practices that promote wellness and progress. And in doing so we have learned that external fixes don't last long.

Taking the role of partner rather than of fixer requires a different way of thinking. We need to tap into clients' talents to come up with the best solutions. Our role is to support people on their journeys, recognizing that solutions can be vastly different even when people are dealing with similar issues.

We hope you will take away a deeper understanding of how organizations and leaders can become more adaptive and learn to create a learning community.

We hope that you, too, will be inspired by the courage the authors—our colleagues in the field—display each day as they make tough choices in a time of uncertainty and guide their organizations' efforts to help chart better futures for children and their families.

Preface

The Strategy Counts initiative of the Alliance for Children and Families is a multiyear pilot project designed to enhance the social impact of nonprofit human services organizations by increasing their focus on strategy and its effective deployment.

Research conducted by the Alliance for Children and Families in preparation for the Strategy Counts project shows that within human services organizations, strategic issues frequently take a back seat to program development, day-to-day operations, managing ongoing changes in the regulatory environment, and the pursuit of new sources of revenue. Consequently, organizations may not be investing in or prioritizing the areas in which they have the greatest impact.

Launched in May 2011, Strategy Counts is supported by a $5.375 million grant to the Alliance by The Kresge Foundation. "Creating opportunity for low-income people is a hallmark of our work at The Kresge Foundation," says President Rip Rapson. "Our programs reflect the inflection points where we think we can actually make a difference in the life trajectories of people who are poor, disadvantaged, or underserved in fundamental ways."

This initiative serves as a pilot project and learning laboratory to explore the role of strategy *as one of those key inflection points*. As Alliance members begin to see and enhance their role in addressing root causes of poverty and other societal challenges, the Strategy Counts initiative serves as a lab for accelerating the transformation of the nonprofit human services sector toward impact and results.

By determining the impact of elevating strategy in 20 pilot organizations, Strategy Counts has sought to identify and evaluate the tools and methods that have the greatest potential to enhance the capacity of nonprofits to more effectively anticipate emerging market forces and adapt strategies to meet those changes and improve the lives of children, adults, and families.

THE CASE FOR STRATEGY COUNTS

The literature indicates that recognition of the power of being strategic is not new to nonprofit management. Studies conducted as early as 2001 stated:

> The nonprofits . . . that experienced the greatest gains in capacity were those that undertook a reassessment of their aspirations—their vision of what the organization was attempting to accomplish . . . their strategy. (McKinsey & Company, 2001, p. 15)

What is newer is discussion and inquiry concerning whether the successful implementation of long-term strategies, which has largely remained in the domain of the chief executive officer (CEO), may be severely limited without either a full-time executive champion for strategy or an organizationwide transformational initiative creating strategic perspective throughout all operating units of an organization.

Like their for-profit counterparts, CEOs of high-performing nonprofits are challenged to meet today's escalating and often competing demands. Faced with funding pressures, accountability demands, expanding operating environments, shifting market priorities, the nuances and intricacies of interorganizational relationships, and the management of multidimensional organizational structures, the nonprofit CEO is increasingly challenged to attend to innovation and is frequently unavailable to ensure that strategy is executed consistently across all departments and line functions of the agency.

Interviews conducted with 45 Alliance CEOs during the planning phase for this project revealed four significant conclusions:

1. In nonprofit organizations, strategy frequently takes a back seat to program development, day-to-day operations, managing ongoing changes in the regulatory environment, and the pursuit of new sources of revenue.
2. Nonprofit CEOs have experienced limited success in the elevation of strategy to a level at which it has a decisive and considerable effect on outcomes.
3. CEOs perceive the most significant obstacles to the elevation of strategy to be a strong cultural and historic focus on funding programs rather than on management capacity.
4. More substantial information and data on the return on investment and benefits of the elevation of strategy will be critically important to supporting any organization pursuing cultural change or transformational initiatives to enhance the role of strategy in its agencies.

In a study conducted by McKinsey in 2006 in which researchers tapped the strategic planning concerns of over 800 executives, only 36% said that their strategic plans were meaningfully integrated with their human resources and processes, and only 56% said that their companies tracked the execution of strategic initiatives. In other words, the planning was done and the plans existed, but they were not aligned with day-to-day operations to the extent that they drove and defined organizational priorities.

In our interviews, all but a few executives worried or recognized that their strategic planning efforts would require significant changes or enhancement to become well aligned or integrated with the achievement of their agency's highest priorities.

A Nonprescriptive Approach

The Kresge Foundation supported further exploration of the role of strategy and its effective deployment by the Alliance by funding the Strategy Counts initiative. The 4-year project launched in May 2011 would have 20 pilot sites, a cohort learning community, and disseminated findings.

In the spirit of serving as a learning lab, the initiative did not impose a specific approach or require all pilot sites to begin from a common starting point. Rather, we recognized that organizations would be at different stages in the cycle of strategy development and implementation. Instead, we have made an effort to not be prescriptive in either defining or ruling out specific activities as organizations build on the progress they have achieved to date.

The Strategy Counts initiative was designed to identify pilot sites that would demonstrate repeatable approaches for developing and deploying strategy into operations. A key activity during the implementation at the various pilot sites involves looking across the sites to glean and distill the principles. This book is one avenue for sharing the insights at the midpoint of the project.

20 Pilot Sites

The first 15 pilot sites began their Strategy Counts projects in January 2012, and the remaining 5 pilot sites started in January 2013. To competitively select the pilot sites, the Alliance released a request for proposals (RFP) in August 2011 seeking nonprofit human services organizations to serve as pilot sites for the Strategy Counts initiative.

Applicants chose between two project types, both of which involved strategy development and its effective deployment. Pilot sites would either employ a chief strategy officer (CSO) or conduct a transformational project. The CSO's responsibilities and activities were to be clearly directed at the elevation of strategy as a means of building organizational capacity to produce a decisive and considerable impact on the organization's most important outcomes for the clients and communities served. An effective transformational project was described as *a catalyst to change the organization for the longer term.*

Nine pilot sites were selected to begin CSO projects in January 2012. Each CSO project was awarded a total of up to $237,000 for the 3-year period. Five transformational projects were selected to begin in January 2012, and a second RFP in August 2012 identified an additional five transformational projects to begin in January 2013. Each transformational project was awarded a total of up to $100,000 for a period of between 18 and 24 months. The RFP required agencies to provide a minimum match of 50% of their total grant. The Kresge Foundation, in awarding the Strategy Counts grant to the Alliance in 2011, included the Alliance as a pilot site, bringing the total to 20.

There was great interest in the Strategy Counts project by Alliance members. During the first RFP process, an Intent to Apply was received from 112 organizations, and 73 Alliance members submitted proposals. Thirty-eight members applied to become one of the nine chief strategy officer projects, and 35 members applied to become one of the five transformational project pilot sites. During the second RFP process, we received an Intent to Apply from 98 organizations, and 72 Alliance members submitted proposals applying to become one of the five transformational project pilot sites.

Chief Strategy Officer Projects

Within Strategy Counts pilot sites, the CSO position reports directly to the CEO, and the CSO role is dedicated to advancing strategy within the organization. The role of CSO is a relatively new management concept that has established its value over the past decade within the for-profit sector. Fueled by the necessity of managing today's complex, dynamic business environments, the CSO has emerged as an important force in executing both short-term strategy and long-term vision. Though the CEO and board retain ultimate responsibility for setting strategy, the CSO serves as the centralized position for integrating knowledge into planning and strategy into operations. As a facilitator between the executive suite and the business units, the corporate CSO serves an important and vital role within the organization, responsible for ensuring that there is shared alignment around the vision and operationalizing strategy to achieve it.

Though the position is less common in nonprofits, the chief strategy officer can offer human services agencies the same benefit and results obtained by companies in the for-profit sector: a focus on strategy that leads to greater organizational impact, enhanced revenues, and a sustainable future. Interviews conducted with six current nonprofit CSOs[1] during the planning phase of this project revealed that those member agencies realized some very tangible results, including the following:

---

[1]Not all executives interviewed carried the formal title of CSO, but these six were singled out as senior executives solely responsible for elevating strategy within their organizations.

- They narrowed core services, focused their organizations' efforts, and attracted more funding.
- They identified better benchmarks for results.
- They put their agencies in better positions to make data-driven proposals and decisions.
- They reduced drifting from strategic goals—when goals were not achieved, clear reasons were given and new goals were mapped.
- They developed their agencies' first comprehensive strategies.
- They developed strategic responses to avert major budget crises.

As the literature suggests, there are three specific roles a CSO can undertake to affect successful strategy execution in high-performing nonprofits. These roles were all identified in some fashion by the six agencies reporting dedicated senior leadership positions focusing on strategy:

1. *Securing commitment to existing strategic plans.* As a 2007 *Harvard Business Review* article said, CSOs "resolve strategy . . . clarify it for themselves and for every business unit and function, ensuring that all employees understand the details of the strategic plan and how their work connects to corporate goals" (Breene, Nunes, & Shill, 2007).
2. *Creating the right changes to implement strategy and achieve results.* As the CEO's eyes and ears on the ground, the CSO has the authority and autonomy to test whether the operational decisions being made on a daily basis are in fact aligned with the organization's strategy and achieving the results envisioned by the board and senior leadership. Where they are not, the CSO is empowered to create new systems, innovate services, and implement structures that will support strategy and promote success.
3. *Facilitating ongoing strategy development.* In addition to leading formalized strategic planning processes within the organization, the CSO assumes the role of continuously challenging the assumptions underpinning a chosen strategy. By keeping in mind the long view in tandem with the pragmatic, and overlaying global trends onto both, the CSO effectively builds knowledge, assesses advantages, constructs opportunities for continuous improvement, and identifies viable options for long-term growth and sustainability.

Transformational Projects

By design, preparing a proposal to fund a transformational project was different from other funding opportunities that an agency might commonly pursue, such as bidding to provide a direct service for a specific population. While some direct services start and stop depending on funding cycles, the transformational project was viewed as a catalyst for providing enduring change. Rather than being at the periphery of the organization as some programs are, the transformational project was to be at the core of the organization and would seek to involve the whole organization.

Each transformational project would be developed to fit the specific agency's needs. Our overall approach was to be nonprescriptive, recognizing that organizations would be at various stages in the cycle of strategy development and implementation. We hoped that sites would build upon the experience and progress they had made to date. Thus, we have not been requiring all sites to restart with a set of assessments that would inform the next steps.

Each agency was encouraged to engage in dialogue, discernment, and even debate to strengthen the design of their transformational project. We provided a line of questions that could help an organization begin to formulate a transformational project, including the following:

What would it take to transform our organization into one that

- Further elevates the role of strategy?
- Expands our long-term view?
- Operates in a more proactive manner?
- Aligns operations with the core mission of our organization?
- Enhances our ability to make data-driven decisions?
- Engages and brings an understanding of and level of ownership for our mission and strategy to our mid-level and direct service staff?
- Increases focus on meaningful client and community impact?
- Helps us see our role, directly or indirectly, in poverty reduction?

An effective transformational project should also diffuse responsibility for strategy throughout multiple levels of the organization. Within that scope, we expected that significant cultural change would need to occur through a formalized, facilitated process so that across the organization, from the board downward, there would be greater understanding, ownership, and empowerment to contribute to strategy development, implementation, and refinement.

The projects were likely to use a variety of methods for driving culture change and elevating strategy throughout the whole organization, including organizational assessments, training, executive coaching, mentoring, utilization-focused evaluation activities, and technical assistance.

The Cohort Learning Group

The pilot projects were established to contribute a new depth of understanding about the role of strategy in nonprofit organizations and to add to our knowledge those tools and methods that have the greatest potential to enhance the resilience and effectiveness of organizations that share our mission to improve the lives of children and families.

A cohort learning group of all the pilot sites is one way we are accelerating the development of transferrable models and expanding the knowledge base to the wider Alliance membership and industry. All pilot project sites have been participating in the cohort learning group facilitated by the Alliance, which is designed to

- Identify and share successes and challenges facing the pilot project participants in their efforts to elevate strategy
- Discuss resolutions to issues that emerge in the pilot sites
- Identify the organizational cultural changes that are occurring, as well as how they are being managed throughout the organization
- Consider the impact on the individuals and communities served by the organizations
- Prepare for and participate in formal presentations of successful practices deployed and lessons learned
- Synthesize the challenges and successes of the piloting experience
- Compile a set of best practices for nonprofits that will help enhance the effectiveness of future initiatives

In addition to joining in periodic conference calls, sharing status updates, and connecting individually across the sites, members of this group convene for a 2- to 3-day in-person meeting each year and gather as a cohort within the annual Alliance National Conference.

THE PURPOSE OF *MAKING STRATEGY COUNT*

Making Strategy Count in the Health and Human Services Sector will show readers how the health and human services welfare agencies continue to use strategy to achieve long-term social impact in communities across the United States with the goal of reducing poverty and increasing opportunities for people to live safe, productive, and healthy lives.

Making Strategy Count in the Health and Human Services Sector is a guide and toolkit based on the lessons learned from 20 organizations and CSOs. Specifically, this book discusses how these organizations, by deploying strategies and having senior leaders in a strategy role, show that nonprofits can be:

- More agile in adjusting to change
- More data-driven in making decisions
- Better positioned to partner
- More able to innovate in ways that meaningfully help reduce poverty throughout America

Through lessons learned and case studies from Strategy Counts participants and experts, *Making Strategy Count in the Health and Human*

Services Sector will share a new depth of understanding about the role of strategy in nonprofit organizations and add to the knowledge of those tools and methods that have the greatest potential to enhance the resilience and effectiveness of nonprofit organizations that share the mission of improving the lives of children, adults, and families.

Featuring writers from various health and human services leadership teams and clinicians in the field, this book promises to be the first and most comprehensive work describing how to create social change and impact by deploying critical strategies in the health and human services child welfare sector.

An Audience With a View to the Future

This book serves to fill in the knowledge gap for leaders, managers, practitioners, students, faculty members, providers, and professionals working in the health and human services sector who are interested in learning about or teaching in the health and human services sectors, as well as for universities educating social workers, counselors, psychologists, nurses, and other health professionals who want to add preparation to work in the health and human services sector into their curricula.

Readers will walk away with the ability to

- Understand the history and growth of the human services sector
- Develop organizational strategies for how child welfare agencies can achieve long-term social impact by reducing the number of people living in poverty; increasing the number of people who have the opportunity to lead safe, healthy lives; and increasing the number of people who have opportunities for educational and employment success
- Recognize the challenges and opportunities within the health and human services sector
- Identify ways to innovate that will meaningfully affect the reduction of poverty throughout America
- Discuss how to use strategy to improve organizational capacity and infrastructure
- Understand how to use data to drive organizational change
- Recognize the need to align services to achieve collective impact, and learn how to do just that
- Recognize the role of culture and strategy within an organization
- Discuss how strategy can be used to create policy impact and systems change
- Learn how to deploy strategy to create purposeful partnerships

The title of this book foreshadows a blending that we see occurring over the next decade of what have historically been the two largely independent sectors of health care and human services. Research on the social determinants of health and emerging practices that link physical health care with behavioral health bring support to what is rather intuitive when it comes to human health: the mind and body are inextricably linked.

Many of the contributors to this book represent leading nonprofit human services agencies and write from that perspective. Coeditor Tine Hansen-Turton and her colleagues at Public Health Management Corporation contribute content to this book as one nonprofit that is bridging these two sectors. Newer funding models are beginning to reflect this link. Some nonprofits are not only blending physical and behavioral health but are also incorporating family and neighborhood or community health. We see promising practices on the horizon as these disciplines connect and collaborate.

REFERENCES

Breene, R. T. S., Nunes, P. F., & Shill, W. E. (2007, October). The chief strategy officer. *Harvard Business Review*. Boston, MA: Harvard Business Publishing.

McKinsey & Company. (2001, August). *Effective capacity building in nonprofit organizations.* New York: McKinsey & Company.

Acknowledgments

We extend special thanks to the Strategy Counts colleagues who encouraged us all to pursue the book while meeting as a cohort learning group in Detroit, Michigan: Vince Hillyer, Great Circle; David DeStefano, Kids Central; Richard Graziano, The Village Network; Dave Paxton, The Village Network; and Greg Ryan, Heartland Family Service.

We would like to extend a note of thanks to Nandi J. Brown and Amanda Karpeuk for their editorial support, without which our manuscript could not have been completed.

We sincerely appreciate the ongoing support provided by Ann Koerner, who has served as the project assistant for the Strategy Counts initiative.

CHAPTER 1

Strategy in Nonprofits

Michael Mortell

The standard of living in our country appears to be higher than ever. For our elders, who were raised during the Great Depression of the 1930s and endured shortages and rationing of goods during World War II, much has changed. Many from that generation can recall substantial portions of their lives when the common comforts and conveniences of today, such as telephones, air conditioning, color televisions, and travel by air, were not so common. Compared with just a half-century ago, today homes are larger while housing smaller families and retailers offer enormous options in massive quantities. Recreation and entertainment are widely available. In the past decade, Internet access, smart phones, and tablets have become near necessities, suggesting an ever-increasing standard of living.

Although our current lifestyle may afford more comforts and conveniences, a closer look reveals a bleaker reality. In a report by the National Poverty Center, 15.1% of all Americans lived in poverty in 2010—the highest rate since 1993. For children, the picture is worse. Although they made up 24% of the total population, children accounted for 36% of all those living in poverty. That translates to 16.4 million of our nation's kids, or more than 1 in 5, who are growing up in poverty (U.S. Census Bureau, 2011).

Poverty is a complicating factor and even the root of many other challenges in the lives of those served by the nonprofit health and human services sector. Nonprofits find themselves not only on the forefront of the issue but also uniquely positioned to make a meaningful difference. Consider these questions: Who, other than nonprofits, has the infrastructure and community presence nationwide to make a difference? Who, other than nonprofits, has the staff with the specialized skills and training needed to address the complex situations that many living in poverty face? Who, other than nonprofits, has the programming in place to take action now?

Our nation's adults, families, and children need this help. And many cannot wait much longer.

What Is Poverty?

Many have argued that the current federal poverty definition does not work because it focuses only on the economics of poverty while overlooking the social and political implications. In their article "Beyond the Poverty Line," Rourke L. O'Brien and David S. Pedulla (2010) elaborate on this definition's shortcomings: "No poverty line, regardless of how well conceived or how well intentioned, can provide the information that nonprofit leaders and policymakers need to better serve their community. A line cannot provide information about the depth or intensity of deprivation. It cannot tell us about the duration of poverty. It does not provide direct information about actual deprivation, such as homelessness or hunger" (2010, 33).

Challenges Complicated by Poverty

It is helpful for nonprofits to fully understand the needs of those who live in poverty and measure which approaches are most effective in bringing about change. Toward this end, the Alliance solicits observations from those who work in nonprofits. The following are excerpts and ideas from the Alliance's report *Scanning the Horizons: Top Five Trends 2009–2010:*

"Society needs to realize that poverty is at the root of all problems: lack of education, unemployment, homelessness, crime, health issues and abuse/ neglect situations," says Jennifer Dale (p. 42). As poverty grows, more people are affected by these conditions, either directly or indirectly, which puts greater strain on our health care system, schools, law enforcement agencies, and social services organizations.

"Because so many programs have been cut and people in need were not able to get wellness exams or health education, there may be increased incidences of diabetes, high blood pressure and other diseases," Undraye Howard says. In addition, some organizations will not be able to provide mental health services to a growing number of uninsured people who cannot afford to pay the minimum fee (pp. 41–42).

"Food bank usage across the country has also increased dramatically, especially from families that never used food banks before," Elizabeth Carey says (p. 41). "When basic issues such as hunger, stable living and employment are not being addressed, it is very challenging to meet the mental health needs of children and families," adds Brigitte Grant (p. 43).

With higher unemployment and more home foreclosures, the nation's school districts report increases in the number of highly mobile and homeless students. Compared with their peers, children with unstable housing are at greater risk of school failure, behavioral problems, truancy, and other challenges (p. 40).

"We're encountering more moms reporting mental health and substance abuse issues, which can be related to environmental stressors, such as money concerns, loss of jobs, and other difficulties. These are often correlated with increased incidence of child abuse and neglect," Mitzi Fletcher says (p. 42). Often when problems such as these go untreated, the cycle of poverty and violence toward children continues.

Scenarios such as these are commonplace. Across the nation, today's human services organizations report an increased need for all types of programs, ranging from quality child care, financial literacy, and vocational training to mental health counseling and addiction recovery. Complicating matters, many human services agencies find themselves facing dramatic funding cuts, making it more difficult to serve their current clients—and nearly impossible to keep up with growing demands.

"As human services organizations adapt to changing social and economic conditions, there's a natural impulse to focus on immediate concerns," says Guillermina Hernandez-Gallegos, director of human services for The Kresge Foundation. "Our Strategy Counts investment is intended to help the leaders of human services agencies step back and take a strategic view, make informed choices and ultimately build stronger and more effective organizations."

STRATEGY COUNTS: A LEARNING LAB

"Creating opportunity for low-income people is a hallmark of our work," says Rip Rapson, president of The Kresge Foundation. "Our programs reflect the inflection points where we think we can actually make a difference in the life trajectories of people who are poor, disadvantaged, or underserved in fundamental ways."

As a pilot project and learning lab, the Strategy Counts initiative seeks to help nonprofits use strategy as a key inflection point—or turning point—from which they can bring positive change to people's lives.

Strategy Counts is a 4-year pilot initiative designed to enhance the impact of nonprofit human services organizations by increasing their focus on strategy and its effective deployment. The Alliance for Children and Families launched this initiative in May 2011, supported by a $5.375 million grant from The Kresge Foundation.

While preparing for this initiative, researchers with the Alliance discovered that many nonprofits' long-term goals—their missions and their visions—get pushed aside as everyday issues and interruptions command immediate attention. Instead of focusing on those areas that have the greatest impact, many nonprofit leaders find their days filled with managing day-to-day operations, adjusting to regulatory changes, pursuing new revenue sources, deploying programs, and putting out proverbial fires.

Strategy Counts has 20 nonprofits serving as pilot sites. Their leaders were asked to identify and evaluate various tools and methods that could help them work more effectively and strategically in achieving their missions and visions. For example, various sites are modeling how to become more agile in adjusting to change, more data-driven in making decisions, better positioned to partner with others, or more innovative when helping children and families move out of poverty and toward greater well-being.

An early observation suggests that there is no lack of compelling vision or of worthy aspirations by nonprofits. More often, the challenge is in the effective deployment of strategy. Thus, this project is less about writing a strategic plan and more about being strategic. While multiyear strategic plans remain useful, the value diminishes if organizations take an episodic approach to strategy. Instead, strategy leaders, from the pilot sites and beyond, are taking a more continual approach to strategy in which the strategy is aligned with and guides daily operations.

NONPROFITS: AGENTS OF CHANGE

Leaders of today's nonprofit social services organizations are called upon to be agents of change in two different arenas—both among those we serve and within our own organizations—helping people become more strategic in bringing about change, more resourceful in environments that require doing more with less, and more focused on accomplishing what really matters.

So what has to happen for nonprofits to be agents of change? During a roundtable discussion with the pilot sites, Guillermina Hernandez-Gallegos asked about how the voices and perspectives of those we serve as intended beneficiaries are helping the pilot sites be more strategic. One of the responses articulated the role of the strategy officer and underscored the value of nonprofits' taking a strengths-based approach that builds on the assets of communities and individuals:

> The old questions of community development were always about lacks, gaps, needs, wants, and whatever was missing and broken. At Neighborhood Centers, Inc., we don't ask, "What's tragic about your life?" Instead, we want to know, "What are you working on? What do you have? What are you able to accomplish? What are your ultimate aspirations?" So the dots that really need to connect are the ones that align their aspirations with resources. A key role for the strategy officer in our organization is seeing where neighborhoods are going and where resources are headed and then finding the intersection of the two. That intersection is critically important, because resources never align perfectly with what needs to be done. So a key part of our strategy work is looking at the way they do align and finding ways to reshape the resources to fit the neighborhoods and neighbors.
>
> —Angela Blanchard, president and
> CEO of Neighborhood Centers, Inc.

To be agents of change for those we serve, it's important to reframe our questions. To be agents of change within our own organizations, it's important to be intentional about strategy and its effective deployment. We can help our organizations run more smoothly and effectively, freeing up our time, energy, and resources to focus on things that really matter: not only reducing poverty and the many challenges that accompany this condition but also enhancing the lives and opportunities of children and families.

This book is one way the Strategy Counts initiative will share information. In the following chapters, pilot site leaders discuss the tools and methods they are evaluating, allowing other nonprofits leaders to consider new strategies for making their time, energy, and resources more effective in realizing their organizations' missions and visions.

By helping people move from poverty and toward greater self-sufficiency, the hope is also to reduce the many challenges that stem from or are complicated by poverty. The ultimate goal is to help nonprofits throughout the nation use strategy more effectively to transform and enhance the lives of the nation's poorest adults, children, and families.

REFERENCES

Alliance for Families and Children. *Scanning the horizons: Top five trends 2010–2011.* Milwaukee, WI. Retrieved from http://www.alliancetrends.org.

O'Brien, R. L., & Padulla, D. S. (2010). Beyond the poverty line. *Stanford Social Innovation Review,* July. Retrieved from http://www.ssireview.org/articles/entry/beyond_the_poverty_line

U.S. Census Bureau. (2011). *Child poverty in the United States 2009 and 2010: Selected race groups and Hispanic origin.* Washington, DC: Macartney. Retrieved from http://www.census.gov/prod/2011pubs/acsbr10-05.pdf

CHAPTER 2

A Century of Service: A History of the Sector

Patricia Winsten and Amanda Dahlquist

PRE-1900s: EARLY PHILOSOPHIES SHAPE THE FUTURE

The early philosophies and practices of American social welfare were rooted in the English Poor Law. Settlers in the American colonies adapted the Poor Law's principles to the new country's beliefs in democracy and in individual rights and freedoms. Social welfare was influenced heavily by religious ideas, such as saving souls and a moral duty to help those in need.

People of sound mind and body were expected to work and take care of their families. Relatives and neighbors were responsible for helping family members in need. If they were unable to do so, the local community, usually organized around a parish, was obliged to help. Ultimately, local officials were responsible for providing relief.

Charity was afforded only to those at the very margins of society—the "dependent, defective, and delinquent." The dependent poor were a plentiful source of cheap labor and were literally "farmed out." Children were bound out as apprentices, and adults were sent to the workhouse. Both children and adults were placed with other families, and the host family was paid for the service. Religious, ethnic, and fraternal groups created almshouses and other programs to look after their own.

The Industrial Revolution Brings Challenges

The 19th century was a period of sweeping transformation. Abundant prosperity alternated with civil war, bank panics, and depression. Rapid

This chapter, edited and updated by Amanda Dahlquist, is based on the book *A Century of Service*, written by Patricia Winsten, which commemorates the Alliance for Children and Families' first century of service, from 1911 to 2011. The book recalls the historical events, perspectives, and societal norms that shaped the nonprofit human services field.

industrialization led to equally rapid urbanization and immigration. The port cities along the Eastern seaboard swelled with vast numbers of new immigrants.

Loosely organized voluntary charitable groups developed to address the emergent problems of the day: pauperism, widows and orphans, the mistreatment of animals, and the epidemics and natural disasters that ravaged entire cities. A sense of humanitarian moral responsibility vied with the belief that the misfortunate were responsible for their plight and should help themselves.

In the first few decades of the 1800s, organizations formed to prevent pauperism and states formed commissions to assess the administration of public charity. Poor farms and public institutions were created for orphans, the deaf, tuberculosis patients, delinquent youth, and prisoners.

The Civil War Heightens Need

The Civil War prompted federal health and social welfare programs. Army camps and hospitals were riddled with disease, lacked trained medical care, and had no preventive sanitary measures. The first national public health group, the U.S. Sanitary Commission, was created in 1861. Private groups mobilized to provide food, clothing, medical supplies, and a nursing coalition. State boards of health were formed and implemented sanitation practices. Numerous charitable organizations were founded to care for widows and orphans, many of them members of today's Alliance for Children and Families.

The United States government created the first federal social welfare organization just before the war ended. The Bureau of Refugees, Freedmen, and Abandoned Lands provided temporary relief to freed slaves, providing rations, education, legal aid, health care, job training, housing, and other resettlement services. The bureau provided relief on an unprecedented scale—the first indication that if poverty and hardship could not be remedied at the local level, the federal government could successfully provide for the welfare of the people.

Orphanages Are Among the First Organized Charities

Since the earliest recorded histories, most cultures have provided for their abandoned, vulnerable children: family helping family, neighbor helping neighbor, and religious congregations helping members. With the population explosion, rampant disease, and peripatetic society of America's 19th century, orphanages proliferated. By 1900, there were about 1,000 orphanages in the United States. Many arose in response to the needs of immigrants living in poverty. Others followed in the wake of war, depression, or epidemic disease.

Many children living in orphanages were not parentless. Some were placed because their parents were impoverished, seriously ill, disabled, or otherwise in crisis. In some cases, the orphanage was intended to be a temporary placement until the child could return home or another suitable home could be found. In others, the orphanage became a home until the child reached adulthood. Residents would be taught a vocation, receive an education, and then "graduate" upon maturation.

Religious institutions were a primary sponsor of orphanages. They instilled the beliefs and values of the religion, and they were also an important means of preserving the language and culture of immigrants. Private charities and public departments also founded orphanages and other forms of institutional care, such as mental asylums and almshouses.

By the early 1900s, the view of orphanages had changed. Homer Folks, a pioneer in the child welfare movement, was among the progressives who argued that the best setting for children was in their own homes. Rather than removing children from dysfunctional families, the focus should be on improving the family situation. Institutionalization was to be avoided. If children could not remain at home, then a foster home or the most homelike setting possible should be provided.

Industrialization, immigration, the discovery of oil and gold, the transportation revolution, and westward expansion brought vast new opportunities—and extraordinary social and economic problems. The decade following the Civil War was marked by a profound depression. Larger cities moved away from providing outdoor relief. State-supported institutions, state boards, commissions of charities, settlement houses, foster homes, orphanages, and voluntary agencies proliferated to address the many urgent needs.

Leaders of public and private social welfare organizations established the Conference of Boards of Public Charities in 1874. Charity organization societies and settlement organizations also joined in the annual conference to exchange ideas and address mutual concerns.

As the nation began to return to prosperity following the Civil War, philosophies about charity shifted. The sense of moral duty to help those in need conflicted with new elitist theories of self-reliance. England had rewritten the Poor Law in 1834 and declared that public assistance was not a right. By the second half of the 19th century, American capitalists were embracing the social Darwinian thought promulgated by Herbert Spencer, whereby survival of the fittest was deemed morally correct. The only remedy for poverty was self-help. Social Darwinism led to abusive labor practices, oppressive government, and, at its most extreme, systematic eugenics programs that sought to rid society of those deemed unfit.

Philanthropy at that time was impulsive and sporadic. For the newly wealthy, philanthropy was a means to demonstrate their social status. But relief was handed out indiscriminately, with little attention to individual hardship, community-wide needs, or duplicative efforts. "Professional beggars" plied the city streets. Immigrants continued to pour into the country, and cities were desperate for a means to control the roiling masses of paupers.

The economic depression of the 1870s profoundly strained benevolent organizations, making it clear that a more organized system of charity was necessary. Like most growing towns at this time, Buffalo, New York was home to hundreds of roving street urchins, who lived in doorways and alleys and drank from gutters. Many were sent to prisons, orphanages, and poorhouses. Some were sent to live with families in the country and worked as farmhands or servants. Untold numbers of children died before reaching adulthood.

Concerned about the orphaned newsboys and bootblacks who worked and lived on the street, the Young Men's Christian Association (YMCA) in Buffalo treated them to a sumptuous Thanksgiving dinner in 1872. The children were sent back to the streets, but the prominent citizens of Buffalo moved swiftly to create permanent solutions. Just 2 months later, the Children's Aid Society was founded to protect orphaned and abandoned children. In 1877, the Charity Organization Society was established, the first such city-wide organization in the United States. It was instrumental in founding the National Association of Societies for Organizing Charity, the predecessor of the Alliance for Children and Families.

These two Buffalo societies worked together to form the city's first joint fundraising effort in 1917, which evolved into the Community Chest and then later into the United Way. They also created a citywide council of agencies to evaluate and plan social services. The societies had the same goal—to promote the well-being of children and strengthen families. They later merged to form today's Child and Family Services of Buffalo, one of the nation's largest nonprofit family services agencies.

Its volunteer workers, who were usually women, carefully interviewed those seeking aid and then matched assistance to individual need. They thoroughly documented their work so that agencies could coordinate services among themselves. This new method was the origin of today's social casework and counseling services.

The charity organization movement spread rapidly throughout the country. Reverend S. H. Gurteen, an Englishman instrumental in the creation of the Buffalo organization, recommended that similar societies be created in every large city in the United States and that a national and international society be created to exchange ideas and share methods. By the turn of the century, there were nearly 140 charity organizations throughout the country. They promoted cooperation and efficiency, collected and shared data, raised standards, and eliminated duplication and fraud among existing charitable organizations in their local communities.

Although rooted in the ideals of humanitarianism and social justice, the charity organization movement recognized that relief was demoralizing and often led to dependence and pauperism. Its proponents wanted not only to be sure that those who needed relief received it but also to uncover and prevent the root causes of poverty and personal distress—and ultimately prevent them. Their work led to countless social reforms in child welfare, health care, housing, labor, and other areas.

The Settlement House Movement Takes Shape

The settlement house movement developed in the United States concurrently with the charity organization movement. The focus of the settlement house movement was not on charitable relief but rather on reform through social justice. Settlement workers directed their efforts toward an entire neighborhood or group rather than on individual needs.

Like the charity organization society, the settlement house movement began in 19th-century England. It was based on the radical idea that social and economic conditions, rather than personal weakness, were the root causes of poverty.

During the Industrial Revolution in England, dramatic advances in technology, transportation, and communication caused a massive population movement from rural to urban areas. City slums emerged where families lived in crowded, unsanitary housing. Health care was nonexistent; disease was rampant. There were few schools, and children were sent to work in factories.

It was in this environment that the world's first settlement house opened in East London in 1884. University students lived on site with neighborhood residents. They provided classes, social gatherings, summer camps, arts programs, clean-milk stations, baby clinics, nursery schools, and other innovative programs. They helped to organize their neighbors into community groups that could leverage more power than they could alone. Student residents and neighborhood residents were equals. This marriage of social justice and the practice of living among the poor, or "settling," came to be called "the settlement way."

These ideas found a welcome reception in the United States, where many social reformers focused on preventing the causes of poverty, not on dispensing charitable relief. The University Settlement Society of New York was founded in 1886. Jane Addams and her friend Ellen Gates Starr founded Hull House in Chicago in 1889 (which became the Jane Addams Hull House Association). The pioneering ideas and values of the settlement house movement spread quickly, and by 1910 more than 400 settlements had been established in the United States. Most were centered in the nation's largest cities to serve indigent immigrants. The National Federation of Settlements was founded in 1911. It is today's United Neighborhood Centers of America, part of the Families International group of organizations.

At the heart of the movement was a belief that healthier communities could be built by fostering healthy relationships among all of its members, not simply by dispensing charity. Rich and poor lived side by side in fellowship. Rather than asking residents, "What can we do for you?" settlement workers asked, "What can we do together?"

Each settlement house provided activities and programs based on the unique needs of its neighborhood. Kindergartens, nurseries, and daycare centers, schools, classes for adults, health care centers, gymnasiums, parks and playgrounds, and cultural activities were common. Many of these ultimately spun off into independent organizations such as urban leagues, legal aid societies, public health clinics, and community centers.

Jane Addams and other leaders of the settlement house movement were fervent social activists and pioneers in the fight against racial discrimination. Their work contributed to progressive legislation on housing, child labor, work conditions, health and sanitation, and countless other social policy measures.

For many people, these settlement houses provided the first safe, clean, and inviting places in which they had ever lived. They enabled many mothers to go to work for the first time. Countless children made friends, found mentors, and learned skills that they would carry with them for the rest of their lives.

As social work became more professionalized, it came to focus more on behavioral issues than on systemic social problems. Reliant on Community Chest or United Way funding, settlement houses became unable to support full-time residents or round-the-clock services. Many evolved into today's community centers, which are as relevant in today's context as they were 100 years ago.

Volunteers' Roles Evolve to Include Professional Techniques

Early caseworkers were friendly visitors who had no formal training and little knowledge about psychology and emotional problems. Their role was to help strengthen their clients' moral character by providing counsel and friendship and by modeling behavior. This, in turn, would lead to improved circumstances.

However, friendly visitors exercised a certain amount of social superiority and moral judgment. It was recognized by those at the forefront of the social work movement that casework needed to be more empirical, more scientific. As the charity organization movement rapidly grew, volunteer support couldn't keep up with demand. Many towns and cities began to employ district agents to do this work. Agencies and universities began to provide training for this new field. Volunteers offering friendly visits rapidly evolved into professional, salaried workers—the precursor of today's professional social workers.

Mary E. Richmond, considered the founder of the social work profession, was one of the founding leaders of the National Association of Societies for Organizing Charities, the antecedent of today's Alliance for Children and Families. She helped develop the country's first professional social casework instruction. These initial efforts eventually evolved into today's Columbia University School of Social Work, the first school of its kind in the United States.

A National Organization Is Formed

Following much correspondence and interviews with leading charity organization executives, a committee was appointed at the National Conference in 1909 to present a plan for a national charity organization association. The committee studied the YMCA, National Consumers League, National Playground Association, Federation of Woman's Clubs, and other national movements to help craft the best model for the new organization.

The National Association of Societies for Organizing Charity was launched in Boston in 1911. The organization began with 59 charter members from New England to the Pacific Northwest. The Russell Sage Foundation provided grants and a national office to help the fledgling organization get off the ground.

1900–1920: THE PROGRESSIVE ERA PROMOTES GROWTH

Dubbed "the progressive years," the first two decades of the 20th century were characterized by a public zeal for social reform and social justice. In 1885, English businessman Charles Booth had created the new concepts of a poverty line and a normal standard of living. His thoughts about social reform were widely promoted by Robert Hunter of the University Settlement in New York, who published *Poverty* in 1904. Muckraking writers of the period aroused outcry among the general populace by exposing corporate and government corruption, and by depicting the shocking conditions in tenements, mental asylums, and factories. Upton Sinclair's book *The Jungle*, published in 1906, exposed abuses in the meat-packing industry and led to labor reforms and the establishment of the Pure Food and Drug Act.

States began passing legislation and creating commissions related to child welfare, labor laws, workplace safety, minimum wage, housing, sanitation, and other social welfare issues. Most state governments created public pensions for widows with dependent children. Between 1912 and 1913, the U.S. Children's Bureau, the U.S. Department of Labor, and the U.S. Department of Commerce were founded. The first White House Conference on Children brought together child welfare leaders from across the country to enact reform.

Against this backdrop, the newly organized National Association of Societies for Organizing Charities had immediate influence. Its extensive fieldwork helped organize new societies and strengthen others. In 1917, this organization became known as the American Association for Organizing Charity. In rural and newly populated areas, the recently organized charity societies often were the only human welfare agencies. In larger, older cities, they operated among a plethora of disparate agencies.

The intent of this movement was to bring all the local philanthropic agencies together in concerted action to prevent haphazard or duplicative relief. The charity organization was also to investigate and record individual cases and then refer clients to the appropriate agency for help.

War Leads to New Services, New Directions

While the U.S. did not enter WWI until 1917, the years leading up to this saw a mobilization of the entire nation with unprecedented growth in social welfare organizations and programs. The American Association for Organizing Charity's fieldwork was essential during these years, organizing charities in "sleeping towns" that grew almost overnight because of new war industries. By 1915, the association's membership had grown to about 175 members.

During this period, the American Association for Organizing Charity and member agencies loaned professional staff to train volunteers for war service. Women's groups mobilized to provide direct aid, raise funds, and work in war-related employment. These volunteers received intensive training in areas from operating office telephones to friendly visiting and investigative casework. During the war, volunteers took on the essential work of the organization as directors of the board and members of district committees.

Future Scope and Policy Put the Focus on Family

Until this time, casework had largely been provided for those living in extreme poverty. Now casework services were being provided to servicemen and families undergoing emotional distress regardless of their economic situation.

With the rapid growth in and increasing demand for services, the charity organization movement had evolved to a new stage of development. A committee on future scope and policy was created. In its 1919 report, it determined that casework with disorganized families was the fundamental purpose for the field of family welfare, whether or not they were destitute.

The American Association for Organizing Charity agreed to promote major social reform by educating and influencing legislation. With this pivotal decision, the business of organizing charities quickly evolved into the business of social work. To reflect this change, the American Association for Organizing Charity dropped the word "charity" from its name and became the American Association for Organizing Family Social Work.

1920s: PROSPERITY FUELS THE GROWTH OF A MOVEMENT

The progressive governmental activism of the earlier decade diminished amid the country's newfound prosperity and optimism, and the 1920s saw a return to political conservatism.

As the United States moved out of a wartime economy, the first years of the 1920s were marked by an employment crisis. But new technology and rapid industrialization quickly altered the country, ushering in a prosperity that seemed to have no limits. By 1920, more Americans lived in cities than on farms. The automobile fostered greater mobility in the population.

Factories were booming and employment was plentiful, although labor and tenement housing conditions were deplorable. The association and many of its member agencies were outspoken advocates for fair wages and other labor reforms, including a child labor law.

New philanthropic organizations were an outgrowth of the decade's prosperity. Service clubs, fraternal organizations, and women's clubs, which had long been a strong force for social good, multiplied rapidly and extended their outreach. Only a handful of philanthropic foundations existed at the turn of the century. Now, with the creation of sudden millionaires, foundations proliferated.

Federated fundraising was not a new idea, but World War I had generated a nationwide mobilization of charitable donations on a scale not seen before. Local communities had created "war chests" to further the war movement and support charitable organizations that assisted servicemen and their families. Philanthropy was no longer just the province of the upper classes; now businesspeople and even people of modest means who had never thought of donating to charity were spurred to action. After the war, these chests shifted to supporting local organizations, and they spread across the country.

Federated financing enabled community leaders to partner with charitable organizations, assess local needs, identify gaps and duplications in service, and arouse community support for local agencies. Greater community involvement also created a strong resource of lay leaders to serve on charitable boards and committees. But while the community chest potentially created new opportunities for funding, it also restricted program innovation and social activism.

Religious organizations founded many of the country's earliest child and family service organizations. The American Association for Organizing Family Social Work appointed a Committee on Case Work and Religion in 1921 to examine how the two could more closely work together on behalf of people in need. A 1926 report noted that Roman Catholic and Mormon communities had the most complete social casework programs among all church bodies.

Social Work Achieves Professional Status

Rapid industrialization and the demands of the war years underscored the urgent need for trained social workers. For some years, social work had been moving from philanthropic activism to a professional vocation requiring scientific knowledge and practice. The White House Conference on Dependent Children and Youth in 1909 highlighted the role of social work, which lent it a new credibility.

The introduction of scientific theory irrevocably replaced the belief that social work required no more than good morals, a caring heart, and a friendly disposition. The fields of psychiatry, clinical psychology, and sociology were exploding with new knowledge and techniques. Sigmund Freud, Alfred Adler, Carl Jung, and others lent fresh understanding of human development, personality, and behavior. Intelligence tests were now in wide use. Child guidance and mental hygiene were new concerns, with a focus on prevention and early intervention. It was now recognized that heredity and the social environment influenced the human condition.

For the first time, this new body of knowledge provided a scientific foundation for the work of charity organizations. Casework and documentation, once the provinces of volunteer friendly visitors, increasingly required technical competence.

Mary Richmond was instrumental in transforming friendly visiting into professional casework. Her book, *Social Diagnosis*, was the first textbook on social casework theory and method. It provided the family-counseling field with a scientific foundation and modern skills to diagnose and treat family problems. It stimulated colleges and graduate schools to provide professional training for social work and was used as a textbook for decades.

1930s: THE DEPRESSION ERA FURTHER DEFINES THE MOVEMENT

During the Depression, many Americans developed a new perspective on charity. Instead of being only for those who were unable to help themselves, charity became invaluable to the millions of Americans who recognized that unbridled capitalism could result in severe economic downturns. The New Deal reflected this change in the public thinking and allowed charities to reevaluate their role in society.

With the stock market crash of 1929 and the Great Depression, family services agencies were overwhelmed with unemployment and relief needs. Now their clientele included middle-class families who were suddenly jobless, homeless, and hungry. State departments of public welfare still were in their infancy, and federal assistance was not forthcoming in the early years of the Depression. Thus, most association member agencies, even if they had not provided financial relief previously, tapped their own limited funds to assist destitute clients.

Agencies struggled just to keep their doors open. In fact, between 1929 and 1932 about one-third of the nation's private agencies disappeared for lack of funds. It was clearly evident to both the volunteer and the public sectors that such massive relief could only be addressed by the federal government. In addition, the federal government needed to institute reforms to prevent the causes of this crisis.

When Franklin D. Roosevelt became president in 1932, he swiftly enacted widespread New Deal social welfare programs to combat unemployment and poverty. With the exception of the short-lived Freedman's Bureau, created to aid former slaves, this was the first time the federal government had accepted responsibility for the social welfare of its citizens. The New Deal programs created a public safety net for those grappling with extreme poverty, unemployment, old age, and physical disabilities.

By 1933, the federal government had created the Civilian Conservation Corps, the Civil Works Administration, and the Federal Emergency Relief Act (FERA). FERA provided federal funds for relief and established public assistance offices in each state. It also required local relief administrators to employ at least one trained social worker, heightening the visibility and appreciation of professional social work in towns nationwide—and straining the demand for personnel who were already in short supply.

The landmark Social Security Act was enacted in 1935 to provide public assistance for such groups as dependent children of single mothers, the aged, the blind, and disabled workers. Although it was widely criticized for not going far enough—particularly for not including health insurance— the Social Security Act and its 1939 amendments expanded social welfare throughout the country and moved responsibility for relief from local municipalities and charitable organizations to the federal government.

A Fundamental Change in the Social Services Role

With the creation of a public safety net for welfare relief, the role of voluntary agencies was fundamentally altered. Both the public and private sectors grappled with shifting boundaries and new roles. Welfare was now to be delivered by public institutions, which allowed charities to offer and promote specialized therapeutic services.

Linton Swift, general secretary of the newly renamed Family Welfare Association of America (FWAA), issued a historic response to the changing social welfare landscape that redefined the role of voluntary family services agencies and welcomed the public sector's assumption of responsibility for the financial safety net.

The FWAA was especially concerned about maintaining and improving service standards amid the rapid transformation of relief programs from voluntary social organizations to public agencies. It also worked in partnership with other local and national groups that shared an interest in family life.

New Opportunities for Service

The FWAA surveyed its membership in 1935 about public versus private responsibilities. It learned that members agreed that providing food, clothing, and shelter for those in distress had passed from the realm of private philanthropy into that of public obligation. They believed that private funds were insufficient to even scratch the surface of relief needs and that private funds should be used to help people deal with problems other than relief.

As the government established public programs for basic relief and the Great Depression eased, family agencies were able to shift funds and attention back to casework. They initiated new programs, implemented new techniques, and served new populations. Family agencies began to focus on relationships between family members, not just on individual situations. They experimented with group work and added group activities such as parent education, recreation, and nursery schools. By the late 1930s, agencies were beginning to discuss a sliding fee scale for clients with the ability to pay for service.

The Depression era created a huge demand for professional social workers and a corresponding demand on training schools and field service. Women in particular were attracted to this new career, which now enjoyed great prestige. The FERA requirement that local and state relief organizations employ experienced social workers had vastly raised awareness of the profession. Prominent social workers were appointed to lead many of the newly created governmental social services agencies, further elevating the profession's status. The new public programs relied extensively on the skill and knowledge of the social work profession, opening opportunities in education, recreation, medicine, social justice, agriculture, and numerous other areas.

1940s: WORLD WAR II FUELS GREATER DEMAND

Once again, a world war brought profound family distress and economic hardship. In the early years of World War II, child and family services agencies were deluged with marital and family problems. With little supervision at home, youth delinquency increased and many communities dealt with the problem of "the victory girl"—a teenager who "demonstrated her patriotism" by having sexual relations with any interested serviceman. Men who were rejected from the armed services because of a mental or physical health reason often required counseling, as did wounded veterans returning home.

The Family Welfare Association of America (FWAA) estimated that 43% of America's families had a recently returned veteran. Upon their return, they faced uncertain employment, marital difficulties, and a greatly increased cost of living. The psychiatric field lent family services agencies a new understanding of the psychological casualties of war.

The latter years of the war brought an influx of refugees resettling in America. Member agencies were especially concerned during these years with aiding new Americans. War brides and fiancées, repatriated Americans, displaced people from the Nazi concentration camps, and other new immigrants needed a wealth of social services to help them acclimate successfully.

Displacement also impacted countless American citizens during this period. During the war years, according to FWAA reports, more than 15 million Americans relocated to war industry towns, leaving behind their family and community ties. Family agencies knew from experience that social instability led to emotional and psychological instability.

The Committee on Current and Future Planning

A second world war, following so closely on the heels of the Great Depression, prompted major changes in the social services field. Child and family agencies now provided greatly expanded services to families of every income level. Responsibilities and alignments between public and voluntary agencies were shifting rapidly. The FWAA board recognized that it was time to take stock of the basic purpose, function, and scope of social services agencies, both individually and collectively.

A Committee on Current and Future Planning was appointed in 1943 to identify the issues in a program, organization, or relationship that were of greatest concern to voluntary family agencies. The committee's findings were reported at the 1946 biennial conference. The primary issues were defined as the following:

- **Marriage counseling.** By 1945, the U.S. divorce rate had reached 1 in 3, the highest in the world. Some of these divorces might have occurred anyway but were postponed by the war. In addition, wartime conditions encouraged hasty marriages between couples who scarcely knew each other.
- **Family life education.** Family agencies had accumulated vast knowledge about the personal attitudes, environmental factors, and social requirements that contribute to a sound and satisfying family life. This knowledge was applied to the diagnosis and treatment of individuals and families and used to educate them about how to prevent family breakdown.
- **Aging population.** Social casework programs had to immediately reorient themselves to the needs of the rapidly growing older adult population. In addition to financial support and institutional care, the case workers also needed to address health, housing, recreation, personal and family adjustment, adult education, and vocational retraining.
- **The role of child and family agencies.** The committee recommended that the structure and function of these agencies be reexamined.
- **The role of family services programs.** The new demands of the war years broadened the range of services within agencies. With the exception of the ongoing crisis in personnel, member agencies were most concerned with the scope of services they should appropriately provide. The committee concluded that the basic goal of the organization should be to prevent family disorganization and breakdown.

Expansion of Services

The demands of the war period necessitated a vast mobilization of social services, including day nurseries, counseling for veterans and their families, and travelers aid. Many agencies, aware of the permanent traumatic effects of removing children from their homes during crisis or family illness, developed homemaker services as part of their casework aid.

The community's need for and use of these services brought an acceptance and reliance on family services agencies. It was now more socially acceptable to seek expert, specialized help for emotional difficulties.

The passage of the National Mental Health Act in 1946 intensified the demand for counseling and mental health services. It opened the door to new community-based services and made public funding available for special projects.

As demand grew, there was a far greater emphasis on graduate training and supervised internships for caseworkers. The newly created FWAA Committee on Family Social Work Personnel helped coordinate recruiting, but agencies realized that they would have to employ some workers with partial or no training. The FWAA helped organize work/study plans and field training so workers could acquire professional training. Still, by 1946 the association declared that meeting demand was the most serious problem facing the association and its members.

Families also increasingly turned to family services agencies for help with problems caused by economic insecurity. Because of the inflationary economy, vast numbers of clients could not afford housing and food, had exhausted their savings, were highly in debt, postponed needed medical and dental care, and were unable to continue supporting ill or aged relatives and dependents. As during the depression, high school students were leaving school to supplement the family income.

An Urgent Need for Community Leadership

It was crucial that family agencies exercise leadership in their communities. Without their leadership and community support, agencies could not hope to extend the quality and reach of their services.

What made a family agency strong enough to play a leadership role in the community? The association and its members acknowledged that professional competence was not enough. Agencies needed to have a vital board of directors that represented the community to the agency, and the board, in turn, had to interpret the agency's work to the entire community, not just major donors. They had to use their knowledge and experience to effect social action.

A New Name Reflects a Changing Focus

In 1946, the Family Welfare Association of America (FWAA) changed its name to the Family Service Association of America (FSAA). Both the association and its member agencies had been moving away from the misleading designation of "welfare" or "charity" to describe their services. *Family* services more aptly described this nationwide program. "Because of long experience in dealing with personal and family problems, thousands of people from every walk of life now come to these agencies for consultation," explained Ralph Uihlein, who served on the board of FWAA.

1950s: SOCIETAL CHANGES MARK THE ADVENT OF SERVICE EXPANSION

The advent of the atomic bomb, the Korean War, and an economy influenced by defense spending had a profound impact on American families. In fact, the 1950 FSAA meeting in New York City was titled "Family Living in a Time of World Tension."

Industrialization and urbanization were booming. But with the readily available automobile, families fled the city for the suburbs. Women, teens, and older adults moved into the workforce in record numbers. Family welfare leaders agreed that these trends were leading to greater depersonalization of family life and interpersonal relationships.

The field was particularly concerned with the effects of continued inflation. A "new army of the poor" had emerged since World War II. Lower middle income and white-collar families had seen their entire savings wiped out by rising taxes and inflationary living costs.

In the field of social services, major developments in the 1950s included the following:

- Greater interest in establishing a family services agency, with a focus on preventing mental illness
- Emphasis on family life education to strengthen families and relationships and to prevent family disruption
- A growing acceptance of fees for casework
- Integrated services, which included new concepts of social interaction, culture conflicts, and psychiatry
- Growing reliance on community chests, which provided nearly 90% of member agencies' incomes
- Increasing numbers of agency mergers, especially between child placement and family services agencies
- Family homemaker services that provided care to children when a mother was temporarily unable to function, which allowed children to remain in their home
- New interest in research, especially in evaluating the effectiveness of services

Information and Education Advance the Field

In addition to field service, information service remained a core function of the FSAA in the 1950s. The association typically received more than 1,200 specific inquiries each year from agencies requesting help on various organizational problems. In 1950, the information service prepared reports on financial assistance practice, salary trends, intake policies, homemaker services, and fee charging policies. The association collected and published monthly statistics on caseloads and service trends in 60 selected agencies and shared the data for comparative planning purposes.

The social work profession evolved rapidly, adding new specialties and research-based methods. By the 1950s, there were more than 50 graduate schools of social work in the United States. Still, shortages of personnel remained a serious issue. FSAA and member agencies created scholarship programs to advance professional education. The FSAA also worked actively with the Council on Social Work Education in developing new and creative ways to call attention to social work as a rewarding career.

Methods Adapt to Current Needs

The population and its evolving needs were growing rapidly in this period. Modern industry required a large, mobile labor force. Families moved often; farm families moved into cities, and city families sought better living conditions in the suburbs. More women were working outside the home than ever before. Compulsory military service promoted the trend to earlier marriage—and a higher divorce rate. Most family agencies had a greater demand for services than they could meet. The predominant characteristic of FSAA and its member agencies was their flexibility of programming and their ability to meet the changing patterns of family living.

FSAA adapted to another change with the defense buildup, which created new communities overnight. Small towns suddenly became urban centers. Where a desert, cotton field, or farm had existed just a few months earlier, there was now a steel mill or a defense material depot. Many of these communities had no social services agencies.

FSAA played a leading role in the development of the United Community Defense Services, which mobilized local leadership to help affected communities plan and create facilities and services to foster sound community life.

1960s: REVOLUTIONARY SOCIETAL CHANGES FORCE RAPID HUMAN SERVICES CHANGES

The 1960s ushered in massive political and cultural upheaval: the civil rights movement, antiwar protests, drug culture, women's rights, and the sexual revolution. Amid these rapidly changing social and economic conditions, the Family Service Association of America examined the range and emphasis of a typical family services agency, and in 1960 noted many new developments since its 1953 report. Some of these changes included a growing interest in mental health, escalating divorce rates and a growing use of marital and family counseling, services for the elderly, and group treatment.

During this tumultuous time, race relations and poverty took center stage. The nation awakened to the future needs of its rapidly increasing older population. There was a new focus on the growing issues of homelessness, drug addiction, and crime. Patterns of family life were changing rapidly; in fact, the very definition of "family" began to be questioned. Child and family services agencies were grappling with significantly increased divorce rates, out-of-wedlock pregnancies, domestic violence, juvenile delinquency, and drug and alcohol use and abuse.

Many thought leaders were questioning the moral fiber of the American people. Did organized religion provide adequate leadership and guidance? Was the family as the basic social institution failing in some of its most vital functions?

Federal Funding Offers Opportunities, Challenges

The federal government instituted social welfare legislation and programs not seen since the New Deal. This infusion of federal funding forever altered the course of human services organizations.

During President John F. Kennedy's term, Aid to Families with Dependent Children (AFDC) eligibility was expanded. Congress passed the Manpower Development and Training Act, the Social Security amendments, and the Community Mental Health Centers Act. These provided a greatly increased role for social workers to provide counseling, job training, and outpatient treatment. FSAA added a mental health consultant to its staff to help craft a preventive approach to mental health care.

In the emerging affluence of the 1950s, poverty went almost unnoticed. In fact, much of the public thought poverty no longer existed. Yet the 1960 U.S. Census revealed that not only was poverty prevalent, it was growing worse.

FSAA conducted a census of its member agencies in 1960 to determine the socioeconomic levels of agency clients. Results pointed out that the greater part of its member agency services were devoted to serving the poor and underprivileged. Like the charity organization societies and settlement houses before them, family agencies of the second half of the 20th century worked to create self-sufficiency and to address the root causes of poverty.

In his 1964 State of the Union address, President Lyndon B. Johnson declared an "unconditional war on poverty." He shortly there-after enacted the Economic Opportunity Act, followed by a plethora of Great Society programs—and the federal funding to back them up. The Civil Rights Act, the Older Americans Act, Medicare, Medicaid, and other legislation launched countless new initiatives to address poverty, racial inequality, health, education, housing, urban decay, and other urgent social problems. In addition, federal funding helped train a new generation of social workers to meet the escalating demand.

Federal money was funneled to the states, which contracted for services from public and private organizations both for-profit and nonprofit. Local community action agencies became a force, contracting with family services organizations for services. FSAA agencies began accepting government contracts, often creating new programs to address specific needs. This was a fundamental shift not only in the way organizations were funded but also in how they developed and operated their services.

At a 1963 meeting, the FSAA board of directors discussed the members' use of public funds. Some felt that under no circumstances could public funds be used. Others felt equally strongly that "you should use whatever you can, whenever you can get it, and for whatever purpose it can be gotten." The board agreed that basic health and welfare needs were the responsibility of the government. Agencies should not take public funds to solve a temporary problem, they concurred. Rather, agencies should make a deep, long-term commitment to the jobs they had agreed to perform.

The FSAA board focused on the safeguards necessary in using public funds. They advised that agencies be prepared to reject public funds if conditions were not appropriate. The board also recognized the dangers of overreliance on this new source of funding. Government funding could come and go.

The Infusion of Public Funds Generates Explosive Growth

Prior to the influx of federal money, most family services agencies could only provide counseling—nothing else. With federal money coming into the states for mental health services and the war on poverty, agencies could offer multiple programs, serving people in multiple ways.

The proliferation of government funding and new social welfare programs birthed many new social services agencies. Existing agencies began to offer multiple programs in response to government funding. Historically responsive to changing social conditions, family services agencies applied new knowledge about behavioral health care to meet the changing patterns of family living.

With the divorce rate at a record high, the family services field and the American public wanted solutions. In addition, the 1960 White House Conference on Children and Youth heightened interest in family counseling. Marital counseling and family life education increased tremendously.

FSAA received a grant from the National Institute of Mental Health (NIMH) in 1962 for a 3-year project involving interagency exploration of causes and treatment of marital problems. Member agencies responded enthusiastically and affirmed that their participation challenged and stimulated their local staff members. NIMH also provided a joint grant to FSAA and the Child Study Association of America to train family caseworkers in leading family life education groups targeted to parents.

Government funding did not come without strings attached. Agencies were burdened with newly restrictive and often onerous regulations. There were also new requirements for accreditation and quality assurance. A master's degree in social work became the standard in the field. Agencies now emphasized fiscal, administrative, quality, and governance standards.

In 1962, FSAA's delegate assembly revised the organization's membership requirements to impose higher standards for casework, staff training, and board and committee participation. Long the recognized body in family services accreditation, FSAA intended these new requirements to be valuable tools in strengthening the structure and quality of all member agencies. In meeting these requirements, agencies had to be disciplined, accountable, and transparent. Accreditation increasingly became the selling point in a competitive funding environment. FSAA continued to raise the bar on standards.

FSAA and other national leaders cautioned in the late 1960s that small private agencies risked extinction. An FSAA conference for large agency executives sounded a warning as valid today as it was more than 40 years ago: Agencies must consolidate to achieve economies of scale and maximize impact.

National Focus and a Demonstration Project
Push Aging Services

The 1961 White House Conference on aging heightened awareness of the needs of the rapidly growing older adult population. FSAA sent four delegates to the conference, which led to passage of the Social Security amendments, Medicare, fair housing legislation, and the Older Americans Act of 1965.

In 1960, the Ford Foundation awarded FSAA $300,000 for a 4-year demonstration project to work with older adults. FSAA added two professionals to the national staff to manage the project. Forty member agencies from 31 communities participated. The funding supported training, innovation, and improved quality in counseling, home care, and other specialized programs for older adults. It also stimulated closer cooperation at the local level between voluntary and public agencies. The FSAA Project Advisory Committee fostered the interchange of knowledge gained by the participating communities. National and regional training institutes promoted cross-fertilization of evolving new concepts and skills.

The demonstration project successfully integrated work with the elderly and their families into the mainstream of agency program and practice.

The Civil Rights Movement Is a Wake-up Call

Even before the civil rights movement necessitated strong action, FSAA had been moving toward greater engagement with and increased recognition of the needs of the Black community. In 1963, the association surveyed its members about their efforts to develop services that strengthened family life for minority groups. Agencies changed their policies to facilitate access by minority families by expanding their office hours to evenings, moving their headquarters, or opening satellite offices in inner-city neighborhoods. Family life education and group techniques were targeted specifically toward minority populations.

The Civil Rights Act of 1964 and other legislation in this decade was targeted at ending racial discrimination. How it played out in the streets, on campuses, in the board rooms, in lawmakers' offices, and around the kitchen tables of America was a different story.

The relatively peaceful sit-ins and marches of earlier years boiled over into riots and violence. Generations of poverty, unemployment, and injustice fueled hopelessness and rage. The "White establishment" was angry, too. Welfare rolls were growing rapidly. It was popularly believed that welfare created a culture of poverty and dependence perpetuated from generation to generation. Welfare programs and those who benefited from them were under growing attack. The social work profession was also seen as part of the problem—criticized on one side for perpetuating dependence and on the other for being out of touch and unresponsive to real problems.

FSAA called for a national policy to end racial and ethnic discrimination, eradicate the causes of poverty, and protect and strengthen American families. The association also worked to end discrimination in its selection of board and staff members. Although it was clear that the official position of the organization had changed, it did not significantly alter the complexion of most association gatherings. A strong working relationship with the National Urban League helped FSAA move more rapidly and effectively toward these goals.

The FSAA 1969 Biennial Conference, "Meeting with Change," was aptly named. By this time, protest was everywhere—in the streets, on campuses, in churches, and at every major national conference. It was no surprise that change took center stage at the biennial.

Just after the conference's opening speech, a group of African American protesters (almost all FSAA members) took over the stage and called for a Black caucus. Brian Langdon, retired president and CEO of Family Services Woodfield in Bridgeport, Connecticut, remembered it well. "The demonstrators challenged this national organization to stand up for the rights of African American families and civil rights," he recalled. "That was a powerful moment that led to rapid and significant change within FSAA. It also helped all of us think about things in a bigger way, both personally and professionally."

The planned program for the following day, designated The Day of Challenge, quickly was changed to The Day of Black Challenge. The Black caucus presented specific demands to the FSAA, including strong action regarding FSAA's commitment to the National Welfare Rights Organization, greater representation on the FSAA board by people of color, and an FSAA task force on White racism. Both the FSAA and the Black caucus regarded these demands as positive challenges, motivated by a mutual concern for the future of the family services movement.

At the first national board meeting following the biennial, FSAA president Paul Neal Averill observed that the experience was a healthy reflection of the prevailing mood. FSAA was challenged to update itself and maximize its potential of opportunity to enhance family and individual functioning. FSAA and member agencies responded with creative and experimental approaches to meet current needs, expand outreach, and broaden the product mix. Most agencies grew to multiservice operations. The cost to do business increased tremendously without corresponding growth in sources of income.

1970s: AUTHORITY AND INSTITUTIONS CHALLENGED

Trends that began in the 1950s and 1960s intensified in the following decades. Advances in psychiatric treatment, new behavioral health care models, and the advent of psychotropic drugs were combined with budget constraints and a public outcry over the custodial nature of mental institutions and orphanages.

The Joint Commission on Mental Illness and Health recommended community-based treatment, and the Community Mental Health Centers Act of 1963 promised federal support. The latter fell far short amid rising Vietnam War expenditures and an economic recession, but outpatient facilities, clinics, employment training, and other community-based services continued to grow.

State asylums and group homes were virtually emptied and residents were moved to less expensive outpatient care, foster care, and community-based services. Both adult and children's institutional facilities saw a radical shift in population. Residential programs became the placement of last resort, for those who had the most severe disabilities.

President Richard M. Nixon came into office on the promise to end the Vietnam War and reduce government services—particularly the welfare programs created by earlier administrations. He said he would eradicate the Great Society and liberal "big spenders." Social workers were a particular target; he vowed to "make sure social workers would be looking for honest work."

The unpredictable Nixon, however, signed legislation that provided federal block grants to local communities for social services; expanded Social Security benefits and the food stamp program; and provided funding for job training, rehabilitation, and occupational health and safety. He even proposed comprehensive health insurance for every American.

Although the National Institute of Mental Health increasingly focused on research, there was little effort to identify and eradicate the causes of social and economic dysfunction. Conservative backlash against the swelling welfare rolls and rising out-of-wedlock births among African American mothers affected a return to the thinking of a much earlier era: Poverty represented a moral defect or other problem within the individual. Hard work and sound moral character were the solution. Legislation reflected this public attitude.

The economic crises of the next two administrations cut funding for welfare and social services programs. President Jimmy Carter's expansion of mental health care policy was immediately rescinded by President Ronald Reagan, who escalated defense spending, reduced spending on social welfare programs, and transferred responsibility for most social welfare to the states.

The National Association of Homes for Children Is Founded

It was within this climate that the National Association of Homes for Children (NAHC) was founded in 1975. The deinstitutionalization movement was intended to place children in more normalized and less restrictive environments. It also resulted in lower costs per child. Unfortunately, for many children, the use of family foster care resulted in children moving frequently, necessitating their adjustment to many different placements. The trauma of each placement was and has been detrimental to these children.

NAHC was a reaction to this movement against residential child care. In banding together, these organizations were large enough to be heard and to influence policy decisions in the best interests of children. By its second year, NAHC had more than 400 member agencies and was working to educate legislators at the regional, state, and national levels. Advocates who had lived in children's homes and now were in government leadership positions testified on behalf of the best interests of children. They agreed that foster care was an important service. They agreed that children should be kept in their own homes whenever possible. But they advocated that above all, children needed to be protected and provided with a stable environment. Not every child's home or every foster home provided such an environment.

NAHC adopted a code of ethics and professional standards, leading to an accreditation program for children's residential group care facilities in 1978. The accreditation program helped establish NAHC as a credible, viable national voice in the child care field, led by NAHC-trained peer reviewers from across the country who could objectively evaluate each other's programs. The NAHC standards defined what the field thought of as appropriate care for children and shared best practices. NAHC achieved success in both the legislature and public opinion surveys.

A Revolution Arrives: Privatization

There was a great deal of new investment in human services organizations by the government. As government funding increased, United Way funding, the traditional mainstay of human services organizations, decreased.

Agencies moved from being largely United Way–supported to being largely government-funded. Foundation support also became an important source of funding. United Way was no longer the sole funder.

The world had changed, and FSAA had to change with it. With the government responsible for the bulk of social welfare funding, FSAA and member agencies realized that it was vital to have a strong voice at the table when policy and funding decisions were being made. FSAA made a concerted decision to strengthen its influence and liaison with government agencies. By the end of the decade, FSAA had established the Washington Office for Governmental Affairs. Today, the public policy office continues to represent the child and family services movement in Washington, closely monitoring developments that impact children, families, and communities.

The Formation of the Council on Accreditation

To be a credible voice for children and families, FSAA, the Child Welfare League of America (CWLA), NAHC, and other organizations understood that their members had to meet high performance standards. Thus, they independently developed accreditation standards.

For decades, FSAA had focused on field service to help member agencies evaluate and improve program operations, management, and governance to meet and exceed accreditation standards. But by the 1970s, government contracts and other funding sources increasingly called upon human services organizations to demonstrate quality standards. It was apparent that there were too many different organizations offering too many accreditation standards for too many different programs. FSAA and CWLA worked together to create the Council on Accreditation (COA) in 1977, each giving up its independent accreditation program.

Today, COA accredits more than 45 service areas for private social service and behavioral health care organizations. Accreditation is viewed as a catalyst for change, building on organizational strengths to achieve ever greater performance.

In 1979, a long-held FSAA goal came to fruition: the establishment of an Office for Families in the federal government's Administration for Children, Youth and Families. Its intent was to identify and eliminate governmental policies that adversely affect families.

1980s: CUTBACKS, RECESSION, AND GENERAL UNEASE BRING NEW DIRECTION

Throughout the 1980s, the Family Service Association of America and member agencies learned to do more with less. Recession, unemployment, and inflation helped swell the ranks of the already poor with the "new poor." More than two-thirds of adults living in poverty were women.

As the government inserted itself into family life through social welfare funding, family problems increasingly became public problems. The White House Conference on Families focused new attention on family issues and generated contentious debate. A conservative backlash to the "big government" social spending harkened back to the prior century: Welfare was criticized as creating a culture of dependency. People living in poverty often were stigmatized as lazy people with poor morals who had to be taught self-sufficiency.

President Ronald Reagan's administration approved cutbacks in federally funded social programs, such as public and mental health, school lunch programs and food stamps, child care, alcohol and drug treatment, and other social services. Many federal functions were transferred back to the states.

The cutbacks hurt doubly. Besides shrinking the basic benefits to which vulnerable families were entitled, the cutbacks also impacted the availability of services to people trying to cope with their worsening living conditions. Child and family services agencies struggled to meet increased demand even as their own revenues shrank. Agencies found themselves in the odd position of simultaneously courting government contracts while also speaking out against government policies that they felt hurt families.

A New Leader for a New Direction

W. Keith Daugherty, FSAA's general director, who was intimately familiar with all the issues facing family services, resigned in 1981. Many FSAA board members recognized that the movement and the national organization were in trouble. The environment for families and the organizations serving them had undergone a marked change. FSAA established a task force on organizational renewal. It redefined its mission and structure, and it chose a CEO to take the association in a new direction.

Geneva Johnson was hired as president and CEO in 1983. With the hiring of Johnson, the FSAA board committed to a significant shift in direction. Johnson was recruited from United Way of America, where she was senior vice president of strategic planning.

"At the time, most FSAA member organizations were relying on the traditional ways of operating, anticipating that United Way would always be a major source of funding and that things would go along pretty much the way they did the last 35 or 40 years," says Reed Henderson, who was executive director of Family Service of Morris County in Morristown, New Jersey, at the time. "Geneva talked to us about the bottom line, the need to be more flexible and nimble or others would take our places. She talked about the need for new funding streams, the need to think in new and different ways about what it means to be a leader in the nonprofit sector in a changing world."

A Volatile and Challenging Environment

As poverty, crime, homelessness, domestic violence, child abuse and neglect, and other social problems continued to increase in the 1980s, new problems emerged. The changes in family makeup and lifestyles that had begun in the past several decades intensified. The number of married-couple households dropped; births to unmarried mothers increased. At a time when its funding was seriously jeopardized, the child and family services field was affected by four main challenges: children living in poverty, aging, adolescent pregnancy, and the AIDS epidemic.

The FSA (Family Service America, formerly FSAA) Washington Office on Government Affairs directed its efforts in the 1980s to opposing cuts to AFDC and other programs that protected vulnerable children and families. FSA created a crucial coalition of several dozen other organizations to oppose AFDC cutbacks and turn administration over to the states. The government affairs staff also worked on legislation affecting child support, single-parent families, pregnant adolescents, and employment leave for new parents. Efforts to improve family violence legislation led to the passage of Public Law No. 98457, which for the first time provided funding to service providers and shelters to help people dealing with violence. The growing issue of small-business competition and protecting the tax-exempt status of nonprofit organizations was a major concern. FSA worked to develop a state-by-state network to strengthen and protect nonprofit agency mission and interests in a changing climate.

"The State of Families 1984–1985," an exhaustive research study commissioned and published by FSA, received extensive national recognition. It was released to the media at the National Press Club. The review of external factors impacting family life outlined current problems, examined trends, and provided a blueprint for short-term and long-range action. This report and the ones that followed were invaluable to FSA and member agencies in generating awareness and making the case for financial support.

Social Enterprise

Child and family services agencies have historically been involved with industrial life. By the turn of the 20th century, they were working to improve child labor laws and workplace conditions. In the mid-1980s, FSA and its member agencies found new ways to reach out to families and industry—and a major source of new revenue for FSA and member agencies. The development of a for-profit employee assistance program (EAP) was a major milestone for the organization.

Geneva Johnson had been with United Way of Rochester before moving to United Way of America. She knew that executives at Xerox Corporation, headquartered in Rochester, New York, had a local counseling service for Xerox employees. She suggested that FSA pursue the idea of a nationwide EAP contract using the FSA national membership network. It was a natural extension of FSA's concern for working families. Some member agencies already were providing employee assistance services on a local basis. Parents spent most of their waking hours in the workplace. What better channel to offer access to human services?

FSA created the National Service to Industry Division in 1979 and entered into a nationwide contract with Xerox. It was the first national EAP founded by a nonprofit organization and remains a pioneer in behavioral health.

Later renamed Family Enterprises, Inc., and today named FEI Behavioral Health (FEI), the program quickly became a leader in the field. Within several years, it added IBM, General Motors, North American Philips Corporation, and other major corporations to its client roster. Services included counseling, information and referral, health education programs, and evaluation and referral for drug and alcohol problems.

In 1989, FEI added two new areas of service in response to changing needs. The Dependent Care Program provided information and referral services to employees with elder care and child care needs in any community in North America. It also created the first comprehensive crisis management program, providing consultation, counseling, and critical incidence stress debriefing for mass-casualty incidents, workplace catastrophes, and community disasters.

Fast-forward to the moment the first plane hit the World Trade Center tower in the terrorist attacks of September 11, 2001. The FEI staff went into action, and some literally lived at the office for most of the next 3 months. FEI operated a national call center for survivors and victims' families, working with the U.S. Department of Justice, the FBI, and the National Transportation Safety Board. Also among FEI's EAP clients were dozens of airlines and corporations whose employees had been affected by the terrorist attack.

FEI has since adapted its crisis response model to serve the needs of customers affected by both major and minor disruptions that have lingering and unintended consequences in the workforce, including interference of service to customers, service delivery, and productivity. Today, in addition to airlines, FEI works with financial service providers, government agencies, retailers, and many hotel and hospital providers.

1990s: COMMUNITY-BASED FOCUS EMERGES

By the early 1990s, new approaches to behavioral health care began to focus on community-centered initiatives. This work encompassed far more than counseling: It provided an array of outreach services and partnered with other resources to help individuals and families maximize self-sufficiency. "Our clients are in the community, and that's where we need to be," says Jerome Johnson, president and CEO, Family Service Association in Egg Harbor Township, New Jersey. "We haven't been a traditional, office-based agency since then. . . . Now our staff understands that they are *community-based providers of service.*"

Brian Langdon, who retired as president and CEO of Family Services Woodfield (FSW) in Bridgeport, Connecticut, in 2009, confirms that getting the clinical staff on board was the biggest hurdle for his agency. In 1988, FSW moved to a new building three blocks from its former office. "That was the most critical area for violence," Langdon explains. "There were guns going off. There was prostitution, break-ins. That move was based on our board's commitment to use our resources in the community that needed them most."

That was a turning point for FSW, where they truly became a community asset and began to employ people from within the community as case aides. They may not have had the educational degree, but they knew the community. Today, the organization has people who started without any degree, have gotten an education and worked their way up the agency ranks. Two women who are vice presidents of the organization obtained their leadership roles because they were able to bring the community together."

As the new FSA CEO in 1994, Peter Goldberg immediately recognized the challenges ahead. He saw that the times were changing more quickly than the agencies could adapt to them. United Way was an imperiled funding stream. The majority of FSA member agencies were small; in an era of increased privatization, they were not well positioned to access government contracts. These agencies were faced with CEOs who were trained in a different time for a different purpose.

In 1996, the Personal Responsibility and Work Opportunity Act forever changed welfare as it was known in the United States. As the name of the legislation makes clear, the act framed economic status in moral terms: The exit from welfare and the path to self-sufficiency lies in accepting responsibility for one's life.

FSA (which became the Alliance for Children and Families in 1998) was alarmed by how this legislation impacted millions of Americans at the bottom of the economic ladder. In 1999, the Alliance launched the Faces of Change project in collaboration with the Community Service Society of New York. Over a period of several years, the project gathered first-person narratives from 415 people whose lives and families had been detrimentally affected by welfare reform. *Faces of Change: Personal Experiences of Welfare Reform in America*, published in 2001, included 100 narratives gathered in the first phase of research. *Faces of Change* gave voice to those who had none and was a critical contribution to the nation's understanding of how public policy affects individuals and their families.

Alternatives to Residential Care

Residential care facilities that provided only long-term custodial care began disappearing in the 1960s. Some closed permanently, while others merged. Those that grew and thrived in the coming decades were large enough and nimble enough to adapt to new opportunities.

The trend—and the funding—favored keeping children in a home environment. A diverse range of services developed rapidly, from short-term residential treatment and foster care to community and in-home services. The National Association of Homes for Children (NAHC) changed its name in 1990 to National Association of Homes and Services for Children (NAHSC) to reflect the growing diversity among its membership.

"Children's organizations across the country were evolving and expanding," explains Marty Mitchell, president and CEO of Starr Commonwealth in Albion, Michigan. "Their goal wasn't necessarily to serve children in residential care alone; it was to serve children at risk, children in need. Evidence-based practices were showing that young people could be treated in less restrictive forms of service." Children's agencies were beginning to understand that treatment wasn't an isolated event, with young people then being sent back into the original environment without the support system they needed. A continuum of care began to emerge, where a young person could come into care at any one point and move seamlessly into other areas of care. In addition to the long-standing residential service, children's agencies began providing early intervention alternatives, community-based services, and adequate follow-up support to make sure the gains that had been secured in the care setting would be maintained and built upon.

"At the same time children's agencies were expanding services, we realized that the traditional emphasis on the child had very little emphasis on family," says Mitchell. "Today, one of the first pieces of a diagnosis occurs with the developmental audit. We ask, 'What is the context of this child's family, school system and community?'"

Numerous child welfare and family services agencies expanded into multi-service, multi-site organizations. As they became more diverse, they became more indistinguishable from one other, and consolidations were increasingly common.

2000s: NEW MILLENNIUM BEGINS WITH TUMULTUOUS EVENTS

The first decade of the millennium opened and closed with profound crises. The terrorist attacks of September 11, 2001, forever altered the country in many ways. After several years of rapid economic growth, the last few years of the decade were marked by a financial collapse followed by massive unemployment, which strained the social safety net to its breaking point and left many nonprofit human services agencies struggling for survival.

By the 1990s, most nonprofit human services agencies were heavily reliant on government funding. Over the past few decades, reimbursement rates had steadily eroded compared to the actual cost of services. Now, amid the economic crisis that befell the nation in 2008 and 2009, states increasingly were shifting their budgetary problems onto the nonprofit organizations that serve the most vulnerable populations.

Peter Goldberg, president and CEO of the Alliance at the time, was a national leader in the call for reform of the government financing system. "The system has been broken for years, even decades," he said. "The economic situation has pushed this to a crisis point."

In 2009, the Alliance, Deloitte, and Alliance member Hillside Family of Agencies in Rochester, New York, convened a diverse group of thought leaders to strategize the transformation of nonprofit human services financing. In their report, "Human Services Financing for the 21st Century: A Blueprint for Building Stronger Children and Families," the group emphasized that the first step in transformation must be the creation of a fundamental national human services strategy committed to serving the entire individual or family.

"Our current system is highly fractured and under-resourced. There is no clear, consistent approach we can all work toward," says Marty Mitchell. "Responsibility for human services planning and funding is spread across countless federal agencies and programs—each with its own priorities and goals, funding patterns, regulations, and reporting requirements. These federal silos are mimicked at the state level and leave no room for flexibility, creativity, and innovation. Most decisions are being driven by economic realities rather than best practices and the best interests of children and families."

Instead of many separate government programs, the forum participants believed that bringing together all funders in a common strategy for human services planning would foster many benefits, including the following:

- Clear priorities
- Synergistic goals and unified outcomes expectations
- Higher-quality service integration
- Innovation in programs, delivery, and funding
- Greater cost-effectiveness

Amid this economic environment the need for advocacy and capacity building was urgent.

Preparing for the Future with Lessons From the Past

In 2006, two important human services movements came together in an affiliation that strengthens children, families, and communities. Both the settlement house movement and charity organization societies began in the late 1800s and were concerned with improving the lives of those at the very margins of society. Whereas the early charity organization societies tended to focus on individual casework with families, the settlement houses worked to improve conditions in entire neighborhoods. Both groups formed independent national organizations in 1911. The settlement houses came together as the National Federation of Settlement Houses, founded by Jane Addams and known today as United Neighborhood Centers of America (UNCA). The charity organization societies formed the National Association of Societies for Organizing Charity, the predecessor of today's Alliance for Children and Families.

In 2013, the Alliance and UNCA announced that they would unite into a sole membership organization. UNCA would transform into a national resource center for civic engagement and neighborhood revitalization dedicated to supporting, instructing, and powering the neighborhood revitalization and community-building movements. As Susan Dreyfus, president and CEO of the Alliance, describes the transformation, "The center serves as an action-oriented learning community that unites and amplifies the voices of neighbors and leading practitioners by embracing person- and family-centered and strengths-based values and pursuing meaningful and sustainable community change."

Public Policy Continues to Make Inroads

With the fiscal crisis of 2008, key public policy issues for the sector included support for programs impacting children, families, and neighborhoods, such as the American Recovery and Reinvestment Act of 2009, a $787 billion economic recovery package. In addition, important public policies included ensuring prompt payment by public agencies to charitable organizations for government-funded services, establishing a low- or no-interest bridge loan fund for agencies facing short-term cash flow problems, and fighting efforts to limit charity advocacy and lobbying rights.

In addition to the American Recovery and Reinvestment Act, key legislation in this decade was the Children's Health Act of 2000, which contained provisions to protect nonmedical, community-based facilities. Changes to Medicaid policies enacted by the George W. Bush administration, which limited funding for mental health services such as therapeutic foster care, was an ongoing issue. The public policy office worked to influence reform of the federal financing of Title IV-E foster care programs. The Fostering Connections to Success and Increasing Adoptions Act passed in 2008 with heavy bipartisan support. Health care reform deeply divided the country, and a bill was passed in early 2010. The implementation of health care reform since becoming law continues to be a contentious issue.

Disruptive Forces That Are Revolutionizing the Sector

With a look at the future for the sector, the Alliance has identified six key forces that are driving change within the sector. Referred to as disruptive forces, the six factors have been identified with the purpose of helping leaders of nonprofit organizations plan for successful futures by illuminating complexity, inspiring tough conversations, and pushing leaders to think outside of their comfort zone (Alliance for Children and Families, 2011).

Disruptive Force 1: Purposeful Experimentation. Increased purposeful experimentation will be required of organizations, driven by (a) risk-taking activities of for-profit competitors, (b) low-cost information technologies, (c) the growing role of social media in communications, and (d) desperation as funding sources decline. Further, the demand for new, innovative solutions will be high.

Disruptive Force 2: Information Liberation. Regulations such as the Health Insurance Portability and Accountability Act go to great lengths to ensure information confidentiality, but they will become outdated. A new generation of consumers will share information about themselves with friends, family, and communities, both live and virtually. Information sharing can improve service delivery models such that they ultimately give consumers more control over how their information is shared and allow other agencies in the same continuum to provide better care.

Disruptive Force 3: Integrating Science. Extraordinary advances in technology will blur the lines between what is possible, what is affordable, and what is acceptable. Advances will alter the ways in which individuals are diagnosed and treated. Successful human services organizations will not only leverage these advances but will also partner with the research community to shape how these sciences can be applied cost-effectively to demonstrate impact.

Disruptive Force 4: Uncompromising Demand for Impact. The ability to demonstrate that particular interventions have efficacy will result in payment. Funders and communities will expect greater impact at a lower cost. Key sector stakeholders will first define the desired impact and then consider what organization or groups of organizations can deliver at the lowest cost.

Disruptive Force 5: Branding Causes, Not Organizations. It will be much more effective for human services organizations to leverage support by emphasizing core issues and causes rather than on their individual agency brands and programs. While brands can seem somewhat artificial and institutional, movements create a vision and goal for change.

Disruptive Force 6: Attracting Investors, Not Donors. The current model of nonprofit funding will shift to an investment paradigm. Performance-seeking portfolios will be aimed at achieving a return on investment that solves a societal problem, contributes to a movement, or eliminates a community issue.

Rather than being predictions for the future, the six disruptive forces are factors that may shape the future and are defined here to spark strategic conversations about the future of the sector. For additional information on disruptive forces, visit www.alliance1.org/disruptive-forces/about

REFERENCES

Alliance for Children and Families & Baker Tilly. (2011). *Disruptive forces: Driving a human services revolution*. Washington, DC: Alliance for Children and Families.

Winsten, P. (2011). *A century of service*. Milwaukee, WI: Alliance for Children and Families.

CHAPTER 3

Forces Shaping the Human Services Sector in the Early 21st Century

Elizabeth Carey, John Hollingsworth, and Alex Reed

This chapter follows a historical perspective of the sector and begins to lay the foundation for where the broader health and human services sector is going, including why the Strategy Counts initiative is so timely for the industry. The chapter begins with Embracing the Industry of Courage, which is an adaptation of a position paper first prepared for the board of directors at Michigan-base Starr Commonwealth. This chapter also shares Eckerd's story: although Eckerd is not a pilot site, the agency has served as an inspiration to the Strategy Counts sites, providing insight into what it really takes to transform an aging health and human services organization.

EMBRACING THE INDUSTRY OF COURAGE

The only constant is change—everything flows. This is the doctrine of the Greek philosopher Heraclitus, and today, in the human services sector, we know that standing still is not an option.

However, the factors and trends to which children and families agencies are now responding are far from unique to our sector. And with change comes opportunity—the opportunity to use new, innovative means to help many more children and families fulfill their potentials.

We operate in a sector that has been placed under enormous pressure. And yet the "quiet revolution" of the nonprofit sector (Salamon, 2003) continues, despite the chaos of our public finance crisis. While numerous organizations in the human services field have succumbed to the contraction of government funding, some green shoots of hope can be found in the nonprofit sector as a whole.

The key to withstanding the pressures of our economy, increased competition, public sector reform, and societal shifts is to be bold—to have the courage to break from tradition and be enterprising, innovative, collaborative, and quick.

Service providers in all sectors are required to be ever more dynamic in how they interact with their clients. It is increasingly naive to assume that children and families will travel to a treatment center for our services when they already prefer to experience banking, retail, education, and entertainment online, at home, and through mobile devices.

Funding streams are also changing. Government funding overall is declining and continues to be threatened by an unprecedented debt burden at the federal and state levels. Foundations are still recovering from a difficult period for their investments and are being asked to meet a broader range of needs.

As demand for its services rises, the nonprofit sector continues to grow. The expectations of nonprofits are also on the rise, with increased focus on performance-based contracting, a need to demonstrate outcomes, and more emphasis on collaborations aimed at efficiency.

The levels of funding available from government sources do not match the costs of traditional, institutional treatment approaches. There are fewer funds available in the juvenile justice and child welfare systems, while mental health is holding strong, particularly with increased coverage from private health insurance and Medicaid.

Society and the populations our organizations serve are changing too. Overall, we are aging. We are more diverse—the populations currently regarded as minorities will account for 90% of the total population increase in the next 45 years. Growth in the U.S. population is increasingly concentrated in the south and west.

Meanwhile, the needs of children and families are greater and more complex. Families are less likely to include a married couple. More children live without their biological parents than ever before. Poverty is a daily reality for over 46 million Americans. Obtaining a good education is a challenging and unfair process, with just over 70% of all school pupils graduating from high school; the figure drops significantly for urban children and for children who are Black, Hispanic, or Native American.

Children are increasingly living with multiple needs that established systems are not prepared to meet. Children in the juvenile justice system, for example, are often in need of mental health services they cannot access. The proportion of children diagnosed with neurological differences is rising—the U.S. rate of autism diagnosis is 1 in 88 children—while children and adults face significant challenges in accessing services for diagnosis and support.

At Starr, we believe such disadvantages are unacceptable: We know there is a better way. This is why we are continually examining how we meet the needs of the most vulnerable people in our society and are constantly striving to improve how our services are delivered. This is the industry of courage, and we plan to lead it.

Your communities have benefited from your bravery. It takes courage to move out of the comfort zone, to take chances, to change, and yes, to innovate. In this field, there is little reward for taking risks, but driven by your mission, and compelled to provide high-quality programs and services, you take those risks in order to better serve your communities.

—Peter Goldberg, president and CEO, Alliance for Children and Families (Alliance for Children and Families, 2011)

Beyond the Knowledge Economy

Revolutions in technology, communication, and consumerism are often seen as revolutions in retail and other private-sector industries. However, the experiences, efficiencies, and conveniences that customers find in other sectors are highly relevant to human services, particularly as collaboration between for-profits, nonprofits, and government become more common.

With such rapid changes, it can be argued that we now operate in a "learning economy," which focuses on the rate of change and the consequential requirements of constantly renewing firms' capabilities and workers' competencies (Morel, Palier, & Palme, 2009). It is not a case just of buying into new technologies but also of being flexible in how you operate and innovative in your response to changes. In this sense, people are still the key to success.

New capabilities emerge just by virtue of having smart people with access to state-of-the-art technology.

—Robert E. Kahn, Internet pioneer

No longer can human services organizations focus only on the delivery of existing programs and contracts: Dynamism and constant connectivity with the external environment are also required. The way individuals and organizations interact with services is fundamental to how human services need to be designed and managed.

Although the basic developmental needs of the children and families in Starr's care today are, in many ways, the same as they were for Starr's very first children in 1913, the manner in which these needs are met is far from the same. The system in which vulnerable children and adults find themselves is changing, in part as a result of the continuous search for efficiency, greater effectiveness, and improved customer experiences. Where technology and for-profit solutions can replace government intervention and expense, they increasingly will.

We can look at a host of industries for examples of services responding to consumer trends. When traveling, for example, we book trips and travel experiences anywhere in the world using the Internet and through mobile devices. Ticketing is electronic, and even security in airports involves fewer people. In health care, reliance on the institution has decreased—we stay overnight less often thanks to improvements in surgical technology, robots, and local outpatient services. In education, colleges and universities are switching to virtual courses, involving less travel, less need for physical facilities, and less overhead.

One of the top consumer trends in 2012 was identified as do-it-yourself health, facilitated by advances in mobile applications (apps; "12 Crucial Consumer Trends for 2012," 2012). At the end of 2011, Apple's App Store offered 9,000 mobile health apps (including nearly 1,500 cardio fitness apps, more than 1,300 diet apps, more than 1,000 stress and relaxation apps, and more than 650 women's health apps).

Other related trends include point-and-know ("12 Crucial Consumer Trends for 2012," 2012), which is the need among consumers for instant information on real-world images and people; this is driven by the growth in augmented reality apps, which allow people to point a device at a real-world scene and make it come to life using images and text.

The way we innovate is also changing. Idle-sourcing is the next frontier for crowd-sourcing ("12 Crucial Consumer Trends for 2012," 2012): It is the practice of obtaining needed services, ideas, or content by soliciting contributions from a large group of people, especially from an online community, rather than from traditional employees or suppliers. Idle-sourcing comes from people seeking to contribute their services, ideas, and content with minimal effort and minimal reliance on technology, enabled only by their mobile devices. It is also making brands more instantly accountable for their actions, with consumers expecting honesty about flaws in a company's service rather than the appearance of flawlessness.

"More!" is as effective a revolutionary slogan as was ever invented by doctrinaires of discontent. The American, who cannot learn to want what he has, is a permanent revolutionary.

—Eric Hoffer, American moral and social philosopher

Continuous learning, development, and improvement are required, and yet these cannot always come from within an existing organization. Just as businesses, particularly technology companies, have embraced "open innovation" (Chesbrough, 2005) for decades, human services nonprofits can look for external innovation and exploit it through collaboration, partnerships, mergers, and acquisitions.

Changes in technology, with the increased potential to reach large audiences with interactive and tailored communications, are opening up new possibilities in business development and fundraising. Realizing this potential is proving to be a challenge, however: Although nearly all nonprofits are experimenting with social media, approximately 80% are unsure how to build real value by doing so (Weber Shandwick, 2009).

To embrace social media, human services organizations must be more open with their information while ensuring that they maintain client confidentiality. Used responsibly, proactive social media strategies can significantly increase an organization's community of interest—and, potentially, its donor base.

Know Your People

Demographics played a significant role in the outcome of the U.S. presidential election campaign of 2012. As Republicans have since acknowledged, their party's campaign did not make full use of data that would have told them how significant the Latino population has become, both nationally and in specific regions of the country.

As shown in Figure 3.1, there are 52 million Hispanic persons living in the United States, comprising 17% of the total population—making Hispanics the largest minority group. This number is projected to reach 132.8 million (30% of the U.S. population) by 2050 (Pew Research Hispanic Center, 2008). In 1980, Hispanic children accounted for 9% of all children in the United States; in 2011, the proportion was 22%. The growth of non-Caucasian populations is undoubtedly changing the politics of the United States and is also changing the dynamic of the communities served by the human services sector.

Although non-Caucasians make up an increasing proportion of the total population, inequality continues to present major challenges. In education, for example, Hispanics, African Americans, and Native Americans graduate from high school at rates consistently below 60%, whereas the national average is 71%. Similar patterns are evident in college and university graduation rates.

Ethnicity, however, is just part of the demographic picture. Approximately 37 million Americans are over 65, and this number will double in the next 40 years. The millennial generation (born 1982–2002) is 81 million strong and, over the next 20 years, will come to comprise the bulk of the population. Family structures are changing: Fewer than 1 in 4 households consists of a heterosexual married couple with children. Meanwhile, 1 in 4 children under 21 in the United States lives in a single-parent family, more than three-quarters of such children supported by single mothers.

For the human services sector, such shifts in families and communities can affect the social needs that organizations are challenged to meet, as well as how culturally appropriate services are and how their delivery should be managed.

FIGURE 3.1   U.S. Hispanic population.

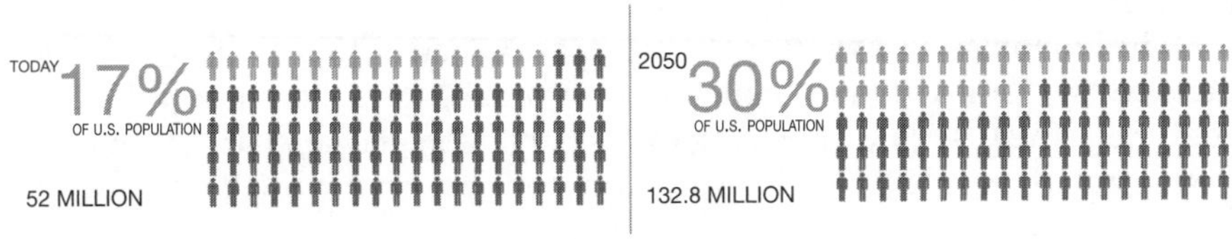

TODAY 17% OF U.S. POPULATION 52 MILLION

2050 30% OF U.S. POPULATION 132.8 MILLION

Where's the Money?

The distribution of government funding arguably reflects what we as a society are accepting as our social priorities, and as funding becomes tighter, scrutinizing the nature of expenditures becomes more important.

Currently, national spending on adult corrections is $81.5 billion, approaching three times as much as that for child welfare ($29.3 billion) and 12 times what we spend on juvenile justice ($6.4 billion). Meanwhile, spending on mental health is much higher, at $113 billion. Typically, less than 10% of the federal budget is spent on children (The Urban Institute & The Brookings Institution, 2010), and although no comprehensive figures are available detailing the mental health dollars spent on children, it is estimated that in 2007, approximately $6 billion was spent on preventive services for children (O'Connell, Boat, & Warner, 2009).

The growth in older populations will continue to draw funds away from other areas of social services. Federal funding spent on children has been decreasing, and this trend is expected to continue. Already the budget allocated to this area has shrunk from 20% of the total budget in 1960 to 16% in 2007, and this is expected to fall to 13.8% by 2018.

Other pressures on public funding include the increased number of Americans living in poverty and on relatively low incomes. With 19% of U.S. children living below the poverty line (a family unit of three living on less than $19,530 per year, for example), and many more adults struggling to support them, the demand for basic services is enormous.

Charitable Giving Under Pressure to Fill the Void

Total charitable donations in the United States are still approximately 11% below their level in 2007 and are recovering slowly—growing only 0.9% in 2011. It is expected that it will take a decade for charitable giving to return to pre–economic crisis levels. Donations to foundations have dropped, resulting in lower levels of grant-making. Despite this, the United States is still the most charitable country in the world, donating approximately $300 billion to charities each year.

Overall charitable giving from corporations is still relatively low, owing in large part to the stress and uncertainty in the banking sector that has long been the largest source of corporate philanthropy. Meanwhile, online giving by the public is growing as a proportion of charitable philanthropy, and fundraising through social media represents an area of opportunity for nonprofits.

The human services sector attracts approximately 12% of the total donations in the United States, compared with 32% for religion and 13% for education. In 2011, 90% of Michigan residents donated to charity, a greater percentage than in 2007 (Michigan Nonprofit Association, 2012). However, competition for donations is also high, and fundraising techniques must be sophisticated for a human services organization to present itself as an attractive investment.

Rethinking Social Finance

Record levels of debt in national, state, and local governments are driving austerity initiatives, leaving fewer and fewer public resources available for human services. At the same time, the funds behind social investment are coming not only from a wider range of sources, but also with greater expectations.

In the wider nonprofit arena, budget cuts and private-sector social innovation are driving the creation of new financing models. The competition among nonprofits for ever-scarcer public funding is encouraging collaboration, partnerships, and mergers.

Socially minded individuals and corporations with integrated approaches to sustainability are seeing social change as an investment opportunity. Social impact financing is beginning to replace traditional corporate philanthropy and has made evidence-based impact a point of entry as opposed to a source of advantage. Government is seeking private sector–nonprofit collaboration to maximize the impact of the dollars it invests.

You cannot have development in today's world without partnering with the private sector.

—Hillary Clinton, U.S. Secretary of State, Clinton Global Initiative, 2012

One example of social impact financing is the social impact bond, a mechanism of funding for social programs in which government agencies pay only for real, measurable social outcomes, and only after results have been achieved, with the private sector providing the upfront financing (Center for American Progress, 2012). Such a model is built entirely on the need to demonstrate impact and creates a new starting point for a nonprofit bidding to obtain funds.

Health Care and Health Reform—New Frontiers for Human Services

The links between physical, mental, and social wellness are better understood than ever, and our health care providers are rapidly realizing the real value of addressing needs more traditionally met by the publicly funded human services sector. Mental health, substance abuse, and behavioral health, for example, are being treated on a more equitable level by private insurers, and this trend is likely to be accelerated by the implementation of the Affordable Care Act.

As the country continues to look for new ways to control health care costs, states have increasingly become laboratories for adopting new financing strategies and moving away from traditional fee-for-service reimbursement models. This means that integrated care delivery models, such as health homes, have begun to take hold in many states.

Health homes provide integrated, coordinated primary and behavioral health and substance abuse services. They represent a person-centered, holistic approach that normally focuses on serving individuals who have been diagnosed with one or more chronic and/or behavioral health conditions. As defined by the Centers for Medicare and Medicaid Services (Center for Health Care Strategies, 2011), a health home provides six specific services beyond the clinical services offered by a typical primary care provider:

- Comprehensive care management
- Care coordination and health promotion
- Comprehensive transitional care and follow-up
- Patient and family support
- Referral to community and social support services
- Use of information technology to link services, if applicable

This trend means that behavioral health organizations and community mental health centers will need to learn how to master different markets. This change and the overall increase in links to the health care sector provide opportunities and challenges. While service areas threatened by public cuts may find new sources of funding, organizations will be required to meet a different set of expectations and measurement standards. Diversification into new areas of service and new client groups can also reduce reliance on public funding and increase support from private health care providers.

Neurological Differences—Emerging and Unmet Needs

The number of people diagnosed with neurological differences, including the most commonly known autism spectrum disorders (ASD), is increasing at an alarming rate.

The nonprofit autism science and advocacy organization Autism Speaks reports that autism affects 1 in 88 children overall, including 1 in 54 boys, and that autism is the fastest-growing serious developmental disability in the United States (What Is Autism? 2013). Research conducted among U.S. parents suggests that the rate of autism is much higher—possibly 1 in 50 children of school age (Centers for Disease Control and Prevention, 2011–2012); the variance in reported rates is thought to be affected by a low but improving level of diagnosis.

White children are more likely than are Black or Hispanic children to be diagnosed—among white children the prevalence is 1.6%; among Hispanic and African American children, the rates are 1.0 and 0.6%, respectively. These figures, in part, reflect disparities in society when it comes to awareness of neurological differences and accessing appropriate services for diagnosis and treatment.

ASDs begin in childhood and continue through adulthood, and although each case is unique, children who have been diagnosed with ASDs have in common problems with social and communication skills. Other features typical of children with ASDs are unusual patterns of learning, paying attention, and reacting to sensory stimuli. These issues, if untreated, make it less likely that an adult who has been diagnosed with an ASD will thrive.

Among those diagnosed with an ASD, socioeconomic status appears to play an important role in mitigating the symptoms. Non-Hispanic white children of highly educated mothers are much more likely to experience rapid improvement in functioning than are other children (Fountain, Winter, & Bearman, 2012).

The lifetime societal costs associated with autism have been estimated at $3.2 million per person who has been diagnosed with autism. These costs are driven largely by behavioral therapies in childhood and extensive adult care, along with large indirect societal costs owing to lost productivity (Ganz, 2007).

In addition to autism, a range of other conditions require special attention from organizations such as Starr. Attention deficit hyperactivity disorder (ADHD), for example, is frequently encountered by Starr and has a significant impact on young people in the United States. The Centers for Disease Control and Prevention (CDC) reports (OPEN MINDS, 2013) that ADHD is one of the most prevalent neurobehavioral conditions in the United States, and that between 4% and 12% of school-aged children have been diagnosed with the disorder. The CDC estimates the societal cost of this illness to be between $36 and $52 billion—that is, between $12,005 and $17,458 annually per individual. National survey data suggest that approximately two-thirds of children who have special care needs such as ADHD are covered by commercial employer-based health insurance (Mathematica, 2004).

Even as the needs of people with neurological differences grow, service provision is lagging behind the demand. In Michigan, for example, significant waiting lists exist for access to services required by people with neurological differences, including assessment and diagnostics as well as day treatment and respite. Many organizations, particularly schools, could also benefit from expert advice on working with children affected by neurological differences.

Fresh Thinking Closer to Home

Just as we've seen deinstitutionalization in mental health in recent decades, a major shift is also under way in the areas of juvenile justice and child welfare. The number of children and adolescents in residential placements is falling, and community-based, in-home care models are more highly prized by public authorities and clients.

This shift is driven by a range of factors, including both cost and the belief that it is better to keep children in their normal environments and find solutions to their behavioral challenges that fit those environments.

There is also a move toward more coordinated and integrated treatments; new systems are being designed to reduce the inefficiencies of moving young people between different care and funding models.

EXHIBIT 3.1

Case Study: Massachusetts Unified Child Welfare Service Model for Congregate Care and Community-Based Treatment (Open Minds, 2013)

A new model of child welfare launched by the Massachusetts Department of Children and Families and the Department of Mental Health reflects some of the emerging trends in child welfare.

The Massachusetts approach is a unified service model called "Caring Together" that integrates congregate care and community-based treatment for youth in the child welfare system. The Massachusetts model has six key elements:

1. Collaborating between human services and mental health with monitoring of outcomes and performance
2. Creating standardized level-of-service criteria for various levels of placement and common criteria for utilization management and network management
3. Contracting for human services through RFPs that can be renewed for as long as 10 years and that have federal grant funding attached (e.g., IV-E demonstration projects)
4. Reimbursing through pay for performance
5. Using congregate (residential) care only for short, intensive stays
6. Focusing on aftercare community programming such as independent living and vocational services

Foster Care

Nationally, the number of children in foster care has been declining for over a decade. From the peak of 567,000 children in 1999, there were 401,000 children in foster care in 2011 (Foster Care, 2012). The challenges faced by children in foster care remain far greater than those faced by most other children. Children who live in foster care are more likely to exhibit physical, learning, and mental conditions: One study suggests that 60% of young children (aged 2 months to 2 years) in foster care are at high risk of slow development and neurological impairment (Child Trends, 2003).

Furthermore, the young people who age out of foster care (i.e., leave because they have turned 18 or have graduated from high school) often find it difficult to progress to a healthy adult life. The largest study of this population in the United States showed that 38% had emotional problems, 50% had used illegal drugs, and 25% were involved with the legal system.

Currently, the funding for foster care does not cover the full cost of delivering services to the high standards most agencies strive for—approximately 14 states cover less than half the cost of foster care.

Education

As change sweeps across all governmental and business sectors, education in the United States is also undergoing some of the most substantial reform in American history. Funding is being cut, teachers and administrators are under immense pressure, and student achievement is struggling.

In recent years, strong emphasis has been placed on standardized testing to measure the academic progress of young people. The role of standardized testing in schools has increased dramatically in response to federal legislation, such as the No Child Left Behind Act, which requires states to administer standardized tests to measure students' yearly progress. Schools not making adequate gains according to the legislation are sanctioned. Opponents of standardized testing suggest that the tests do not accurately measure progress, and they cite the significant cost of administering and grading the tests as wasteful spending.

Education is also becoming increasingly integrated with the business world. In an effort to raise student performance and close the achievement gap, the United States has seen a large rise in private investment in education in the form of for-profit charter schools. Nonprofits are also having a greater influence in the educational arena, with many helping to open public charters alongside local public schools to meet the needs of communities.

As in all areas of everyday life, technology has had a huge influence on education. From online learning opportunities to entirely virtual schools, the way students receive educational services is constantly evolving. Traditionally reserved for post-secondary learning, online schools are on the upswing in K–12 education, and are now becoming serious alternatives to traditional public schools.

Courage in Our Communities

The growth in demand for community-based services is one of the most important shifts in our field and is evident not only in traditional service lines such as juvenile justice. More flexible, tailored, often in-home models of service are proving to be effective and efficient in the support of people who have developmental disabilities, neurological differences, and mental health conditions. To respond to these opportunities and serve a wider range of needs, we must be innovative and customer-focused at an organizational level as well as in our sector as a whole.

Having led bold, inventive initiatives in its first century of service, Starr will continue to meet children, families, and communities where they are and, with a focus on resilience and courage, be a part of where they are going. We know that on that journey, our business model, our programs, our people, our culture, and our customers will change and keep changing—the challenge is to ensure that we are leading the changes, not following them.

To achieve this, we must continuously scan not only Starr's landscape, but that of other innovators, service leaders, partners, and customer champions, linking macro trends to how we achieve local impact. Only then can we identify the leaps we must make to stay ahead of the curve, master our own horizon, turn courage into success, and ensure that children and families flourish.

ECKERD: A DRAMATIC TRANSFORMATION

Founded by Jack and Ruth Eckerd in 1968, Eckerd is a nonprofit youth services organization dedicated to ensuring that every child has the opportunity to succeed. Through a continuum of life-changing behavioral health and child welfare services nationwide, Eckerd has given much-needed second chances to nearly 150,000 children and families.

In 2007, Eckerd operated 47 programs serving 9,500 youth annually on revenues of $80 million, with 86% of this revenue derived from residential programs for which state and local agencies were rapidly reducing funding because of the costs. As a result of this industry shift toward more cost-effective community-based services for treating at-risk and troubled youth, since 2007, Eckerd has had to exit 46 of those original 47 programs along with $78 million of the $80 million in revenue. To put this into perspective, Eckerd today would be a $2 million nonprofit with only one program serving

TABLE 3.1 The Eckerd Transformation

	Eckerd in 2007	Programs Exited Since	Today If No Transformation	New Programs	Eckerd in 2014
Youth Served	9,500	9,400	100	14,000	14,100
Total Programs	47	46	1	32	33
Revenue	$80M	$78M	$2M	$158M	$160M
Residential %	86%	85%	100%	4%	5%
Community %	14%	15%	0%	96%	95%
Overhead Rate	17%	N/A	17%	N/A	5%

Source: Reed (2013).

100 youth annually had it not embarked on a significant transformational effort over the past 6 years.

Rather than facing closure, since 2007, Eckerd has opened or is in the process of opening 32 new programs serving 14,000 youth on $158 million in revenue, with 96% of this new revenue being community-based. Additionally during this period, Eckerd has reduced its overhead rate from 17% to 5%, significantly improved its program quality, and eliminated the use of nearly $3 million annually from its endowment for sustaining base operations. Table 3.1 provides a snapshot of this dramatic transformation.

How did Eckerd make this transformation a reality? The answer starts with a reflection on how a nearly 40-year-old nonprofit found itself in the position of possibly having to close its doors.

Jack Eckerd: The Genius Leader

Management consultant Peter Drucker wrote in *The Effective Executive* (2006), "Organization is, to a large extent, a means of overcoming the limitations mortality sets to what any one man can contribute. An organization that is not capable of perpetuating itself has failed" (p. 56). Unfortunately, history is littered with organizations large and small, for-profit and nonprofit, that were so dependent on the "genius" of a single leader that when the leader ultimately left—whether by choice or the wear of time—the organization floundered and even eventually collapsed.

Jack Eckerd was a business titan with a gift for innovation and deal making. After acquiring three failing drugstores in Clearwater, Florida, Jack reengineered the drugstore experience and built Eckerd Drugs into a national chain that was on the road to becoming the preeminent drugstore company. However, as Jim Collins wrote in *Good to Great* (2001) when comparing Eckerd Drugs with Walgreens, "But then Jack Eckerd left to pursue his passion for politics, running for senator and joining the Ford administration in Washington. Without his guiding genius, Eckerd's company began a long decline, eventually being acquired by J. C. Penney" (p. 46).

Collins describes Eckerd Drugs' organizational model in *Good to Great* as being one of a "genius with a thousand helpers" (p. 47), with the primary guidance mechanism for Eckerd Drugs' strategy being "inside Jack Eckerd's head" (p. 46). How does an organization not just survive, but thrive after its iconic leader leaves? That was the daunting task faced by Eckerd the nonprofit—not the drugstore chain—after its founder, Jack Eckerd, died in 2004.

1968—"It's the Kids"

It was Jack's desire to give back to the country that had given him so much that fueled his calling to create a nonprofit providing and sharing solutions for children in need of a second chance. When asked what was most important to him over the years, Jack, despite his extensive professional accomplishments, always said: "It's the kids."

In the late 1960s, Florida's juvenile justice system often approached working with "incorrigible youth" by confining them in punitive institutions for years at a time. Believing there had to be better treatment alternatives, Jack researched the programmatic landscape and discovered therapeutic wilderness programming, a strengths-based, 12-month residential model operated in a wilderness setting that was an innovation for its time. Utilizing this model, he opened the first outdoor therapeutic program for boys in Florida in 1968, followed by the first outdoor therapeutic program for girls in the southeastern United States a year later.

Over the next 4 decades, at the request of state leadership in Florida as well as in Georgia, New Hampshire, North Carolina, Rhode Island, Tennessee, and Vermont, Eckerd opened 16 more therapeutic wilderness camps, accompanied by additional types of residential programming. Additionally, Jack's innovations in youth services programming extended beyond wilderness camps and residential services. Understanding the need to prevent younger at-risk youth from needing residential treatment in their teens, he personally funded school-based character education pilots in Florida elementary schools, leading to the creation of Eckerd's early intervention and prevention "Hi-Five" model of services. Jack also led the charge—again with his own funding—for launching aftercare and reentry services throughout Florida to help youth leaving juvenile justice residential treatment facilities successfully transition back to their home communities.

2007—"It's the Camps"

In the late 1990s, Jack suffered a stroke that reduced the time he could dedicate to Eckerd; with his subsequent death, in 2004, the nonprofit organization found itself in a precarious position, much as Eckerd Drugs did in the 1970s after Jack began focusing on politics and philanthropy. By 2007, just 3 years after his death, the nonprofit Eckerd stood paralyzed on a dangerous precipice.

Over the previous 10 years, Eckerd had been led by five different CEOs. Outcomes had deteriorated and were not driven by data. Annually, $2.8 million was siphoned from a dwindling endowment to support an overhead rate that had ballooned to 17%. And 86% of the organization's $80 million in annual revenue was generated largely by wilderness camps with declining census levels.

After Jack died, Eckerd's primary driving force of "It's the kids" morphed into "It's the camps." Instead of perpetually trying to develop better and more cost-effective treatment alternatives for youth based on research and best practices, the organization had come to identify itself inextricably as "the wilderness camping organization." Faced with this dilemma, and sensing the organization teetering, Eckerd's board of directors knew change had to happen. In 2006, they launched a national search for a transformational leader who could not only "put out the fires and right the ship," but also embed systems within the organization that would ensure that the ship was adaptable enough to sail successfully into perpetuity, regardless of the mortality of any future leader.

With these objectives in mind, in April 2007, David Dennis was hired as chief executive officer. A licensed marriage and family therapist, David had a 30-year history in the child welfare and juvenile justice sectors, with a particular emphasis on leading turnarounds and startups. In addition to his professional experience, David brought personal passion to his work, born out of a childhood journey that included being removed from his alcoholic mother's care by child protective services after his father's death and later being adopted and given the second chance every child deserves.

Transforming the Organization

After engaging numerous stakeholders and assessing Eckerd's existing services and systems, David put in motion a plan to begin transforming the organization and ensuring its future adaptability:

- Reaffirm the mission and vision and operationalize the values
- Face reality with courage and plant a flag on the moon
- Codify strategic building blocks, execution paths, and measurable milestones
- Install systems to drive execution and perpetually improve

Step 1: Reaffirm the Mission and Vision and Operationalize the Values

As Peter Drucker wrote in *The Effective Executive*, "Any organization also needs a commitment to values and their constant reaffirmation, as a human body needs vitamins and minerals. There has to be something 'this organization stands for' or else it degenerates into disorganization, confusion and paralysis . . ." (p. 56). Because Eckerd was disorganized, confused, and paralyzed when the new leadership took over in 2007, company leadership decided to begin the journey of transformation by focusing staff on the answer Jack gave when asked what was most important to him: "It's the kids." He never said, "It's the camps." It was always: "It's the kids."

Eckerd engaged a wide variety of stakeholders, including staff, the board, and customer agencies, to weigh in on its mission ("Provide and share solutions that promote the well-being of children and families in need of a second chance") and vision ("Ensure that each child has the opportunity to succeed"). It quickly became clear there was universal agreement by all and, aside from minor editing, the mission and vision remained intact as Eckerd's overarching compass points. The values, however, were a different story. At the time, Eckerd had 10 organizational values and seven guiding philosophies, all of which were being followed haphazardly at best. As a result, Eckerd leadership culled the list to the following values:

- We base our concepts upon a belief in God and respect for all.
- Youth always come first.
- Services should focus on the family.
- Local communities must be engaged and empowered.
- We hold ourselves accountable for achieving superior outcomes.
- We engage people from a strengths-based perspective.
- We are good financial stewards.
- We build strong and lasting partnerships.
- We have the courage to innovate and change.

With agreement on the values, leadership reflected on how well Eckerd had recently been "living" its values with sobering results. Was Eckerd really holding itself accountable for achieving superior outcomes when it had programs on conditional status for poor quality? Was it being a good financial steward with a 17% overhead rate and an annual withdrawal of $2.8 million from the endowment? And how was Eckerd demonstrating the courage to innovate and change when it actively refused customer requests to transition away from wilderness camps toward community-based services? After Eckerd pondered these questions, it became clear that a system was needed to ensure that the values were embedded and operationalized throughout the organization so that Eckerd could never again stray from them.

As a result, an organizational operating construct was created called "The Eckerd Wheel." It consisted of both performance and person sides. As shown in Figure 3.2, the performance side of the Eckerd Wheel has as its hub Eckerd's second through fourth values regarding youth, families, and communities, to ensure that each operational decision or action is made with its effects on these values in mind.

Surrounding the hub are Eckerd's five "spokes" of quality, staff, finance, external relations, and growth and transformation, with each spoke mapped to one of values five through nine. In turn, each spoke (and hence each value) is championed by one of five spoke departments located at Eckerd's support

FIGURE 3.2   The performance side of the Eckerd Wheel.

Source: Reed (2012).

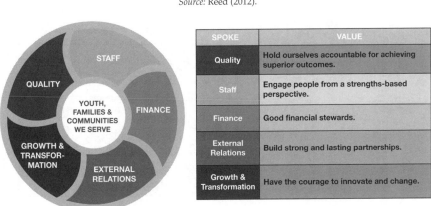

SPOKE	VALUE
Quality	Hold ourselves accountable for achieving superior outcomes.
Staff	Engage people from a strengths-based perspective.
Finance	Good financial stewards.
External Relations	Build strong and lasting partnerships.
Growth & Transformation	Have the courage to innovate and change.

center, with each department chief a member of the executive leadership team that reports directly to the CEO. For example, the quality spoke/value of "We hold ourselves accountable for achieving superior outcomes" is championed by Eckerd's quality team, which is led by the chief quality officer.

On a bike, if one spoke is bent, the wheel wobbles. Analogously, the Eckerd Wheel dictates that each spoke contributes equally to decision making to ensure that all points of view are heard and equally considered. The systemization of this dynamic tension ensures that each spoke (and thus each value) operates as a peer and fosters balanced decision making while keeping the hub values always at the center of the decision. Ultimately, by continuously championing Eckerd's values, the Eckerd Wheel reinforces a strong sense of organizational identity and ideology while simultaneously acting as a thread binding the organization together as it forges a stronger ability to drive and adapt to future change.

Whereas the performance side of the wheel ensures Eckerd's perpetual performance, the person side of the wheel (Figure 3.3) ensures that all staff members are focused on attending to each other's, and their own, needs as human beings. The person side balances the performance side, making sure that Eckerd never loses sight of superior performance's total reliance on an engaged and fulfilled workforce.

At the hub of the person side is "Respect for All," which reflects Eckerd's first value: "We base our concepts upon a belief in God and respect for all." This value recognizes that each person is uniquely special and has inherent worth. Surrounding the hub are the five person-side spokes:

- *Integrity:* Totally ethical behavior at all times and in all situations
- *Responsibility:* Knowing and doing what is expected of you
- *Empathy:* Seeing the world through another person's eyes
- *Caring:* Meeting another person's needs
- *Happiness:* Having a smile on your face

FIGURE 3.3 The person side of the Eckerd Wheel.

Source: Reed (2012).

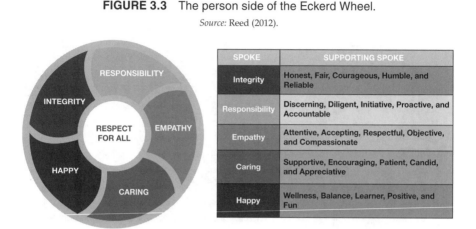

SPOKE	SUPPORTING SPOKE
Integrity	Honest, Fair, Courageous, Humble, and Reliable
Responsibility	Discerning, Diligent, Initiative, Proactive, and Accountable
Empathy	Attentive, Accepting, Respectful, Objective, and Compassionate
Caring	Supportive, Encouraging, Patient, Candid, and Appreciative
Happy	Wellness, Balance, Learner, Positive, and Fun

Eckerd's five-dimensional leadership development system is designed to develop and evaluate all staff with respect to both the person and the performance sides of the Eckerd Wheel. Methods of developing staff include on-the-job experiences, mentoring, interactive training, employee appreciation events, team-building exercises, cohort groups, and more. This is one way that the organization attempts to weave the Eckerd Wheel and its corresponding values into the everyday fabric of the staff.

Step 2: Face Reality With Courage and Plant a Flag on the Moon

By 2007, a vast majority of youth services agencies were far into the process of moving away from residential services. Eckerd, however, had refused to face this reality, believing that wilderness camps were the end-all solution and hoping that eventually the tide would turn. Knowing this tide would never turn, Eckerd's new leadership held frank discussions with staff, the board, and stakeholders about the hard realities Eckerd faced and the courage needed to overcome these challenges. Although these were not always comfortable conversations, they were necessary ones, at times waking people up to Eckerd's situational realities, which included the prospect of program closures. So important were these reality-check conversations that Eckerd has integrated them into its annual planning process. An example from 2007 of "Facing Reality with Courage" is shown in Table 3.2.

It has been said that without a vision, the people perish, and as Eckerd faced the harsh realities of 2007, leadership did not want staff to lose sight of the possibilities ahead. To this end, leadership decided to "plant a flag on the moon," establishing in measurable terms a "2020 Vision" for the organization that projected Eckerd to increase the number of youth served annually from 9,500 to 20,020 in the year 2020, and also to achieve national thought leadership recognition. Additionally, Eckerd established "Program 2020

TABLE 3.2   Eckerd 2007: Facing Reality With Courage

Eckerd's 2007 Reality	The Courage Needed
• Shrinking residential funding	• Exit or transform camps
• Increasing community-based funding	• Grow community base
• Under-engaged families	• Focus on families
• Reluctance to use data	• Become data-driven
• Bloated overhead	• Reduce overhead
• Investments being drained	• Leverage investments
• Customers not partners	• Build customer partnerships

Source: Reed (2013).

Visions": Each program has painted a picture of where it intends to be by the year 2020. Over time, Eckerd's 2020 Vision has become a rallying cry for staff, and because the organization has transformed and now serves 14,000 youth annually, the staff have taken great pride in their accomplishments to date.

Step 3: Codify Strategic Building Blocks, Execution Paths, and Measurable Milestones

Having a 2020 Vision, leadership next defined for each performance-side spoke its own strategic building block and execution paths marked by clear and measurable near-term, midterm, and long-term horizon milestones. Each spoke's strategic building block is meant to represent the spoke's foundational competency, while the execution paths represent the directional expectations over the next 18 to 24 months for each spoke (and hence building block) in pursuit of achieving the upcoming horizon milestones. For example, Table 3.3 shows the quality spoke and its strategic building block, milestones, and midterm execution paths, and Table 3.4 shows those for the growth and transformation spoke.

Eckerd's recent transformation of its North Carolina wilderness camps is a good illustration of how the strategic building blocks work. The building block for Eckerd's growth and transformation spoke emphasizes "actively engaging and partnering with customers to develop solutions to better meet their needs." At the height of Eckerd's wilderness camp programming, the organization operated seven such programs in North Carolina, even though the Department of Juvenile Justice wanted to transform to more community-based services. The department was effectively hampered in doing so because the camps were included in their budget as a non-compete line-item that Eckerd had successfully fought to protect. With the establishment of the growth and transformation strategic building block, Eckerd's new leadership engaged the department, asking them (much to their surprise) what their needs and desires were and offering to partner on the corresponding changes. Over the years that followed, Eckerd then supported the elimination of the Eckerd budget line-item and

TABLE 3.3   The Quality Spoke's Strategic Building Block, Milestones, and Midterm Execution Paths

Building Block	Milestones	Midterm Execution Paths
Thought leadership with respect to operating family-focused, data-driven services that deliver cost-effective outcomes and impact	*Near-Term (by June 2013)* Make the use of data central to each program's operations by deploying a Perpetual Performance Improvement (PPI) system (milestone achieved).	• Develop and deploy throughout all programs a "Youth Success Wheel" using evidence-based principles with the objective of generating positive long-term impact.
	Midterm (by June 2016) Achieve the best contractual outcomes in each operating state for each program operated.	• Focus each program's PPI efforts on exceeding the performance of the other providers in their state.
	Long-Term (by June 2021) Demonstrate the long-term impact for the youth served of each service operated.	• Engage other organizations on ways to improve services and performance.

Source: Reed (2013).

TABLE 3.4   Growth and Transformation Spoke's Strategic Building Block, Milestones, and Midterm Execution Paths

Building Block	Milestones	Midterm Execution Paths
Thought leadership with respect to system reform and to actively engaging and partnering with customers to develop solutions to better meet their needs	*Near-Term (by June 2013)* Serve 12,000 youth annually (milestone achieved).	• Support each program's 2020 Vision in engaging customers and communities as to their needs.
	Midterm (by June 2016) Serve 16,000 youth annually.	• Pursue mergers and acquisitions as a means to strengthen both organizations and scale.
	Long-Term (by June 2021) Serve 20,020 youth annually.	• Secure investments to pursue strategic resource needs.

Source: Reed (2013).

the refocusing of state funds on competitively bid, short-term residential and community-based services. While this did result in the closure of all seven North Carolina Eckerd camps, the department's needs were met and Eckerd competitively won two short-term residential programs and five community-based programs, which enabled Eckerd to serve more youth annually with lower costs and better outcomes.

One particularly exciting area of future focus for Eckerd is the quality spoke's execution path strategy to develop and deploy a "Youth Success Wheel" to drive substantive longitudinal youth impact. This path represents Eckerd's determination to shift programmatic outcomes from transactional outcomes, such as completion rates and 12-month post-success rates, to impact outcomes, such as whether an Eckerd program is truly a driving force in giving children a second chance to ultimately grow up into successful adults.

Step 4: Install Systems to Drive Execution and Perpetually Improve

With strategic building blocks and measurable milestones in place, leadership next set out to develop and install a system of execution that maximized the impact of the Eckerd Wheel and ensured perpetual improvement. What emerged was Eckerd's Perpetual Performance Improvement (PPI) process, which identifies, for both the overall organization and individual programs, support center spokes, as well as the individual staff, performance data, reports, and improvement processes that will be utilized. Three examples of performance tools and systems defined by the PPI process follow:

- *Program Performance Scorecards*
  Each Eckerd program has its own performance scorecard populated with key performance indicators (KPIs) spanning the five performance spokes of the Eckerd Wheel. This ensures that each program maintains alignment with the Eckerd Wheel and hence Eckerd's values. Program scorecards are reviewed monthly by program operations and spoke staff during program PPI meetings; areas of high performance are highlighted and areas of low performance are targeted for improvement.
- *Spoke 5×5 Performance Scorecards*
  Each performance side spoke has its own performance scorecard with five "subspokes," and each subspoke has its own top five KPIs. For example, the staff spoke has as its five subspokes stability, engagement, development, exit satisfaction, and recruiting, with each of these having its own five KPIs that are reviewed on a monthly basis for performance improvement opportunities. By having both the 5×5 spoke performance scorecards and program performance scorecards, Eckerd is able to view performance from two important perspectives.
- *Eckerd Execution Status Report*
  Each month, Eckerd produces an overall organization execution report that includes strategic and tactical (annual operating plan) scorecards, both containing KPIs for each of the spokes of the Eckerd Wheel. For example, the strategic scorecard tracks Eckerd's execution relative to the spoke execution paths and upcoming horizon milestones. This report is available to all staff every month and is provided to the board on a quarterly basis.

In short, the PPI process was engineered with the Eckerd Wheel at its core to ensure that Eckerd's values were being lived and measured throughout the organization.

Six Years Into the Journey: A Dramatic Transformation and an Exciting Future

First and foremost, the Eckerd Wheel and its supporting planning and execution systems provided Eckerd with the capacity to adapt, to be able to react swiftly and nimbly when "the cheese has been moved" or to be a "cheese mover"—and thus, in turn, to be able to overcome the limitations mortality places on what any one person can contribute. As Peter Drucker wrote in *The Effective Executive*, "An organization which just perpetuates today's level of vision, excellence, and accomplishment has lost the capacity to adapt. And since the one and only thing certain in human affairs is change, it will not be capable of survival in a changed tomorrow" (p. 57).

In 2007, Eckerd was an $80 million nonprofit with 86% of its revenue derived from residential programs that agencies no longer wanted. Six years later, and having closed $78 million of that original $80 million in programming, Eckerd approaches its 2014 fiscal year as an organization of $160 million, of which 95% is community-based. And while the organization does have strong leaders, there are no genius ones. Instead, the organization's values are lived in a systematized manner every day; reality is faced with courage; people strive to plant a flag on the moon; building blocks, execution paths, and milestones are clear; execution is not optional; and, most important of all: "It's the kids."

However, although progress has been made, the journey is far from over. There is much room for improvement, and there are 20,020 youth annually yet to be reached.

REFERENCES

Alliance for Children and Families & Baker Tilly. (2011). *Disruptive forces: Driving a human services revolution.* Washington, DC: Alliance for Children and Families.

Center for American Progress. (2012, December 5). *Social impact bonds: Frequently asked questions: Social impact bonds.* Washington, DC: Costa, Shah, Ungar, & the Social Impact Bonds Working Group. Retrieved from http://www.americanprogress.org/issues/economy/report/2012/12/05/46934/frequently-asked-questions-social-impact-bonds

Center for Health Care Strategies, Inc. (2011, June). *Implementing health homes in a risk-based Medicaid-managed care delivery system.* Hamilton, NJ: Hasselman & Bachrach. Retrieved from http://www.chcs.org/usr_doc/Final_Brief_HH_and_Managed_Care_FINAL.pdf

Centers for Disease Control and Prevention. (2011–2012). *National survey of children's health* [Data file]. Retrieved from http://www.cdc.gov/nchs/slaits/nsch.htm

Chesbrough, H. (2005). *Open innovation: The new imperative for creating and profiting from technology* (1st trade paperback ed.). Boston, MA: Harvard Business Review Press.

Child Trends. (2003, December). *Children in foster homes: How are they faring?* Retrieved from http://www.childtrends.org/?publications=children-in-foster-homes-how-are-they-faring-2

Collins, J. (2001). *Good to great.* New York, NY: HarperBusiness.

Drucker, P. (2006). *The effective executive.* New York, NY: HarperBusiness.

Fountain, C., Winter, A. S., & Bearman, P. S. (2012). Six developmental trajectories characterize children with autism. *Pediatrics, 129*(5), e1112–e1120. doi:10.1542/peds.2011-1601

Foster care. (2012). *Child Trends*. Retrieved from http://www.childtrends.org/?indicators=foster-care

Ganz, M. L. (2007). The lifetime distribution of the incremental societal costs of autism. *Archives of Pediatric and Adolescent Medicine, 161*(4), 343–349. doi:10.1001/archpedi.161.4.343

Mathematica Policy Research, Inc. (2004, November). *Children with special health care needs: Building a quality-of-care initiative*. Princeton, NJ: Nyman & Ireys. Retrieved from http://www.mathematica-mpr.com/publications/pdfs/cshcn.pdf

Michigan Nonprofit Association. (2012). *Snapshot on volunteering and giving in Michigan*. Detroit, MI. Retrieved from https://michigan.michigan.gov/documents/mcsc/GivingandVolunteering2007_282129_7.pdf

Morel, N., Palier, B., & Palme, J. (Eds.). (2009). *What future for social investment?* Stockholm, Sweden: Institute for Futures Studies.

O'Connell, M. E., Boat, T., & Warner, K. E. (Eds.). (2009). *Preventing mental, emotional, and behavioral disorders among young people: Progress and possibilities*. Retrieved from http://www.nap.edu/openbook.php?record_id=12480&page=346

OPEN MINDS. (2013, March 5). *The cost of ADHD*. Gettysburg, PA: Oss. Retrieved from http://www.openminds.com/market-intelligence/intelligence-updates/030512-more-adhd.htm

Pew Research Hispanic Center. (2008). *U.S. population projections: 2005–2050*. Washington DC: Passel & Cohn. Retrieved from http://www.pewhispanic.org/2008/02/11/us-population-projections-2005-2050/

Reed, A. (2012). *The Eckerd strategic plan snapshot*. Clearwater, FL: Eckerd.

Reed, A. (2013). *The Eckerd transformation*. Clearwater, FL: Eckerd.

Salamon, L. M. (2003). *The resilient sector: The state of nonprofit America*. Washington, DC: Brookings Institution Press.

12 crucial consumer trends for 2012. (2012, January). *trendwatching.com*. Retrieved from http://trendwatching.com/trends/12trends2012

The Urban Institute & The Brookings Institution. (2010). *Public expenditures on children through 2008*. Washington, DC: Macomber, Isaacs, Kent, & Vericker. Retrieved from http://www.urban.org/UploadedPDF/412003_public_expenditures_on_children.pdf

Weber Shandwick. (2009). *Social media in the nonprofit sector: A survey of nonprofit communications executives*. New York, NY: Author.

What is autism? (2013). *Autism Speaks*. Retrieved from http://www.autismspeaks.org/what-autism

CHAPTER 4

Early Reflections on the Strategy Counts Initiative: A Pilot Site Roundtable Discussion

Elizabeth Kunde

Strategy Counts, an initiative of the Alliance for Children and Families supported by the Kresge Foundation, embarked on its second year by gathering the Cohort Learning Group for a 3-day peer-learning experience on February 6–8, 2013, in Detroit. On February 7, leaders from the pilot sites discussed their work and how it connects to the overall sector and current trends, as well as the challenges they face, the opportunities they embrace, and what keeps them leaning forward against the headwinds of what feels like relentless change.

What follows are excerpts from the event's discussion, which was moderated by Susan Dreyfus, president and CEO at the Alliance for Children and Families, Guillermina Hernández-Gallegos; human services program director at the Kresge Foundation; Ruth McCambridge, editor-in-chief of the *Nonprofit Quarterly*; and Michael Mortell, director of Strategy Counts at the Alliance for Children and Families.

Ruth McCambridge: What have been your experiences in engaging staff?

Mona Swanson: Part of our project involved having an outside consultant hold focus groups throughout the organization, and it was very difficult to hear what they had to say—how staff felt unsure of how we were mission-focused at this point. While it was kind of earth-shattering to us, it has been very helpful and has given us plenty to do in terms of figuring out how we bring the organization together and build our strategy.

Rob Myers: With 675 employees—echoing what Mona said—we have had our challenges with getting the message across. But, one of the things we created, in helping us deliver the message, is a group called Process Council. That's a group of 10 individuals who were hand-selected from throughout the organization, all different levels of staff members. Many of the individuals have become our voice for process excellence transformation. It has been very effective.

Tim Johnstone: The staff responded quite well. Management is where we had problems. We've done strategic plans for a number of years. We talked about how we needed to look across all of the services, and not just at what we offered, but what is offered throughout the community to help clients and client families achieve self-sufficiency. We realized quickly that we had to collaborate better internally before we could start to think about collaborating better externally.

Guillermina Hernandez-Gallegos: What role do constituent voices play in helping you be strategic?

Angela Blanchard: We have to be incredibly good listeners—that is fundamental. But, even more important is framing questions in a new way. I like to say that change begins with the first new question. The old questions of community development were always about lacks, gaps, needs, wants, and whatever was missing and broken. At Neighborhood Centers, Inc., we don't ask, "What's tragic about your life?" Instead, we want to know, "What are you working on? What do you have? What are you able to accomplish? What are your ultimate aspirations?"

So, the dots that really need to connect are the ones that align their aspirations with resources. A key role for a strategy officer in our organization is seeing where neighborhoods are going and where resources are headed—then finding the intersection of the two.

That intersection is critically important, because resources never align perfectly with what needs to be done. So a key part of our strategy work is looking at the way they do align and finding ways to reshape the resources to fit the neighborhoods and neighbors.

I think it's the willingness to not go in asking the question and dutifully go through the motions of chronicling what you are assuming you are going to hear so that you can say you did it. But it's putting yourself in a place of humility. Humility's a very powerful word in this work.

Denise Roberts: JFCS was just involved in a very competitive process and the last question was, "What are your mission, vision, and values?" And I wrote something boring. But, then we asked the participants what they value. Well, they said, "I like to be looked right in the eye. I want you to remember my name." And so that's what we put in. We shredded what I wrote. And we got the project. In fact the feedback we got had one panelist saying that, while this application was the best all around, it shone because of the extensive use of participant input at every stage.

Tine Hansen-Turton: First of all, I want to say that strategy is a luxury asset. What Kresge has enabled us to do is really ask the right questions. I mean, most of us in the human services sector have been driven by what government funders want.

Susan Dreyfus: If you were in charge of all of the federal and state money that flows through your agency, what would you do differently to be more strategic?

Alan Mucatel: I would think about our social safety net in a complete picture. Our funding sources should be thinking about the comprehensive needs of all members of our communities. But even easier than that, I think some longer-term thinking about funding is a nice place to start. We are wasting dollars each time we stop the flow of money and then start it up again.

Dave Paxton: Several years ago, unfortunately, Ohio had a couple of horrible, tragic incidents where two foster children died largely because they fell through cracks in the system. That said, the reaction of the State Legislature was to pile on all these new regulations that were expected of us. And meanwhile, they provided the same amount of fees. So they were expecting more oversight, more outcomes for the same amount of funding. It was hard to track back how their new rules were going to prevent what had actually happened.

Angela Blanchard: We need to try to get away from the notion that neighborhoods can be transformed by a single service. You can't build a clinic and expect it to change a neighborhood in some heroic, miraculous, transformational way—for good. Not going to happen. We've wasted so much money on this notion[,] and [we] need to move on.

Michael Mortell: How do we, as a sector, increase the percent of giving to nonprofit human-serving organizations?

Tine Hansen-Turton: You've got three generations in this workforce right now. Each thinks very differently about philanthropy. And I think that's driving a lot of this. A few things are going on in the corporate sector, too, such as benefit corporations. We must align ourselves with them. It's about how we—rather than going out parading our own social mission—how do we align ourselves with that larger social mission and become a partner in that.

Angela Blanchard: I think it stems from a very major language change. They're changing from the language of charity to one of investment. The intent is to stop talking about people's needs and focus on what we're trying to build together—a healthier economy and a region of industry, innovation, and investment.

Rob Myers: I think it's important not to get lost in all of this. The Alliance had Andy Goodman speak at the National Conference about learning to tell our story. So, it's really learning, I think, on a real simple, basic level, how to tell your story.

Guillermina Hernandez-Gallegos: What is the role of philanthropy in this strategic process?

Angela Blanchard: I just feel appalled by the way we view a nonprofit's need for infrastructure versus that same need in a business. We would never invest in a business that lacked the capacity to build systems to track customers or find out how their sales were doing and so forth.

But some people seem to think you can run a human services organization in some magical way. Just dream up something and not have any tools. I think that one of the key things that philanthropists do is to support organizations with the tools and platforms.

They can use the considerable power of philanthropy to demand from the sector a higher-quality product.

Ruth McCambridge: When an organization transforms, it often closes programs and activities that do not fit its strategic vision. What have been your experiences?

Amelia Blake-Dowdle: A little over a year ago now, our Senior Leadership Team found ourselves in a spot where we were losing hundreds of thousands of dollars each year. We knew that, obviously, we couldn't continue with that gap. We had been losing revenue, but weren't reducing the associated expenses, so we had some tough decisions to make. We had to separate several folks and redeploy some folks in order to sustain the organization and fill that gap. Last January was very difficult for us, but I'm happy to say that we're in a much better place a year later.

Now we have surpluses and need to figure out how to best use those surpluses. So it's been a good year for us, most recently in looking at profitability in terms of particular programs. We have an eating disorder program, and we got rave reviews on how well we do with the youth from the surrounding county.

But because only 1 of every 20 youth was eligible after restrictions around insurance companies and private-pay situations, we were just losing hundreds of thousands of dollars every year. So unfortunately, we did have to close that program.

Tim Johnstone: We have a number of food banks that we operate as part of our emergency services. We created a program a couple years ago called Nourishing Networks, which was a grassroots food program where each community could identify the biggest need for supplemental food. While it was a really, really valuable and important program in the community, we realized that our program didn't fit with our model, because it didn't allow us to have case management to help coach clients towards self-sufficiency, which is our mission. And so we didn't want to just close it. We ended up spinning it off. Now a former employee is the executive director and has received the funding for the program so it could go off on its own.

Glenn Wilson: Our focus on strategy has us looking at our complete business. After careful reflection and analysis, we concluded that because of the distance between our headquarters in Pittsburgh and site in Philadelphia, we may not be in the best position to carry out our mission. Our first and foremost thoughts were of youth we serve, our staff, and the positive impact our work has on the community. We wanted a solution that limited and reduced any trauma that may be felt by the children, families, and staff. We sought a partner with like values and like programs—one that would be willing to continue our programs and services, and continue to employ our staff.

We found that partner in Public Health Management Corporation. As a Philadelphia-based organization, it seemed to have all of the perfectly aligned political connections, which is an important aspect of running a social service organization that relies on government funding. The assets, program, services, and staff transferred to the organization April 1, 2013. It's been a wonderful partnership, and the relationship will continue. We are extremely confident that the organization will continue to carry on our mission, while growing the programs and services offered to the community. The transfer was the perfect solution for the people we serve, for our employees, and the community.

Ruth McCambridge: How has Strategy Counts impacted your board?

Greg Ryan: One of the things that we've done over the last year with Strategy Counts is create a strategy task force of the board. Previously, we had a task force that convened only once every 4 years to do long-range planning. Now, that has become a regular standing task force that monitors how we're doing in implementation between those 4-year cycles.

Elizabeth Carey: In these last 2 years we've taken a lot of risks—meaning we've engaged in a process with our board of trustees to try to shift into new directions and use organizational resources that we wouldn't have used in the past. We plan to impact kids and families in some different ways and in new places and in new efforts. That takes resources and we're trying to gather them from everywhere. And so, Board, can you go with us to try and do that?

It has been an invigorating experience because we had board members absolutely get that and step up, saying, "We can't do anything else but that. Of course. Let's go." And then, because it means changing old ways of doing business, we had others say, "Help me understand how that is what I came to do."

It has made us ask questions we hadn't asked of ourselves and it is ever changing. I described it the other day as being on a highway, seeing the final destination, and then construction happens. And you think "Darn it, where's the exit ramp to go around this one?" But, you search for the appropriate detours, you find the way, and you end up headed in the right direction again.

Alan Mucatel: Our board is taking ownership in a way that is somewhat unexpected. About a year after they participated in the creation of our strategic plan, they decided to create, on their own, a committee to keep all of the board members informed about where our state was going. They took full ownership of making sure the organization stays on top of current trends.

They've also been very proactive in wanting to understand evidence-based practices, where we should be in that space, what programs we should be taking on, and how they might change the culture of the organization.

Guillermina Hernandez-Gallegos: How are you using data to inform your strategic direction?

Greg Ryan: Data's always been embedded in our culture. But sometimes decision making can become very driven by funding and compliance, and data collection becomes just another task or a report that needs to be done.

I think Strategy Counts has allowed us to take that to the next step. It's not just about collecting the data in order to satisfy a compliance issue. It's about using that data to make better decisions. We've put together a scorecard, a strategic scorecard that brings together data elements from across the organization.

How do you measure whether you improve the lives of the individuals and families in the community? That's tough. But that's really what we're here to do. And if we're not figuring out a way to measure that, then we're not really realizing our mission.

Tim Johnstone: We have to do a better job of demonstrating that we have a lasting impact on the clients that we serve. The health care community, hospitals particularly, are way ahead of us. Look how many hospitals, for example, have applied for Baldrige awards and other quality-based awards and are measuring outcomes and improving health outcomes for patients. And we're way behind on that. So for us to catch up, we have to do a way better job of being able to demonstrate that.

Jim Bettendorf: For our organization, we're on a journey of creating a theory of change for each of our eight program areas. We started our first theory of change with a project team of staff who provide services to people coming back from prison. In terms of outcome expectations, the staff has always set the bar at whatever the Federal Bureau of Prisons said they were supposed to do.

After the discussion, the project team realized they could have a greater community impact than before. The project team set their bar to a level where they will need to track these people for a lot longer, so the people will become responsible members of society, which means a lot of things have to happen before that point. So the team set the standard, it wasn't set for them. The project team set the metrics. They weren't set for them by the funder, the leadership team, or a strategy team.

Ruth McCambridge: How have your partnerships and choices related to working with other groups changed?

Tine Hansen-Turton: PHMC noticed that another Alliance member agency in Philadelphia does work in human services and behavioral health. Because we have health care expertise, we came together over a 2-year period and said: If we help you bring health care to your agency, can we create a joint venture? We both have a stake in its success.

From the Strategy Counts initiative, we have learned that we have an obligation to partner the right way and make sure that each partnership has a purpose directly related to client and community impact. It goes back to the luxury of being able to think more deeply and strategically.

It's not a mistake, and you're not a failure, if you let things go. This has changed the way we are partnering, because we are now putting what I call divorce clauses into our partnership agreements—that if it doesn't work out, there's a way out for both parties. And now, quite frankly, organizations are coming to us because they know that we are open to walking away if it doesn't work out.

Dave Paxton: It isn't so much who we're partnering with, but who we're not partnering with. More recently, we have been contracting with local juvenile courts to keep kids out of detention. One of our largest programs now is in Franklin County and in Columbus, Ohio, with the local juvenile court to keep kids out of detention who otherwise would have no place to go. Kids come to our foster care programs for respite for the weekend or a week assessment.

What's interesting about that and quite different for us is that Children's Services is not involved at all. I think it's a matter of Children's Services' focus and lack of funding. The shift is going to juvenile justice rather than Children's Services.

Susan Dreyfus: What is it that worries you and keeps you up at night?

Glenn Wilson: I'm most worried about low-performing organizations potentially diluting the amount of work that we actually do. We want to serve more and we want to do more, but to do that, we need to have more people to serve. If we have too many organizations in a geographical area providing the same type of service, the process is diluted. It would be a shame if we lost the best of the best only because of the inability to have enough force and enough magnitude of work to keep us sustaining.

Jim Bettendorf: I worry that I'll wake up one day and our sole funding provider will be a managed care organization of some sort, and we won't be ready or capable of proving our worth and value to them. At some point, the government's going to be less and less a provider. Insurance or managed care entities will be the funders, and I'm not sure what they are going to ask of us. And that's what keeps me up at night.

Greg Ryan: Something that I worry about is being able to continue to grow the quality of staff that we can hire. We've really focused on trying to do a better job of providing better compensation and benefits to our staff, and that takes resources. But it's important because you want to have the best people delivering services, making connections, fostering those relationships, and helping people build the skills that they need to be self-sufficient.

Guillermina Hernandez-Gallegos: What inspires you and allows you to continue to think differently?

Elizabeth Banwell: I guarantee that the human services sector is going to continue to demand change. The best news is that we, as an organization, are going to be able to make that shift, and we are going to be able to retain the passion and connection to the grassroots.

Mona Swanson: Similarly, the work we've been doing since Strategy Counts has a lot to do with hearing from our staff and making sure that they are a strong part of the process, that they understand their roles, that they are heard, and that they have all shaped how we plan to get where we're going. And that excites me, because we have a lot of fantastic people.

PILOT SITE ROUNDTABLE PARTICIPANTS

Greg Ryan, CSO, Heartland Family Service, Omaha, NE
Amelia Blake-Dowdle, COO, Villa of Hope (formerly St. Joseph's Villa), Rochester, NY
Tine Hansen-Turton, CSO, Public Health Management Corporation, Philadelphia, PA
Dave Paxton, CSO, The Village Network, Smithville, OH
Elizabeth Banwell, CSO, The Opportunity Alliance, South Portland, ME
Angela Blanchard, president & CEO, Neighborhood Centers, Inc., Houston, TX
Alan Mucatel, president & CEO, Leake and Watts Services, Inc., Yonkers, NY
Jim Bettendorf, CSO, Volunteers of America of Minnesota, Minneapolis, MN
Denise Roberts, consultant, Jewish Family and Children's Service, Sarasota, FL
Rob Myers, executive vice president of Fund Development, Hathaway-Sycamores Child and Family Services, Pasadena, CA
Elizabeth Carey, executive vice president and chief strategy and administration officer, Starr Commonwealth, Albion, MI
Tim Johnstone, CSO, Hopelink, Redmond, WA
Mona Swanson, COO, The Children's Village, Dobbs Ferry, NY
Glenn Wilson, CSO, Holy Family Institute, Pittsburgh, PA

CHAPTER 5

Reshaping Organizations Through Culture and Strategy

Kathleen O'Brien, Ellen Katz, Shannon Starkey-Taylor, Timothy Johnstone, Richard Cohen, Tine Hansen-Turton, Anne Callan, Nancy Bradberry, and Richard Benoit

CULTURE EATS STRATEGY FOR LUNCH

This chapter gives the reader an insight into how organizations use different approaches to change their cultures to successfully deploy strategy. Included in here are perspectives from Great Circle, The Children's Home of Cincinnati, Hopelink, and Public Health Management Corporation.

Authors of this chapter were asked to consider the phrase "culture eats strategy for lunch," which is widely attributed to Dr. Peter Drucker, often referred to as the father of modern management. This phrase is a popular topic among business leaders today and is the subject of various articles, many blog posts and comments, and a forthcoming book, *Culture Eats Strategy for Lunch* by Curt W. Coffman, coauthor of *First, Break All the Rules,* and leadership expert Dr. Kathleen Sorenson.

Workplace Culture: People and Relationships

Workplace culture is the collective behavior of people within an organization, including individual and collective values, norms, systems, processes, symbols, and habits. It reinforces the organization's mission, vision, goals—its overall strategy. The culture influences the brand image of an organization. Although each workplace culture is unique, culture is based on the following elements:

- How the work gets done
- How decisions are made
- Communication within, between, and among work units

In *First, Break all the Rules,* Buckingham and Coffman differentiate between two types of office culture: the "big C," referring to mission, vision, core values, and strategy, and the "little c," the day-to-day work unit, team, or department. They suggest that a strong predictor for growing, high-performing organizations is the alignment of these two cultures (Buckingham & Coffman, 1999).

Cultures within organizations evolve and change over time. The behaviors of the senior leadership, primarily the CEO, largely shape the culture of an organization. Changing the culture of an organization must be a conscious decision by the senior leadership, demonstrated by changing and modeling desired behavior in words and actions.

Strategy: Articulating the Big Picture Direction

Strategy involves determining the direction of the organization by defining the mission or purpose, the vision or aspiration, and the goal measures for achievement. It is an ongoing, iterative process that evaluates the core business model of an organization and includes assessing a changing environment or industry, outlining core competencies, leveraging competitive advantages, and responding to social, economic, and political forces that determine long-term performance mission impact.

The organization's leadership is responsible for clearly articulating the vision and direction, which involves identifying strategies for responding to industry changes, defining accountability for results, clarifying work processes and systems, allocating resources for priorities, communicating within and among the workforce, and decision-making within the organization. The ways that work gets done and decisions are made and communicated parallel how culture is created, thus reinforcing that culture and strategy are intertwined. In effective, high-performing organizations, strategy drives the execution of the operational day-to-day activities measuring performance targets that link strategies to outcomes and results. Decisions across the organization are focused on strategy implementation, and resources are allocated per defined strategic direction and initiatives.

Culture Eats Strategy; When There Is a Disconnect

Business experts, including Michael Porter of Harvard University, suggest that if there is a conflict or misalignment between culture and strategy, culture will win every time. A frequently cited example of misalignment is when an organization's strategy is to aspire to growth through innovation and creativity, yet the culture is highly autocratic and hierarchical and bureaucratic systems require that all decision-making be controlled from the top—the CEO and senior leadership. Hierarchical management requires that suggestions or decisions travel up and then down the chain of command, taking time and reducing an organization's agility. A stall in strategy performance may indicate a disconnect or misalignment between the culture and the strategy. It may be time for a "culture assessment," including evaluations of systems, procedures, attitudes, behaviors, and incentive rewards. Senior leaders may not have a solid understanding of the real culture and may be out of touch with the existing cultural norms and behaviors of the organization's workforce. Even though there may be stated core values, frequently those values may be vague and meaningless to the entire workforce. Values are based on a person's biases, beliefs, personal experience, and perceptions, and no two people experience an organization's culture the same way. Thus it falls on the shoulders of the CEO and senior-level leadership to embrace and demonstrate any expected and desired behaviors. A large part of changing a culture to ensure greater alignment with strategy starts with building trust and effective two-way communication and *walking the talk* of the stated core values—that is, linking them with the direction and strategies of the organization.

Research over the years has clearly demonstrated that people frequently depart their workplaces because of the poor or negative quality of relationships at work, particularly those with their managers or supervisors. People leave organizations by (1) being terminated or dismissed, (2) departing voluntarily, or (3) remaining with the organization but disengaging from the culture, working with less motivation and inspiration to accomplish the mission strategies. All three groups can negatively affect the culture. Buckingham and Coffman suggest that the "little c" cultures, the work unit relationships between managers and employees, are critical catalysts for high performance (1999). Jim Collins, author of *Good to Great*, exemplifies the tension between culture and strategy in his famous "bus" metaphor: Get the right people on the bus and the wrong people off the bus, then decide where to go.

Even though there is no "right" culture, whether there's top-down, hierarchical senior leadership, cross-department collaboration, or some balanced combination, culture drives performance. Culture is difficult to measure and cannot be purchased, imported, or demanded. Changing the culture within an organization is a slow, long-term process and will not happen in a month, or 6 months, or a year. Change can be even more troubling, difficult, and slow if there is a long history of silos with little integration or interdepartmental collaboration on short- or long-term strategies and directions. Change doesn't happen just because top leadership declares that things have changed. Change is about developing good processes and procedures and solid, effective communication with feedback loops from the workforce, customers/clients, and critical stakeholders.

Notably, there are some situations in which a culture change may occur more quickly or in which the current state is disrupted—for example, during a CEO transition, whether through an abrupt dismissal or through the hiring of someone from outside the organization or industry. A new CEO with a clear directive from the board of directors to make significant changes should develop specific strategies to change the culture or direction of the organization. There is less likelihood of culture change when there is a long-term CEO succession plan, including an internal candidate, a clear strategic direction, and plan priorities and effective work processes already in place.

Another situation likely to result in culture disruption is after the merger of two organizations. Although on paper and in the decision-making process the joining together may make a lot of sense and appear to be a win–win, there can be a natural divide based on each entity's unique history, traditions, values, and ways of operating—its culture. Often when a merger is followed by revenue loss or the departure of leadership or other key workforce, the disruptions stem from a culture clash between the merging organizations, and the "us" vs. "them" blame game begins. Inevitably, time is needed for the board of directors, the remaining workforce, and other key stakeholders, possibly from organizations that were previously competitors, to join as one with a common culture, shared goals, and a strategic direction that aligns with those goals. The correct approach by the new senior leadership in aligning the strategy and merging the two cultures will minimize the time needed for a successful integration.

Another factor that can greatly impact the culture of any organization is the fast pace of changing technology, particularly around communication now with email, texts, and Facebook, Twitter, and other social networks. And some industries and organizations have been affected by this century's globalization, which can also influence culture and strategic direction.

In addition, there is a potential disconnect between culture and strategy in the generational differences, both in workplace attitudes and behaviors, among mixed workforces (e.g., baby boomers, Generation X, Generation Y [the so-called millennials]). As noted in numerous articles, these groups differ significantly in their approaches to work, attitudes toward authority, work style preferences, and need and/or desire for feedback and supervision. These differences can greatly influence the culture of an organization. If marshaled in a positive direction, the blend of these differences can provide the energy and momentum for a highly engaged culture aligned with the strategy direction of the organization.

Culture and Strategy Aligned = High-Performing Organization

The current reality is that all organizations face demands for constant change to meet ever-changing needs and industry trends. Thus organizations, particularly senior leaders, must create a culture that is agile, innovative, and able to adapt and improve. Developing effective strategies to meet or adapt to those changes is not about an occasional senior-level retreat to develop a future plan. It is about engaging and involving all key stakeholders in establishing the strategic direction by revisiting and clarifying the mission (purpose), the vision (future), and the goals (achievable priorities). High-performing organizations have well-aligned business models that leverage their workforce cultures as catalysts for change. Alignment will determine the direction and pace of change. It includes a clear direction with measurable goals, accountability for getting the work completed, progress checks on accomplishments, adjustments as warranted to the goals per the strategic direction, and clarity on the roles, procedures, processes, and allocation of human and dollar resources needed to accomplish the strategic direction.

Mario Morino, author of *Leap of Reason: Managing to Outcomes in an Era of Scarcity*, states, "there's one common denominator among organizations that manage outcomes successfully: courageous leaders who foster a performance culture" (2011, p. 22). Morino underscores Collins's tenet that it is about having the right talent and leadership to execute a mission. It is critical to recruit leaders who exemplify the performance culture that the company hopes to instill in the workplace. Expectations must be defined, clarified, and measured. Organizations need a balance between strategic leaders who drive the vision, direction, or change and leader-managers focused on the day-to-day operations with disciplined execution. An imbalance may result in chaos, resulting in an organization's inability to sustain long-term high performance. When a performance culture is aligned with the strategy direction, all stakeholders (e.g., workforce, board of directors, customers) will be moving in the same direction and heading for the same destination, and thus the organization will leverage its unique advantage with value-added services, achieving strategic goals and ensuring sustainability.

One method that has become more widely deployed is the use of scorecards that channel performance achievement measures from the strategic plan to the annual operating plan to a department or work unit and then to individual employee performance (see Figure 5.1). Such scorecards should include not only program and financial results but also human resource measures

FIGURE 5.1   Aligning strategic initiatives with individual performance goals.

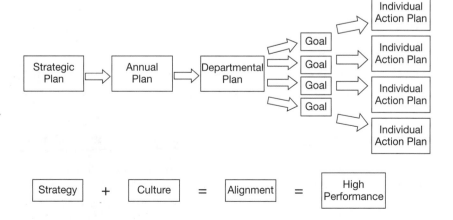

such as retention, engagement, work systems satisfaction, effectiveness of the board of directors, marketing awareness/public relations, advocacy, customer satisfaction and engagement, and internal operations and systems. Defining such measures is an iterative process and will take time—time that will be well spent toward demonstrating key results and high performance. Adopting and adapting this type of measurement is outside the scope of this chapter, but numerous resources and samples are available for various sectors.

Warning Signs of a Disconnect or Misalignment

There are a number of cues that can let an organization know there's been a disconnect between culture and strategy:

- Not having a clear strategic plan or direction
- Having a plan that is not consistently deployed across the entire organization, as exemplified by independent, silo-type work units rather than a team-based, integrated work culture
- Having a CEO who is mired in day-to-day operations and who doesn't have the capacity to stay focused on the more external, strategic issues (which is not intended to suggest that the CEO should not be well informed)
- Lack of role clarity between the CEO and the COO; lack of trust and confidence that the COO and/or senior leadership will manage the day-to-day operations
- High turnover, whether throughout the organization or in individual work units
- Lack of clear processes and procedures
- Lack of clear, measurable expectations and outcome results
- Senior leaders who think they're thinking strategically but who are actually narrowly focused on a particular business unit
- Lack of strategy direction alignment from the board of directors to the direct, on-the-ground staff
- Having a "crisis of the moment" or "crisis of the week" culture in which constant adrenaline rushes result in varying degrees of chaos or mistrust. (This can be a risk for some social services agencies that have a mission to help people at risk or help them meet their basic needs.)
- Senior leaders who feel they don't have time to pursue strategy–culture alignment because they are too busy/overwhelmed or are out of touch with the real culture of the company

Hallmarks of an Organization With Strategy and Culture Aligned

There are also ways to tell when an organization's strategy and culture have been effectively aligned:

- Clear mission, vision, and core values
- A workforce culture built on
  - trust and respect
  - performance, continuous improvement, innovation, and cycles of learning
  - collaboration rather than silos and integrated planning and plan execution
- Clear, measurable short- and long-term goals that flow from the strategic plan to individual employee performance
- Well-defined programs, services, or products, including expected outcomes, integrated into and throughout the organization
- Effective two-way communication up, down, and across work units; clear direction and progress
- Ongoing market research for new programs, services, or product development
  - Use of a business product development model to test the proposed new programs, services, or products

Effective alignment between strategy and culture promotes increased engagement, both staff and customers, to build emotional loyalty to the brand.

GREAT CIRCLE'S APPROACH TO ALIGNING STRATEGY AND CULTURE

In Missouri, Boys and Girls Town and Edgewood Children's Center merged in 2009, creating an organization—Great Circle—with a budget of close to $50 million and over 780 staff serving about 11,000 children and families through a continuum of services. In Great Circle's inaugural strategic plan, a high-priority strategic direction was to establish a continuous, consistent model for quality improvement. The agency decided to embrace the Baldrige performance excellence model as its transformational initiative with the support of The Kresge Foundation through the Alliance for Children and Families.

Initial first steps included (1) performing a Baldrige Organizational Self-Assessment, the Show Me Challenge, which surfaced opportunities for improvement (OFIs) that were incorporated into the 2013 annual plan, (2) identifying senior leaders to participate in Baldrige Examiner Training, (3) distributing a comprehensive staff survey called "Are We Making Progress?" (based on Baldrige Criteria for performance excellence) to determine a baseline for comparison every 6 months, and (4) establishing the Great Circle Strategy Council.

The strategy council met for the first time in mid-March, 2013. Members, selected by senior leadership, represent all departments, all regions, and all levels of staff from department and program directors to direct care and maintenance staff. The council will meet monthly. The council's role is to do the following:

- Help promote a culture change within Great Circle.
- Learn to apply the Baldrige Model and Principles of Performance Excellence.
- Increase the alignment of goal priorities between senior leadership and direct staff.

The council reviewed the "Are We Making Progress?" survey results and identified four OFIs that needed to be addressed to strengthen the alignment between strategy and culture at Great Circle:

1. Clarifying the understanding of Great Circle's vision for the future and how individual staff roles fit into that vision
2. Improving internal communication and interdepartmental teamwork
3. Improving understanding of the financial status of Great Circle
4. Aligning individual performance evaluation goals with the 2013 annual plan and overall strategic plan

Great Circle's Baldrige journey continues as the agency strives to increase the alignment between its strategy and its culture.

CREATING AN "ALLOY" OF STRATEGY AND CULTURE AT THE CHILDREN'S HOME OF CINCINNATI

Many of us have heard the saying "culture eats strategy for lunch." A natural conclusion to draw from this assertion may be that culture matters more than strategy, but that is not the case. Many leaders consciously or unconsciously separate the two. Culture influences strategy, but it cannot achieve the strategy. Similarly, strategy can impact culture, but it cannot create or maintain it. Strategy and culture are different, yet both matter equally. What is most important is how they meld together.

At The Children's Home of Cincinnati, we believe that strategy and culture are like oars in a boat: You can't get where you are going (vision achievement) by rowing with just one oar; you will of course just go around in a circle, because you need both to move forward. As with rowing, emphasis on either strategy or culture alone will impede progress, and neither alone will enable winning versus competitors. The key is creating what we call an "alloy" of strategy and culture.

An alloy, by definition, is a new, stronger metal formed from a combination of elements. For example, iron and five or six other elements are mixed in an alloy to form a stronger metal: steel. The same concept applies to organizations. The combination of both culture and strategy makes an organization stronger in its capacity to deliver superior products and services, demonstrate results, and excel beyond its competitors' capacity to do the same.

The key catalyst in creating the alloy is leadership. Napoleon once said, "There are no bad regiments [organizations]; there are only bad colonels [leaders]." All organizations are a reflection of their leaders. The key to building the alloy is focused, involved, committed leadership that promotes both strategy and culture. Leaders must be clear and specific in "what," "why," and "how" by providing solid rationales and clear plans. Leaders must be visible and interacting (leading) with all levels in the organization daily to ensure results. Leadership means not merely observing but engaging in hands-on activity and ensuring that the troops are involved.

The creation of the alloy of strategy and culture requires a framework for understanding. We start with simple definitions. Strategy can be defined as best positioning your organization's services, versus those of your competitors, to meet the needs of your customers. Strategy is about choices—whom to focus on, where to play, and how to win (what customers in what markets, and how to meet their needs). Strategy considers the four Cs: deeply understanding the "voices" of the *consumer* (the end user of the service), the *customer* (who helps you reach or deliver the product or service), the *competition* (those who compete against your organization), and the *company* (your own agency's capacity, capabilities, strengths, and weaknesses) (Hickman & Silva, 1986).

Culture can best be defined as the attributes that reflect the organization (values and beliefs, practices, rituals, skills, and behaviors). Culture defines the capacity and capability of an organization to organize or mobilize effectively to deliver the strategy of the business: It is the spirit of your organization. Culture can also be expressed in terms of the three Cs: the business's *characteristics* (its competence in achieving its goals and strategies), *commitment* (to the staff's and leadership's understanding of their "stake" in winning, motivated by the Adult Business Deal we describe below), and *consistency* (its ability to develop individuals, teams, and an overall organization with a common understanding and point of view as a basis for delivering strategy) (Hickman & Silva, 1986).

The entire framework for creating the new alloy must be structured around what we call an "Adult Business Deal." This "deal" between employees and the organization is the cornerstone of culture and answers the question affectionately known as WIIFM: *What's in it for me?*

The Adult Business Deal supports the reality that an organization's entire staff, whether they think it or not, are not only contributors to business but also part "owners" because of their stakes in the organization. The interests of the employees and the interests of the business are truly inseparable.

The deal is that each of us comes to work seeking certain basic fundamental needs: Employees are looking for pay and benefits so they can provide for their families, job security so they don't have to fear unemployment, a safe working environment where they don't have to worry about injury or illness, and professional development opportunities to support their growth and natural drive toward self-actualization. In turn, businesses seek people who are committed and competent in delivering services to ensure competitiveness and the long-term ability to stay in business.

Employees must embrace the reality that if the organization is not successful or does not achieve its goals, they will not benefit or achieve their goals. It's only when the business is successful that both the needs of employees and the needs of the business are achieved. And the business can only be successful if its employees clearly understand the integral roles their particular functions play in creating overall business success. At The Children's Home, we love to tell the story of the consultant who paid a visit to NASA. As he was leaving the building after a long day of talking to its leaders about their objectives and the way they involve their employees, he came upon a custodian in the stairwell who was sweeping the floor. The consultant asked the custodian what he was employed to do at NASA. His response? "I'm putting a man on the moon."

We want our employees to embrace the notion that The Children's Home is a place where we contribute our time, skills, and effort to help the organization achieve its vision. As a result, we as an organization are then able to satisfy our own needs. This makes us feel that we are truly owners of the business, and so we treat it as if we own it. And we are more apt to recognize the importance of teamwork required to support our culture, which in turn supports the achievement of our strategic goals—the ones that ensure the success of consumers, the organization, and employees.

Returning to the four C's of strategy and the three C's of culture: These can be modeled into a framework useful for creating and developing this alloy. Figure 5.2 presents the Hickman and Silva model for creating the alloy:

FIGURE 5.2   The Hickman-Silva model.

From *Creating Excellence* by Craig R. Hickman and Michael A. Silva, copyright © 1984 by Craig R. Hickman and Michael A. Silva. Used by permission of Dutton Signet, a division of Penguin Group (USA) LLC.

A *key* element of winning in the marketplace is creating an "*alloy*" of *strategy* and *culture* in your business...

Strategic Elements \ Cultural Elements	Committed	Competent	Consistent
Consumer	Match	Match	Match
Customer	Match	Match	Match
Competition	Match	Match	Match
Company	Match	Match	Match

The key task for leadership in creating this alloy is matching the strategic and cultural elements and creating a framework of structures, actions, and interventions that focus on constancy of purpose (delivery of direction) and continual improvement (in delivery of service). First, the organization must have a system focused on creating long- and short-term direction that incorporates a deep understanding of the voices of the four Cs. This system should include an assessment of the competition (who they are, what they are doing, and their skills and capabilities as best as the organization can understand them), the consumer (understanding the voices of clients and stakeholders as well as the voice of the organization's own capabilities and strengths), the customer (individuals or organizations that supply the organization and serve as the channels through which clients and stakeholders reach it), and finally the company (looking closely at how the company itself performs and interacts with the other Cs). This information informs the organization's strategic plan. Development and deployment of the plan must be rigorous: Plan, plan, plan, and then execute with precision and a high level of accountability. At The Children's Home, we employ a quarterly audit process to ensure that all elements of our strategy are on track; those that are not are retooled with support to get target measures back on track for the next quarter.

In addition to effective strategy deployment, it is also critical to building the alloy to have a system that supports delivery of the strategy and captures deep understanding of the voices of the three Cs. Employees are a key aspect of this system. At the Children's Home, we look for employees who are competent (in their work), committed (to the agency as well as to continually finding ways to make better contributions), and consistent (staying long-term, understanding the four Cs, and consistently making their best contributions). This system operates by principles rather than rules. The Children's Home has built its culture around three sets of cultural platforms: values (what we believe), standards of behavior (how we act), and core competencies (what we're really good at). These platforms build the commitment, competence, and consistency of our workforce. Most organizations have a set of values, which should be limited in number (we have six) and clearly defined. Our standards of behavior define in specific statements what it looks like to live our values. Our core competencies are the abilities that each individual (and therefore the organization) must have to ensure flexibility, responsiveness, and speed in managing the changes required for the organization to achieve our vision.

To ensure that the desired culture and its strategic competencies are fully integrated into the organization, work processes must be in place that support the system and allow for speed, strength, and innovation (hallmarks of a higher-performing organization) to meet consumers' needs better than the competition does. Some examples of these processes are found within the employee life cycle system: recruitment and selection of staff, performance evaluation, and staff development. Each must have embedded within it the strategic and cultural aims of the organization to ensure accountability to the entire system.

The system and supporting processes that operationalize the alloy of strategy and culture must also be driven by a system of measures. Nothing should be left to chance or opinion—all must be verified by data and held accountable to measures. Our motto at the Children's Home is "In God we trust—all others bring data." Aligning data-based strategic decisions with cultural principles ensures constancy of purpose and continual improvement.

The new alloy will require consistent testing, assessment, care, and feeding. Data, data, data is the key. Assessments of inputs, the system, and its outputs are critical. Ask yourself the following questions:

- Are the four Cs changing?
- How should we adjust or renew the system?
- Are the three Cs fit, robust, and working in sync?
- Is the lodestar (a satisfied customer) always the focus?
- Do we understand the voice (needs) of our consumers?
- Are our products and services best meeting or exceeding their needs?

There is an old adage that says that if you're not meeting your consumers' needs, it's you who has lost touch, not the consumer. Employees and teams feeling like owners and making individual and team contributions keep the focus, the processes, and the system operating. The system must regularly be evaluated and assessed for efficiency and effectiveness in meeting consumer needs.

Again, making the alloy work is the role of the leaders. The experts in the alloy are the top leaders in the organization. Lapses or inconsistency in leadership cost the agency results. Everyone has a role and responsibility, and leaders need to hold themselves and each other accountable. Leadership is action-oriented and face-to-face. Each top leader should be visible, engaged, and interacting daily. Good leaders use a common theme or platform message to ensure competence, consistency, and commitment to the culture via routine reinforcement.

To recap: The fit between strategy and culture is the key to forming the new alloy, which is the key to winning. Strategy is critical but is insufficient by itself to win—yet some focus on it to the exclusion of anything else. Strategic thinking aims at getting and keeping consumers. On the other hand, a strong culture builds, develops, unifies, and motivates employees—but consumers need to perceive better services or the culture is wasted. We are reminded of the boat rowing with two oars rather than one: Winning (i.e., satisfying the consumer) requires that both elements be designed in tandem, perfectly matched and melded together. Strategy and culture should complement each other, responding individually and together to drive forward progress with the ultimate aim of winning in the marketplace with the consumer. Without this alloy, an agency can never achieve sustainable results, including constancy of purpose (the role of strategy) and continuing improvement (the role of culture).

We live and work in a competitive marketplace, whether we recognize this or not. Understanding culture and its winning attributes is important for all employees at every level in the organization. When employees recognize that all the work we do with our clients is about winning (i.e., helping clients achieve the goals that are meaningful to them), it changes the old perception of a focus on "winning" as being too competitive or too much like a business. Winning in the marketplace requires an effective, competitive strategy and an efficient culture. Both are necessary and need adequate attention and resources to ensure success. A handful of brilliant leaders leading an organization are not enough. The entire organization must work as a team and in harmony with a clear focus and a clear framework in which to operate in order to win the consumer.

HOPELINK'S STRATEGY AND CULTURE

With his famous quote that "culture eats strategy for breakfast" (later changed to "lunch" by Dick Clark at Merck (@drkellypage, 2013) and many others), Peter Drucker started what turned out to be a fierce debate about whether culture or strategy is more important to organizational success. There has since been no shortage of smart people chiming in to support one side or the other, and plenty more voting for a tie. But given the volume of the debate over the past decade or so, it is impressive how many current nonprofit thought leaders are silent on the subject of culture as it relates to strategies featuring collaborative social impact.

The current wisdom in the nonprofit world is that the only way to really make a profound and lasting difference for clients and in the community is by working outside the organization's borders through broad collaborations (Crutchfield & Grant, 2008, p. 19). Yet the major "how-to" works in this area do not appear to consider the tremendous stresses that the prescribed levels of institutional and systems change might have on the cultures of the participants. More importantly, and with a nod to Peter Drucker, there is no mention of the impact *organizational culture might have on the desired systems change.*

Culture in the Nonprofit World

There is plenty of material written on nonprofit organizational culture, but for many it remains an elusive concept. The general agreement is that culture is mostly invisible (Merchant, 2011), is often misunderstood and therefore discounted (Parr, 2012), and generally operates at an emotional level rather than a cerebral one (McLaughlin, 2011). A favorite description comes from Shawn Parr: "Culture is a balanced blend of human psychology, attitudes, actions, and beliefs that combined create either pleasure or pain, serious momentum, or miserable stagnation" (2012).

Regardless of how it is defined, culture is built slowly in the nonprofit world and is therefore particularly deep-seated. The nature of the work nonprofits do inspires, and often requires, a high level of passion; employees and volunteers choose this work because helping others resonates on a personal level. Their beliefs in and about the organization's mission are therefore often much more foundational than are the beliefs of their counterparts in the for-profit world. This strong emotional commitment to mission provides a basis for organizational culture that is rock-solid and magnificent yet that can be highly resistant to change.

The complex elements of culture that overlay this emotional foundation include how decisions are made, how people are treated, and "how things are done," both internally and with clients. The amount of trust people have in senior leaders and their styles of leadership, as well as the levels of inclusion, are also important components of organizational culture. Over time, these and other elements combine to form the habits and norms that enable people to cooperate by assumption rather than by negotiation (Merchant, 2011).

Contrast this with the environment in which nonprofits must operate today. The external environment for the nonprofit industry has never been in as great a state of flux—particularly for those organizations with a mission to deal with tough social problems that are difficult to measure quantitatively. Funding is highly volatile, and scarce dollars are coming with ever greater demands for demonstrated success in the form of increased and measurable impacts on clients and the communities the organizations serve.

This level of intense scrutiny will only increase as governments, foundations, and individual supporters continue to wrestle with tighter budgets in the face of sharply increased demand for services and an economy that is still in recovery. These forces have inspired some nonprofit pioneers to explore new ways of delivering services in better, more collaborative, and more cost-effective ways.

Studies of early collaborative successes are highly encouraging, and point to even more promising results. It is clear that agency success will no longer be measured only by how well agencies manage their programs but also by how they manage programs *and* mobilize all sectors of society to attack social problems collaboratively (Crutchfield & Grant, 2008, p. 19).

As a result of these environmental forces, new approaches to service delivery, and the need to collaborate closely with organizations that are quite different, agencies and their cultures are being battered on all sides and are in danger of being ripped out of the ground by their roots. Let's examine why.

Cultural Stress

First, nonprofit cultures were mostly built upon the passion all constituents had for delivering personal services one-to-one with clients through isolated interventions. Now, both because of things learned from new data and also to position themselves for better funding opportunities, organizations are shifting rapidly to cross-sector, multiservice coordination. This shift will often require nonprofits to change the way they deliver services so that they will fit into the collective, holistic approach to client service. Change of any kind is a source of cultural stress, but because nonprofit programs often are foundational, these types of changes can be particularly stressful.

Second, everything is in motion. Not only is the funding environment in flux, but results from cross-sector collaborations are still coming in, and pay-for-performance funding models are being developed. Though the sea change to collaborative service delivery is itself an assault on long-standing cultures, nonprofits are further stressed by the need to be ready to change course flexibly and quickly (Burns, 2007, pg. 39) as more data becomes available and funding restrictions sort themselves out. Most organizations do not respond well to change, so the very need to be prepared to shift on a moment's notice creates an additional source of cultural stress.

Third, in an effort to build processes that are both holistic and collaborative, organizations may find themselves in situations in which competing theories of change and approaches to service delivery and policies may contradict each other. These contradictions make it very hard for leaders to decide what to do to move their agencies and collaborative processes forward. The resulting compromises can further stress organizational culture (US DOJ, 1999).

Fourth, in an attempt to rapidly increase both their efficiency and their program effectiveness, nonprofits are more often looking to for-profit models for help. Unfortunately, for-profit models are difficult to apply in a world in which outcomes and impacts resist measurement (Collins, 2001, p. 5). Attempting to force-fit for-profit methods and tools can drastically undermine a nonprofit's culture, mission, and public image (Landsberg, 2004), and even efforts that by and large are successful can be a source of stress on organizational cultures.

It is clear that all these stresses on culture can cause nonprofit employees and volunteers to reject the strategy and thus "eat the strategy for breakfast." The manifestations of this rejection will vary and can range from the passive-aggressive behaviors of ignoring it or subtly undermining it to the extremes of outright sabotage. Paying attention to the early warning signs of these behaviors can prevent many of these potential difficulties.

But there are other possible outcomes as well, as represented by the flip side to the Drucker paradigm. One possibility is the opposite of "culture eats strategy"—namely, one in which the "strategy crushes the culture." The likely outcome of this scenario is that the talented people the organization has recruited, hired, and developed over time start leaving. Seldom do departing employees state "cultural stress" as their reason for leaving, but when their passion has been snuffed out, they will leave to seek re-inspiration elsewhere.

Another, more subtle possibility is that rather than make internal changes, employees and volunteers will react to the stresses described above by forcing most of the change and imposing their organization's culture on that of their collaborative partners, overwhelming them. Despite agreements, memorandums of understanding, and apparently aligned missions, collaborations then fail to achieve the expected results and may break apart.

What Peter Drucker's quote means for nonprofits is that leaders who impose on their organizations the kind of strategic changes that most nonprofits are developing right now, without considering the cultural impact, do so at their peril. Culture is a lot like oxygen—you can't see it, smell it, or taste it, and we often take it for granted, but if you ever find yourself underwater you appreciate its importance and, often too late, wish you'd paid it more attention.

How Culture Becomes a Positive Force for Strategic Change

So what does this mean for strategy development? Very little. But it means *everything* for the *execution* of strategy. Execution is all about how well managers, employees, and volunteers understand the organization's strategy, appreciate how it reinforces and lifts up their core values and beliefs, and realize how what they do each day makes a difference in achieving organizational goals and positively affecting clients' lives as well as the community.

A nonprofit's culture can be a powerful ally and force for change, and some believe that it is actually the most powerful driver of organizational success available to nonprofit leaders (Schneider & Schneider, 2007). For example, in a recent Bridgespan study of 130 nonprofit management teams, culture rated as one of the top two organizational assets across the board (Kramer & Matthews, 2012, p. 1). Smart leaders are harnessing this power to dramatically increase their odds of success.

To tap into this power, three things must happen when organizational strategy needs to change. First, leaders need to ensure that as they make strategic choices for the organization, those choices fit and are aligned with and *informed by* the current culture—and that necessary changes are within reasonable reach from the existing culture (Katzenbach, Leinwand, & Kleiner, 2011). Understanding the degree to which a new strategy must move the existing culture should highly influence the execution plan. If a significant change is necessary, a wise leader will guide changes incrementally over time.

Second, to ensure that strategic decisions support organizational culture and nurture and grow the underlying passions of the organization, leaders should involve more people in the decision-making process

(McLaughlin, 2011). This way, staff and volunteers can help the organization make changes that build on their shared commitment to the organization's mission and can articulate the aspirational elements of strategy (Venture Philanthropy Partners, 2001). Because they helped create it, the staff are also more likely to support and champion it.

Third, personal communication and visible leadership from the CEO are critical. The organization must be led through changes of this magnitude, not managed through them. A well-developed and well-understood strategy is a powerful tool for change (McLaughlin, 2011), and it is the role of the leader to communicate the aspirational nature of the new strategy, how it will positively affect clients in compelling new ways, and how it fits with and appeals to employees' and volunteers' passion for their work (Kramer & Matthews, 2012).

Organizational effectiveness in the face of the impending metamorphosis in the nonprofit world depends on how well the organization can balance and align its culture, its leadership, and its strategy (Schneider & Schneider, 2007). Marshaling the forces of culture through visible leadership and a well-articulated strategy can yield transformative results even in the most volatile of times.

Bill and Kristine Schneider go a step further and talk about how organizational effectiveness can be maximized *only* when an organization's approaches to strategy, culture, and leadership align. Figure 5.3 depicts this graphically (Schneider & Schneider, 2007).

An understanding of how these three forces balance can help leaders make better decisions about strategy development and execution. When all three are aligned, organizations can not only handle change but also lead it to the benefit of their communities.

FIGURE 5.3   When strategy, culture, and leadership align.

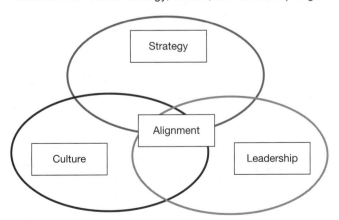

People are highly resilient, and cultures are as well. Because of the complexity of nonprofit organizations, it is very difficult to "nail" a strategy development and execution plan perfectly every time. The key to success is for leaders to be intentional about the creation and development of culture in their organizations and then to pay attention to early warning signs of trouble and make course corrections as quickly as possible.

A Nonprofit Case Study

Consider the case of a medium-sized nonprofit that had been working for several years on developing and executing strategic plans, creating dashboards, and improving its processes. At the encouragement of its board, the agency decided it was time to take this work to the next level and hired a chief strategy officer from outside the sector.

There immediately ensued a flurry of activity, including very deep dives into strategy, success measurements, and results with the senior leadership team. The work was spectacular. There was clear direction capped by a new 10-year vision and strategic plan, as well as an execution plan complete with delineated goals and initiatives that both directly tied to the strategic plan and had direct accountability assigned to individual members of senior management. The board was happy. The CEO was happy. The managers were miserable!

Nothing as exciting as a coup attempt ensued, and most of the staff went about business as usual. But realizing that things were not right was a seismic event for the CEO. As part of the ensuing diagnosis and intervention, the CEO discovered that even after 6 years with the agency, there were some parts of the organization's culture that were well disguised. It turned out that as the organization was evolving and its culture was changing, not everyone was on board. What the CEO uncovered during the diagnosis and then did about it is illuminating.

The CEO began noticing two seemingly conflicting things happening. The first was that people were reporting that they and their staffs were burning out. Because historical strategic plans had no associated work, division heads were used to running their own ships and loading up themselves and their teams with local-level initiatives and attendant tasks. Initiatives that came from the agency as a result of the new strategic planning effort included additional work that was layered onto this already overfull workload. While most worked hard to accomplish both, when one had to be chosen over the other, senior leaders were most often prioritizing their own initiatives over agency initiatives. As resentment over agencywide initiatives grew, and "rounding down" of scope also occurred, further diminishing the effectiveness of agencywide initiatives. Together, these actions formed a clear case of "culture eating strategy."

In addition to, and in part as a result of, this workload stress phenomenon, people were losing their passion for their work as well. Because of her vision and enthusiasm, the CEO was pushing people hard to accomplish agency goals, which included some of the external, cross-sector, and collaborative initiatives described here and elsewhere in this book. The changes these initiatives were causing resulted in increased lateral stress and were causing employees and volunteers, particularly in the service delivery divisions, to lose their enthusiasm for their work. Reports of disgruntlement began surfacing through the ongoing performance review process and regular meetings between employees and managers. These were clear symptoms of "strategy crushing culture." Enough was enough.

As both "Drucker symptoms" were occurring, they both had the same causes: While there was a history of inclusion in the organization, the direction and pace of change had overrun the normal level of inclusion and pushed people into a state of mistrust. Even if the historical level of inclusion had been ample for the situation, the managers clearly felt that the addition of a CSO was a new barrier to inclusion in decision making and in fact actually diminished it.

Further, the focus on evaluation and measurement was viewed as both diminishing the value of the work being done and an indication of a lack of respect for the expertise and experience of program staff. The combination of growing staff mistrust and resentment over the perceived exclusion from the decision-making process, the perceived diminished value of their work, and the higher workloads combined to create unrest.

Finally, as a part of agency strategy, the CEO was spending more and more time on external advocacy and collaboration initiatives. These efforts had the unintended consequence of reducing internal communication at a time when greater clarity and reassurance were needed.

All was not lost, however. The leadership team was solid, and the CEO and CSO were able to slow things down, work on repairing and rebuilding relationships among senior leaders, and revisit the visioning and planning process to help senior managers reengage. A key component of the reengagement was a new focus on the plan for executing agency strategy. As is the case with many organizations, the CEO recognized that there was a disconnect at the point where strategy and its attendant long-term initiatives met short-term operational needs. Care was taken to incorporate short-term, division-level initiatives into the prioritization process with the agency-level strategic initiatives.

The senior leadership team spent additional time refining the strategic 10-year vision and the agency's theory of change to create a clearer message around how broader initiatives were more effective in creating positive client outcomes and adding social value to the community. This served the dual purpose of increasing the overall level of inclusion and improving the ability of senior managers to communicate roles and tasks to their teams.

Lessons

While the transition was a difficult one, the end result was transformational for the organization. The experience brought the senior leadership team closer together as a group and led to more clarity around the organization's theory of change and its long-term vision. It also resulted in a more collaborative internal process for informing decisions that led to better decision-making and that better prepared the organization for external collaboration as well.

This was intentional. The CEO knew she needed to repair and strengthen the culture if the organization was to be successful in the long term. She took great pains to improve communication and engage a broader cross section of managers in the visioning and planning processes, and she particularly focused on demonstrating listening skills.

The broader lesson, and one for the smart people who debate the meaning of Peter Drucker's famous saying, is that it isn't always strategy *or* culture that wins out in a fair fight. People, and the organizations that unite them, are highly complex, and dysfunction can occur in both directions simultaneously.

The big lesson is that with the amount of stress being placed on non-profit culture and the need for broad-scale change, nonprofit CEOs must be on the lookout for the symptoms of cultural bruising. Intentionally designing, building, and nurturing organizational culture must be a cornerstone of any strategy and execution plan. Higher levels of communication, a pace of change informed and dictated by the effects on culture, and an understanding of the unique effects on individual team members will dramatically improve the odds of success.

DEPLOYING STRATEGY TO CHANGE CULTURE: THE PUBLIC HEALTH MANAGEMENT STORY

For Public Health Management Corporation (PHMC), the Alliance's Strategy Counts initiative in 2011 came at a particularly critical and opportune time for the organization. PHMC was teetering on turning 40 years old, and although it was known to be entrepreneurial because of its serial social entrepreneur CEO, in many ways PHMC looked like the health and human services organization of the past. PHMC had grown organically for four decades and had a relatively flat organizational leadership structure. Although PHMC was considered a high-performing nonprofit and had enjoyed tremendous growth, with a current budget above $170 million, its management structure had remained decentralized and thus had created a silo mentality among its leaders, many of whom had spent their full careers in the organization.

For background, PHMC is a Philadelphia-based 501(c)(3) nonprofit corporation and long-standing Alliance member. Founded in 1972, PHMC now operates 70 sites and serves over 200,000 clients annually in more than 350 programs that include behavioral health/recovery, nurse-managed health care, health promotion, early intervention, parenting supports for families, and emergency preparedness for southeastern Pennsylvania, and that are augmented by research and evaluation to assess and target health issues effectively. Services are provided in health centers, homes, shelters, and agencies, on the street, and in other sites by diverse, highly qualified staff members who understand and reflect the racial, ethnic, cultural, and linguistic characteristics of the communities they serve. Nine out of 10 PHMC clients are low-income and at higher risk for health and social problems because of issues related to socioeconomic status and discrimination based on gender, sexual identity, race/ethnicity, language, and culture. PHMC has a record of delivering high-quality services and serves as a convener, bringing together multiple stakeholders to understand and solve the complex issues facing vulnerable communities. To advance public health, PHMC also serves as a fiscal and management entity for local government, foundations, and nonprofit affiliate organizations. The five southeastern Pennsylvania counties make up PHMC's main service area, but other parts of Pennsylvania, Delaware, and New Jersey are also served, and some initiatives have a national scope.

In late 2010, senior managers recognized and agreed that for PHMC to better compete in a troubled economy amid a changing health and human services industry, corporationwide structural changes were going to be necessary to grow and scale programs. Thus, the organization and its leadership over the previous 18 months underwent its first corporationwide strategic positioning process, involving all levels from front-line staff, the next generation of leaders, to executive staff and the board of directors. As a result of this process, PHMC decided to restructure in early 2011, starting with top-line management, to realign business across the organization. In the process, the need also became apparent for the creation of a chief strategy officer (CSO) position to assist the president/CEO in the preparation and implementation of the restructuring, the achievement of strategic plan results, and the facilitation of ongoing strategy development across PHMC.

In January 2012, PHMC appointed a CSO to work with a new team of leaders including a chief operating officer (COO), a chief financial officer (CFO), and a chief human resources officer (CHRO), who would work together with the president/CEO and the CSO to carry out the strategic plan and the new structure.

SWOT Analysis

As part of its first corporationwide strategic positioning process, conducted over an 18-month period, PHMC conducted a SWOT (strengths, weaknesses, opportunities, threats) analysis that included all levels of staff, management, and board and that revealed consensus across the *organization and key information regarding opportunities and needs. The analysis found that* PHMC was recognized for strong management expertise, excellence in fiscal management, sustained partnerships with government and foundations, a "can-do" approach to emerging issues, and a research/evaluation capacity that positioned it to support public health and social services programming based on science, along with high-quality programs and services. There was agreement that growth opportunities existed for PHMC to expand its direct services as well as its intermediary and supporting role with govern-ment and other nonprofits. However, there was also agreement on barriers to growth, such as limited funding owing to the economy; federal, state, and local budget reductions; and insufficient philanthropic funding, which restricted investments in programs and facilities.

As a result of the strategic positioning process, PHMC broadened its mission. It is now a nonprofit public health institute that creates and sustains healthier communities beyond the immediate region and has committed to the following values:

- PHMC works to ensure access for all to the full array of public health services.
- PHMC provides high-quality services.
- PHMC works with government, foundations, academic institutions, businesses, and community-based organizations to meet public health challenges.
- PHMC supports growth and fiscal responsibility.
- PHMC values its employees and their contributions and maintains an inclusive environment where all are treated with dignity and respect.
- PHMC recognizes strong governance and ethics as the foundation for success.

PHMC's new strategic priority goals and objectives are:

- **Goal 1:** *Public Health Issues:* Lead in the identification of and response to existing and emerging public health issues.
- **Goal 2:** *Service to People and Communities:* Initiate, expand, and maintain programs and services that are aligned with the needs of the people and communities served and that are always inclusive of the underserved and those hardest to reach.
- **Goal 3:** *Quality of Service:* Identify and implement metrics to assess the quality, safety, and effectiveness of programs and services provided, to ensure accountability.
- **Goal 4:** *Infrastructure:* Create and maintain the organizational and operational infrastructure needed to support programs, services, and growth.
- **Goal 5:** *Financial Viability and Growth:* Promote financial viability and growth through existing and new programs, services, and affiliations.
- **Goal 6:** *Organizational Vitality:* Support and recognize staff contributions with career pathways across the organization; ensure future leadership and governance through succession planning; ensure and promote a positive public image and reputation for the organization.

In the SWOT process, there was broad agreement that PHMC was an organization where a flat *hierarchy had fostered a silo environment and created an unmanageable platform for the central service functions.* To be fully effective, it was necessary for PHMC to rethink its organizational structure and service strategies and improve communication, consultation, and learning across the organization, including management, direct programs, and affiliates. All levels of the organization recognized that for PHMC to continue its success and pursue growth opportunities, its structure needed to change and the role of strategy needed to be elevated and owned by a leader who could support the president/CEO in this effort. A further opportunity was the strategically planned *retirement of several management staff, which made the restructuring* possible.

The Right Moment for a Strategy Role

Participation in the Strategy Counts pilot initiative immediately accelerated the integration and success of the CSO role within the organization.

PHMC focused on a three-pronged approach to the chief strategy officer:

- Structural realignment and building internal capacity
- Strategic support to grow existing business
- Strategic support to grow new business

The focus on structural realignment and building internal capacity was to operationalize the new infrastructure to support PHMC's strategy and values. Realignment was guided by PHMC's strategic plan and new organizational structure, and the CSO would have an important role in the cultural transformation that would allow the leadership to more effectively support not only their operating components but also one another. A close partnership with the chief operating officer, the next level of component leaders (termed managing directors), and the affiliate directors helped create the right balance of new strategy while maintaining successful service outputs.

In order to provide central strategy support to grow existing business, the CSO utilized systems and tools for maintaining oversight for the broad range of service areas that often overlapped but could also be quite disparate. Early on, the focus was on creating strategic partnerships between the previously siloed programs and services to foster *communication, consultation, and learning across the organization.* Multiple funding types and sources, various programmatic targets and objectives, and a range of revenue levels made this responsibility particularly complex and reliant on information technology.

Leading the strategic vision for growing new business through technical assistance, business incubation, and new mergers and affiliations was the third key function of the CSO. As a science-driven public health institute, PHMC bases its objectives on data, and its nationally respected Community Health Data Base (CHDB) will be an important tool in the strategy for impact and sustainability. (The central component of the CHDB is the Household Health Survey, which is administered every 2 years across the five Philadelphia-area counties. It provides timely information, at multiple levels, about health status and needs, personal health behaviors, and access to and utilization of area health services. Since 1983, CHDB data has greatly enhanced the capacity of PHMC and local health and social service organizations to plan and design health programs to address the needs of local residents and communities.) PHMC used CHDB data to identify community needs, determine new lines of business, and collaborate with other public and community organizations and potential affiliates. The incubator function in the new organizational structure is the space where new business lines can build capacity, begin collaborations with PHMC partners, and focus their purpose within the institutional network. This is where strategy meets infrastructure, and the strategy officer will be accountable for ensuring the successful integration of new business into a niche that complements PHMC's existing business and organizational culture while fostering growth and innovation.

Results and Impact

The Strategy Counts initiative, as expected, has had a significant impact on PHMC's ability to implement its new strategic plan by accelerating the process of integrating the CSO. In the first year of the rollout of the role, more clients were served and enhanced services were provided to the community as the organization grew and expanded. As an example, in the first year, PHMC absorbed a treatment facility that served children and youth with behavioral programs and it affiliated with a children and families agency to work with foster care children. The CSO monitored and evaluated programs and services corporationwide against the strategic plan and goals and reported progress to the president/CEO, the board of directors, the other PHMC chiefs, and the managers of all business lines, functions, and programs. The impact of the Strategy Counts initiative was felt across the goals of the strategic plan as noted below.

Impact on Organizational Capacity

The CSO worked in partnership with the chiefs, managing directors, and affiliate directors to build PHMC's organizational capacity and focused on the following strategic goals and tasks in this area:

- *Quality of Service*
  Identify and implement best business and service practices, organization-wide electronic medical/client record systems, and quality assurance processes, as well as consumer and employee satisfaction systems.

- *Infrastructure*
  Implement systems to enhance organizationwide coordination and information systems, communication, database systems, and integrated operations; enhance educational offerings and measure impact across staff skills; and develop centralized operational support services.
- *Financial Viability*
  Identify for replication successful internal programs and other models; build on PHMC's long-term strength in financial management; initiate organizationwide fundraising and development activities; identify cost savings, including consolidation of functions; and explore new models of funding.
- *Growth and Organizational Vitality*
  Expand efforts to retain and develop staff through training, education, and development; create "career ladders"; design a competitive compensation program, including performance-based incentives; implement organizationwide succession planning; and highlight expertise and successes with internal and external audiences.

Community impact was to be measured by growth in quality services to clients. With the implementation of the strategic plan and growth strategies, PHMC expected to see growth and improvements in all direct services, and had the goal of an additional 20,000 clients over the next 3 years, which it reached in the first year. To impact clients and the community, the new COO and CSO worked closely together with service-managing directors, who oversaw the health (behavioral health and primary care), health promotion, and social services and who focussed on the following strategic goals and tasks in this area:

- *Public Health Issues*
  Promote intraprogram data collection and analysis to identify public health issues and trends; create strategic alliances/partnerships with researchers, practitioners, and organizations, and work with CHDB to identify existing and emerging public health issues; promote increased collaboration among PHMC programs and affiliates; explore development of additional services/centers to address public health issues; increase public awareness of public health issues; and centralize tracking systems to identify trends and issues. A key tool in meeting this goal was the recently created Project Connect, PHMC's new data warehouse integration project, through which PHMC client program databases can develop connections to help identify geographic/demographic groups served and develop crosscutting performance indicators, including client satisfaction. Through Project Connect, client data was available for decision making and to show client impact.

- *Service to People and Communities*
  Expand public awareness of and trust in PHMC services and operations; identify and engage community partner agencies and government agencies at all levels; integrate services internally to provide the best services possible; and utilize data and other resources to identify new service areas.

PHMC Board- and Executive-Level Buy-in

PHMC's new corporationwide strategic plan and reorganization were owned and supported by all levels of its leadership, including the president/CEO and the board of directors. The board believed that the appointment of the CSO would lead to better organizational performance, enhanced revenues, and a sustainable future for PHMC and believed that the Strategy Counts project would accelerate the integration and success of the CSO role within the organization.

Early Results

PHMC's taking charge of its future as a health and human services agency has shown results early on. In terms of structural realignment and building internal capacity, within an 18-month period of the implementation of the initiative, PHMC determined that its internal financial management and human resources information systems needed overhauling. It invested in two new systems that would enable the organization to grow and scale. Simultaneously, PHMC's CEO set out with the CSO and senior leadership to identify a new home for PHMC and create a new open office environment. The move, which is detailed in the next segment of this chapter, is expected to create ultimate culture change as the open space architecture allows for better collaboration among different entities.

In terms of strategic growth for existing and new business, PHMC's partnership affiliation model was accelerated with the focused effort of the CSO working in close partnership with the CEO to execute partnership deals. Whereas PHMC would usually do one affiliation a year, in the first year of the Strategy Counts initiative it was able to complete three. The future is still being built, but there is a general feeling that the silos have been broken and that PHMC has a bright future ahead of it.

Vision–Strategy–Space–Design–Culture: The New Paradigm

In early 2010, as the not-for-profit field faced a time of increasing complexity, PHMC began forging a direction to take its mission and its programs into the next decade. PHMC, begun in 1972, had enjoyed significant growth and success over the previous 10 years. Its budget and staff had doubled and its impact, measured by the number of programs run and clients and communities served, had increased in scope by an even larger percentage. PHMC's work in mergers and acquisitions, serving as a governance and back-office resource to programs strong on services but needing administrative support, was increasing in recognized value, and the number of new affiliates was growing each year.

At the same time, the board and executive leadership recognized the impending challenges not only facing PHMC and its affiliates but rapidly looming over the sector. Funding mechanisms were changing, and governments looked increasingly at their not-for-profit partners as vendors. With the emergence of for-profit entities competing in the sector, impact and outcomes were nonprofits' only stated metrics of success, and there were no clear definitions; in addition, talent was increasingly difficult to recruit and maintain, and myriad factors were increasing the management and financing challenges faced by the boards and staffs of high-functioning nonprofits.

The board and management of PHMC did an environmental scan of the field and fully realized that past success and a level of outstanding service were not enough to ensure the organization's ability to serve and succeed in these new realities. They recognized that change would be necessary at multiple levels—strategy, governance, management, talent, facility, and culture—and created a process to identify, evaluate, and execute a set of responses that would help ensure the continuation of PHMC's and its affiliates' strong missions for years to come.

As a first step in this work, the executive management of PHMC, working closely with the board leadership and using an outside consultant to facilitate and staff resources to manage the process, entered into a focused review of its strategy aimed at the creation of a succinct and practical strategic direction for the enterprise. This development phase included a review of past strategic plans, town hall meetings with staff of all levels, board discussions, and discussions with community stakeholders, all leading to the board-led approval of a new strategic direction for the organization. The process culminated in establishing a practical action-driven set of brief statements reflecting the refined principles as the categories of vision, mission, approach, values, and goals.

This new strategic direction for the corporation required a more dynamic governance structure that could support and drive change while offering flexibility in movement with strong oversight capacity. The board of directors of PHMC actively engaged in this change process, using a board bylaws committee with members who understood that 40 years of past success with little modification in governance structure during that time did not guarantee an ability to adapt and succeed in a new environment. Members put personal biases and needs aside, focusing only on creating the best governance framework for PHMC while never losing focus on the crucial oversight role of a board. For the first time in PHMC's corporate history, stringent term limits were put into place. Board seats were realigned with more meaning-ful representation. Committees were updated based on the needs of a high-functioning corporation facing new challenges. After a robust process, new bylaws were unanimously approved by the PHMC board.

With a new strategic direction and an updated governance structure and rules of engagement in hand, senior management looked closely at the organizational structure in place and assessed the ability of this staff-ing alignment, as well as the incumbent talent and capacity base, in order to determine whether what existed would allow for maximum delivery on the new strategic direction. After a thorough review both internally and with assistance by outside consultants, it was determined by management and supported by the board that a new organizational structure would be needed. Again working with the strategy consultant and including full input from the board and staff, the team worked together to craft a structure that would allow for the best delivery of service and output on the new strategic vision of the enterprise. Beginning with a "C suite" of five chiefs, it was clear that a chief strategy officer position would be essential in driving the organ-ization to its new level of delivery and achievement. Also proposed were chiefs for finance, human resources, and communications, all working under the chief executive officer. Each "book of business" (major program area) was identified with a managing director (MD) who would oversee and guide that area toward success in terms of growth, revenue, service excellence, client outcomes, and a positive bottom line. After a thorough review and vetting process, there was full support for the new structure at the board, executive, management, and service levels of the corporations.

The new structure required an assessment of the current talent as well as the alignment of available managers and executives. Much of the success of PHMC over its 40-year history had related to the consistency of its staff and leadership team, as well as to its rich set of relationships with funders, com-munity leaders, service experts, stakeholders, and friends. Because there was a new set of realities, defined by the need for flexibility and change, as well as required new relationships and partnerships, it was important to assess the role of incumbents as change agents. In order to provide options, the executive leadership, working with senior members of the board, sought and engaged an outside HR consultant to construct an early retirement option for long-term employees who might prefer retirement to engagement in a process by which to be considered for a position in the new structure. In researching the early retirement option, it was discovered that there was little to no precedent for this kind of option in the not-for-profit public health and human services fields. After a careful development process, the option was rolled out and, with full and open choice for the long-term employees, was implemented with incumbent management staff with more than 20 years of service. Six of these staff chose to accept the option and leave at a specified time, receiving transition pay and benefits. With this new structure and a number of key positions available, executive leadership at PHMC recruited a dynamic, diverse innovation-focused team prepared to implement the new strategic direction and structure and committed to driving the enterprise to mission and business success.

- PHMC, with strategy, structure, and leadership staff in place and beginning to engage in the challenges ahead, focused its next change management initiative on the working space, design, and culture of the corporation, beginning with a review of the literature and discussions with experts in the field. Strategic innovation through the use of spatial workspace design driving cultural change was the goal, with a commitment to using the same kind of energy focus on this area that had been placed on governance, strategy, structure, and talent leading up to this phase of the corporate change initiative. PHMC looked to a global business context for perspective on the highest standards in workspace design. Current realities include the following:

  ○ The rapid pace of technology evolution, facilitating unprecedented access to information and knowledge while altering people's values and behaviors across departmental and international boundaries
  ○ A globalized economy in which an increasingly aware and diverse workforce demands respect and the provision of its social, psychological, cognitive, and physical needs
  ○ The recognition that wealth creation centers on social, intellectual, and knowledge capital, demanding a humancentric approach to strategic management
  ○ The geometric growth of complexity and available information in a competitive innovation landscape, requiring organizations to encourage collaboration across distinct and specialized disciplines to remain competitive
  ○ Devising means to shift from a task-oriented to a results-oriented corporate culture in which the emotional and social aspects of work, largely hidden in social network bonds, are as important as hierarchy and direct compensation were to traditional work (Steelcase, 2011)

Utilizing theory espoused by Steelcase, a global leader in the office furniture industry and the contractor eventually selected to help direct this new initiative, PHMC was eager to adopt many of the values that were contributing to sustainability and workforce strength throughout the world. Acknowledging that organizations succeed through reinvention and that technology is disrupting our traditional methods of gathering, comprehending, and sharing information was a key value in PHMC's initiative toward physical transformation.

As the issues faced at work increase in complexity, so do potential solutions. The paradigms for workplaces today were developed 40 years ago. Many of the jobs we do today didn't even exist back then, let alone the tools used to do them. Yet workplaces are sometimes designed with a one-size-fits-all approach that disregards individual work styles and preferences. Lifestyles have evolved as people juggle competing demands and priorities from all directions, and the modern challenge is managing a balance between work and personal lives. How work gets done reflects these changes. Productive work is all about new ways to solve problems, not processing yesterday's activities. Individuals can create value with new ideas alone, but giving them access to each other, to the leaders, and to information and processes, can foster latent skills that many workplaces currently don't have access to. An ideal workspace allows people to spend time getting to know their colleagues, learning from them, sharing personal experiences, and building trust. In the new ideology for successful work environments, "the office" provides a variety of settings that support the work being done, not necessarily the position on the organizational chart.

The contemporary workplace provides choice. Providing spaces where people can work by themselves without distraction, spontaneously connect with others for a quick update on a project, or conduct a team meeting in a space where others are free to drop in can break down many of the typical barriers that exist in older offices. But removing the physical borders is just a start. Generating continuous and appropriate innovation often requires more flexible work processes, different structural relationships, the forging of new trust relationships between staff and management, cultural evolution, and staff ownership of the decisions and financial well-being of the company (Klein, 1998). Many organizations think of themselves as strictly businesses, but people are the wheels in motion that operate that business. Human beings are social creatures, and they want to be part of a community, not a business strategy. Thinking of the work environments and technologies more broadly as active tools in the organizational change process makes the discussion richer and potentially more valuable (Steelcase, 2011).

The opportunity to redefine the boundaries so that a new engagement model can support higher-order processes such as innovation and informed decision making was one that PHMC could not afford to miss. Understanding how to use the workplace as a tool to uncover and leverage behavior and culture change allowed for aligning workspace design with strategy and goals beyond cost. The basic paradigm shift was to design with and from an engaged employee and executive point of view rather than by designing simply "for" staff. Techniques to do this without lengthening the design process have been developed and used by Steelcase's Applied Research and Consulting group, in concert with leading design thinkers, for organizations globally (Steelcase, 2011).

The models used acknowledge and act as though organizations are made up of both formal structures and informal social networks. It is this deep and dynamic relationship that is culturally embedded in the accomplishment of knowledge work. Staff are first engaged in thinking about how value can be created in an organizational future state, and through these discussions they help frame a new mix of tools that are active elements in "becoming the change." Staff involvement in needs definition helps bridge the often disparate languages of business and design, linking design meaningfully to business needs through human engagement (Steelcase, 2011).

In developing its own plans for a reenvisioned workspace, PHMC was extremely fortunate to have the assistance of the architectural design firm Bradberry and Kheradi (B&K) in the design of its facilities for almost two decades. The B&K team knew the work of PHMC and its team. They had worked closely with the leadership and understood the mission, personalities, needs, and cultural drivers central to the corporation and its objectives in this change management process. They shared its vision, style sensibilities, and drive for disruptive innovation in the work. Most important, B&K brought the industry knowledge that design drives culture and change and became the lead partner in this essential component of the PHMC drive towards a strategic future. B&K's projects are always a collaborative effort, combining good design with efficient plans and meeting the optimal operational needs of its clients. The process to get to a great design and the most efficient space is a very involved one, and when working with PHMC, B&K knew that direction from the executive team would be critical with regard not only to design but also to the function of the space.

As with any change-driving process, first steps included extensive discussions, research, and in-field activities. Over a period of months, visits to identified "forward designed" office facilities were made, continually refining the vision of an office space most aligned with PHMC and its work. Early outreach was made with the cutting-edge office furniture companies. B&K principals joined with PHMC executive leadership in reviewing furniture options, understanding competing value propositions, and using the rich experience of the furniture companies that are among the leaders in understanding worksite and employee behavior in an extensive process of field review of workspaces. As the work continued, the full PHMC leadership team engaged in these discussions and processes, with several field visits by the full team.

In this series of visits and meetings, it was clear that one of the office furniture providers stood out as the most closely aligned with the PHMC vision for workplace and cultural change. After an extensive set of discussions and negotiations with full engagement, input, and assistance from the B&K partners, the aforementioned Steelcase was selected as the furniture partner for this project. From the outset, there was clear and close alignment between PHMC, B&K, and Steelcase. In addition, Corporate Interiors, the local Steelcase franchise, worked closely as a key player in this partnership. B&K, as the architectural design professionals, led the process, serving as the central point of contact, the vision leaders, and the project managers in moving this concept and mission to the reality of the newly envisioned PHMC corporate headquarters.

At about this time, the actual office space was identified. After a wide-reaching search throughout Philadelphia, undertaken while working closely with B&K and without the use of a real estate broker for strategic as well as financial reasons, PHMC identified an outstanding building with the full array of class A facilities in the central core of the city. A lease was negotiated and actual office planning was initiated quickly, and B&K continued to serve as the leaders in this activity, calling on each of the partners but taking responsibility for getting to the actual construction in a timely fashion. With the actual space selected, the time and activity pressure to move the process from search and decision to execution was heightened.

When preparing to begin the exploration and visioning process, B&K knew that thinking through the overall design itself needed to be an effort involving all members of the staff, not just the executive team. PHMC took the information gathering to a new level on this project, to give a range of individuals the chance to help visualize what type of space might help them best perform their work. Staff were enlisted to help through surveys, questionnaires, and tours of office spaces and similar relocation projects. The response was overwhelmingly positive, with tremendous ideas emerging from these discussion sessions and interviews, including how best to use technology in meeting spaces, the importance of collaborative work, and the need for specific types of space that nurtured staff well-being in both design and function. Much of the vision of upper management was echoed in the staff's voices, and all of it was then translated into the plans for the new building.

Many visions were presented to B&K, all of which would influence the size and quality of PHMC's new office space. Among the key values communicated by PHMC staff were the following:

- Designing a space that would inspire everyone
- Affording staff more ways to communicate with one another for better collaboration
- Enjoying brighter personal workspaces with more daylight
- Creating a casual central gathering place where staff could socialize
- Promoting healthy lifestyles by providing a fitness center and nutritious meals/snacks for staff
- Building in abundant meeting places with the right support technology in place and abundant private spaces for staff who need to focus on individual tasks or take private calls

All involved were clear that the new space would include significant shared space. Offices would be at a minimum, more open space would be available, and there would be shared window spaces and access to natural light, opportunities for collaboration and discussion, private spaces, and a number of innovative space concepts that would serve the needs of staff and visitors. On behalf of PHMC, B&K drove these ideas throughout the concept and design phases. An emerging theme that was central to planning was the idea of a "town square," an office area to which staff would be drawn for practical as well as enjoyment and personal purposes. B&K and the wider design team envisioned a fitness facility, a cafe, and a "help room" as key components of this town square. The square would be open and inviting, contiguous to conference rooms and meeting space. While these ideas were being calibrated, the data gathering process was taking place. B&K interviewed key PHMC personnel to obtain specs regarding staff quantities, growth projections, and departmental, program, and staff adjacencies. Meeting space size and frequency needs were qualified; storage and file areas were assessed; and procedures on how much to store and archive were challenged so that organizational standards and protocols could be revisited.

The next step for B&K was to give staff a way to understand how these ideas could be executed, in the form of a pilot or test space that would incorporate all of the above. The combined vision has resulted in an efficient, attractive, brightly lit space that occupies a full quadrant of an entire floor of PHMC's current building. Varied private and collaborative spaces make the office a better place to carry out the functions of everyday work, as do comfortable and inviting meeting spaces with amenities, as all had envisioned. Constructing this test space allowed staff to be immersed in the simulated environment so that they could work with the team to modify and perfect the space and suggest improvements. The first of the teams to take up residency in the pilot has been truly pleased, with one of the program directors commenting, "Staff really enjoy the space. They want to be in the office more now. They talk to each other during the day, sharing resources and problem solving how to work with families through each other's experiences." Reflecting the information gathered in this way has been particularly rewarding for all involved and certainly establishes a best practice in ensuring that the new building will ultimately embody the best design possible.

A significant milestone in this project was the launch of the pilot space, which featured informal presentations from PHMC's president, B&K, and Steelcase cycled repeatedly over the course of 2 days. Hundreds of staff attended to hear about the process that had unfolded in the previous year based on PHMC's goals and values, while learning more about the worldview and changing workforce dynamics that pointed to an open floor plan. Each session concluded with a tour of the space led by B&K, who described the thought process behind the layout and functionality of the furniture. Team members created a celebratory tone for the launch with decorative touches around the space, a whiteboard wall where staff were encouraged to leave messages and first reactions, and a taste-testing station provided by a potential food vendor for the new building. This celebratory opportunity was utilized to its fullest in informing staff about updates and reinforcing the background and history inherent in the present, a type of messaging critical in a large organization in which channels of communications can be difficult to manage. Explaining the vision that went into the design provided clarity and context for staff who had not been central to the planning conversations. Staff feedback was extremely positive, with Steelcase consultants commenting that it was one of the more successful events of the kind that they had seen.

Another important element of the pilot launch was a "Spring Cleaning Day" held at the end of that week. On the heels of seeing the new workspace model, staff had a better understanding of the level of reduction of paper and materials that would be necessary for them to be comfortable in the new space. Facilities and administrative services staff accommodated the disposal of close to six tons of recycled paper and almost as much trash across the roughly 700 staff in the building that day. Going paperless has been a major area of focus throughout PHMC's change management process, and not solely because the new building will not be able to accommodate current levels of paper usage—both in individual workspaces and storage as a whole. Nor is it primarily an issue of ecological consciousness, although both the environment and the new space restrictions are compelling and pertinent motivators. What was most important was that the many transitions inherent in an organization of PHMC's size make going paperless a tremendous business decision that ultimately impacts infrastructure and technological systems across all central and administrative units of the organization.

An example of a tool in this transition is the multifunction device, or MFD, which combines printing, scanning, faxing, and photocopying in one device. On a surface level, the major area of change in the new space is that instead of printers in individual workspaces, all staff will be networked to just a few central MFDs shared across the entire floor; plans estimate roughly four to six MFDs and approximately 150 staff per floor. More fundamentally, however, this shift marks a transformation of how back-office systems are structured and utilized every day, most notably in the HR, fiscal, and information systems areas, as paper-and-pen forms and carbon copy materials become obsolete. In tandem with these revisions is a movement toward document imaging, which will employ scanners to feed paperwork into these electronic systems, ultimately resulting in a comprehensive filing system comprising internal documents, along with electronic file storage for the over 150,000 individuals whom PHMC serves.

Throughout these types of change decisions, more questions have emerged that reveal a need for additional changes in PHMC's operational systems and infrastructure. Targeting key elements of organizational culture, such as technology, central support roles, and policies, has put PHMC on track for true strategic change. Everything from how internal mail is distributed to establishing a universal standard for personal conduct in the workplace points to a true investment in and commitment to strategic culture change. A primary area of focus for carrying out PHMC's change management process, through which workflow and infrastructure and culture can be truly transformed, is communications with staff. Through emails, surveys, meetings, focus groups, decentralized communication chains, and events such as the pilot launch, PHMC has been able to successfully communicate with its 1,500 staff and, in particular, the 700 staff who will be moving in 2014. The main goals associated with these communications were and continue to be to inform staff, to collect staff input, to answer questions and clarify rumors, to prepare staff for upcoming changes, and, when possible, to begin to implement changes in the current space.

The first all-staff communication was an email that linked to a survey provided by Steelcase. Exemplifying the strong partnership between the two organizations, PHMC was able to create custom questions and develop a free response section of the survey that Steelcase integrated into the existing format. Staff answered questions about space, including how they worked at the time, the environmental factors that contributed to an ideal workspace, and what PHMC could do to enhance the health and well-being of staff through space. Shortly thereafter, a change management advisory group (CMAG) was created to develop an opportunity for open communication within a network of leaders and key stakeholders at PHMC, including the executive team/C-suite, managing directors, deputy-level and key future leaders, and staff involved in daily PHMC facility activities or administrative decision making. The first CMAG meeting was led by Steelcase, who painted a broad picture of where PHMC fell in the grand scheme of today's workforce, and the research and data that led PHMC to its reenvisioned space philosophy. Two other key workgroups were also formed: the change agents, a diverse group of program staff with strong relationships and peer networks throughout the organization, and the administrative assistants and office managers, who provide critical input on day-to-day workflow issues, including mail, purchasing, supplies, room reservations, and other administrative areas.

Regular all-staff communications mainly comprise a series of biweekly emails branded "On the Move" that cover a range of issues related to the relocation and that have helped give structure to the pace of the change management process. Additional forms of reinforcement and, likely, the more effective means of disseminating messages are through staff workgroups. The executive team meets with the managing directors who oversee PHMC's 11 divisions every two to three weeks, and the MDs then disseminate updates and information to their staff while bringing questions to the executive team as well. Throughout these practices, a critical dynamic among staff has emerged in which individuals have adopted organizational messages as their own and now help facilitate understanding among friends and peers in a way that management never could. Because they were empowered from the beginning of the process through regular opportunities for discussion and input, staff at all levels throughout the organization have become perhaps the most important leaders in changing the culture.

With the extensive involvement of partners in a complex change process, management, direction, and staff tactical efforts are essential, as exemplified throughout this process for PHMC. In addition, leadership and detailed project management are essential to a positive outcome. As PHMC began to explore the real estate portion of the project, the relocation discussion was included in existing weekly real estate meetings in which multiple construction and space discussions were reviewed for all of PHMC's 70 locations throughout southeastern Pennsylvania. Each discussion included an extensive update on the various metrics critical for project completion. This continues to be done on each of the PHMC real estate projects, but as the relocation process has developed, the space discussions have become the highest-priority subject at each meeting, and the PHMC team of staff assigned to manage the work has increased accordingly. A key member of the strategy team was enlisted to manage many of the internal processes, in particular the staff-focused change management strategy. An outside consultant, an expert in facilities management, was recruited to play a key role in the facility development planning. Throughout these steps, B&K has strongly managed the process, pushing all team members to consistent movement toward the targets and task completion that will keep the project aligned with an aggressive schedule. Throughout this process, various staff teams have continued to meet and provide input, within the context of a relevant worldview from B&K and Steelcase.

Thus, PHMC is moving this process forward to the key point for true change. The governance, strategy, structure, and talent are in place. These will all help drive the corporation and its affiliates toward delivery of the strategic direction outlined at the beginning of this process. The new home for the organization comes with a vision to create a physical facility that supports communication, collaboration, interaction, excitement, and change. PHMC's physical transformation will drive a new culture of disruptive innovation toward the creation of robust and forward-thinking public health and social services for the communities we serve. That is PHMC's vision, responsibility, and mission.

RESOURCES

For more information, see the following websites:
   Public Health Management Corporation: www.phmc.org
   Steelcase: www.steelcase.com
   Bradberry and Kheradi: www.bradberrykheradi.com

REFERENCES

@drkellypage. (2013, January 18). Re: Culture eats strategy for lunch [Web article comment]. Retrieved from http://www.fastcompany.com/1810674/culture-eats-strategy-lunch

Buckingham, B. & Coffman, C. (1999). *First, break all the rules: What the world's greatest managers do differently*. New York: Simon & Schuster.

Burns, D. (2007). *Systemic action research: A strategy for whole system change*. Bristol, UK: The Policy Press.

Collins, J. (2001). *Good to great*. New York: Harper Collins.

Crutchfield, L. & Grant, H. M. (2008). *Forces for good*. San Francisco: Jossey Bass.

Hickman, C. & Silva, S. (1986). *Creating excellence: Managing corporate culture, strategy and change in the new age.* New York: Plume.

Katzenbach, J., Leinwand, P. & Kleiner, A. (2011, December 6). Culture eats strategy for breakfast. (Webinar for Booz & Co). Retrieved from http://www.booz.com/global/home/what-we-think/katzenbach_center/kc_webinars

Klein, D.A. (1998). *The strategic management of intellectual capital.* Woburn, MA: Butterworth-Heinemenn.

Kramer, K., & Matthews, C. (2012). "Four actions nonprofit leaders can take to transform organizational culture," White Paper for the Bridgespan Group, February, 2, 2012.

Landsberg, B. (2004). "The nonprofit paradox: For-profit business models in the third sector," White Paper for the Pikes Peak Foundation for Mental Health.

Marino, M. (2011) *Leap of reason: Managing to outcomes in an era of scarcity.* Washington, DC: Venture Philanthropy Partners.

McLaughlin, T. (2011, April 1). Work is a battlefield. *The NonProfit Times.* Retrieved from http://www.thenonprofittimes.com/news-articles/work-is-a-battlefield/

Merchant, N. (2011, March 22). Culture trumps strategy, every time. *Harvard Business Review* Blog Network. Retrieved from http://blogs.hbr.org/cs/2011/03/culture_trumps_strategy_every.html

Parr, S. (2012, January 24). Culture eats strategy for lunch. *Fast Company.* Retrieved from http://www.fastcompany.com/1810674/culture-eats-strategy-lunch

Schneider, B., & Schneider, K. (2007, March 7). Executive forum: *Aligning culture, strategy and leadership.* Lake Oswego, OR: Bill Schneider & Kristine Schneider.

Steelcase (2011). Engaging users for a better work experience.

U.S. Department of Justice. 1999. What is systems change? In *CCITools for Federal Staff.* Retrieved from http://www.ccitoolsforfeds.org/systems_change.asp

Venture Philanthropy Partners. (2001, August). The seven elements of nonprofit capacity. In *Effective capacity building in nonprofit organizations* (pp. 37–68). Washington, DC: McKinsey & Company. Retrieved from http://www.vppartners.org/learning/reports/capacity/assessment.pdf

CHAPTER 6

Strategy, Sanctuary, and Turnaround

Editors' note: This chapter features two perspectives on the Sanctuary Model®. The chapter begins with a case study on a Strategy Counts initiative pilot site based in Rochester, New York, in which the Sanctuary Model is applied as one component of the organization's turnaround effort. Following this practical example of the Sanctuary Model in one organization is a reprinted article highlighting the theoretical framework of the Sanctuary Model from the peer-reviewed Families in Society: The Journal of Contemporary Social Services.

FINDING HOPE: A CASE STUDY ON STRATEGY REDESIGN AND TURNAROUND

Michael Mortell, Christina Gullo, and Patricia Winsten

Christina Gullo estimates that when she joined St. Joseph's Villa as CEO in late 2010, the 68-year-old agency was just months from closing its doors. It was entering its third year of operating with a deficit and projected a loss of $1.2 million in 2011, the largest thus far.

Gullo undertook—and achieved—a dramatic 1-year fiscal turnaround. The change in executive leadership also presented the opportune time for the Villa to take a critical look at its strengths, weaknesses, and future. Agency leaders understood that to survive and thrive, the Villa would have to transform its strategic focus and organizational structure to become change-agile, competitive, and continuously innovative. Today, Villa of Hope continues to work toward transformation in four key areas: strategy, leadership, culture, and performance evaluation.

Now, midway through its journey of transformation, Villa of Hope is elevating its strategic capacity, identifying areas of growth, strengthening its infrastructure, and reshaping its identity with a new name, mission, vision, and culture.

On the Journey to Reinvention

When St. Joseph's Villa unveiled a new name, logo, and tagline in April 2013, it was the most visible manifestation of the transformational journey underway. Now called Villa of Hope, the agency that was on the brink of closure is looking ahead to a hopeful future.

Even though the agency had downsized from 72 residential beds to 48 just before Gullo arrived, a consistent drop in residential occupancy and a high rate of unplanned discharges added to the fiscal crisis. Gullo gathered an entirely new executive leadership team and immediately tackled the agency's finances. Programs that were not financially or operationally feasible and did not fit the core service area were cut or eliminated, space was consolidated to buildings owned in order to reduce fixed expenses, and a number of staff members were laid off. At the same time, the agency achieved a rate increase that resulted in $500,000 annually, and it submitted proposals for new programming. It reduced its $3.5 million line of credit to $1.5 million and secured it with property assets, freeing foundation dollars for major initiatives. New metrics were designed to track cash flow, assess fluctuations, and project discharges. Every program now has a monthly profit-and-loss statement, instilling a new accountability among leadership and management. A major gift campaign is raising unrestricted funds.

The result? Since mid–fiscal year 2012, the Villa has been operating with a surplus and has invested resource dollars to start new programs and build upon existing infrastructure.

Transformation. The board and senior leadership realized that they could not merely plug holes in the budget. Nothing less than transformation would enable the agency to remain viable and impactful into the future. A strategy team was formed to drive the transformational project, comprising the board chair, the CEO, and 10 cross-functional staff members. In August 2011, the strategy team began preparing a proposal to become a Strategy Counts pilot site that identified four areas for transformation: strategy, leadership, talent/culture, and performance evaluation.

With a great deal of the foundation in place, had the Villa not been selected as a pilot site, the transformation work most certainly would have continued. When the selection process ended in December, Gullo and the strategy team learned that the Villa would be one of the pilot sites conducting a transformational project. Becoming a pilot site provided $100,000 for an 18-month period beginning in January 2011, engagement with peers in the cohort learning group, and, to some degree, an external vote of confidence to carry on with the transformation effort.

The Villa used the expertise of a local consulting firm with a reputation for assisting in strategy creation that empowers leaders and improves client results. The consultants coached the strategy team and provided a neutral voice to objectively assess the agency's weaknesses, navigate conflict, and clarify thinking in the strategic process.

Why Invest in Strategy?

Previously, the agency had a strategic plan that it considered "evergreen" limited metrics to map progress. For a turnaround to begin, leaders needed to know how the agency was doing relative to similar organizations.

The strategy team identified several factors that underscored the need for transforming the Villa. These included the rapid pace of change within the human services sector at the state and community levels, the ability to implement and share knowledge at all levels of the organization, and the need to track and measure progress on objectives on a timely basis.

An extensive assessment of agency needs led by the strategy team revealed elements that needed addressing if the Villa was to realize its potential and expand its impact on youth. The assessment included a SWOT analysis, competitive analysis for each program area, and 26 interviews with internal and external stakeholders, including the senior leadership team, cross-functional staff, board members, donors, family members, clients, and municipal and community collaborators.

The following were identified as areas of weakness in the Villa's capacity:

- Slowness to change in response to changing economic and social conditions
- Programs not aligned with changing community needs (e.g., residential vs. community-based services)
- Focus on short-term program funding rather than building long-term capacity and fiscal viability
- Strategic plans poorly aligned with day-to-day operations
- Lack of outcome data to use in reporting and responding to successes and challenges
- Outdated organizational structure; role confusion

The organizational structure, Gullo observed, was inefficient, outdated, and incapable of reacting quickly. Throughout the organization communication was poor, there was a lack of accountability, and staff were only minimally included in decision making. "It was a deficit-focused, crisis-driven culture," Gullo says. "The staff members were operating in firefighting mode."

Anticipated Outcomes. Transformation of the organization was expected to provide widescale, far-reaching, and sustained results to the Villa's stakeholders and, critically, to youth and families in crisis. The strategy team articulated the following seven outcomes in their strategy counts proposal:

- *Expansion of successful core services*
  As a result of strategically designing our vision, goals, and objectives, we anticipate expansion in areas identified by growth potential and financial viability such as after-care, juvenile justice programs, skill building, and specialized residential and outpatient clinics.
- *Elimination of nonaligned programs and services*
  Utilizing the results of our needs assessment, revised mission, and information from the strategy-mapping process, we will "right-size" our organizational structure according to our core services and eliminate or adjust programs that are not responsive to the current economic and social environment. Database performance tracking will guide our ongoing evaluation and alignment of programs and services.
- *Reconfiguration of existing services and capturing greater program efficiencies*
  The strategic mapping process will reconfigure our services to be more efficient because of the development of performance targets and tracking client outcomes. Human resources, finance, and development functions will be aligned to support agency objectives, and database tracking will ensure that goals and objectives are met.
- *Development of new value-added services through innovation*
  Greater organizational efficiency will allow us to collaborate with other organizations. Agencywide culture change will take place through implementation of the Sanctuary Model, ensuring that services are client-informed and achieve lasting results.
- *Greater resilience in the face of economic downturns, enhanced sustainability of effective programs, and enhancement of revenues for service delivery*
  Strategic expansion of successful programs, key collaborations with municipal and community partners, clarification of our vision and mission, and tracking of performance data will build capacity for revenue and position us to benefit from federal, state, and local funding opportunities—increasing our fiscal capacity to endure economic downturns.
- *Successful reorientation of board energies to issues central to the responsibilities of governance*
  Board involvement at all levels of our strategic process will ensure engagement and reap benefits from board expertise/knowledge. Aligning board members with our clarified vision, mission, and goals allows them to better represent the Villa in the community and focus attention on governance and the cultivation of donors.
- *Greater social impact on the communities served*
  All transformation efforts are directed toward this all-important goal. Organizational development will change agency culture to be driven by client need. Clear strategic goals and ongoing measurement of objectives will allow us not only to serve more youth and families in crisis but to serve them better.

Early Steps

Gullo soon realized that as the agency was forging ahead in transforming, it had to stabilize a few aspects that affected day-to-day operations. Over the next 6 to 8 months, the agency planned for and developed new policies and procedures. New safety measures were put in place, and each operational area was assessed to begin to reduce inefficiencies and redundancies.

Getting the right talent in the right seats was also important. A clinical director position was created. The management team was restructured, making sure people were in the jobs best suited to their skill sets. Roles and responsibilities across the organization were revised and clarified.

Although the Villa was financially fragile, it invested $270,000 to align compensation and benefits with competitive market data. The agency also committed to extensive training and development.

Throughout these changes, Gullo communicated with staff transparently and frequently. She knew that with knowledge comes buy-in, and that buy-in leads to higher performance and, ultimately, to improved outcomes.

With a more solid foundation underpinning it, the Villa worked with a consultant to define its strategic intent and objectives. The goal was to be competitive, change-agile, and continually innovative.

Culture and Talent. Gullo observed that the client population had changed and that the staff were not trained to respond to their high levels of trauma. After extensive research, the Villa implemented Sanctuary, a trauma-informed model of care that not only guides treatment but also shapes the culture and values of the entire organization. "The selling point was that Sanctuary is a whole-system approach," Gullo says. "It focuses on the people who seek treatment, and equally on the community of people and systems that provide it."

The Sanctuary Model brings a perspective that asks: "What's happened to you?" rather than "What's wrong with you?" when organizing goals and assessing strengths and challenges. Sanctuary's seven commitments have become Villa of Hope's guiding principles, the overarching philosophy for how the agency provides services and works within the community (Esaki et al., 2013):

- Nonviolence
- Emotional Intelligence
- Social Learning
- Open Communication
- Social Responsibility
- Democracy
- Growth and Change

The Sanctuary Model's recognition of the inherent resilience in people and the belief that they can heal makes it the very core of the agency's cultural transformation.

A pilot group of 50 cross-functional staff members was trained first; after that a handful of them trained the remainder of Villa employees. From March to June 2012, 350 employees participated in a 3-day "Sanctuary 101" course.

The Sanctuary Model brings families directly into the treatment planning process, which previously had not been followed throughout all Villa programs. Combined with Villa of Hope's growing capacity to effectively measure outcomes and impact, this new approach is transforming agency programs into ones that are client-driven and that are informed by current research and best practices. Recently, the Villa began using an evidence-based screening tool to assess 40 developmental assets on intake, midway through treatment, and on discharge (Scales et al., 1999). These data are incorporated into treatment plans to help customers strengthen their life skills.

Gullo recognizes that culture change takes time, but she is encouraged by the new sense of cohesiveness, accountability, and willingness to work together toward a shared vision.

Transformational Leadership. Innovation is a critical component of Villa of Hope's transformation strategy. Each member of the strategy team receives training and skill building to become an innovative leader. These newly empowered leaders in turn infuse their work teams with the skills they need to understand and execute the mission, vision, and strategic objectives. Ongoing, focused work sessions throughout the organization are designed to stimulate staff to gather performance data, contribute innovative ideas, and report challenges and successes. The Villa is now working on an internal curriculum for ongoing supervisory and management training. This was piloted in June 2013 to all existing managers and supervisors.

Financial Turnaround. In the 3 previous years, including 2011, the Villa had experienced a steady decline in revenue and significant structural deficits in the budget. While the services were moving from being residential-based to being community-based, costs were not reduced in proportion. The Villa relied heavily on cash reserves and asset sales. In addition, over $1 million of a $3 million line of credit was being used to cover operations. Though the agency has a foundation, a restrictive debt structure made accessing the Villa's foundation funds difficult, even for strategic investments.

Several steps were taken to address the fiscal issues facing the Villa, including hiring a Rochester-based financial management firm as a consultant. In 2012, a total of $1.2 million in cost reductions were made, primarily by reducing head count of staff members. The agency secured a rate increase from the New York State Office of Children and Family Services that was made retroactive to July 1, 2012, shortened delays in Medicaid reimbursement by two weeks, and improved the organization's capital structure.

The Villa's organizational structure was revised to create clearer roles and responsibilities while focusing on improving residential program performance. While this was already common practice in many agencies, the Villa now budgets at the program and department levels with a monthly profit-and-loss statement. Further, each program undergoes an assessment of its fit with the mission and its overall profit or loss, which helps ensure that the agency breaks even and helps staff anticipate shortfalls before they occur. Since mid–fiscal year 2012, the Villa has been operating with a surplus and has invested resource dollars to start new programs and build upon existing infrastructure.

Forging a New Identity

A critical component of the agency's new strategic direction was revision of the mission, vision, and value statements—that is, of its very identity. In preparation for rebranding, the agency spent more than a year in extensive research and conversation with crucial stakeholders. The challenge was to honor the agency's rich legacy while positioning the organization not as a *place for troubled youth* but as a *partner* helping youth and families achieve a *hopeful future.*

In spring 2013, St. Joseph's Villa emerged as Villa of Hope. "Hope is what we are all about," Gullo says. "Our name, our vision, our values, and our treatment philosophy offer the hope that youth and families can rebuild, recover, and renew."

Performance Evaluation. Lack of resources and infrastructure has hampered the Villa's ability to measure outcomes and community impact. Currently, most data are extracted manually. The balanced scorecard demands an investment in information technology. Consultants recently analyzed Villa of Hope's IT needs based on each program area's newly defined targets and metrics. The Villa issued a request for proposal for a data system to track outcomes related to client profiles and activities, performance measures, and fiscal controls and expenditures.

"New technology to track outcomes will allow us to consistently evaluate our progress and determine outcome success," Gullo says. "It also will foster innovation and accountability, giving staff the data to make programmatic decisions that are client-informed, embedded in best practices, and responsive to change."

The Villa is moving to a pay-for-performance system, with the new vision and guiding values translated into operational goals. They are being written into job descriptions and linked to new performance appraisal and supervisory tools. Managers are currently being trained in the tools for the upcoming fiscal year, and the tools will be used for a full year before staff begin being rated in real time in the summer of 2014.

Villa of Hope's Priorities for 2013

The strategy team recently implemented the balanced scorecard tool. A one-page strategy map translates the vision into clearly defined quarterly goals and objectives, performance targets, and metrics (see Figure 6.1). The map also informs the organizational structure needed for success. The senior leadership team reviews the scorecard at least monthly, if not weekly.

In fiscal year 2013, the agency focused on continuing to be a more competitive, and therefore more sustainable, agency. The Villa recognizes that a key to driving sustainability is matching qualified, enabled, and motivated direct-care staff with youth and families in need.

In 2013, the Villa has strong program performance, and occupancy is at its highest level in years. The agency added new programs were added, generating significant revenue and resulting in operating surpluses for the second half of fiscal year 2012 and for fiscal year 2013.

A strategic program analysis highlighted opportunities to increase efficiencies, expand programs with high growth potential, and identify emerging opportunities. Programs continue to be assessed using a mission-and-margin basis. Villa of Hope added an eight-bed critical care residential program for girls in June 2012. The agency's new day respite program for children living at home is the only one of its kind in the area. Recently the Villa received a state grant to provide home- and community-based services for juvenile offenders. Revenue is now up 8%.

This was achieved through the investment of funds in direct-care staff, safety, compensation, strategy development, training, the Sanctuary model, and rebranding. The Villa has also invested in leadership development, communication, transparency, empowerment, accountability, improving morale, and attracting very strong talent for key positions.

Next Steps. The transformation work is still in process. After the agency has completed its infrastructure-building phase, each department will create its own strategy map, aligned with the overall agency map. "This is very different from how the organization used to do strategy," says Gullo. "We are embedding it at every level of the organization. Strategy now drives our decision making."

Looking ahead, Villa of Hope will continue to focus on specialized residential care and will leverage its expertise in care management, addiction services, and community-based programs. It sees a niche in trauma-informed treatment that increases the functionality of the youth served, with a focus on building life skills in young adults ages 18 to 25.

Lessons Learned. Gullo learned that eagerness to move forward quickly actually set them back. "I think we got ahead of ourselves because the infrastructure wasn't there yet. We had to pull back and do things in the right

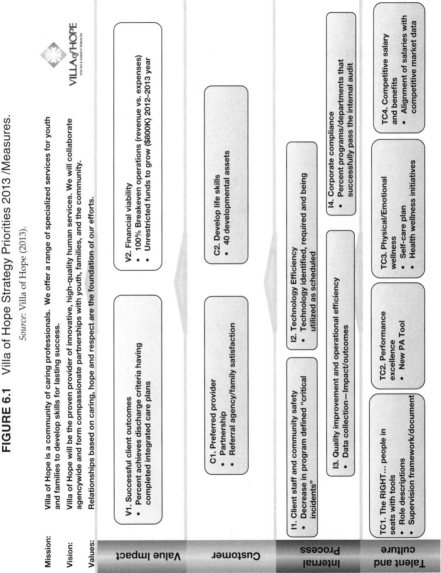

FIGURE 6.1 Villa of Hope Strategy Priorities 2013 /Measures.

Source: Villa of Hope (2013).

Mission: Villa of Hope is a community of caring professionals. We offer a range of specialized services for youth and families to develop skills for lasting success.

Vision: Villa of Hope will be the proven provider of innovative, high-quality human services. We will collaborate agencywide and form compassionate partnerships with youth, families, and the community.

Values: Relationships based on caring, hope and respect are the foundation of our efforts.

VILLA *of* HOPE
YOUTH & FAMILY SERVICES

Value Impact

V1. Successful client outcomes
• Percent achieves discharge criteria having completed integrated care plans

V2. Financial viability
• 100% Breakeven operations (revenue vs. expenses)
• Unrestricted funds to grow ($800K) 2012–2013 year

Customer

C1. Preferred provider
• Partnership
• Referral agency/family satisfaction

C2. Develop life skills
• 40 developmental assets

Internal Process

I1. Client staff and community safety
• Decrease in program defined "critical incidents"

I2. Technology Efficiency
• Technology identified, required and being utilized as scheduled

I3. Quality improvement and operational efficiency
• Data collection—Impact/outcomes

I4. Corporate compliance
• Percent programs/departments that successfully pass the internal audit

Talent and culture

TC1. The RIGHT... people in seats with tools
• Role descriptions
• Supervision framework/document

TC2. Performance excellence
• New PA Tool

TC3. Physical/Emotional wellness
• Self-care plan
• Health wellness initiatives

TC4. Competitive salary and benefits
• Alignment of salaries with competitive market data

117

order," she says. "If we had pushed through, we would have been trying to grow an organization on a very unstable foundation."

The experience also reinforced the importance of having the right people, in the right seats, with the right skill set. Gullo recognizes that culture change has to start at the top: "The CEO and senior leadership team have to all be on the same playing field, saying, doing, and modeling the same behaviors."

With the strategy to drive them and the Sanctuary model to guide them, Villa of Hope's progress toward transformation has been nothing short of astonishing: a fiscal turnaround, high occupancy, new sources of revenue, dramatic performance improvement, accountable leadership and staff, greater resilience and agility, new collaborations, a renewed sense of hope, and a culture driven by client need and empowered by innovation. It all adds up to another word vital to the Villa's future: reinvention.

References

Esaki, N., Benamati, J., Yanosy, S., Middleton, J., Hopson, L., Hummer, V., & Bloom, S. (2013). The Sanctuary Model: Theoretical framework. *Families in Society: The Journal of Contemporary Social Services, 2*(92).

Scales, P. C., & Leffert, T. (1999). *Developmental assets: A synthesis of scientific research on adolescent development.* Minneapolis, MN: Search Institute, p. 5.

Villa of Hope. (2013). Strategy map of priorities and measures.

THE SANCTUARY MODEL: THEORETICAL FRAMEWORK

*Nina Esaki, Joseph Benamati, Sarah Yanosy, Jennifer S. Middleton,
Laura M. Hopson, Victoria L. Hummer, and Sandra L. Bloom*

This article provides a theoretical framework for the Sanctuary Model. The Sanctuary Model is a trauma-informed organizational change intervention developed by Sandra Bloom and colleagues in the early 1980s. Based on the concept of therapeutic communities, the model is designed to facilitate the development of organizational cultures that counteract the wounds suffered by the victims of traumatic experience and extended exposure to adversity. Details of the Sanctuary Model logic model are presented.

Implications for Practice

- Emerging research suggests the importance of organizational culture in the delivery of evidence-based mental health services and, thus, the need for organizational interventions such as the Sanctuary Model.
- By creating a restorative culture through the Sanctuary Model, service providers can be emotionally available to each other and their clients, resulting in positive relationships that create the conditions for resilience.

The Sanctuary Model represents a theory-based, trauma-informed, evidence-supported (National Child Traumatic Stress Network, 2008; Rivard, Bloom, McCorkle, & Abramovitz, 2005), whole-culture approach that has a clear and structured methodology for creating or changing an organizational culture. The objective of such a change is to more effectively provide a cohesive context within which healing from physical, psychological, and social traumatic experience can be addressed. As an organizational culture intervention, the Sanctuary Model is designed to facilitate the development of structures, processes, and behaviors on the part of staff, clients, and the community as a whole that can counteract the biological, affective, cognitive, social, and existential wounds suffered by the victims of traumatic experience and extended exposure to adversity (Bloom, 2011).

Reprinted with permission from *Families in Society: The Journal of Contemporary Social Services* (www
.alliance1.org/fis), published by the Alliance for Children and Families.

History

Beginning in 1980, Sandra Bloom, Joseph Foderaro, and Ruth Ann Ryan worked in both hospital and outpatient settings with people who survived overwhelmingly stressful and often traumatic life experiences. Building on the concept of therapeutic communities, in which staff and clients collectively participate in creating a system of healing (Jones, 1953, 1968; Lees, Manning, Menzies, & Morant, 2004; Main, 1946), and using the work of Silver (1985, 1986), who described "sanctuary trauma" as expecting a welcoming and healing environment and finding instead more trauma, Bloom and her colleagues formed the Sanctuary, a trauma-specific program for adult survivors. The Sanctuary Model, an outgrowth of the Sanctuary, is a blueprint for clinical and organizational change that promotes safety and recovery from adversity through the active creation of a trauma-informed community. Today, the Sanctuary Model has been expanded to include both adult- and child-serving agencies across the United States and in seven countries around the world (Sanctuary Institute, 2012).

Theoretical Framework

The Sanctuary Model is an organizational intervention that is grounded in constructivist self-development theory (CSDT; McCann & Pearlman, 1990; Pearlman & Saakvitne, 1995), burnout theory (Maslach & Jackson, 1981; Maslach, Schaufeli, & Leiter, 2001), and systems theory (Bertalanffy, 1974), utilizing the valuation theory of organizational change (Hermans, 1991; Weatherbee, Dye, Bissonnette, & Mills, 2009) to improve organizational culture. Its goal is to improve organizational culture by educating staff on the effects of trauma and stress on behavior, changing the mindset of staff regarding behavior of clients from being pejorative (i.e., sick) to being the result of injury, and providing tools to change individual and group behavior. The theoretical framework addresses dynamics at both levels, and by so doing, the model aims to improve the quality of service delivery and, ultimately, improve client outcomes.

Constructivist Self-Development Theory

CSDT (McCann & Pearlman, 1990; Pearlman & Saakvitne, 1995) is an integrative personality theory that provides a framework for understanding the impact of childhood maltreatment on the developing self (Saakvitne, Tennen, & Affleck, 1998). With origins in psychoanalytic theory, self-psychology, social learning, and cognitive development, this theory describes the unique impact of traumatic events that arises from interactions among aspects of the person, the event, and the context (Brock, Pearlman, & Varra, 2006); thus it is a constructivist theory of personality development. Because it highlights those aspects of development most likely to be affected by traumatic events, it is also a clinical trauma theory (Saakvitne et al., 1998).

CSDT describes three self-capacities: the ability to maintain a sense of connection with benign others (inner connection); the ability to experience, tolerate, and integrate strong affect (affect tolerance); and the ability to maintain a sense of self as viable, benign, and positive (self-worth). Drawing from theory and research on attachment (Bowlby, 1988), CSDT suggests that self-capacities develop through early relationships with caregivers and allow one to learn to regulate one's inner state. The capacity to maintain a sense of connection with others is posited to form the basis from which the other self-capacities (affect regulation and a sense of self-worth) develop (Brock et al., 2006).

CSDT establishes the foundation for understanding the disruptions in social and behavioral functioning that accompany exposure to trauma and the strong relationship between attachment and emotion regulation. Sanctuary draws from this knowledge and focuses on creating a community environment within the treatment system that allows clients to restore connections with others. A primary goal of establishing this organizational community environment is to allow the development of multiple relationships that will ultimately help clients regulate their internal states.

Burnout Theory

The term *burnout* was coined by Herbert Freudenberger (1974), a clinical psychologist familiar with the stress responses exhibited by staff members in "alternative" institutions such as free clinics and halfway houses (Jackson, Schwab, & Schuler, 1986). Burnout is typically referred to as a condition in which workers become worn out or exhausted because excessive demands have been placed on their energy, strength, and resources (Freudenberger, 1974).

Maslach and Jackson (1981) developed a multidimensional construct of burnout that encompasses three components: emotional exhaustion, increasing depersonalization of clients, and decreased feelings of personal accomplishment. Emotional exhaustion is the depletion of emotional resources and the feeling that one has nothing left to give psychologically. Depersonalization occurs when a worker develops negative and callous attitudes toward their clients and begins to treat clients as objects rather than persons. Decreased feelings of personal accomplishment result when a worker begins to develop a negative view of their achievements on the job or begins to believe that personal expectations are not being met (Poulin & Walter, 1993).

Of the three components of burnout, it is most commonly associated with emotional exhaustion (Poulin & Walter, 1993). It is the most widely accepted and recognized aspect of burnout and is also the one that most resembles traditional measures used to study job performance (Jackson et al., 1986). Various types of job-related stressors, such as work overload, role ambiguity, role conflict, limited job autonomy, and client demands, have been shown to contribute to burnout (Kowalski et al., 2010; Peiro, Gonzalez-Roma, Tordera, & Manas, 2001; White, Edwards, & Townsend-White, 2006).

The individual experiences stress and, without adequate resources for coping, may face strain, exhaustion, and attitudinal and behavioral changes indicative of burnout (Maslach, 1982).

Workplace support has been identified as an important organizational factor for worker outcomes such as burnout or job satisfaction (Himle, Jayaratne, & Thyness, 1991; Yoo, 2002). For example, social support from supervisors serves as preventive of burnout and also provides emotional relief to workers (Swanson & Power, 2001; Yoo, 2002). The Sanctuary Model suggests that worker burnout, particularly emotional exhaustion of direct service providers, can be a barrier to their emotional availability to serve as adequate attachment objects for clients who need positive relationships in order to begin to self-regulate. The Sanctuary Model is informed by burnout theory through attention to the well-being of staff and their need for adequate support within the environment.

Systems Theory

Bertalanffy (1974), one of the architects of systems theory, asserted that a system is defined as a constellation of components in mutual interaction (Iglehart, 2009). In an open system, energy is imported from the environment (inputs), transformed to create a technology, and then exported back into the environment (outputs). Significant features of an open system are interrelatedness of subsystems, boundary maintenance, system equilibrium, system functions (socialization, social control, communication, and feedback), system adaptation and maintenance for survival, and the relationship between the system and its environment (Katz & Kahn, 1978; Netting, Kettner, & McCurtry, 2008).

One of the guiding assumptions of most organizational theory is that organizations are systems. Organizations are a confluence of interlocking parts. Programs, work units, frontline staff, clientele, boards of directors, administrators, and organizational constituents are components of organizational systems. A common understanding among participants differentiates the organization and its members from those people and structures that are not part of the organization (Norlin & Chess, 1997). A change in one part of the system produces change in the entire system. In addition, organizations are subsets of larger systems, often referred to as the organization's *suprasystem* (Hasenfeld, 1992; Norlin & Chess, 1997). For example, organizations are affected by what happens in the surrounding community, or by events in social, economic, or political systems. The Sanctuary Model incorporates this understanding of organizations as systems, in that the organization itself is seen as the primary target for the intervention, with staff, clients, and other stakeholders composing that system as recipients of the intervention.

Valuation Theory of Organizational Change

As explored by Weatherbee et al. (2009), Hermans' valuation theory (Hermans, 1991) with its related self-confrontation method (SCM; Hermans, 1976; Hermans, Fiddelaers, de Groot, & Nauta, 1990) is a therapeutic approach that can facilitate access and insight into deeper structures of organizational change through a focus on the valuations or personal meanings that organizational actors bring into the workplace (Hermans & Hermans-Jansen, 1995; Weatherbee et al., 2009). Valuation theory, which draws on the work of Mead (1934), is rooted in the metaphor of the person as a storyteller giving special significance to particular events or groups of events that function as units of meaning for them (Hermans & Hermans-Jansen, 1995). As individuals and organizational groups perceive organizational change in different ways, with a variety of attributed meanings and interpretations, this may lead to significant differences between the valuations held by individuals, work groups, or the organization as a whole. Thus there exists significant potential value in the use of the SCM to elicit organizational valuations and bring them to the surface so that they may be discarded, reinforced, or molded to facilitate change processes in organizational environments (Weatherbee et al., 2009).

The valuation theory allows for clinical research methodologies to be integrated into the study of organizational change, because psychotherapeutic methods access interpretations and understandings of organizational culture and change (Kets de Vries, 1991; Schein, 1993). Similarly, the context in which the change occurs, including historical elements, must be considered (Pettigrew, Woodman, & Cameron, 2001). Valuation theory is a proven method for accessing and understanding the underlying or deeper interpretations, cognitions, beliefs, and values held by individuals (Weatherbee et al., 2009). SCM, which assesses attitudes toward the past, present, and envisioned future of individuals' experiences, can shed light on those contextual, temporal, and historical elements that influence attitudes toward organizational change (Weatherbee et al., 2009). The Sanctuary Model introduces training, skill building, and tools into an organization to generate self-confrontation among individual staff members as well as among groups within the organization, culminating in change in the system as a whole.

A Socioecological Logic Model for the Sanctuary Model

Organizations are the primary vehicles for delivering positive changes on multiple levels to consumers and are also an integral part of any social service system; therefore, organizations have a significant role in effecting change in the system. The Sanctuary Model uses a logic model to connect activities and outcomes at each socioecological level: individual, interpersonal, organizational, and community (see Figure 6.2). From left to right, the model identifies common input and activity logic model components leading to outcomes. From top to bottom, the model depicts the levels of the socioecological model, beginning with individual-level activities and outcomes at the top and progressing down and ending with community-level activities and outcomes.

FIGURE 6.2 Sanctuary Model Logic Model.

Inputs

Training:
- 5-day leadership
- Core team
- General staff
- Clients/families
- Stakeholders
- Orientation
- Boosters

Skill Building:
- On-site TA
- Phone TA
- Implementation manuals
- Practice-based learning materials

Tools:
- Fidelity checklists
- Toolkit lessons
- Psychoeducation manuals

Relationship Building Time

Activities

INDIVIDUAL
- Training participation
- Acceptance of role on Steering Committee and Core Team
- Use of safety plans and self-care plans and rescripting

INTERPERSONAL
- Core team practice of year 1 implementation tasks
- Community meetings, S.E.L.F. treatment plans/problem solving, psychoeducation and supervision

ORGANIZATIONAL
- Seven Commitment monthly themes
- Implementation tasks related to certification
- Policy and practice work group activities

COMMUNITY
- Sanctuary Network Conference and events
- Social media participation
- Policy and advocacy work by regional groups

Outcomes

Short-Term

Individual
- Self-reflection regarding power and conflict
- Adoption of new lens through which to view organizational dynamics
- Perception of clients as injured
- Increased knowledge of milieu dynamics
- Increased awareness of vicarious trauma

Interpersonal
- Staff share a common language
- Increased focus on future
- Increased hope and morale
- Improved recognition of feelings by both staff and clients

Organizational
- Increased sense of staff inclusion in decision making
- Leaders feel more hopeful and efficacious
- Decreased turnover in staff

Community
- Increased knowledge by staff of the Sanctuary Network of organizations, their missions, and potential collaborations
- Demonstrated social responsibility among community members
- Increased knowledge by outside stakeholders of the Sanctuary implementation process

Mid-Term

Individual
- Changes in self-perception for clients
- Improved conflict management skills
- Personal commitment to organizational change
- Willingness to serve as a role model and representative for others

Interpersonal
- Exploration of organizational change
- Reduction in untoward events
- Increased team collaboration
- Stronger sense of community
- Awareness of coworker strengths and vulnerabilities

Organizational
- Increase in Seven Commitment behavior by leaders and staff alike
- Changes in policy and procedures to align agency practice with the Seven Commitments of Sanctuary
- Increased Core Team involvement in organization decisions

Community
- Sanctuary organizations share best practices (i.e., presentations at Sanctuary Network Days)
- Increased altruism—sharing information, practices, and products with others, such as federal and state policymakers outside the Sanctuary Network

Long-Term

Individual
- Improved treatment outcomes for clients
- Improved emotional regulation demonstrated by a majority of staff
- Improved stress management demonstrated by a majority of staff

Interpersonal
- Increased ability of staff and clients to avoid and reduce reenactment
- High-functioning multidisciplinary teams

Organizational
- Improved staff recruitment and retention
- Staff and client satisfaction
- Appropriate distribution and use of power

Community
- Demonstrated social responsibility among members
- Improved regulations and enhanced funding streams that give priority to evidence-supported trauma interventions

Inputs

Inputs refer to the resources needed to initiate and sustain a program. In implementing and sustaining organizational change through the Sanctuary Model, inputs fall into three categories: training, skill building, and tools.

Training. This consists of 5-day leadership training; Core Team training; general staff training; psychoeducation for clients, families, and internal and external stakeholders; new staff orientation training; and ongoing staff booster trainings. The Core Team is a multidisciplinary team with representatives from each level of the organization who are agents of change within the organization. These various training courses are facilitated by Sanctuary Institute faculty using a specially designed curriculum for each of the training courses this above, in conjunction with written materials and film clips. The content of all of this training consists of some combination of didactic and experiential learning activities in four areas known as the four pillars (described in Table 6.1).

Skill Building. This consists of technical assistance through on-site consultations, phone calls, written materials for staff training, and a series of activities for the Core Team that are executed by Sanctuary Institute faculty in the following areas: embedding the Seven Commitments in policy and practice, using the S.E.L.F. (safety, emotion management, loss, and future) framework for problem solving, applying trauma theory to systems, interpreting many client behaviors as trauma responses, managing conflict, and using the concepts of the Sanctuary Model in supervision.

TABLE 6.1 The Four Pillars of the Sanctuary Model

Trauma Theory

Overview of information about how traumatic experiences affect the brain and therefore influence thoughts, feelings, and behaviors.

Seven Sanctuary Commitments

Philosophical underpinnings of the Sanctuary Model that describe how community members agree to behave with each other and the values to which the organization subscribes.

S.E.L.F.

Acronym for the organizing categories of safety, emotion management, loss, and future, used to formulate plans for client services or treatment as well as for interpersonal and organizational problem solving.

Sanctuary Toolkit

Set of 10 practical applications of trauma theory, the Seven Commitments, and S.E.L.F., which are used by all members of the community at all levels of the hierarchy and reinforce the concepts of the model.

Tools. The inputs category of tools consists not only of training in the Sanctuary Toolkit but also of support from Sanctuary Institute faculty through ongoing phone and on-site consultation for troubleshooting when there are problems implementing any of the tools. In addition, a set of fidelity checklists are provided that can be used to measure adherence to the practices and the Sanctuary Certification Standards, which detail the manner and frequency of practice of the tools for different types of settings. Finally, staff members can use four Sanctuary psychoeducation manuals to deliver lessons to clients about the four pillars of the Sanctuary Model in either group or individual settings. Each manual is designed to apply to clients who are operating at a specific developmental level. The 10 tools in the Toolkit are detailed in Table 6.2.

Individual-Level Activities and Outcomes

The individual-level activities that contribute to implementation of the Sanctuary Model are participation in training and acceptance of a role in the Sanctuary Steering Committee and Core Team. In addition to engagement in these forums for individual activity, the practice of safety plans, self-care plans, and rescripting traumatic reenactment also contribute to outcomes on the individual level.

Generally, organizational leaders participate in the initial 5-day training with the outcome of individual engagement in a self-reflection and a new lens for looking at their own organization's functioning. The 5-day training also results in the experience of leaders in understanding their own behaviors, their use of and experience of power within the organization, and an appreciation for their own as well as the staff's and clients' experience of personal and organizational adversity. These leaders who attend the initial training are expected to accept a role in the organization's Sanctuary Steering Committee, a small group of five to seven leaders who are charged with organizing the process of Sanctuary implementation and maintaining contact with the Sanctuary Institute faculty. The outcomes of participating in the Steering Committee are (a) recognition of oneself as a role model to all staff practicing the model and (b) greater insight into one's use of power and one's own role in conflict and organizational reenactments.

Accepting a role in the Core Team is another individual-level activity in creating organizational change through Sanctuary. Participation in the Core Team means that an individual agrees to represent his or her peers as part of an implementation team that participates in structured activities to reinforce the practices of the model and explore opportunities for change in the organization. Participation results in a change in practice with clients that includes a perspective that moves from judgmental to one that assumes that clients are using ineffective skills for managing distress, and that one must use relational opportunities to teach new and more effective skills. Similarly,

TABLE 6.2 Tools in the Sanctuary Model Toolkit

Core Team

Primary vehicle for implementation of the Sanctuary Model, which consists of a cross section of staff from all levels of the organization's hierarchy charged with executing the implementation steps.

Supervision

Individual or group meetings to review performance that include opportunities to discuss issues of vicarious trauma, self-care, and updating safety plans.

Training

Ongoing support to staff in use of the Sanctuary Model concepts through educational materials and interactive learning opportunities.

Community Meetings

All community members begin meetings by answering three questions designed to promote feelings identification, a focus on future, and a connection to community.

Team Meetings

Way to structure meetings among staff members that allows for them to reflect on the work, discuss team functioning, and service delivery issues.

Self-Care Planning

Practice of identifying and committing to practice a set of activities that one can do to manage stress both inside and outside the workplace.

Red Flag Reviews

Response to critical incidents that follows a protocol to focus on solutions over problems.

Safety Plans

Visual reminders of emotion management practices represented as a list of activities, techniques, or skills to be used in situations that may trigger inappropriate behaviors.

S.E.L.F. Service Planning

Framework for organizing service planning meetings and documents that explores functioning, challenges, goals, and progress in the areas of safety, emotion management, loss, and future.

Sanctuary Psychoeducation

Educational materials about the effects of trauma; the Sanctuary Tools and Concepts delivered to clients and families.

team participation also results in the capacity for individual participants to apply this understanding and practice to peers and administrators, thereby improving knowledge of milieu dynamics.

Participation in regular staff training is an individual-level activity for all staff that results in a clearer understanding of the organization's expectations for relational interactions among and between clients and staff. The use of safety plans and self-care plans, part of the Sanctuary Toolkit, are individual activities in which practitioners create immediate and long-term ways of managing stressful situations. The resulting outcomes of practicing both of these tools are increased awareness of vicarious trauma and improved emotion management skills and personal stress management skills. The application of rescripting, which is the recognition of one's prescribed role in a conflict and the conscious and decisive action to do something outside of that role as a way to disrupt traumatic reenactment, results in an increased sense of agency in the individual in resolving interpersonal conflicts. Overall, the practice of applying knowledge obtained in training results in a stronger commitment to positive organizational change and increased knowledge of trauma symptoms and strategies for effective intervention, which eventually lead to changes in client perceptions of themselves as well as improved outcomes for clients.

Interpersonal-Level Activities and Outcomes
Interpersonal activities consist of the practice of several tools as well as execution of specific Core Team actions detailed in the first-year tasks of the *Sanctuary Implementation Guide*. These include creating a communication plan; having a kickoff event; engaging in self-assessment; learning the organizational trauma history; holding a conflict retreat; and exploring the power, values, beliefs, and assumptions across the agency. These activities result in deeper exploration of organizational change, development of a shared language for understanding and solving problems, increased team collaboration, and increased hope and morale among workers.

The community meeting tool among staff and clients brings groups of people together for a very short meeting in which each member reports a feeling, a goal, and a person to ask for help. The outcomes of this practice are increased awareness of the feelings of others, improved ability to focus on the future rather than dwell on the past, and a stronger sense of community among members of the organization. Team meetings offer similar outcomes for staff, in that team members who meet together in this forum have an increased understanding of each other's triggers, can use this knowledge to intervene more appropriately with each other in the milieu, and have a clearer sense of each individual's vulnerability to reenactment within the team. This increased knowledge allows for faster resolution of interpersonal conflict as evidenced by disrupted reenactment, fewer untoward events, and improved teamwork. Red Flag Reviews, which allow anyone in the community to bring a concern to be addressed and to use the trauma-informed, problem-solving framework of S.E.L.F., result in more collaborative and creative solutions to client and organizational issues, and encourage higher levels of functioning in multidisciplinary teams.

Service planning using a multidisciplinary approach and the S.E.L.F. framework as a way to organize client problems, goals, and interventions results in an increased focus on resolving issues of emotion management, loss related to trauma or exposure to adversity, and sense of hope for the future rather than overemphasizing client behavioral control in the service of safety as the exclusive priority. Psychoeducation for clients and supervision for staff are tools that reinforce the common language of trauma and adversity and that help clients and staff avoid traumatic reenactments.

Organization-Level Activities and Outcomes

The organization-level activities are represented by operationalizing the Seven Commitments, since these are the values to which organizations using Sanctuary aspire. The purpose of each of the Seven Commitments is to combat the negative effects of exposure to trauma and adversity through construction of an environment that systematically exposes a traumatized individual to repetitive restorative experiences within the treatment setting. Each commitment is described in Table 6.3.

Operationalizing these commitments, aligning policies and practices with these commitments across all areas of the organization (leadership, human resources, admissions, milieu, and treatment/clinical), and evaluating progress against the Sanctuary Certification Standards are the organizational activities. The results of these activities are alignment of practices and policies as well as behavior of leaders and staff with the Seven Commitments. Leaders report feeling more hopeful and effective, and they demonstrate appropriate use of and distribution of power. The active role of the Core Team in operationalizing the Seven Commitments results in members' increased participation in decisions, often also reflected in the general experience of all staff. Increased participation correlates with increased client and staff satisfaction, reduced turnover, and improved recruitment and retention.

Community and Societal Activities and Outcomes

Community activities fall into two categories: (a) the community of Sanctuary agencies, also known as the Network, and (b) the society at large, which includes funders, regulators, referents, stakeholders, and colleagues. Both types of "community" have an evolutionary quality to the way in which Sanctuary concepts and tools get applied within their respective settings.

Within the Network, agencies learn early on about other Network agencies and their client base, as well as a little about what products and practices they use. The purpose is to help Network agencies begin not only to see each other as potential resources and partners in the implementation process but also to function as a community that can ultimately speak with a stronger voice regarding issues of trauma and the healing process—and a community that is data-driven. The result of this effort is that Network agencies become increasingly confident about sharing their effective practices with others (demonstrating social learning).

TABLE 6.3   The Sanctuary Model's Seven Sanctuary Commitments

Nonviolence

The community works toward ensuring that all members are safe and refrain from hurting each other.

Emotional Intelligence

Recognizing and anticipating the influence that emotions have on behavior and using that information to guide practice.

Democracy

Encourages community members to share decision making in whatever ways are most appropriate for their group. This is based on the premise that diversity of opinion yields a better result and that people are more likely to support something they have helped create.

Open Communication

Members agree to be aware of how they communicate with each other. Community members agree to talk about issues that affect the whole community, no matter how difficult they may be, and to do so in a direct and open way. Leaders practice transparency in regard to decisions or issues that affect everyone. All community members have the information they need to be successful.

Social Responsibility

Agreement that the community will take care of itself and its members. Members share responsibility for doing good work, adhering to the rules of the community, and being accountable for their behaviors and decisions.

Commitment to Social Learning

Creating an environment that allows people to learn from each other, their experiences, and their mistakes.

Growth and Change

The belief that individuals, groups, and systems can grow and heal. We create situations that promote growth out of our comfort zones and create a sense of disequilibrium that forces movement. Growth and change are achieved through inquiry, self-reflection or assessment, and acquiring knowledge.

The second category of community involves the society at large. In this context, the goal is to reach out to colleagues, consumers, and governmental bodies in order for them to recognize the effects of trauma on children and their families and those who serve them. The results of these activities are improved regulations and enhanced funding streams that give priority to evidence-supported trauma interventions.

Discussion

Application of a socioecological logic model to the Sanctuary Model intervention process is beneficial is several ways. First, the logic model highlights positive systems change as a primary goal of Sanctuary Model implementation by clearly articulating potential change at higher socio-ecological levels. Second, the model differentiates between activities and outcomes at each level of the social ecology, providing a framework for corresponding trauma-informed activities and outcomes. This framework promotes outcome measurement at all levels, potentially informing individual organizational intervention projects, as well as the overall development and evaluation of the Sanctuary Model across various settings. Third, because the Sanctuary Model itself is informed by systems theory, the socioecological logic model is theoretically complementary and allows for a trauma-informed, systems-inclusive approach that is useful in planning, implementing, and evaluating Sanctuary Model organizational interventions.

Although useful, there are some limitations related to the application of the socioecological logic model to the Sanctuary Model for trauma-informed organizational change. First, though the proposed logic model provides a solid framework distinguishing activities and outcomes for each discrete level, changes in organizational culture and at the community level are complex and may require efforts from multiple agents. As such, it is often difficult to attribute change to a single program or intervention when measuring change across organizations and systems. Second, an organization's or community's capacity to and readiness for change will influence its ability to successfully implement and achieve systems-level changes. For example, child welfare organizations often suffer from *change fatigue* associated with repetitive organizational restructuring, which may detrimentally affect their workers' readiness for change and capacity to take on new initiatives. Third, the theoretical frameworks that inform the Sanctuary Model do not distinguish between the constructs of organizational culture and climate and do not specifically account for climate factors, which may be an important consideration when examining the social context within which large-scale change occurs. Enhanced testing is critical seeing that the Sanctuary Model is the only trauma-informed organizational intervention of its kind, currently being implemented in over 250 agencies in a variety of settings and communities across the nation (for implementation details, see Sanctuary Institute, 2012, n.d.).

Conclusion

Individuals who have experienced trauma continue to suffer from suboptimal physical and mental health. Yet, research demonstrates that survivors of trauma can be resilient if they are connected to positive, caring service providers (Harney, 2007; Larkin, Beckos, & Shields, 2012). Unfortunately, high turnover and emotional exhaustion among staff who work with traumatized individuals threaten to create an environment in which it is difficult for these clients to build meaningful connections with providers.

The Sanctuary Model aims to reverse these trends through a set of tools that create an emotionally and physically safe environment for traumatized clients and everyone connected with them. Although more rigorous evaluation of the Sanctuary Model is needed, the emerging research demonstrates that it is a promising approach for creating a healthy environment that promotes emotional health and well-being for agency personnel and the clients they serve (Rivard et al., 2005; Stein, Sorbero, Kogan, & Greenberg, 2011). By protecting the emotional health of agency personnel, the Sanctuary Model creates a context in which service providers can be emotionally available to each other and their clients, resulting in positive relationships that create the conditions for resilience.

References

Bertalanffy, L. (1974). General systems theory and psychiatry. In S. Ariete (Ed.), *American handbook of psychiatry* (2nd ed., Vol. 1; pp. 1095–1117). New York: Basic Books.

Bloom, S. L. (2011). The Sanctuary Model. Retrieved October 18, 2011, from http://www.sanctuaryweb.com/trauma-informedsystems.php

Bowlby, J. (1988). *A secure base.* New York: Basic Books.

Brock, K. J., Pearlman, L. A., & Varra, E. M. (2006). Child maltreatment, self capacities, and trauma symptoms: Psychometric properties of the Inner Experience Questionnaire. *Journal of Emotional Abuse, 6*(1), 103–125. doi:10.1300/J135v06n0106

Freudenberger, H. J. (1974). Staff burnout. *Journal of Social Issues, 30*(1), 159–165.

Harney, P. A. (2007). Resilience processes in context: Contributions and implications of Bronfenbrenner's person-process-context model. *Journal of Aggression, Maltreatment & Trauma, 14*(3), 73–87.

Hasenfeld, Y. (1992). *Human services as complex organizations.* Newbury Park, CA: SAGE.

Hermans, H. J. M. (1976). *Value areas and their development: Theory and method of self-confrontation.* Amsterdam, The Netherlands: Swets & Zeitlinger.

Hermans, H. J. M. (1991). The person as co-investigator in self-research: Valuation theory. *European Journal of Personality, 5*(3), 217–234.

Hermans, H. J. M., Fiddelaers, R., de Groot, R., & Nauta, J. F. (1990). Self-confrontation as a method for assessment and intervention in counseling. *Journal of Counseling & Development, 69*(2), 156.

Hermans, H. J. M., & Hermans-Jansen, E. (1995). *Self-narratives: The construction of meaning in psychotherapy.* New York: Guilford.

Himle, D. P., Jayaratne, S., & Thyness, P. (1991). Buffering effects of four social support types on burnout among social workers. *Social Work Research & Abstracts, 27*(1), 22–27.

Iglehart, A. P. (2009). Managing for diversity and empowerment in human services agencies. In R. J. Patti (Ed.), *The handbook of human services management* (2nd ed.; pp. 295–318). Thousand Oaks, CA: SAGE.

Jackson, S. E., Schwab, R. L., & Schuler, R. S. (1986). Toward an understanding of the burnout phenomenon. *Journal of Applied Psychology, 71*(4), 630–640.

Jones, M. (1953). *The therapeutic community: A new treatment method in psychiatry.* New York: Basic Books.

Jones, M. (1968). *Beyond the therapeutic community: Social learning and social psychiatry.* New Haven, CT: Yale University Press.

Katz, D., & Kahn, R. (1978). *The social psychology of organizations* (2nd ed.). New York: Wiley.

Kets de Vries, M. F. R. (1991). *Organizations of the couch.* San Francisco, CA: Jossey-Bass.

Kowalski, C., Driller, E., Ernstmann, N., Alich, S., Karbach, U., & Ommen, O. (2010). Associations between emotional exhaustion, social capital, workload, and latitude in decisionmaking among professionals working with people with disabilities. *Research in Developmental Disabilities, 31*(2), 470–479.

Larkin, H., Beckos, B. A., & Shields, J. J. (2012). Mobilizing resilience and recovery in response to adverse childhood experiences (ACE): A restorative integral support (RIS) case study. *Journal of Prevention & Intervention in the Community, 40*(4), 335–346. doi:10.1080/10852352.2012.707466

Lees, J., Manning, N., Menzies, D., & Morant, N. (2004). *A culture of enquiry: Research evidence and the therapeutic community.* London, UK: Jessica Kingsley.

Main, T. F. (1946). The hospital as a therapeutic institution. *Bulletin of the Menninger Clinic, 10,* 66–70.

Maslach, C. (1982). *Burnout: The cost of caring.* Englewood Cliffs, NJ: Prentice Hall.

Maslach, C., & Jackson, S. E. (1981). The measurement of experienced burnout. *Journal of Occupational Behavior, 2*(2), 99–113.

Maslach, C., Schaufeli, W. B., & Leiter, M. P. (2001). Job burnout. *Annual Review of Psychology, 52,* 397–422.

McCann, I. L., & Pearlman, L. A. (1990). Vicarious traumatization: A framework for understanding the psychological effects of working with victims. *Journal of Traumatic Stress, 3*(1), 131–149.

Mead, G. H. (1934). *Mind, self, and society.* Chicago: University of Chicago Press.

National Child Traumatic Stress Network. (2008, August). Sanctuary Model: General information. *Trauma-Informed Interventions.* Retrieved from http://www.nctsnet.org/nctsn_assets/pdfs/promising_practices/Sanctuary_General.pdf

Netting, F. E., Kettner, P. M., & McCurtry, S. (2008). *Social work macro practice.* Boston, MA: Allyn & Bacon.

Norlin, J., & Chess, W. (1997). *Human behavior and the social environment: Social systems theory* (3rd ed.). Boston, MA: Allyn & Bacon.

Pearlman, L. A., & Saakvitne, K. W. (1995). *Trauma and the therapist: Countertransference and vicarious traumatization in psychotherapy with incest survivors.* New York: W.W. Norton.

Peiro, J. M., Gonzalez-Roma, V., Tordera, N., & Manas, M. A. (2001). Does role stress predict burnout over time among health care professionals? *Psychology and Health, 16,* 511–525.

Pettigrew, A. M., Woodman, R. W., & Cameron, K. S. (2001). Studying organizational change and development: Challenges for future research. *Academy of Management Journal, 44*(4), 697–713.

Poulin, J., & Walter, C. (1993). Social worker burnout: A longitudinal study. *Social Work Research & Abstracts, 29*(4), 5.

Rivard, J. C., Bloom, S. L., McCorkle, D., & Abramovitz, R. (2005). Preliminary results of a study examining the implementation and effects of a trauma recovery framework for youths in residential treatment. *Therapeutic Community: The International Journal for Therapeutic and Supportive Organizations, 26*(1), 83–96.

Saakvitne, K. W., Tennen, H., & Affleck, G. (1998). Exploring thriving in the context of clinical trauma theory: Constructivist self-development theory. *Journal of Social Issues, 54*(2), 279–299.

Sanctuary Institute. (2012). Our network. Retrieved September 5, 2012, from http://www.thesanctuaryinstitute.org/our-network

Sanctuary Institute. (n.d.). Sanctuary Model® implementation: An overview of the process. Retrieved from http://www.sanctuaryweb.com/PDFs/A7c.%20Sanctuary%20Model%20Implementation.pdf

Schein, E. H. (1993). Legitimating clinical research in the study of organizational culture. *Journal of Counseling & Development, 71*(6), 703–708.

Silver, S. M. (1985). Post-traumatic stress and the death imprint: The search for a new mythos. In W. E. Kelly (Ed.), *Post-traumatic stress disorder and the war veteran patient.* New York: Brunner/Mazel.

Silver, S. M. (1986). An inpatient program for post-traumatic stress disorder: Context as treatment. In C. R. Figley (Ed.), *Trauma and its wake* (Vol. 2; pp. 213–231). New York: Brunner/Mazel.

Stein, B. D., Sorbero, M., Kogan, J., & Greenberg, L. (2011). Assessing the implementation of a residential facility organizational change model: Pennsylvania's implementation of the Sanctuary Model. Retrieved from http://www.ccbh.com/aboutus/news/articles/SanctuaryModel.php

Swanson, V., & Power, K. (2001). Employees' perceptions of organisational restructuring: The role of social support. *Work and Stress, 15*(2), 61–178.

Weatherbee, T. G., Dye, K. E., Bissonnette, A., & Mills, A. J. (2009). Valuation theory and organizational change: Towards a sociopsychological method of intervention. *Journal of Change Management, 9*(2), 195–213.

White, P., Edwards, N., & Townsend-White, C. (2006). Stress and burnout amongst professional carers of people with intellectual disability: Another health inequity. *Current Opinion in Psychiatry, 19*(5), 502–507.

Yoo, J. (2002). The relationship between organizational variables and client outcomes: A case study in child welfare. *Administration in Social Work, 26*(2), 39–61.

CHAPTER 7

Using Data to Drive Change and Achieve Impact

Greg Ryan, John Jeanetta, Michael Bedrosian, Francine Axler, Amy Friedlander, and Alex Lehr O'Connell

Editors' note: This chapter features two case studies on the role data plays in transforming a nonprofit organization.

DEVELOPING A DATA-DRIVEN CULTURE: A CASE STUDY

Twenty years ago, few human services organizations made use of much data other than budget information used to ensure that costs were being covered. Today, the amount of data that is collected, organized, and analyzed by human services organizations can rival that collected by any commercial business in the private sector. Depending on an organization's capacity to manage it, this torrent of data can be overwhelming or it can be leveraged to improve strategic and operational decision making. This chapter will evaluate key factors that have been instrumental in fostering a data-driven culture at Heartland Family Service.

Heartland Family Service is a nonprofit human services organization founded in 1875, serving the Omaha–Council Bluffs metro area and surrounding communities in east central Nebraska and southwest Iowa. To fulfill its mission to improve the lives of individuals and families in the community through education, counseling, and support, Heartland Family Service operates over 40 programs in eight service categories: addictions, child abuse, community services and centers, domestic violence, early childhood development, juvenile delinquency, mental health, and poverty and homelessness. These services are provided in diverse settings, including office-based outpatient, in-home, residential, and community-based drop-in locations. With an annual budget of $22 million, the agency serves 37,000 community members each year.

In their article "Building Capacity to Measure and Manage Performance," Matthew Forti and Kathleen Yazbak outline five key components of organizational capacity for measurement: leadership commitment, a spirit of learning and improvement, outside expertise, a measurement director, and a flexible structure (Forti & Yazbak, 2012). The importance of each of these components has been evident in the evolution of the culture at Heartland Family Service since the early 1980s, when the agency first made a concerted effort to begin collecting and monitoring performance data.

Inception

In 1977, the Child Welfare League of American and Family Service America (now the Alliance for Children and Families) founded the Council on Accreditation (COA). COA was formed to define national standards of service quality for organizations that serve children and families and to ensure that those standards were being met. As this national accrediting body was being formed, the leadership at Heartland Family Service (then known as Family Service) was taking notice. They realized that if the agency was to be effective and to create lasting change for individuals and families in need, it was imperative that it become accredited. However, the accreditation process demanded that the organization demonstrate, in real and concrete ways, how it delivered services and created change. For the first time, leadership and staff were challenged to become very specific and systematic about how services were delivered.

To accomplish this goal, agency leaders identified local experts in quality improvement and recruited them to the board of directors. They tapped into the knowledge and expertise provided by national organizations such as the Alliance for Children and Families. And from this consultation they formed a quality council. The council was an internal team of staff representing all parts of the organization. The team reported directly to the president and CEO and monitored different kinds of information than had been typical up to that point. Instead of counting dollars collected and expenses paid, this group measured client satisfaction and staff safety. Instead of balance sheets and budget reports, it was file audits and clients served. Through proactive leadership and the efforts of a passionate group of staff, practices were established to ensure that the effectiveness of their services was being monitored on a regular basis. Their early efforts paved the way for the agency to remain continuously accredited from 1983 to this day.

Leadership commitment, outside expertise, and a spirit of growth and improvement fostered by the accreditation process were critical factors that set Heartland Family Service on its journey to become data-driven. Without strong, visionary, and supportive leadership determined to realize the value of accreditation, it is hard to imagine that a group of staff would have gotten together to start monitoring service quality on their own. Without the expertise provided by local quality improvement professionals, or national organizations providing guidance and technical assistance, it is hard to imagine that effective practices would have been established. And without a focus on learning and improvement rather than deficiencies and faults, it is hard to imagine that staff would have tolerated such scrutiny of their performance.

Leaders wanting to strengthen a datacentric culture within their organization could start by setting a goal of becoming accredited through one of a number of national accreditation bodies. COA accredits a variety of human services and behavioral health organizations; the Joint Commission is geared toward health care organizations; and the Commission on Accreditation of Rehabilitative Facilities (CARF) is a third alternative. For organizations that are already accredited, the Baldrige Criteria for Performance and Excellence could be used to challenge a culture that has gotten complacent with regular accreditation cycles. The Baldrige Criteria have more recently gained popularity among human services agencies as a way to benchmark their performance both within and outside of the human services sector.

Expansion

Because the quality council reported directly to the president and CEO and was integral to the accreditation process, it played an increasingly important role in the operation of the agency. In addition, members of the quality council were seen as leaders within their respective job roles across the agency, and membership on the council was viewed as a staff development opportunity. Third, beginning in the late 1990s, United Way was leading a national effort to move beyond merely tracking outputs to identifying and measuring outcomes (Hendricks, Plantz, & Prichard, 2008). Instead of simply counting the number of clients served, meals provided, or sessions attended, human service organizations were being challenged to identify how their services created tangible positive changes for clients. This challenge forced organizations to be more sophisticated in their approaches to measurement, data management, and analysis. Instead of simply distributing a survey and averaging results, organizations were expected to collect information multiple times during the delivery of services and compare scores across time, analyzing the differences. The combination of internal stress on the quality council and external pressure to track more complex information resulted in two significant changes in the structure of the data monitoring and reporting systems at Heartland Family Service.

The amount of information the agency needed to track for accreditation purposes, the new United Way initiative, and other internal and external reporting requirements added up to more than a single team of staff could manage. So the quality council was disbanded in favor of four quality improvement teams (QITs), each designed to manage a specific type of performance data. The Outcomes QIT was developed in direct response to the United Way's effort to measure outcomes. The Record Review QIT met the accreditation-related need for internal file audits. The Utilization Review QIT helped manage program capacity. And the Internal Care Monitoring QIT was responsible for measuring satisfaction among clients and employees and ensuring a safe workplace. In addition to building capacity for managing a wider variety of data, this reconfiguration provided opportunity for more staff involvement. Whereas the quality council was made up of 9 to 12 members, the new QIT structure included 40 or more members. With increased staff involvement, the value of measurement and analysis was being communicated to an ever-widening audience within the organization and was permeating deeper into the culture of the agency.

The second change that was implemented during this expansion period was the hiring of a director of quality improvement. Not only was this role needed to manage the rising number of staff involved and increasing complexity of the performance measurement process, but it also showed how dedicated agency leaders were to using data to make strategic and operational decisions at all levels and in all facets of the organization. The director became an important champion of the structural changes the agency implemented in going from a single quality council to multiple QITs. The position has always had special support from the president and CEO, which gave the director the necessary authority to hold the agency accountable for supporting the growing culture. And although proficiency with measurement and data was an obvious requirement, it was equally important for the person selected for the role to be an excellent communicator and connector, allowing him or her to help translate the concepts and language of outcomes and quality improvement into everyday tasks and practices that all staff could understand and to which they could relate. In this way, the director became a respected resource for helping program managers and vice presidents promote the success of their programs and craft competitive funding applications.

Changes that Heartland Family Service implemented during this expansion phase demonstrated a maturing of the organization's data-driven culture. Leadership remained flexible in their approach to dealing with the changing needs of the agency. They understood that these new data challenges could not be addressed with the same structure and practices that had created their initial success. They also understood that a more complex structure required guidance and oversight from a director dedicated to managing the process. External expertise, this time from the United Way, was once again an important factor in refining the agency's understanding of performance management. And the spirit of learning and improvement originally fostered by the quality council was perpetuated as more staff became involved in the process through the QITs.

Every organization eventually gets to a point at which it is necessary to consolidate the management of measurement and evaluation systems into a specific person's role. This consolidation should not relieve the rest of the staff from continuing to foster a datacentric culture. Instead, this role is intended to accelerate the culture by creating more opportunities for involvement, increasing everyone's knowledge and expertise through training, clarifying roles and responsibilities, and ensuring that responsibilities are met systematically and regularly. A good measurement director needs change management skills that are at least as good as his or her proficiency with data.

Refinement

Over the last 3 years, Heartland Family Service has continued to refine its data-driven culture. Decades of regularly monitoring, reporting on, and improving performance across all different facets of the organization have been useful and rewarding. But the work has also often led to fragmented data silos within which it is difficult to relate performance data in one aspect of the organization to another.

For example, the agency's juvenile evaluation program is required to complete interdisciplinary psychosocial assessments within 10 working days of receiving a referral. This is a demanding time frame in light of the number of professionals involved in each assessment. Key performance indicators for this program include the number of assessments completed per month and the percentage of those assessments that are completed on time. Without regard to any other factors, the more assessments completed and the higher the on-time percentage of completed assessments, the better. But at what cost? Without taking into account wear and tear on staff, it could appear that the sky is the limit when it comes to these performance indicators. Monitoring staff satisfaction alongside the productivity data described above would paint a more complete and accurate picture of the program's performance, but historically this has been difficult—because these groups of data have been managed separately.

Three years ago, the agency began experimenting with the balanced scorecard concept (Kaplan & Norton, 1992). A balanced scorecard is a diverse collection of performance indicators reflecting the most critical measures across all parts of an organization. Rather than concentrating solely on financial metrics, a balanced scorecard brings together data from a variety of areas such as human resources, quality improvement, programs and services, clients, volunteers and stakeholders, and fulfillment of mission. Much of this data was already being tracked separately within each functional area, but the balanced scorecard created an opportunity for these measures to be monitored side by side. This led to new thinking about the relationships between different parts of the agency. Limits placed on the number of indicators that could be included on the scorecard also challenged agency leaders to identify the critical few measures that provided the most information about how a department was performing.

As this concept has been refined over the last several years, programs are now encouraged to implement their own scorecards. These program-level scorecards are designed both to meet the day-to-day management needs of the program and to connect the program's work back to the agency's strategic initiatives and overall performance. Making these connections between data collected at all levels and across all parts of the organization reinforces for agency staff the value of measuring and monitoring performance.

Another factor that can either facilitate or frustrate a data-driven culture is the types of tools and data systems that are available to help manage and make sense of all the information that is collected and stored. At Heartland Family Service, the quality improvement reporting system has gone through many iterations of development. Initially, performance was reported in word processing templates. Aggregating data across the agency based on these templates was labor-intensive, time-consuming, and error-prone. Eventually, the reporting templates were re-created in spreadsheet software in order to leverage pre-populated formulas and reduce errors. But data aggregation was still a difficult task. Next, advanced spreadsheet programming was used to automate the aggregation process. In addition, visually based interactive dashboards were created to assist program staff in analyzing their results, identifying trends, and making ad hoc comparisons in their data. As the agency's quality reporting system has evolved, QITs have been able to go from checking to make sure the math is right to evaluating whether changes in procedures are resulting in improvements for clients.

The next step in Heartland Family Service's journey to becoming increasingly datacentric is to implement a unified data system that will consolidate client data across all of its programs. Up to this point, programs have used all different kinds of tools for managing client data. Some programs have used spreadsheet software, some have developed simple desktop databases, and others have used an enterprise-level database. By moving everyone to a unified data system, leadership and decision-makers will have better access to more comprehensive, up-to-date, and accurate information about the clients the agency serves. Clearly, having the right tools in place plays an important role in supporting a data-driven culture.

Incorporating ideas from external experts, including ideas such as the balanced scorecard concept, continues to be an important strategy for refining the agency's datacentric culture. A flexible infrastructure that can incorporate new tools and solutions has become increasingly important as the agency's capacity for data analysis has grown more sophisticated. Finally, a strong spirit of continual growth and constant improvement is especially important at this mature stage to ensure that the agency does not become complacent.

Depending on the size of the organization and the types of services being provided, data systems do not need to be complex. For a small organization providing straightforward services such as information and referral, well-organized paper-based tally sheets paired with a simple spreadsheet could be an effective way of tracking the most important data needed to optimize performance. As the level of complexity and amount of data increase, it becomes increasingly necessary to invest in enterprise-level databases that provide more power and flexibility when it comes to data entry, management, analysis, and reporting. At the extreme end of complexity, large organizations require ways to connect and relate data between databases, often creating data warehouses that coordinate data across software applications. Regardless of the level of sophistication, it is useful to manage data in some type of electronic system in order to leverage tools that can automate routine data management tasks.

Conclusion

Of all the lessons learned during the journey that Heartland Family Service has taken to become a data-driven organization, the most surprising is that after a clear and compelling direction was set and supported by leadership, there were very few radical breakthroughs in the evolution of the culture. Instead, by and large, the culture was created, strengthened, and sustained through thousands of tiny improvements brought about by a wide range of people over many years. Often the changes were so simple and obvious as to hardly even be celebrated as improvements: A simple revision to a complicated record review checklist that saves a reviewer 10 minutes of flipping back and forth in a client file during an audit; adding the previous quarter's data to a quarterly report in order to put current performance into context; sharing client success stories on the agency's intranet to remind staff how their work makes a difference. None of these changes by itself was all that revolutionary, but taken together they create a kind of positive momentum that persists in an organization.

Knowledge is power. And one of the richest sources of knowledge is the data that an organization collects about its people, clients, services, and finances. The challenge is to create an environment in which every person has the capability to extract knowledge from the data at his or her disposal. By employing the key components identified by Forti and Yazbak and adapting ideas that have served Heartland Family Service well on its journey, you, too, can accelerate your organization's capacity to become data-driven.

USING DATA AND INFORMATION SYSTEMS TO DRIVE AN INTEGRATED HEALTH AND HUMAN SERVICES ENTERPRISE: THE PUBLIC HEALTH MANAGEMENT CORPORATION APPROACH

Today's social service environment depends on the effective use of data to measure the impact of the services rendered to clients. Data are at the center of every measurable and sustainable program. Funders, whether at the federal, state, or local level, require increasingly detailed reporting on utilization of services, including data regarding client participation, adherence to program guidance, and completion of interventions. The Public Health Management Corporation (PHMC) recognizes this and has created a model of data collection and information system development that complements existing databases maintained by funders or regulators but that also goes well beyond the obvious basic financial drive. The PHMC model incorporates specific, measurable, attainable, realistic, and timely program metrics into every system developed. This approach to system development is central to PHMC's mission of improving the health and welfare of residents in its region.

PHMC, headquartered in Philadelphia, Pennsylvania, is a large, private, nonprofit health and human services agency. Since its inception in 1970, PHMC has invested heavily in its infrastructure and core management support services, including information systems technology. At PHMC, the information systems (IS) group and the Center for Data Innovation (the Center) are charged with continually improving the quality of the data collected to improve the services delivered to clients. To achieve this, PHMC has created a model of data collection and system development that is fueled by teamwork, collaboration, and commitment to the PHMC mission. The model is guided by one unified principle—building information systems that will help enhance the client experience and increase client success rates. Working with various program, quality management, and fiscal staff, the PHMC model creates systems addressing the requirements of funding agencies but that remain tightly aligned with the goals of the programs they support. Several case examples follow that illustrate PHMC's unique approach to developing rigorous program data collection and information systems. As you will see, the end result of the PHMC model is enhanced social service delivery for the most vulnerable populations.

Case Example #1

PHMC operates a network of substance abuse treatment programs (behavioral health treatment programs) providing a range of comprehensive services throughout the city of Philadelphia. These treatment programs target the most at-risk and vulnerable population groups: low-income women, women with children, adolescents, and individuals caught up in the criminal justice system. Each of the treatment programs utilizes a holistic approach to service delivery. The goal of all of these programs is to help individuals living with addiction to drugs or alcohol develop the skills and support they need to become free of their disease. PHMC's goal is to link clients with specific needs to additional services such as primary care, aftercare case management, early intervention, and specialized employment services.

To meet the needs of these high-risk clients cost-effectively, PHMC built a comprehensive data collection system called the client registry service (CRS). The CRS quickly and easily stores client and service data including authorizations, financial history, drug screening results, contacts, and progress notes. These data are connected directly to PHMC's fee-for-service billing system, reducing the effects of human error on clients by automatically linking intake data to financial claim data. This allows the immediate generation of claims to multiple payers. Most importantly, the CRS helps clients get services faster by allowing for the ad hoc exporting of data so that any issues in treatment can be analyzed and addressed quickly when clients are most receptive to behavior change.

Case Example #2

Since 1985, PHMC has directed the Health Care for the Homeless program. Funded primarily by the Federal Department of Health and Human Services, this program has the primary goal of improving the health status of homeless persons by improving their access to primary health care, drug and alcohol treatment, and mental health services in order to increase their ability to obtain permanent housing, stable employment, and access to needed social supports.

To develop an information system that allowed for gathering data on a very hard-to-reach population, the PHMC model was utilized for this program. PHMC staff worked collaboratively with several partners, including service providers, case managers, and funders, to develop a system that would allow program managers to capture data on more than 85,000 homeless clients and manage productivity 24/7 without relying on IS programmers. The end result was that the system enabled case managers to do their jobs better and faster while adhering to the mission of the program of providing targeted services. PHMC's model was extremely effective in capturing data for this population group and has built on this core capability by designing and implementing an electronic health record to support the provision of primary care services by PHMC nursing staff at the city's homeless shelters.

Case Example #3

The County of Philadelphia maintains an early intervention program known as ChildLink. This program provides service coordination to help children from birth to age three who have developmental delays or disabilities and their families living in Philadelphia. PHMC's ChildLink program works in partnership with parents and early intervention specialists to evaluate each child's needs, identify outcomes, and develop an Individualized Family Service Plan (IFSP) comprising supports and services appropriate for each eligible child and family. The program serves approximately 9,000 clients annually. To meet the needs of this program, PHMC developed a system to automate the coordination of provider services and monitor compliance with the IFSP. As with other PHMC data collection systems, the system was designed to facilitate the export and exchange of data for detailed analysis of the program's performance at the client level and to be compatible with funder-mandated reporting systems.

Case Example #4

PHMC's Center for Data Innovation provides an unmatched set of information on local community economic and health needs that can be used to develop focused programs supported by actual community data. The Center for Data Innovation combines current data initiatives at PHMC with external programs to monitor, track, and evaluate the health of the public.

The primary data source within the Center is the community survey. The community survey has served as a key data resource in developing priorities and rationales for strategic plans for health and human service providers since 1983. The survey collects data from over 10,000 households in Bucks, Chester, Delaware, Montgomery, and Philadelphia counties every 2 years, providing a rich data set for longitudinal analyses of a variety of health, economic, and community topics affecting adults and children. The survey is one of the largest local surveys in the country; no other population survey collects the depth of public health information at small levels of geography that allow for analysis by legislative district, neighborhood, and clusters of census tracts and ZIP codes.

One of the primary goals of the Center for Data Innovation is to enhance the capacity of health and human services programs by improving access to and increasing utilization of data. To meet this goal, the center worked with PHMC's IS team to create tools that would allow users access to the data in a "friendly" way. The tools were created using the PHMC model of meeting funding requirements but with a commitment to aligning with the goals of the program. Two online analysis tools were created utilizing over 40 health variables that can be examined by six demographic subgroups for any geographic area in the five-county region of Southeastern Pennsylvania for each survey year from 2000 through 2012. Users can compare their service area with the county and the region on a set of key health indicators.

The data and online tools help to expand organizations' planning, funding, and marketing capabilities and are used as critical tools to support fund development and community health needs assessments. There are infinite uses for data of this type including strategic planning, target area analysis, policy and program development, community health needs assessments, market analysis, and program evaluation. Currently, over 350 organizations such as major health departments, nonprofit organizations, and hospitals and health systems utilize PHMC's Community Health Data Base for health data. In addition, Pennsylvania legislators utilize the data to support policies that improve the health and well-being of residents, and the academic community utilizes the data for ground-breaking research in the areas of nursing, criminal justice, social work, and more.

Case Example #5

PHMC operates five federally qualified health center (FQHC) sites, each of which provides comprehensive health care to homeless and public housing residents and their surrounding communities regardless of an individual's insurance status or ability to pay. FQHCs are the only culturally competent, affordable, accessible health care providers for over 19 million of the nation's most vulnerable residents. By providing access to cost-effective primary care and prevention services, FQHCs have been shown to reduce emergency room visits by 20% and hospitalizations by 10% (Falik et al., 2006) when compared with private practices. Funding authorized by the Patient Protection and Affordable Care Act is poised to double the nation's network of FQHCs to serve 40 million patients annually by 2015. Such expansion will require careful assessment of existing capacity and demonstration of need sufficient to qualify for grant funding in an increasingly competitive funding environment.

In response to changes in legislation, PHMC analyzed data from the 2010 Census, along with surveillance data on disease prevalence, outcomes, and health disparities, and identified a neighborhood in Eastern North Philadelphia as prime for investment. Specifically, this predominantly Latino community had seen rapid population growth in the previous decade. With over 80% of the population living below 200% of the federal poverty level (the federal designation for low-income in the FQHC program), the area met and exceeded the high bar set to compete for federal funding. Community and client surveys collected demonstrated very high prevalences of chronic conditions such as diabetes, hypertension, and asthma and high utilization of emergency rooms, indicating poor management of those conditions. Data from existing FQHCs on their market penetration that were made publicly available for the first time in 2010 revealed over 133,000 residents of the area who were low-income and had not visited an existing FQHC grantee for even a single visit in the previous year (The Health Foundation of Greater Cincinnati & the American Academy of Family Physicians, 2010).

The area had been served for over 30 years by the Congreso de Latinos Unidos (Congreso), a robust education, health, and social services provider that had only primary care missing from its on-site resources. Sharing PHMC's focus on data-driven, impact-oriented service provision, Congreso was already tracking the outcomes of its programs, through the Efforts to Outcomes (ETO™) social services platform. This allowed Congreso to demonstrate the positive steps their clients had been able to take towards economic independence, including obtaining necessary industry certifications, gaining and retaining employment, obtaining a GED or associate's degree, purchasing a home, and other indicators of success.

Armed with a multifaceted analysis of existing need and capacity, a long history of providing efficient, effective, culturally competent care, and an ideal community partner in Congreso, PHMC competed for and won federal funding to open a new FQHC site. The Congreso Health Center began serving patients in December 2012. By connecting data collected through the PHMC's electronic health record system and Congreso's ETO platform, the partnership will be able to track client outcomes across health and social service programs, truly demonstrating an impact on the whole person and the whole community.

Deep Dive: Putting It All Together and Examining Real-Time Data Across Programs With the Goal of Improving Client Outcomes

So what does PHMC do with all of the various data systems it has developed? PHMC connects individual data systems through one enterprisewide data integration warehouse called PHMC Connect. Data for PHMC Connect are first aggregated into standard reporting metrics to ensure that key indicators are measured across programs. Each night, data from individual programs are selected and transferred automatically to the Connect warehouse.

PHMC Connect was created by applying the PHMC model of teamwork, collaboration, and commitment to the PHMC mission. Connect allows PHMC senior management and nontechnical users to filter comprehensive information regarding PHMC services using a variety of filters, including age, gender, ethnicity, location, and diagnosis. Aggregate information from PHMC programs can be culled and is immediately ready for presentation. Alternatively, a deep dive of the data can be conducted, and the standard metrics developed for Connect can be examined at the program level and compared with other programs at PHMC.

PHMC Connect demonstrates that using tested techniques similar to those employed in the design of individual program systems produces a unified system. For example, rather than writing a client specification and then coding and deploying to that specification, the design team based Connect on a core prototype comprising client demographics. This prototype facilitated ongoing quality projects in each source program database, simultaneously improving the source data and the aggregates in the warehouse. Connect is a stellar example of PHMC's IS philosophy: A data system should be seen as a process, not as a product, and should be created in collaboration with providers, program managers, and financial staff to meet the changing needs of clients. By integrating these processes into each of its programs, PHMC promotes the efficient operation of the programs. And by using the same approach to look across programs, PHMC seeks to provide coordinated care to its clients to create a healthier community.

REFERENCES

Falik M., Needleman, J., Herbert, R., Wells, B., Politzer, R., & Benedict, M. B. (2006). Comparative effectiveness of health centers as regular source of care. *Journal of Ambulatory Care Management, 29*(1), 24–35.

Forti, M., & Yazbak, K. (2012). *Building capacity to measure and manage performance.* Boston, MA: The Bridgespan Group. http://www.bridgespan.org/getattachment/d0076a96-47e9-4c4c-9ad4-106d4a3aa270/Building-Capacity-to-Measure-and-Manage-Perfor.aspx

The Health Foundation of Greater Cincinnati & the American Academy of Family Physicians. (2010). *Uds mapper.* Retrieved from http://www.udsmapper.org

Hendricks, M., Plantz, M. C., & Prichard, K. J. (2008). Measuring outcomes of United Way–funded programs: Expectations and reality. *Nonprofits and Evaluation: New Directions for Evaluation, 119*(Fall), 13–35. doi:10.1002/ev.266

Kaplan, R. S., & Norton, D. P. (1992). The balanced scorecard—measures that drive performance. *Harvard Business Review,* January–February, 71–79.

CHAPTER 8

Improving Organizational Capacity and Infrastructure

Jim Bettendorf, Maria Cristalli, Glenn Wilson, Rose Chapman,
Denise Roberts, and Dave Paxton

Editors' note: This chapter features case studies on capacity and infrastructure of five organizations: Volunteers of America of Minnesota, Hillside Family of Agencies, Holy Family Institute, Jewish Family and Children's Services of Sarasota-Manatee, and The Village Network.

VOLUNTEERS OF AMERICA OF MINNESOTA: DISCOVERY FOR TRANSFORMATION

Volunteers of America of Minnesota (VOA-MN) is an organization that has provided more than 117 years of service to the Minnesota community, serving the most vulnerable at the edges of our society. Its legacy spans several chapters in social services history: the Gospel mission, the Great Depression, the New Deal, and professional social services. VOA-MN was organized under the leadership models of a Christian military and standard nonprofit corporate hierarchy.

The organization is proud of its ability to opportunistically respond to community needs as they have arisen. This "bigger equals better" model led to a time of significant growth, doubling VOA-MN's size during a 10-year period from 1999 to 2010. A change in executive leadership in 2011 was the catalyst to use this increased organizational capacity and pursue an era of excellence—to "make bigger better." At its foundation is the organization's vision for the year 2020: *to become a nationally recognized model of excellence in health and human services.*

In applying for the Strategy Counts grant, our desire was to capitalize on an opportunity to transform the organization's culture from opportunistic to strategic. As part of the grant proposal, it was initially projected that a new strategic plan would be in place within 6 months of engaging the chief strategy officer role. It became apparent quite early that a longer period of discovery would be necessary to move the organization in the right direction. A comprehensive discovery process was developed to provide the necessary context for the future design of the organization. This section will discuss the discovery components, which included well-structured discussions with the board of directors, staff, clients, and external stakeholders.

The Discovery Process: Baldridge Assessment

One of the key outcomes of a high-level operation plan, completed in 2010, was to join with the Minnesota Council on Quality and conduct a Baldrige assessment. The Malcolm Baldrige assessment engaged staff and the board to evaluate the maturity of the organization's management. This assessment became the baseline for the assimilation of a new president and CEO in 2011, as well as the motivation to elevate the organization's strategic thinking.

FIGURE 8.1   VOA-MN 2011 Baldrige Performance Excellence Assessment.

Source: Bettendorf (2011).

The Baldrige process identified strengths and "opportunities for improvement" (OFIs). The greatest opportunities were clearly in the area of business processes. The assessment also established a baseline for what information would be required to develop a strong future for the organization.

Figure 8.1 ranks the relative organizational strengths and OFIs that came out of the assessment.

New Leadership Leads to Strategy Counts Grant

In June 2011, VOA-MN welcomed Paula Hart as its new president and CEO. Using the Baldrige assessment findings as a known, the decision was made to pursue the Strategy Counts grant. The many steps and institutional time requirements necessary to plan and implement new strategies were not immediately apparent. Following the grant award and the selection of a chief strategy officer, it became clear that a multilayered timeline spanning more than a year would be necessary to create a fully developed, ready–to–implement strategic plan. The strategic planning process evolved to the timeline shown in Figure 8.2.

New Mission, Vision, Values, and 2020 Vision Statements

As a first step, a series of cumbersome, multiple-page mission, vision, and values statements were revised through a process that included staff and board input. The new statements were intentionally compact while continuing to describe the organizational impact on the community and how the organization provided services.

The previously stated future vision was also established in order to set the stage for developing a strategic plan. The 2020 Vision strives to recognize our considerable service components in the fields of behavioral and senior health care and to prepare for the changes occurring in the health care field with the effective date of the Affordable Care Act in 2014. The 2020 Vision was further articulated with three strategic priorities for 2014–2016, as shown in Figure 8.3.

Stakeholder Input—Clients, Employees, External Community

Three methods were used recently to gather stakeholder data:

- An initiative was developed to review programmatic surveys and identify consistent client service themes from information about VOA-MN programs gathered through customer satisfaction surveys.

FIGURE 8.2 Strategic planning process timeline.
Source: Bettendorf (2013a).

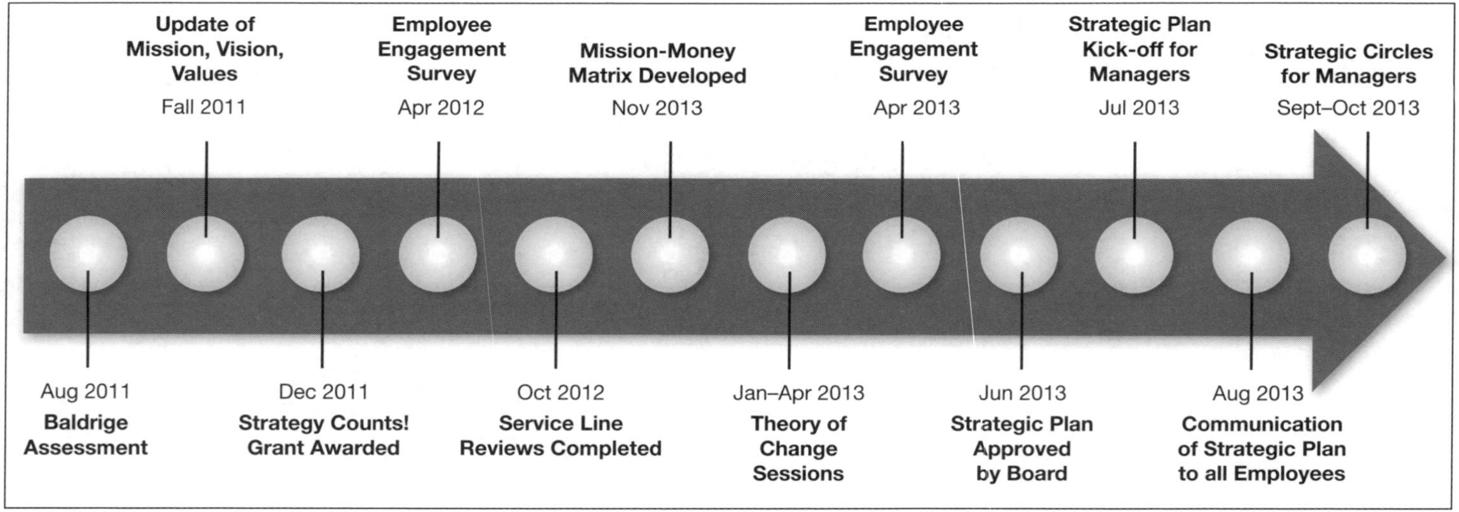

Update of
Mission, Vision,
Values
Fall 2011

Employee
Engagement
Survey
Apr 2012

Mission-Money
Matrix Developed
Nov 2013

Employee
Engagement
Survey
Apr 2013

Strategic Plan
Kick-off for
Managers
Jul 2013

Strategic Circles
for Managers
Sept–Oct 2013

Aug 2011
Baldrige
Assessment

Dec 2011
Strategy Counts!
Grant Awarded

Oct 2012
Service Line
Reviews Completed

Jan–Apr 2013
Theory of
Change
Sessions

Jun 2013
Strategic Plan
Approved
by Board

Aug 2013
Communication
of Strategic Plan
to all Employees

FIGURE 8.3 VOA-MN Strategic Direction for 2014–2016.
Source: Bettendorf (2013b).

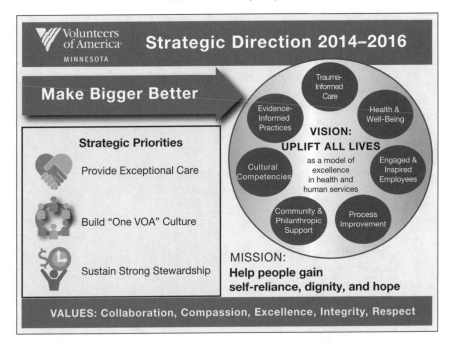

- VOA-MN participated in the 2012 Workplace Dynamics Employee Engagement Survey, permitting a neutral, third-party analysis of employee satisfaction. The survey was a component of the "Top Workplaces" process sponsored by the *Minneapolis Star Tribune*. While we did not rank in the top 100 workplaces in Minnesota, VOA-MN was named a "National Standard Top Workplace" based on the results. More important, several opportunities were identified for improvements.
- A sampling of key external stakeholders was identified and a personal connection was established through an interview process conducted by the vice president of external relations, with questions regarding public knowledge, organizational reputation, and areas for opportunity.

Service Line Reviews and Mission-Money
Matrix Development

For many years, the board of directors had called for a system for providing a broad analysis of our operating programs that could yield a tool for governance decisions. As part of the discovery process, we implemented "service line reviews." In this process, the senior leadership team asked all operating managers to prepare a review document that contained the following information:

- Quantitative Factors
  a. Number of clients served
  b. Per participant cost to provide services
  c. Number of employees
  d. Client satisfaction
  e. Funding sources
- Qualitative Factors
  a. Competitive environment
  b. Differentiating factors vs. competitors
  c. Capacity to refer to our VOA continuum of services (adjacencies)
  d. Competency
  e. Mission impact
  f. Community impact
  g. Organizational impact
  h. Gaps in services
- Future of the Service Line
  a. Community need
  b. Availability of funding
  c. New initiatives
  d. Market demand
  e. Financial impact and investment needed
  f. Risk factors
  g. Exit strategy

In addition to these evaluative points, a 3-year financial projection was completed.

After the service line review information was assembled, the senior leadership team, working with an ad hoc committee of the board of directors, began work on a tool called "The Mission–Money Matrix." The concept of the matrix is derived from the book *Nonprofit Sustainability: Making Strategic Decisions for Financial Viability* by Jeanne Bell, Jan Masaoka, and Steve Zimmerman (2010). The matrix recognizes that in addition to generating resources to be financially viable, nonprofits must also have an impact. The matrix map does more than showcase the organization's business model. It provides strategic imperatives for each service based on its placement on the map, offering the basis for strategic discussions leading to strategic choices.

The map can be used to identify the current programmatic fit with mission success as well as to evaluate areas for expansion, acquisition, and divestiture. With this clear understanding of how the organization accomplishes its mission and generates and allocates its resources, a shared understanding between board and leadership allows for ongoing strategic decisions. Figure 8.4 illustrates the Mission–Money Matrix.

FIGURE 8.4 Mission–Money Matrix.

Source: Bell, Masaoka, and Zimmerman (2010). Copyright © 2010, John Wiley and Sons.

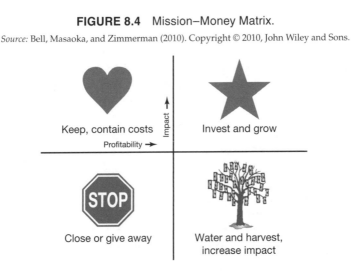

During the process of developing the matrix tool, VOA-MN entered into exclusive negotiations to acquire a nonprofit that provided complementary services in our adult reentry service area. The tool was invaluable in evaluating the mission and financial fit and assisted in making the decision to acquire the organization.

Programmatic Theory of Change Development

Rounding out our qualitative look at our organization provided a deeper opportunity for our staff (at all levels) to assess where they fit and to identify opportunities for greater impact from their services. As a multiservice provider of health and human services, we often have difficulty identifying our specific outcomes and the measurement points that best describe our success. The programmatic "theory of change" development not only allowed our staff, from direct care to management, to describe their ultimate goals, but it also provided the metrics that will be necessary to measure our success moving forward as we strive to achieve our 2020 Vision.

A theory of change starts by identifying a clear ultimate goal and working backwards to establish preconditions for reaching that goal. At each step, assumptions are examined. The next step is to identify indicators. Only when these steps have been completed are the activities or interventions identified. A good theory of change specifies how to create a range of conditions that help programs deliver on the desired outcomes. These can include setting out the right kinds of partnerships, technical assistance, tools, and processes that help people operate more collaboratively and be more results-focused.

Programs need to be grounded in good theory. By developing a theory of change, managers can be better assured that their programs are delivering the right activities for the desired outcomes. Our hope is that this process will make our services easier to sustain, bring to scale, and evaluate, since each step—from the ideas behind it to the outcomes it hopes to provide to the resources needed—is defined within the theory.

Using our higher-level breakout, we conducted 4-hour facilitated sessions for each of eight service lines to develop program-specific theories of change. The service lines were

- Community services for families
- Community services for seniors
- Education
- Mental health services
- Rehabilitative and veterans services
- Residential treatment
- Service-enriched housing
- Services for people with special needs (SPSN)

These theory of change sessions provided eight models of service with ongoing metrics for defining success. Going beyond our expectations, these sessions became team-building environments that often brought together programs with similar clients while helping to identify commonalities and adjacencies of service that had previously been unidentified by our staff.

Figure 8.5 illustrates the outcome of a theory of change session for our rehabilitative and veterans services area:

Capital Vision, Financial Projection

An analysis of our future capital and infrastructure needs and a 3-year operating projection will be the final discovery in this process. Of critical importance are the improvements to our facilities that provide direct care (especially residential) and the technology infrastructure to move forward with requirements under the Accountable Care Act. This will provide our board and leadership with the financial information necessary to manage to the 2020 Vision.

Conclusion

The discovery phase of our strategic planning process will conclude this summer (2013), culminating in a 3-year strategic plan designed to carry the organization into the future of our services. It was clearly our intent to investigate every perspective on how we provide services and where we need to go, not only to survive but to thrive in an era of excellence and change.

After nearly 2 years of discovery, Volunteers of America of Minnesota looks forward to the next step of infusing the new strategies into the organization, measuring our success, and altering our plan to ensure ultimate mission adherence and outstanding financial stewardship.

FIGURE 8.5 Theory of change—community services for families.

Source: Bettendorf (2013c).

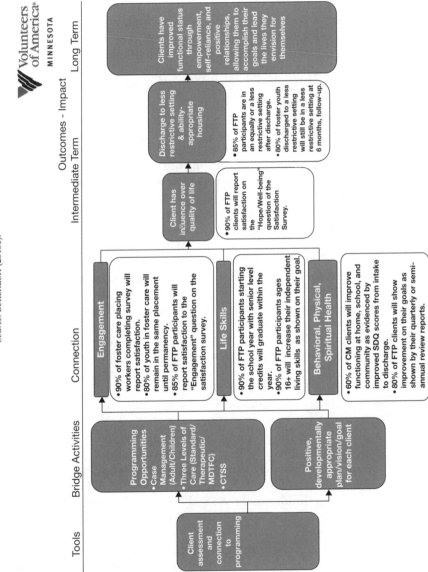

HILLSIDE FAMILY OF AGENCIES: OFFICE OF
STRATEGY MANAGEMENT CASE STUDY

The Hillside Family of Agencies (HFA) provides individualized health, education, and human services in partnership with children, youth, adults, and their families through an integrated system of care across more than 40 locations spanning western and central New York and in Prince George's County, Maryland. HFA is the umbrella organization that provides strategic direction and administrative services, such as marketing, human resources, finance, strategic planning, and quality assurance to six affiliate organizations [all separate 501(c)(3) nonprofits]. Throughout its history, Hillside has always been focussed on embracing change to successfully meet the evolving needs of the communities we serve. Guided by organizational strategy, HFA has undergone organizational transformations that have enhanced service delivery and improved outcomes for youth and families.

The focus on strategy began in the mid- to late 1990s. Dennis M. Richardson began his tenure as president and CEO of Hillside Children's Center in 1994. He led a transformational effort to achieve real change, a breakthrough change that would be required in order to achieve a high level of sustained success for years to come. This effort included creating a shared vision followed by a "fundamental rethinking and radical redesign of business processes" (Collins & Porras, 1996, p. 13). In part, a targeted goal for redesigning the new business processes was to address the fragmented nature of the service delivery system for children and families. Families needed to go to multiple agencies to obtain services, dealing with a different social worker from each agency, each one with different goals. In effect, families had to coordinate their own services and navigate the administrative bureaucracies that deliver, regulate, and fund those services. While each program might have functioned in the best interests of the children and families it served, the resulting inefficiency and conflicts in the overall system generated less than optimal outcomes (New York State Coalition for Children's Mental Health Services, 2003).

Hillside adopted the strategic intent to be the nationally recognized leader and preferred provider of an integrated system of care for youth and their families. Strategic intent is meant to provide a clear, focused long-term goal for the future (Hamel & Prahalad, 2005). The shift in Hillside's strategic plan required significant organizational changes. To begin with, a change was needed from fragmentation to a systematized fluent service delivery system. Furthermore, a shift from decentralized, nonstandard business support processes to centralized administrative functions was necessary to create economies of scale and support a larger organization. This strategy required commitment and alignment across the organization.

In order to be successful, the Corporate Consultancy Department was established in 1996 to oversee organizational planning and alignment to the strategy. This department was led by a corporate resource leader, who served as a member of the executive team. The primary function was to provide strategic management processes and internal consulting and project management services to support Hillside's strategic intent. The consultancy staff were responsible for facilitating a process to determine and subsequently refresh the organization's strategic plan in partnership with executive leadership. It was necessary to achieve agreement on the strategic intent and include relevant constituents in the process: staff and executives, board members, families, children, and the community. As opposed to having strategic decision making be exercised only by the executive staff, Hillside wanted to gather an in-depth understanding of what stakeholders thought might be helpful to achieve improvement in service delivery and organizational functions.

It became clear that an organizing framework was needed to help align the organization to successfully implement the strategy. HFA executives believed that they needed to become better strategists in order to allow the organization to become much more active in decision and policymaking. Instead of simply being reactive to government policies and decisions, HFA wanted to help shape those policies. To accomplish this, a tool was needed to articulate the strategy and monitor the execution of the plan. HFA selected the balanced scorecard (BSC) (Kaplan & Norton, 1996) to articulate and execute the strategy.

The BSC is a framework that helps organizations translate strategy into operational objectives that drive behavior and performance. It was developed at Harvard Business School by Drs. Robert S. Kaplan and David P. Norton and was first introduced in 1992. The balanced scorecard provides a holistic measurement system tied to the strategic intent of the organization. It is based on cause-and-effect relationships between performance drivers (e.g., leading indicators) and outcomes (e.g., lagging indicators) across four perspectives, with financial measures supported by customers, internal work processes, and learning and growth. The process involves a formal performance measurement reporting system that allows executives to view an organization through multiple perspectives simultaneously (Kaplan & Norton, 1996).

The HFA attempted to implement the BSC on its own, with a BSC developed by the corporate consultancy team, but after a year and a half, significant shortcomings became evident. Leadership and staff had not been integrated into the development process. This approach failed to create the buy-in and alignment necessary for successful execution. Therefore, HFA sought consulting help from the Balanced Scorecard Collaborative and built a renewed BSC using the six-step process developed by Robert Kaplan and David Norton (Kaplan & Norton, 2001). Through consultation and support from the Balanced Scorecard Collaborative, a company under the Palladium Group, Inc., changes were made to the HFA BSC that resulted in substantial improvement.

HFA began the BSC renewal effort in March 2002 and included a fifth perspective to the scorecard, the stakeholder perspective. This perspective was critical to connecting HFA's strategic objectives to the communities it serves. The primary objective was to create a sense of ownership in each community so HFA would be perceived as a valuable partner that positively and substantially impacts the lives of children and their families. HFA implemented the new enterprise BSC in July 2002. Two foundations, the Crestwood Children's Foundation and the Hillside Children's Foundation, subsequently became the first affiliates to build their own BSCs. The BSC planning process helped them integrate staff and reduce unnecessary overhead. The service affiliates then began to create their own BSCs. The BSCs helped the affiliates to establish a diverse and well-coordinated array of services, community resources, and informal supports tailored to the needs of children and their families by building linkages among services and reducing cycle time from referral to service enrollment.

In 2004, HFA aligned the entire organization with the corporate scorecard. All strategic business units (SBUs) (service affiliates and foundation affiliates) and all shared services units (SSUs) (support departments) implemented BSCs. The HFA executive team completed the personal and team alignments to the strategy. Each executive team member has a personal scorecard, which is either the SBU or the SSU scorecard of the unit the team member represents. Personal balanced scorecards were added to the annual performance appraisal process.

At the same time, the consultancy department evolved and changed to become Strategic Planning and Quality Assurance (SPQA) in 2003 to serve as the second-generation Hillside entity to manage strategy and related processes. Their primary functions included strategy development and management processes, quality improvement, project management, and data reporting and management. In addition, SPQA provides in-house BSC consulting services for the organization. The chief strategy and quality officer (CSQO) leads this department, reporting directly to the CEO. The CSQO has three key functions: (a) that of an architect designing and executing performance management processes, (b) that of a process owner of organizational planning, and (c) that of an integrator, coordinating and aligning key processes to the strategy (e.g., budgeting, HR) (Kaplan & Norton, 2008). Strategy management is different from managing operational functional areas in that strategy management requires cross-functional processes that span the organization.

The CSQO role developed by participation in global learning communities focused on strategy management. In 2006, Hillside participated in the Balanced Scorecard Collaborative's New Science Learning Community on Strategy Execution, which included organizations worldwide; HFA was the only not-for-profit organization in the cohort. The purpose of the group was to work with balanced scorecard experts to identify the principles and processes needed to build an effective Office of Strategy Management (OSM). Organizations that participated worked with Drs. Kaplan and Norton to define and confirm the general OSM model and the processes associated with this model. We had an opportunity at each session to network and learn about best practices being implemented in other organizations globally. This group met for 24 months, in person three to four times per year.

In 2008, the Hillside Family of Agencies was invited to join the Linking Strategy to Operations Executive Working Group sponsored by the Palladium Group. This working group leveraged the theory highlighted in *The Execution Premium*, written by Drs. Kaplan and Norton, by linking empirical evidence to organizational operations to help the participating organizations operate more efficiently and effectively. The group consisted of chief strategy officers, CEOs, and other C-level roles representing a variety of organizations. The work group interacted through in-depth working program sessions, conferences, and webinars over 2 years. Members had opportunities to identify best practices and share their work at the program sessions. In addition, organizational assessments were conducted to advise participants on their progress with implementing strategy. This helped us build in performance improvement strategies as we learned from the experts and our colleagues.

Capitalizing on best practices learned from these experiences, Hillside's CEO, in partnership with the CSQO, established a priority to design and implement the next iteration of the Office of Strategy Management. Using *The Execution Premium* as the theoretical framework, HFA took a systems approach to linking strategy to operations in an integrated way. As a result, the key responsibilities of Hillside's SPQA organization evolved to include service and clinical practice, program evaluation and research, quality and risk management, business intelligence, and strategy management. This implementation required a human capital strategy that focused on the recruitment of talent from different sectors. Specifically, individuals from the for-profit commercial and academic research sectors joined Hillside to assume director-level roles in the SPQA department.

For over a decade, HFA has been using the BSC as an organizing methodology to articulate strategy and monitor the execution of the plan. Hillside's SPQA consulted with the Balanced Scorecard Collaborative and built our BSC using the six-step process developed by Kaplan and Norton. As a result, Hillside achieved significant outcomes. In 2005, recognizing our breakthrough performance results using the BSC, the Collaborative named Hillside to the BSC Hall of Fame for Executing Strategy™. This milestone validated our initial strategy implementation at HFA, yet we recognize that our strategy practice needs to be continually updated and renewed in order for us to remain competitive. We have learned that a distinct OSM positioned at the executive level of the organization, with responsibility and authority for coordinating the strategy management processes, can help organizations achieve dramatic performance improvements by sustaining a focus on strategy implementation.

HOLY FAMILY INSTITUTE: IMPLEMENTING STRATEGY USING HUMAN-CENTERED DESIGN

Whether at the leadership level or at the point of client interactions, people are thinking, planning, and taking action to close the gaps between what is and what can be. The larger the gap, the more deliberate and strategic the thinking will need to be to make the kinds of decisions that drive the types of behaviors that create the desired future states.

Most of the time, decisions are made quickly and implicitly with little time and energy needed. Implicit decisions work well when we find ourselves in simple, repeating, or familiar situations. When we find ourselves in complex situations or unfamiliar territory, dealing with disruptive factors, or working to create something new or innovative, the decision-making process will take longer, be more deliberate, involve more people, and be supported by research conducted by ad hoc teams.

The following provides a brief insight into one of the problem-solving methods we use to enhance the way we think about our organization—Human-Centered Design (HCD). Examples of how we have applied HCD in developing strategy and improving service to our customers are presented below.

Thinking and Designing for a Change

Paraphrasing Charles Darwin, "It is not the strongest nor the most intelligent of a species that survives. It is the one that is the most creative in adapting and responding to change." One way people and organizations creatively adapt and respond to change is by thinking strategically and that doesn't happen by accident—it happens by design.

At Holy Family Institute (HFI), strategy is continuously and simultaneously driven from two directions: top down, which serves the business, and bottom up, which serves the client. From the top, strategies help answer the following question: *Of all the things that could be done, what will have the greatest impact on achieving increased levels of organizational success?* From the front line, strategies help answer the following question: *How can we improve the client experience in ways that lead to higher levels of sustainable impact in shorter periods of time?* Thinking from both directions is necessary when developing a process for improvement—a strategic plan.

Human-Centered Design: A Strategy for Social Change

Human-Centered Design blends the fields of anthropology and industrial design into one problem-solving process. Until recently, HCD had primarily been used by IDEO for inventing and developing commercial products for market. In 2009, a grant from the Bill and Melinda Gates Foundation funded a special project with the thought of applying the same approach used to solve the toughest commercial enterprise problems to overcoming tough challenges in the nonprofit world.

One of the outputs of that work was the development of a toolkit specifically designed for NGOs and social enterprises that work with impoverished communities in Africa, Asia, and Latin America. The toolkit to date has been used to solve large community problems (e.g., tackling the issues of safe drinking water for the world's poorest people).

In January 2012, Holy Family Institute integrated some of the process, thinking, and tools of HCD into our current problem-solving and design methods to deliver improved business success and client services. This updated process has led us away from looking at our services as solutions to problems toward a more systemic approach to improving the lives of people in context.

Human-Centered Design Defined

HCD is a descriptive and iterative approach for identifying people's articulated and unarticulated needs, generating potential solutions to best address those needs, testing those potential solutions, and implementing the most promising solutions. What makes HCD unique is that the process is driven by the needs, desires, personalities, and contexts of the people who benefit from its use.

HCD uses a three-component model consisting of the following:

Hear: Understanding people's needs, hopes, and aspirations for the future.

Create: Translate what you heard from people **into opportunities and solutions** that lead to strategic directions and tangible solutions.

Deliver: Move your top ideas **toward successful implementation and track** the **impact** of the solutions.

Hear, Create, and Deliver are areas of activity in which specific tools are applied to help users think in ways that advance movement toward the goal. The following are a few examples of how HFI has used HCD to improve our business performance as well as service to our clients.

Using HCD to Co-Create and Execute Strategy

Our first attempt at implementing HCD focused on finding ways to use the process and tools to improve business performance. One of our earliest applications of HCD came in the development of the 2012–2013 strategic plan. Three organizational objectives led to the development of four strategic priorities and five ongoing planning activities for the 2012–2013 fiscal year. Design sessions were conducted using select tools to focus staff thinking on developing departmental strategies for each of the priorities. Each strategy developed was assessed as to the value it could bring to the organization (increase in revenue, reduction in expense, etc.). Strategies found to have little value (time wasters) were eliminated.

In one of the design sessions, the entire management and leadership team was trained in the "Ladder of Abstraction" tool. This tool, using the  questions of "who" and "how," allows the user to either move up in abstraction (getting to the bigger picture) or move down to the more concrete levels of how something might be done. The tool was utilized using each of the four strategic priorities as the most abstract level in the tool, and then, for each strategic priority, moving down the tool to create a wide variety of strategies. From there, the most important strategies were selected. A prioritization tool such as "What's on Your Radar" is perfect for focusing on which strategies to take forward. Once a tool was selected, the process continued for developing tactics (the next level below strategies), and once the most important tactics were selected, the process continued down another level to develop the action plans for implementing the tactics.

This activity was repeated for all 18 service lines for all four strategic priorities. The outcomes of this one HCD tool, starting with the strategic priorities and the development of the strategies, tactics, and action plans, fed into a focused, elegant yearly action plan map for each service line. That action plan map was reviewed monthly for strategic alignment, actions achieved, and actions not achieved, all leading to developing a new action plan for the following month. Using a process that cocreated the strategies, tactics, and action plans for each of the 18 service lines, with the full involvement and support of the senior leadership team, was shown to have significant impact on the organization from a financial perspective (a reduction in expenses of over $400,000) as well as a shift in mindset perspective.

One of the things learned by using HCD in the business side of the organization is that when staff are asked for input, when they are built into the process, and when action plans are cocreated, increasing levels of accountability shift lower into the organization. No longer is the pressure of accountability uniquely reserved for the senior leadership team—*everyone* becomes an owner of the outcomes.

Using HCD to Improve Service to Our Clients

In February 2012, one of the first targets for improvement was food service. Our kitchen served over 300 breakfasts, lunches, and dinners to our students, our residential youth, our Chinese students in our Holy Family International College Preparatory Program (HFICPP), and our staff. New federal food nutritional guidelines, which increased serving sizes for fruits, vegetables, and grains while reducing the amounts of protein and fats as well as overall calorie content, were being introduced. As always, our focus was and continues to be improving the quality of the lives of those we serve. Immediately, we started updating our current menus to not only meet the new federal guidelines but improve on them when we could. Our goal was to provide the best-tasting, most appealing, and most nutritious food we could.

To start the process (Hear), we conducted ethnographic research observing and tracking how food was being delivered, how it was served, and how it was consumed. We also conducted food surveys looking for insights into ways to improve our food and services because we knew some schedules would prohibit participation in our design sessions. We engaged all three components (Hear, Create, and Design) of the HCD process by conducting five design sessions over the next 2 months involving as many as possible of those we serve in cocreating solutions that would lead to healthier lives and lifestyles. Participants in those sessions included the youth who resided  in our in-community homes, their parents, the staff who oversee those youth and their activities, local experts from the fields of health, nutrition, and food service, food vendors, and so forth.

Some of the HCD design thinking tools used from our toolbox were Fly-on-the-Wall Observation, Stakeholder Mapping, Brainstorming with Sticky Notes, Hits, Rose Bud Thorn, What's on Your Radar?, the Importance/Difficulty Matrix, Affinity Mapping, and the Short–Medium–Long Action Plan, among many others. Those sessions were designed to give voice to our customers, which led to our gaining focused insights that we would not have been able to get any other way. We discovered what was most important to our customers and what they saw as the best solutions to the problems at hand.

One of the barriers for implementing the solutions developed was the need to hire additional staff, including a chef and two cooks to cook in our group homes, along with some other additional equipment and printing costs. To solve that problem, a 2-year grant proposal, *Healthy Youth and Family Living*, was developed and submitted to a large local health care corporation. The grant was approved, the staff were hired, the menus were completed, and the work began.

So far, the food and service delivery are getting rave reviews. Consumption is substantially increasing, and our design thinking work is having a huge impact on our ability to hit our success metrics. For example, in a quick statistical study of the eating habits of the students in our HFICPP program, our initial ethnographic study reveled that only about six (15%) of the students ate breakfast, and at the time, there was no lunch option. Our success metric goals were to have 10 of the students (40%) eating breakfast each day and at least 10 (25%) students carrying a lunch to school. With continuing feedback, within one week of implementing the cocreated solutions, between 37 and 40 students (93%–100% consumption rate) were eating breakfasts in the home or taking advantage of the newly implemented "grab-and-go" options (an insight from the observations), which was well beyond our 40% goal. In addition, 34 to 38 students were ordering prepacked lunches (85%–95% consumption rate), which easily beat our 25% projected success metric for having students take packed lunches to school.

Conclusion

There are hundreds of problem-solving processes and thousands of tools used throughout business every day. The art of thinking is to be able to align the right processes and tools to create the desired outcomes in the most productive ways possible. Having a "thinking toolbox" that helps diverse sets of individuals, teams, and groups "think on demand," in the same direction, with the same focus, is critical to organizational success.

HCD is an effective tool for managing social change because it is a descriptive process that is user-centered and cocreative, provides for sequential activity and provides evidence, and is holistic and iterative. However, as Abraham Maslow stated: "If all you have is a hammer, everything looks like a nail." HCD should not be used as an all-purpose hammer. No one process or set of tools can serve that function. From the things we've learned, we have developed a more focused process, framework, language, and set of tools to use in our daily operations: *Holy Family Institute's Human Centered Design Thinking Toolbox for the Nonprofit Social Service Industry.*

JEWISH FAMILY AND CHILDREN'S SERVICE OF SARASOTA-MANATEE: A STRENGTHS-BASED VIEW

In 2009, the Jewish Family & Children's Service of Sarasota-Manatee, Inc. (JFCS) had the opportunity both to work on an exciting project with funding from the Harry and Jeanette Weinberg Foundation and to change the way it did business. The Weinberg Foundation issued a call for proposals to address issues related to caregiver stress in family members who care for older adult spouses, parents, and others. With a long history of providing caregiver support, JFCS created a better and more economical way of providing services and named it Sarasota CARES (Caregivers Accessing Resources & Essential Services).

In issuing its request for proposals, the Weinberg Foundation cited these statistics:

- It is estimated that at least 75% of all care received by older adults in the United States is provided by family members and friends, and many do not consider themselves caregivers.

- Unpaid family caregivers will likely continue to be the largest source of long-term care services in the United States.
- There will be some 37 million informal caregivers in the United States by 2050, an increase of 85% from 2000.
- An estimated 59%–75% of caregivers are female, handling the most difficult caregiving tasks—for example, bathing, toileting, dressing.
- Most caregivers are middle-aged (35–64), but many caregivers of older people are themselves elderly. Among those caring for someone 65 or older, the average age of the caregiver is 63 (Harry and Jeanette Weinberg Foundation, 2009).

As the oldest large county in the United States, Sarasota has thousands of unpaid family caregivers. Anticipating an 85% or greater increase in the number of such caregivers over the next few decades and looking for a cost-effective and sustainable way to provide caregiver support, JFCS turned to a philosophy that has worked well with young children and their families—the wraparound approach—and applied its principles to a new model of caregiver support services. The wraparound process is driven by 10 key principles: family voice and choice; natural supports; individualized services; strengths-based services; persistence; cultural competency; team-based approaches; collaboration and mutual commitment to team goals; community-based services; and outcome-based activities (Miles et al., 2006).

Jessica Campbell, a JFCS wraparound coordinator, shares this story:

Soon after I started with Sarasota CARES, my supervisor assigned Peggy to me. At 78 years old, Peggy was the sole caregiver for her partner, Mary, who suffered from numerous health concerns associated with congestive heart failure. I scheduled an appointment to visit the couple and explain how Sarasota CARES utilized the wraparound process to alleviate as much stress as possible for the caregiver. During the first visit, I got the sense the women were interviewing me to gauge whether or not there was an issue with them being a same-sex couple. I can only imagine what type of prejudice and negative judgment they encountered during their 40 years together. Although Peggy did not sign up for the program that day, I was able to share some community resources with her, and I encouraged her to call JFCS when/if she found it hard to handle her situation.

A week later, I followed up with Peggy and, to my surprise, she said she wanted to participate in Sarasota CARES. We scheduled another home visit to complete paperwork and begin the wraparound process. When I arrived at the house, a panicked Peggy met me at the door. She said, "I really need your help! I just called 911. Mary is having an episode." I thought she meant Mary was experiencing chest pain or shortness of breath, but quickly realized Mary was having a paranoid psychotic episode. She was yelling obscenities and was largely incoherent. Peggy was understandably anxious. I sat with her in the living room while EMT technicians were in the bedroom assessing Mary. Peggy told me that in addition to physical health problems, Mary also suffered from a number of mental illnesses. As a young adult, Mary participated in electroshock therapy and occasionally had "episodes" during which she became paranoid and detached from reality. I stayed with Peggy until she was able to contact a friend to accompany her to the hospital.

The following day, Peggy called me to thank me for supporting her during Mary's episode. She disclosed that normally the couple lived in secret for a number of reasons, but she felt a sense of safety with me. Peggy and Mary have since been able to utilize the wraparound system to organize their medical records, find home health agencies they are comfortable with, and develop an emergency plan that reduces stress during an episode or if other health problems present themselves. The couple identified reliable neighbors, friends, and family as their wraparound team who help support the women physically and emotionally. Peggy recently stated that as a result of Sarasota CARES, she has less anxiety, more time to socialize with loved ones, and a better understanding of what resources are in the community. The wraparound process has helped her organize herself, involve friends and family who can provide additional support, and approach crisis in a manageable way.

Peggy and Mary are resilient women who have overcome enormous obstacles in their lives. They have adopted the wraparound system to ensure they remain as independent as possible and continue to build upon the strengths they possess.

Caregivers participating in JFCS's existing caregiver support programs reported their greatest challenges. These included financial stressors, lack of information, dealing with unhelpful family members, role reversal (parenting one's parents), the strains caregiving puts on other family relationships and responsibilities, and the toll on caregiver physical and emotional health. They want to have the skills and knowledge to provide good care, to stay healthy and continue their current lifestyles, to direct care received and make informed decisions, and to provide quality care for as long as they can.

To address these challenges effectively, the Sarasota CARES system of care is driven by teams of professionals, family members, and volunteers who collaborate and share a commitment to reaching the goals articulated by the family. Caregivers and those they care for determine the services they need and how they wish to receive those services. The program enforces caregiver strengths and reduces the stressors that negatively affect their lives. Other elements of the program that have proved effective in attaining family goals are individualized assessments and plans that can be used by multiple providers, as well as education, respite, help with transportation, streamlined access to services throughout the community, and coordination of community assets and leveraging of community resources. The program is evaluated on an ongoing basis under the guidance of a professor of social work and gerontology from the University of South Florida. The comprehensive evaluation measures (a) success in alleviating caregiver stress, (b) the success of the wraparound process in meeting caregiver and care recipient needs and enhancing strengths, (c) success in integrating volunteers, and (d) the successful replicability of the system of care in other communities.

Each caregiver and family is assigned a wraparound facilitator, a JFCS staff member who is able to see the whole picture and help coordinate all services. The facilitator helps to engage as many individuals and organizations as necessary to develop the best caregiver support system. Those receiving care are central to the process from the outset so that they feel ownership of the plan, want to cooperate, and understand what is happening throughout the process. Of utmost importance is that the family makes the decisions—the JFCS facilitator does not decide for them.

Another family's story gives a good picture of how the CARES model helps people recognize their strengths and use those strengths to improve their lives. Iris describes her experience:

> My husband, Lance, and I moved to Sarasota in 2010 to be closer to our son and his family but we didn't know anyone else in the area. Our financial situation was disastrous with Lance's mounting medical bills and my inability to understand all the complicated insurance and billing. I felt incompetent and alone and started to think that I was just worthless. My pastor knew I was at wit's end and told me I had to call JFCS. They sent a CARES wraparound facilitator, Char, who sat with Lance and me and helped us see that we still were able to do lots of things well. We just needed help with some of the things going on in our lives. I love to cook and I love to talk—I just didn't know who to cook for and talk to! Char encouraged me to call a few people I had met at church and invite them to our apartment for homemade pastries and coffee. Everyone had a nice time and members of the congregation volunteered to spend time with Lance so I could go get my hair done and shop for groceries. Other people offered to give me rides when I needed them. Char encouraged me to attend weekly bingo in our apartment complex. I made many acquaintances and two or three real friends. One of them introduced me to her nephew who has lots of experience with medical bills and insurance companies. He was wonderful! He helped sort through the medical bills and showed me how to fill out claims. When our son learned about this, he said he would help me out, too. I joined JFCS's caregiver support group and I've made friends at the weekly meetings while Lance visits with a mental health counselor at JFCS to deal with his depression. The therapist and volunteers who work with Lance and me have become like family. We now have a whole group of people we can trust and who can trust us, too.

After a year of assistance from the CARES facilitator, Iris and Lance had developed a circle of friendship and care. While they continue their weekly visits to JFCS for caregiver support and therapy, they no longer need the assistance of the CARES facilitator. The size of the team CARES helped them build has grown along with the size of their circle of friends. Iris has stretched beyond activities in her building and attends weekly events at the local senior center with a group of women she met at JFCS's caregiver support group who share her interests and who are or have been caregivers themselves. She established and leads a group in her apartment complex that prepares potluck meals that the members share with their spouses, neighbors, and friends. A neighbor who has improved her cooking under Iris's tutelage is teaching Iris how to play bridge so that she can join another social group in the building. Iris shares her story with newcomers to JFCS's weekly group and has become a member of several other caregivers' support teams.

Iris is typical of most caregivers who come to JFCS. They want to care for their family members but become overwhelmed and feel that they can't cope with responsibilities they were ill prepared to assume. There is usually one major, time-sensitive crisis that has to be dealt with before real progress can be made, such as sorting out medical bills and making calls to insurance companies, doctors' offices, and hospital billing departments. Once the crisis is under control, caregivers are better able to see those areas of life where they do have strengths and talents. Once these caregivers have their lives under control and recognize that they are strong in many areas, they want to share their knowledge with others.

Building on its success in using the wraparound philosophy with young children and older adults, JFCS has expanded its application. Wraparound is central to our parenting services, our healthy fatherhood initiative, our veterans support services, and our jail reentry program, among other programs. In each case, participant strengths are identified and participants drive what services will be received and how they will be offered.

INTEGRATING STRATEGIC PLANNING AND STRATEGY IMPLEMENTATION INTO CORPORATE CULTURE

The Village Network has a long history of providing high-quality services to abused and neglected children across the state of Ohio. Perhaps even more impressive is the Village's rate of growth. In the last 12 years, the Village has grown approximately threefold, going from a $10 million organization to today having an annual budget of $30 million.

Over the last 20 years, The Village Network has completed several 3-year strategic planning cycles. Similar to other organizations, The Village Network committed significant resources to developing its 3-year strategic plans. Unfortunately, also like many organizations, the strategy plans soon lost priority and eventually ended up collecting dust on a bookshelf. Many of the staff recruited to implement the plans were not fully engaged or aligned with the goals and objectives of the plan. Very typical of many organizations, the state of strategic planning at the Village is attributable to a culture that is focused on short-term results. In Patrick Lencioni's terms, the agency has experienced an imbalance in favor of being *smart* over *healthy.*

The culture of the Village has been focused on short-term, bottom-line financial results. There have been benefits to this focus—for example, it has contributed to the agency's tremendous growth and success over the last decade. However, the agency was placed under significant corrective action. Further, as of late, there is a sense that the Village has begun to lose some of its competitive advantage because of a lack of innovative programming.

An assessment of the agency's capacity and culture was completed. The Core Capacity Assessment Tool (CCAT) revealed that a gap exists between the programs and the agency's mission. In other words, the program staff are not making a connection between the agency's mission and its program outcomes. The Village staff do not know the goals and objectives the agency is working toward. Further, according the results of the CCAT, staff have not been provided with outcome data needed to assess and improve performance. All of this has contributed to a culture that is focused on short-term results while leaving strategic planning on the sidelines.

Jeff DeGraff's exercise, based on his Competing Values Framework (CVF) (2007), was utilized to help the Village gain insight and an appreciation for the varied strengths, values, and frameworks from which staff operated. This exercise enabled staff, especially those favoring "soft" skills, to appreciate their contribution to the agency and to strategic planning in particular.

Moving forward, strategic planning will become an annual process incorporated into the Village Network's business cycles alongside annual budgeting and program planning. Moreover, Patrick Lencioni's framework of *smart* versus *healthy* (as found in his 2012 book *The Advantage: Why Organizational Health Trumps Everything Else in Business*), along with DeGraff's CVF, will be used to help change the agency's culture. The desired culture is one that allows for both short- and long-term goals and is characterized as healthy as defined by Lencioni.

Assessing The Village Network

Kaplan and Norton (2005) report that most large organizations fail to achieve profitable growth despite ambitious strategic plans. Moreover, the authors also report that 67% of human resources and information technology departments' strategies do not reflect corporate strategy. According to one recent report, on average, a staggering "95% of a company's employees are unaware of, or do not understand, its strategy" (p. 2). With such dismal statistics regarding the impact of strategic planning, what is one to conclude about the futility of a strategic plan? According to Kaplan and Norton, these trends demonstrate a disconnect between strategic formulation and strategy execution.

Over its nearly 70-year history, The Village Network has rolled out many strategic plans. Unfortunately, as noted above, the plans lost priority and were abandoned. Jeff DeGraff, in his book *Leading Innovation*, describes a strategic-planning scenario that could be used to describe the strategic planning at The Village Network. DeGraff writes: "Staff were frustrated with the firm's lack of rigor and honesty in developing its strategic plans. A typical strategy retreat started off with wishful thinking by senior leaders and support staff and was quickly followed by a stream of practical considerations voiced by operating leaders, leaving little room for great ambition" (2007, p. 39).

As is typical of many organizations, at the Village, day-to-day operations take precedence over the long-term goals of the strategy plan. Consequently, the shorter-term financial returns have taken the focus off of the longer-term, 3-year strategy goals. Patrick Lencioni (2012), in his book *the Advantage*, offers a good framework to help describe the current situation at the Village when it comes to organizational culture and strategic planning. Lencioni claims that smart organizations are good at the classic fundamentals of business such as finance and strategic planning. However, Lencioni also points out that an organization, to sustain true growth and "maximize its success, must come to embody two basic qualities: it must be smart (financials), and it must be healthy (culture)" (p. 5). In Lencioni's terms, the Village Network is a smart organization, but needs to become healthier and incorporate strategic planning into its culture.

At the Village Network, there has been a very real disconnect between the design of our strategy plans and the implementation and execution of the plans. Consequently, very few of the long-term goals of the strategy plans are being achieved. The strategic planning process and strategy execution are not infused in the culture.

The Strategy Counts project has focused on improving the impact of strategic initiatives at the Village Network. More specifically, this project proposes to incorporate strategic planning and strategic initiatives into the organization's culture. It is hoped that by the end of the project, strategic planning and execution of the strategy plans will be a part of the everyday routine and will be integrated into the operations of the agency.

The results of the CCAT, among other data, were utilized to provide feedback to the organization. The CCAT, an online survey administered by a third party, was used to measure, among other things, the extent to which the organization was engaged with the implementation of the strategic plan and connected to its mission and vision. The CCAT also measured the organization's culture.

The results of the CCAT got people's attention. Many of the items on the CCAT were ranked lower than many had expected. Consequently, the assessment was impactful, as indicated by some strong negative reactions. For this reason, the dissemination of the results was done in a planned, intentional manner. Initially, the results were given to a select group of employees and only in summary form. This author held a "town meeting" and discussed the results. It should be noted that the full results of the CCAT were given to the agency's CEO and board chairperson. Eventually, as time elapsed, the shock of the results wore off and they began to be accepted.

The results of the CVF exercise were very positive and helpful to the staff. The exercise was combined with a training session about the differences between strategic thinking and actions versus the thinking and actions of tactical approaches. The CVF exercises allowed staff to recognize the value that they contributed to the agency's success. Combined with the training about tactical versus strategic thinking, staff came away with a sense that they did have value to add to the strategic plan. This began the process of engaging them in the strategic planning process.

Implementation

The results of the CCAT also had an impact on the board of directors of the Village Network. In fact, the board asked that the issues brought to light from the CCAT be addressed by way of a new strategic plan. The human resources strategic planning workgroup has been charged with improving the cultural issues highlighted in the CCAT results. Among these issues is a gap between the programs and the agency's mission as well as an apparent disconnect between performance and outcomes.

To help incorporate strategic planning and implementation into the culture of the organization, strategic planning will become a routine, regular process. The goal is that strategic planning will take place as expected, as routine and required as such processes as annual budgeting or CQI audits. To accomplish this, strategic planning will be done annually rather than every 3 years. Critical to this process is that the strategic planning will be coordinated with the development of an annual business plan that supports the strategic plan. Moreover, the strategic planning process will also be coordinated with the agency's annual budgeting process and succession planning.

Additionally, the employee's performance evaluations have been changed to align each employee's efforts with the goals and objectives from the strategic plan. Moreover, succession planning has been tied in to the strategic plan by way of performance improvement plans tied to the strategic plan. Finally, the line of reports and board meetings has been restructured to support the strategic plan.

RESOURCES

For more information, see the following websites:
HCD Toolkit: www.ideo.com/work/human-centered-design-toolkit
HCD Tool Worksheets: www.hcdconnect.org
Free 90-minute crash course in design thinking: dschool.stanford.edu/dgift
Research articles on the Four Innovation Imperatives: www.cpsb.com/research/articles

REFERENCES

Bell, J., Masaoka, J., & Zimmerman, S. (2010). *Nonprofit sustainability: Making strategic decisions for financial viability*. San Francisco, CA: Jossey-Bass.

Bettendorf, J. (2011). *2011 Baldrige Performance Excellence Assessment*. Minneapolis, MN: Volunteers of America of Minnesota.

Bettendorf, J. (2013a). *Strategic planning process timeline*. Minneapolis, MN: Volunteers of America of Minnesota.

Bettendorf, J. (2013b). *Strategic direction for 2014–2016*. Minneapolis, MN: Volunteers of America of Minnesota.

Bettendorf, J. (2013c). *Theory of Change*. Minneapolis, MN: Volunteers of America of Minnesota.

Collins, J. C. & Porras, J. (1996). Building your company's vision. *Harvard Business Review, September*, 13.

DeGraff, J., & Quinn, S. (2007). *Leading innovation: How to jump start your organization's growth engine*. New York, NY: McGraw-Hill.

Hamel, G., & Prahalad, C. K. (2005). Strategic intent. *Harvard Business Review, July*, 15.

Harry and Jeanette Weinberg Foundation. (2009). *Care giver request for proposals*. Owings Mills, Maryland: Author.

Kaplan, R. S., & Norton, D. P. (1996). *Balanced scorecard: Translating strategy into action*. Boston, MA: Harvard Business Press Books.

Kaplan, R. S., & Norton, D. P. (2001). *The strategy-focused organization: How balanced scorecard companies thrive in the new business environment*. Boston, MA: Harvard Business Press Books.

Kaplan, R. S., & Norton, D. P. (2005). The office of strategy management. *Harvard Business Review, July–August*, 2, 39.

Kaplan, R. S., & Norton, D. P. (2008). *The execution premium: Linking strategy to operations for competitive advantage*. Boston, MA: Harvard Business Press Books.

Lencioni, P. (2012). *The advantage: Why organizational health trumps everything else in business* (1st ed.). San Francisco, CA; Jossey-Bass.

Miles, P., Bruns, E. J., Osher, T. W., Walker, J. S., & National Wraparound Initiative Advisory Group. (2006). *The wraparound process user's guide: A handbook for families*. Portland, OR: National Wraparound Initiative, Research and Training Center on Family Support and Children's Mental Health, Portland State University.

The New York State Coalition for Children's Mental Health Services. (2003). *A children's mental health system of care blueprint*. Albany, NY: Comstock and Schimmer.

CHAPTER 9

Research, Evaluation, and Assessment as Key Strategic Engagements in the Nonprofit Health and Human Services Sector

Jennifer Keith, Lisa R. Kleiner, Archana Bodas LaPollo,
and Lynne Kotranski

Discussions about strategic initiatives within nonprofit health and human services organizations most often focus on programmatic growth opportunities and expansion of services, and on how these align with organizational mission and values. Within the Research and Evaluation Group (REG) at Public Health Management Corporation (PHMC), they see assessment, evaluation, and research as key components of strategy and its effective deployment and as a critical function—whether using in-house talent or external experts—for any health and human services organization.

PHMC's Research and Evaluation Group (REG) has been in existence for almost 40 years and has always been an integral part of PHMC. Initially, REG focused more on health planning and policy studies (it was called the planning department at that time) when PHMC was a small organization with a focus more on managing, planning, and program oversight than on direct client services.

In 1977, PHMC created a formal research and evaluation department with the intent of engaging in scientific research and program evaluation as one programmatic growth area. At that time, there was very little discussion about "documenting outcomes," "evidence-based practices," or "using data to drive strategic decisions." Moreover, because PHMC itself was not a service provider, most of the evaluation and research work REG completed was for external organizations and governmental funders. As PHMC grew and expanded its direct services portfolio of programs, REG started to partner with the programs in evaluating their efficacy as well as serving as a natural laboratory for developing service interventions and evaluating their impact on client behavior and other outcomes.

Today, REG comprises a multidisciplinary team of researchers whose diverse sets of skills and experience allow for a wide range of data-related activities across a broad spectrum of health issues that affect many vulnerable populations, and who have a long history of collaborating with other PHMC divisions and affiliates as well as outside community-based organizations (CBOs), private and government funders, academic institutions, and service agencies locally and nationally. These efforts have driven both short- and long-term impacts on health for the past 4 decades.

The REG's program priorities include health promotion and disease prevention, health status and access to services for vulnerable population groups (e.g., older adults, the uninsured, low-income populations, and cultural/ethnic minorities), HIV/AIDS intervention research, and tobacco and chronic disease research. PHMC's REG capabilities include population and community needs assessment, study design, qualitative and quantitative data collection (e.g., primary surveys, focus groups, key-informant interviews, participant observation), quantitative statistical and qualitative analyses, and preparation of practical technical and policy reports.

We partner with internal, direct-service PHMC programs, with external service providers, with foundations, and with other research and technical assistance providers. Our content expertise and technical knowledge are used to help the organizations and programs with whom we partner use assessment, evaluation, and research findings to directly inform their strategic decisions (see Figure 9.1; PHMC, 2013).

FIGURE 9.1   PHMC Research and Evaluation Group approach to assessment, evaluation, and research.

Below are several case studies demonstrating how community health needs assessments (CHNAs), evaluation and technical assistance to statewide tobacco efforts, and scientific research related to HIV/AIDS have directly affected the guidance of strategic programmatic and organizational directions.

COMMUNITY HEALTH NEEDS ASSESSMENTS

Community health needs assessments are an important element in the strategic planning process for many nonprofit organizations providing health and social services. A community health needs assessment is a community-based process for assessing a broad range of individual, environmental, cultural, and health-related information to identify unmet health care needs and to inform future decisions and actions impacting the health of the community. CHNA findings on unmet needs are used to guide program development and implementation and to measure outcomes to assess program impact, all of which are important components of defining and refining nonprofit programmatic and strategic initiatives. PHMC has more than 25 years' experience conducting CHNAs for hospital conversion foundations, nonprofit hospitals, and government agencies. PHMC also works together with these different nonprofit organizational models to identify new programmatic areas, create outcome-measurement systems and implementation plans, and measure the effects of programs on the populations they serve, as shown in the following paragraphs.

Foundations

In recent years, many nonprofit, tax-exempt Pennsylvania hospitals have been converted to non–tax exempt, for-profit entities. Pennsylvania law requires hospitals to create and endow a nonprofit foundation if the hospital is sold to a for-profit corporation. The purpose of the "conversion" foundation is to meet the unmet health care needs of the community, using the funds formerly set aside by the nonprofit hospital for community benefit. These new foundations are also required to conduct community health needs assessments in their service areas to determine unmet health care needs and direct their grant-making.

PHMC assists each foundation and its stakeholders to achieve consensus on the priority health needs of the community by developing a vision of how a CHNA will meet their needs; identifying the information that will be needed to conduct the CHNA; convening community groups; agreeing on survey, focus group, and informational interview questions and data collection methods; collecting and analyzing data and identifying and prioritizing unmet needs; convening community planning processes; and creating implementation plans.

Hospitals

PHMC has also provided CHNA support to a large number of area hospitals through its Community Health Data Base. In fall 2011, PHMC's REG was chosen as the CHNA provider for Delaware Valley Health Care (DVHC) Council's member nonprofit hospitals and health systems. In 2012, PHMC completed CHNAs for 28 of DVHC's nonprofit hospitals to meet the CHNA requirements of the Affordable Care Act (ACA). The ACA requires a description of the unmet health care needs of the population of the service area; community input on health needs; and information on existing health care facilities and resources. PHMC's REG has also assisted the hospitals in identifying and prioritizing unmet health care needs, information that is used to develop the hospitals' community benefit programs and the required implementation plans. This process is an important part of the hospitals' strategic planning and is essential to establishing a baseline against which to measure the impact of the hospitals' programs on the community.

Government Agencies

CHNAs also are used by many government agencies to determine whether they are providing services to their target populations, identify the unmet needs of the populations they serve, plan more effective programming, meet government reporting requirements, and establish a baseline against which to measure the impact of their programs. PHMC has assisted several large local government agencies with assessments of the need for their services among their target populations, the effectiveness of their outreach efforts, and the impact of their services. Findings in these areas are then used for prioritizing limited resources, directing outreach efforts more effectively, developing new areas for services, and lobbying for additional funding. This assistance is invaluable to these agencies in the current climate of extensive cuts in government funding.

Many nonprofits also find that creating an outcome-measurement system aids in their strategic planning, improves fundraising capacity, and identifies new programming initiatives. The relationship between outcome measurement and strategic planning is described below.

Nonprofit Service Providers

Developing a way to measure the positive impact of services on clients is important to nonprofits as a means of obtaining funding in an increasingly competitive environment, improving programming, and communicating successes to the community. Developing an outcome-measurement system involves creating a program logic model that identifies positive changes in program participants, a plan to collect and analyze information from clients about the impact of the program on their lives. In our 20 years' experience with outcome measurement, PHMC's Research and Evaluation Group has developed expertise in working together with other nonprofits to create effective outcome measurement systems.

Identifying agency outcomes is often the first step in the strategic planning process if a comprehensive approach has been taken to developing the outcome-measurement system. Many nonprofit agencies think of logic models and outcome measures as information that can be used internally to guide program planning or, at best, as information that is required to be reported to a single funder on an annual basis. At PHMC, we often help other nonprofits to view their logic models in a new light as communication tools for advertising their programs' successes and developing new strategic initiatives. A well-thought-out logic model with outcomes supported by program results can provide potential funders and partners with a clear snapshot of what an agency or program is capable of achieving. Many agencies also discover that they can clarify their visions for their programs and are better able to inform and inspire staff, volunteers, community contacts, and board members.

STRATEGIC ASSISTANCE IN TOBACCO CONTROL EFFORTS IN PENNSYLVANIA

Pennsylvania Department of Health, Division of Tobacco Prevention and Control (DTPC)

The Division of Tobacco Prevention and Control (DTPC) runs a dynamic statewide program. Their contractors work across goals for prevention, cessation, clean air, and addressing health disparities. At the core of the program are eight regional primary contractors who work on all four goal areas in different parts of the state. Each region and its stakeholders are diverse, so tailored work is necessary. However, it is the collective impact (Kania & Kramer, 2011) of all program partners that drives change to reduce tobacco-related morbidity and mortality.

To facilitate ongoing discussion about mutually reinforcing program activities, REG and DTPC developed goal-focused annual work plans. The work plans contain both standardized and individualized goals. DTPC examines goals for each region and across regions to ensure that, as a unit, the statewide program will be positioned to achieve its goals. For example, each region provides cessation services, but not to equal numbers of clients. Variation in client-cessation goals may be related to the specific needs of the region, differences in program emphasis, or even geography. By using a coordinated and goal-focused work plan across regions, DTPC is able to discuss expectations and monitor each region's client-cessation goals within the context of other regions' client-cessation goals as well as of other goals within the region itself.

Coordinated work plan development has proven to be useful at several points in time. During template development, DTPC and REG discussed contractual requirements, program priorities, and success to find the right balance of uniformity and customized expectations. Regional primary contractors completed the template by looking at their past experiences, their areas of expertise, and their current priorities. Regional primary contractors and DTPC discussed each proposed work plan and made adjustments to goals across the service continuum within a programwide context. The work plan is also used over time to facilitate discussion between DTPC and contractors, as well as between counterparts. Work plan progress is examined midway through the year and at the end of the year, if not more frequently, but the best part of this strategy is that it promotes combined success, complementary efforts, and coordinated planning all year long.

American Lung Association in Pennsylvania (ALA)

The American Lung Association (ALA) is a long-standing and dedicated leader in lung health. As a leader, the ALA has worked on in-house as well as partner strategies to promote positive change. In 2012, the ALA in Pennsylvania, in coordination with the Pennsylvania Department of Health and other partners, developed and began implementation of a strategic plan for a comprehensive tobacco control program in Pennsylvania. The plan is intended to serve as a framework to inform action across the Pennsylvania tobacco control community. This tool can be used by both funded and unfunded stakeholders to coordinate and focus tobacco control efforts and, ultimately, to drive change.

REG is working with ALA to gather partnership, action, and impact data throughout the strategic plan development and implementation process. Evaluation of the strategic planning process will examine whether and how the plan affects dynamic and coordinated planning and action to facilitate sustained, positive change. A mixed-method evaluation (using both qualitative and quantitative data) is in place. Several surveys are being used to collect feedback from strategic planning partners and potential partners. For example, during the development process, feedback was collected after core partners met for a full-day meeting. During early implementation, two surveys were used to identify partners and their potential roles. Additional data are collected through partner agreement forms, key informant interviews, network analyses, and action tracking.

ALA plans to use ongoing feedback and data to identify additional partners, communicate progress, and identify needs. Evaluation of the strategic planning process will help inform current efforts to leverage resources to raise awareness, provide services, improve health equity, and strengthen tobacco control policies in Pennsylvania. Overall strategic plan evaluation will help to measure impact and also inform future strategic planning efforts, including strategy and partner identification and deployment.

Please refer to the following link for more information: http://www. lung.org/associations/charters/mid-atlantic/assets/docs/a-strategic-plan-for-a.pdf

DEVELOPING STRATEGY AND DRIVING CHANGE IN HIV/AIDS PREVENTION AND SERVICE DELIVERY

PHMC's REG has powerfully used the collection, analysis, and sharing of data to drive change and positively influence the health of communities at risk for or living with HIV and AIDS at the local and national levels. Since 1987, REG has been at the forefront against the HIV/AIDS epidemic in the city of Philadelphia, conducting evaluation and research studies that aim to understand the factors and behaviors that increase and protect against the risk for acquiring or transmitting the virus, understand factors related to HIV testing and linkage to care and treatment, develop and/or evaluate HIV prevention interventions, and reduce HIV-related stigma among both HIV-infected and uninfected individuals. HIV/AIDS is a health issue that affects everyone, including both infected and uninfected children, women, and men across all racial, class, and sexual identities, but is also deeply and inextricably linked with poverty, discrimination, reduced economic opportunities, trauma, and substance abuse. Below, we describe three examples of REG epidemiologic research and evaluation efforts that illustrate different ways that data have driven long-term social impact.

Evaluation of the PALMS Project: Using Data to Demonstrate Efficacy and Reach a Wider Audience

The PALMS project, a program of PHMC's behavioral health services unit (PHMC/BHS), is a homegrown, theater-based, group-level HIV prevention intervention for high-risk, hard-to-reach, minority adolescents. PALMS seeks to help adolescents reduce risky sexual behavior, increase their self-efficacy in practicing safer sex, and empower them to protect their sexual health through theater-based strategies using popular culture elements such as peer actors who model appropriate behavior and opportunities to actively participate in problem-solving and practice skills. Each PALMS group-level intervention combines a dramatic performance with additional intervention activities. The three group sessions each last approximately 2 hours, involving 8 to 15 participants. Since 1993, PALMS has evolved from a single-session intervention to a three-session intervention with separate groups for females and males and has been implemented in a variety of settings, including schools, community centers, juvenile justice facilities, and drug treatment centers.

Using limited resources, the PALMS project partnered with REG to conduct a small evaluation in which pre- and posttest survey data were collected to assess changes in HIV-related knowledge, awareness, and attitudes and to monitor intervention implementation. Positive findings from these data resulted in the choice by the Centers for Disease Control and Prevention (CDC) of the PALMS project as one of nine Reputationally Strong Programs (C-RSP) Projects in 1999 to serve as a model in designing and developing HIV prevention programs. Then, in 2004, PHMC was awarded a grant from the CDC to conduct a more rigorous evaluation that used a nonrandomized, concurrent-comparison group design in which 289 youth (predominantly Black, heterosexually active males aged 12–18 from two Philadelphia juvenile justice centers). The evaluation found that at 6 months' followup, PALMS had been effective in improving HIV-related knowledge and attitudes as well as maintaining high levels of condom use with nonmain female partners, particularly among youth aged 15–18 (Lauby et al., 2010). Based on these findings, PALMS has been identified by the CDC as an evidence-based intervention and will be listed as such in its *Compendium of Evidence-Based HIV Behavioral Interventions* (www.cdc.gov/hiv/prevention/research/compendium/index.html), a well-known national resource for researchers, policy decision makers, and prevention providers that lists the strongest HIV behavioral interventions in the scientific literature to date that have been rigorously evaluated and that have demonstrated evidence of their efficacy. Through rigorous program evaluation methods and collaboration with intervention staff, this effective homegrown intervention will now be able to be replicated and disseminated to a much wider population of high-risk adolescents beyond Philadelphia.

Evaluation of New Pathways for Women: Using Data to Ensure Sustainability

For the past 10 years, PHMC/BHS's New Pathways projects, the New Pathways Project (NPP) and New Pathways for Women (NPW), have provided voluntary drop-in recovery support and referral programs that partner with individuals who are at high risk for HIV through their drug use and sexual behaviors and who are seeking help in initiating their recovery and increasing their readiness for treatment. These programs have met a critical need in Philadelphia's continuum of substance abuse treatment by filling the service gaps between active addiction, substance abuse treatment, and posttreatment recovery maintenance. NPP and NPW were initially funded by federal grants (2002–2007 and 2007–2012, respectively) through the Center for Substance Abuse Treatment and were evaluated by PHMC's REG staff. Evaluation of these programs entailed quantitative data collection at baseline, at discharge, and at 3 and 6 months postbaseline to assess the programs' effects on participants' drug use, sexual risk behaviors, readiness for treatment, enrollment and participation in substance abuse treatment programs, participation in HIV testing and care, health care utilization, and other factors, as well as a process evaluation to monitor implementation and attendance in program activities.

Both New Pathways projects demonstrated strong outcomes at 6 months' follow-up. For example, analysis of NPW's intake and 6-month follow-up data showed significant decreases in substance use over time: the percentage of women reporting any use of illegal drugs decreased from 100% to 41%; the percentage of women reporting daily use of drugs decreased from 31% to 8% at follow-up; and the mean number of days of use of any drug fell from 15.7 days to 5.4 days. At 6 months' follow-up, 42% of women reported having entered substance abuse treatment since joining NPW. Two-thirds (66%) of women who had never been in treatment reported that they had been in a drug or alcohol treatment program between intake and 6-month follow-up (Evans, 2011). Findings from the program evaluations for both projects have been shared at both the local and national levels, and the City of Philadelphia's Department of Behavioral Health and Intellectual disAbility Services has identified the New Pathways Project as a model program in alignment with the department's transformation to recovery-oriented systems of care (Evans, 2011). Subsequently, when federal funding ended for each program, the City of Philadelphia's Office of Addictions Services awarded first NPP and then NPW funding to sustain both programs so that their doors could remain open beyond their initial grant periods and for the foreseeable future.

Brothers y Hermanos: Using Local Data to Contribute to National Epidemiologic Research

In 2001, the REG was awarded a 5-year grant from the CDC to participate in a large, multicity (Philadelphia, New York, and Los Angeles) study to examine HIV risk among Black and Latino men who have sex with men (MSM). Black MSM were recruited in New York and Philadelphia, and Latino MSM were recruited in New York and Los Angeles. The objectives of this study were to describe Black and Latino MSM with respect to their demographic, psychological, behavioral, social, cultural, and environmental characteristics; assess HIV prevalence using rapid testing (OraQuick oral testing) and standard confirmatory tests; assess recent HIV infection using the serologic Testing Algorithm for Recent HIV Seroconversions (STARHS); examine the characteristics that promote or protect against sexual behavior that places Latino and Black MSM at risk for contracting or transmitting HIV infection; examine the characteristics that distinguish between HIV-positive and HIV-negative status; and examine risk-promoting and risk-reducing behaviors among both HIV-positive and HIV-negative men.

As part of this study, REG staff collaborated with several Philadelphia community-based organizations to recruit and conduct cross-sectional quantitative surveys with 540 Black MSM in Philadelphia. Approximately 500 additional Black MSM were recruited in New York City, and approximately 500 Latino MSM were recruited in New York City and Los Angeles each, resulting in a sample of over 2,000 Black and Latino MSM. Findings from this national study have been widely disseminated at the city, state, and national levels, have leveraged funding for additional research, and have informed HIV prevention programming for Black and Latino MSM at the local and national levels. REG staff have conducted approximately 20 local oral presentations to share findings with CBO staff, program planners, and government entities, convened one large local community forum to share findings with Philadelphia community members, conducted one presentation at a Pennsylvania statewide public health conference, conducted six oral presentations at national conferences, and collaborated on the publication of 12 articles in peer-reviewed journals (Bond et al., 2009; Carlos et al., 2010; Han, Lauby, Bond, & LaPollo, 2010; Han, Rutledge, Bond, Lauby & LaPollo, 2013; Jeffries, Marks, Lauby, Murrill & Millett, 2013; Joseph et al., 2011; Lauby et al., 2008; Lauby et al., 2012; Marks et al., 2009; Marks et al., 2010; Millett, Ding, Lauby, Flores & Stueve, 2007; Millett et al., 2011). Black and Latino MSM continue to be the populations most disproportionately impacted by HIV in the United States (Centers for Disease Control and Prevention [CDC], 2010; Lauby et al., 2012). The REG's participation in the Brothers y Hermanos study shows how epidemiologic research contributes greatly to the knowledge base about HIV risk among high-risk communities, providing crucial data that directly inform strategic program planning to improve health at both the local and national levels.

As the descriptions and case studies demonstrate, the PHMC Research and Evaluation Group's work in conducting community health needs assessments and providing technical assistance through work plan and strategic plan development for statewide tobacco control efforts, as well as the role of scientific research and evaluation in driving strategic change in the development of programs targeted at having a positive impact on persons at risk of HIV/AIDS, are all illustrative of the importance of using assessment, research, and evaluation to enhance the capacity of nonprofit organizations and other human service providers to more effectively adapt their programmatic strategies and financial and other resources to meet the existing and changing needs of the varied and diverse populations they serve, to create new service synergies, and to demonstrate long-term impact and relevance.

REFERENCES

Bond, L., Wheeler, D. P., Millett, G. A., LaPollo, A. B., Carson, L. F., & Liau, A. (2009). Black men who have sex with men and the down low: The association of DL identity with HIV risk behavior. *American Journal of Public Health, 99*(S1), S92–S95.

Carlos, J. A., Bingham, T. A., Stueve, A., Lauby, J., Ayala, G., Millett, G.A., & Wheeler, D. (2010). The role of peer support on condom use among black and Latino men who have sex with men (MSM) in three urban areas. *AIDS Education and Prevention, 22*, 430–444.

Centers for Disease Control and Prevention. (2010). Prevalence and awareness of HIV infection among men who have sex with men—21 cities, United States, 2008. MMWR. 59:1201–7.

Evans, A. (2011). *Transformation of Behavioral Health Services in Philadelphia.* Philadelphia, PA: Department of Behavioral Health and Intellectual disAbility Services. Retrieved from http://www.facesandvoicesofrecovery.org/pdf/eNews/Phila.PracticeGuidelines May2011.pdf.

Han, C. S., Lauby, J., Bond, L., & LaPollo, A. B. (2010). Magic Johnson doesn't worry about how to pay for medicine: Experiences of black men who have sex with men living with HIV. *Culture, Health & Sexuality, 12*(4), 387–399.

Han, C. S., Rutledge, S. E., Bond, L., Lauby, J., & LaPollo, A. B. (2013). You're better respected when you carry yourself as a man: Black men's personal account of the down low "lifestyle." *Sexuality and Culture*, doi: 10.1007/s12119-013-9192-3

Jeffries, W. L., Marks, G., Lauby, J., Murrill, C. S., & Millett, G. A. (2013). Homophobia is associated with sexual behavior that increases risk of acquiring and transmitting HIV infection among black men who have sex with men. *AIDS and Behavior, 17*(4), 1442–1453.

Joseph, H., Marks, G., Belcher, F., Millett, G., Stueve, A., Bingham, T. A., & Lauby, J. (2011). Older partner selection, sexual risk behaviour and unrecognised HIV infection among black and Latino men who have sex with men. *Sexually Transmitted Infections, 87*(5), 442–447.

Kania, J., & Kramer, M. (2011). Collective impact. *Stanford Social Innovation Review*, 36–41.

Lauby, J. L., LaPollo, A. B., Herbst, J. H., Painter, T. M., Batson, H., Pierre, A., & Milnamow, M. (2010). Preventing AIDS through Live Movement and Sound (PALMS): Efficacy of a theater-based HIV prevention intervention delivered to high-risk male adolescents in juvenile justice settings. *AIDS Education and Prevention, 22*(5), 402–416.

Lauby, J. L., Marks, G., Bingham, T., Liu, K. L., Liau, A., Stueve, A., & Millett, G. A. (2012). Having supportive social relationships is associated with reduced risk of unrecognized HIV infection among black and Latino men who have sex with men. *AIDS and Behavior, 16*(3), 508–515.

Lauby, J. L., Millett G. A., LaPollo, A. B., Bond, L., Murrill, C. S., & Marks, G. (2008). Sexual risk behaviors of HIV-positive, HIV-negative, and serostatus-unknown black men who have sex with men and women. *Archives of Sexual Behavior, 37*(5), 708–719.

Marks, G., Millett, G. A., Bingham, T., Bond, L., Lauby, J., Liau, A., . . . Stueve, A. (2009). Understanding differences in HIV sexual transmission among Latino and black men who have sex with men: The Brothers y Hermanos study. *AIDS and Behavior, 13*(4), 682–690.

Marks, G., Millett, G. A., Bingham, T., Lauby, J., Murrill, C. S., & Stueve, A. (2010). Prevalence and protective value of serosorting and strategic positioning among black and Latino men who have sex with men. *Sexually Transmitted Diseases, 37*(5), 325–327.

Millett, G. A., Ding, H., Lauby, J., Flores, S., & Stueve, A. (2007). Circumcision status and HIV infection among black and Latino men who have sex with men in 3 U.S. cities. *Journal of Acquired Immune Deficiency Syndromes, 46*(5), 643–650.

Millett, G. A., Ding, H., Marks, G., Jeffries, W., Bingham, T., Lauby, J., . . . Stueve, A. (2011). Mistaken assumptions and missed opportunities: Correlates of undiagnosed HIV infection among black and Latino men who have sex with men. *Journal of Acquired Immune Deficiency Syndromes, 58*(1), 64–71.

Public Health Management Corporation (PHMC). (2013). *Research and evaluation group approach to assessment, evaluation, and research.* Philadelphia, PA: Author.

CHAPTER 10

Deploying Strategy to Create Purposeful Partnerships

Richard Cohen, Tine Hansen-Turton, and Glenn Wilson

One of the core functions of a chief strategy officer is to help execute the vision of the CEO. In several of the Strategy Counts sites, organizational growth and diversification of the organization's portfolio have been major focuses. There are two ways of growing—either through organic growth or through strategic partnerships. This chapter explores a variety of approaches to strategic partnerships.

PARTNERSHIPS: FROM COLLABORATIONS TO MERGERS

Few nonprofits in the health and human services sector, other than hospitals and insurers, merge or affiliate with other nonprofits. This is in stark contrast to the private sector, where part of business growth and development is mergers and acquisitions. When nonprofit leaders are asked in annual surveys from the Nonprofit Finance Fund and others, in spite of their financial situations, only a fraction (2%–3%) of leaders respond that they are in discussions with other organizations about mergers and affiliations. For every one successful nonprofit affiliation or merger, there are hundreds that did not happen but should have. Why is this? And, more important, what will it take for nonprofits in the human services sector to begin to work together more strategically to consolidate operations and focus on their missions?

In the wake of the Affordable Care Act (ACA), the future of the health and human services sector will change dramatically. Health and human services agencies will be financially incentivized to work together. Just as managed care has taken over how health care providers are being reimbursed, so is the recent trend of creating a managed care system within the human services sector to take on the risk of managing foster care through the Improving Outcomes for Children initiative in Pennsylvania, Florida, and Nebraska, among other places, only the beginning of what the future will look like for traditional child and family human services.

The Public Health Management Corporation (PHMC), in its Strategy Counts Proposal, set out to make strategic partnerships a major focus of the role of the chief strategy officer (CSO). This chapter describes PHMC's affiliation models with several organizations, as well as tips from the lessons it learned as a pioneer in the nonprofit health and human services affiliation and merger marketplace.

Since 1989, PHMC has strategically used its infrastructure and size to partner with mission-aligned nonprofit colleagues through its affiliation model. The focus with these affiliations has mainly been on driving down costs, wrapping services around clients, and enabling the affiliate organizations to better focus their operational costs to better compete. PHMC has usually undergone one affiliation a year. However, with the introduction of the CSO role to support the vision of the CEO, PHMC was able to ramp up its strategy and increase to three affiliations a year while having researched 30 other potential partners prior to focusing in on the right ones.

For background, PHMC is a nonprofit health and human services agency that creates and sustains healthier communities using best practices to improve community health through direct service, partnership, innovation, policy, research, technical assistance, and a prepared workforce. PHMC has served the greater Philadelphia region since 1972 and has become one of the largest and most comprehensive health and human services organizations in the nation.

At the beginning of the Strategy Counts initiative, PHMC had 10 affiliates, of which three were support affiliates, with a consolidated annual operating budget of over $175 million, in addition to a foundation with close to $40 million in assets. Through its more than 350 direct services programs and 10 affiliate partner organizations, its work in emergency preparedness across the region, and its various partnerships with government, foundations, businesses, and community-based organizations, PHMC and its work affect every household in the Philadelphia region. In 2013, PHMC served over 200,000 clients. The combined annual impact of PHMC and its affiliates on the Philadelphia community's economic vitality is estimated to be in the range of $500 million. Of every dollar received, on average 92¢, or a total of $161 million, goes toward program services.

The PHMC Affiliation Model: Strategic, Purposeful Partnership

Affiliations are strategically different from mergers. In a traditional merger, one of the organizations usually ceases to exist. Some or all staff and board leadership are absorbed into one of the organizations or into the newly merged corporate entity. Affiliations are different. In this model, staff and board leadership usually remain intact after some back-office consolidation. In the nonprofit sector, an affiliation is akin to the relationship between a subsidiary corporation and its parent corporation in which the parent corporation has some level of control. However, in general the corporations operate independently but rely on economies of scale, for example, common back-office services such as finance, human resources, information technology, and communications support.

PHMC strongly believes in the missions of the organizations with which it partners and wants them to keep their identities and leadership as they affiliate. PHMC's management style is to stay in the background and support its affiliate organizations. The PHMC affiliation model works as follows:

- The partner agency retains its own 501(c)(3) status and federal tax ID number, files its own 990, and completes its own individual agency audit.
- The partner agency has its own board of directors and keeps its own assets and liabilities. There is a firewall between PHMC and the affiliate nonprofit organization.
- PHMC and the partner agency sign an affiliation agreement. The partner agency amends its articles of incorporation and bylaws to reflect the affiliation agreement and its new legal structure as a membership corporation, with PHMC as the sole member of the corporation. Within the affiliation agreement is the ability for the two organizations to part ways should the partnership not flourish.
- Existing partner agency staff are retained; HR policies and benefits are changed to better mirror those of PHMC.
- Existing board members remain on the board of the partner agency, but PHMC also appoints two board members. PHMC also has a seat for affiliate board representation on its own board.
- Following a due diligence process that analyzes the partner organization's need for back-office support, the partner agency enters into an annual management contract with PHMC for PHMC's provision of information systems, fiscal, human resources, communications and marketing, program and strategy development, quality assurance, and related infrastructure services with an arms-length negotiated contract for service.

Why Should Nonprofit Health and Human Services Organizations Affiliate?

With the introduction of ACA, the health and human services landscape will change as we know it in the next decade. There will be tremendous challenges and opportunities on the horizon, and one could speculate that there will less of a need for traditional human services once all aspects of health reform have been implemented. However, each side of the sector needs the other. As an example, for a newly insured adult in an underserved community to be healthy, access to good physical health through the ACA will not be enough. The other traditional human services supports, for example caseworkers who assist and empower individuals, groups, families, and communities to prevent, alleviate, or better cope with crisis, change, and stress to enable them to function more effectively in all areas of life and living will be essential to ensuring good health. Health care practice is rather narrow, whereas the human services sector uses a broader model to assess and deliver services. This model views people, services, and the social environment as integrated entities. This perspective helps individuals, families, and communities address and overcome issues and barriers that arise from a variety of social problems and adverse societal conditions. The sooner health and human service agencies realize they need each other, the more successful both will be in the future.

For any affiliation to be successful, the process starts with the support of both the senior leadership and the board members of both parties. This is key to the success of these strategic partnerships. PHMC has built its model around attracting agencies that are mission-aligned and whose services can be wrapped around existing consumers within the PHMC family. Furthermore, PHMC believes strongly that there is strength in numbers and that through affiliation, both organizations can have a broader community impact. However, there are some key strategic indicators that should be in play before considering an affiliation. Both agencies should have the same goals in mind when exploring an affiliation and should ask themselves whether the affiliation would do the following:

- Strengthen existing compatible missions?
- Increase opportunities to assist in preserving critical community assets and extend programs offered by both organizations?
- Enhance financial stability and create economies of scale?
- Strengthen programmatic and operations infrastructure capacity?
- Grow new relationships that will support each organization's mission?
- Provide new opportunities for staff career advancement and benefits, as well as access to academic programs and training to retain talent?

In PHMC's case, the affiliate organization leadership is usually looking for specific opportunities and is looking to grow and scale. Primarily, they want the following:

- Access to a network of new partners, clients, and funders
- Access to new sources of philanthropic and public funding
- The ability to bid on and secure larger private and public contracts by having the backing of a larger parent organization
- Administrative and infrastructure support as needed, including but not limited to human resources, IT, accounting, and marketing

- The ability to accelerate the growth of existing programs, services, and markets and enter new markets
- Access to a line of credit

The Affiliation Process: How It Works

PHMC's affiliation process usually takes up to 6 months of mutual organizational due diligence. In the first 2 months, PHMC's affiliation team, currently led by Tine Hansen-Turton as chief strategy officer, meets with a prospective affiliate partner's board and leadership to determine the interest in exploring an affiliation. Before the beginning of the formal process, PHMC would already have done some preliminary financial analysis of the health of the nonprofit. One of the challenges in the nonprofit sector is that often when an organization's leadership begins to think about strategic partnerships, it's usually when the organization has begun to lose money, except by the time that has happened, it's usually too late for the process to be initiated.

Once there is overall leadership support, both parties sign a nondisclosure agreement. Over a 60-day period, both agencies complete a mutual programmatic and fiscal due diligence analysis. As a management company, PHMC specifically focuses its efforts on assessing back-office support needs and developing a management contract, based on the needs of the organization in the areas of human resources, information systems, and finance support. PHMC management services are determined by the needs of the affiliate partner organization, which usually makes PHMC more competitive compared with agencies that charge a flat back-office overhead rate. Over the 60- to 120-day period of the due diligence process, program staff explore program development opportunities, including exploration of funders and contracts. PHMC also does an analysis of what impact this new potential affiliation could have on other affiliates and partners. In this period, the affiliation agreement is negotiated, quality management issues are identified, and marketing and communication strategies are developed. Finally, in the 120- to 180-day period, both boards finalize the approval of the affiliation agreement and the change of bylaws and complete and sign the management contract. Staff of the affiliate partner organization are introduced to the transition plan. All administrative issues for on-boarding and ongoing maintenance are finalized, such as consolidating human resource policies and financial management, including accounts payable, billing, and purchasing arrangements and integration of information systems.

The affiliation process can end at any given point during the 6-month period. The process typically ends based on board and leadership's discomfort with parent-control issues and when it is obvious that the missions are not aligned and the parties have fewer prospects than initially believed. Nevertheless, while the due diligence process is key to the success of affiliations, the leadership of both organizations takes a leap of faith that a strategic partnership will bear fruit for both.

Affiliation Impact and Why Relationships Matter

To date, all PHMC affiliate organizations have increased their budgets and community impact up to tenfold or more within a short period: The wholes have clearly been greater than the sums of their parts.

Contrary to mergers and acquisitions in the private sector, nonprofit sector mergers and affiliations are a relationship business. The common theme behind the success of all of the affiliations is relationships—built on trust and over time. These include relationships between the leadership of PHMC and the affiliate organization leadership as well as in the funding community, including the City of Philadelphia and other government agencies, which has a vested interest in ensuring that the organizations it supports are strong both fiscally and in their management.

PHMC's story is no different. The following summaries tell a background story of relationships among leadership and staff of both organizations that have been built over time and on a foundation of trust.

Interim House. Interim House was PHMC's first venture into the affiliation model. Richard Cohen had a strong relationship with the organization and its leadership. Interim House services were considered exceptional by the women served in the residential treatment facility in Mt. Airy. However, the organization and the program were in financial distress. Funding agencies such as the city's Offices of Substance Abuse and Drugs and Alcohol were very supportive of PHMC's helping the program, which started with PHMC entering into a management contract to turn the agency around. PHMC provided management services with support from city government agencies, and the board ultimately turned into an affiliation in 1989, eventually creating a program for women and their children at Interim House West in West Philadelphia. However, it was the relationships that PHMC's leadership had with the organization and the funding community, including the city, that enabled the affiliation to happen.

The Bridge. In the early 1990s, the Bridge, a residential program for adolescents, was in serious financial trouble such that it was at risk of going out of business. The program was strong and well liked by funders such as the city, but it was losing significant amounts of money. PHMC was retained with support from the city's drug and alcohol office to do a management intervention. At the point when PHMC intervened in 1993, the program was losing over $500,000 per year. PHMC and its lawyers did something unheard-of in the nonprofit sector at that time, yet common in the private sector: It put the Bridge through bankruptcy to be able to resolve all of its debt issues. PHMC negotiated with all of the Bridge's creditors and came to a common agreement on payback terms for funding earned—within a 6-month period, the debt was resolved. The Bridge became an affiliate of

PHMC in 1994. Since then, the Bridge has been well managed within a fee-for-service environment and with strong leadership and is poised to grow in the coming years.

Health Promotion Council. The former executive director of Health Promotion Council (HPC) had been a long-time colleague and friend of Richard Cohen and other senior management of PHMC. However, the affiliation idea was initiated by Philadelphia-region consultant Don Kligerman, who introduced the leadership of HPC to the possibility of affiliating with a larger mission-aligned organization that could help it grow and scale. HPC affiliated in 1999 and has seen tremendous growth and expansion in services through the affiliation, including the ability to successfully bid on state funding, which it would not have been able to secure without a strong infrastructure such as PHMC's. Most recently, another PHMC affiliate, Resources for Children's Health, consolidated its programs with HPC and is now operating as a program of HPC.

National Nursing Centers Consortium. PHMC manages a network of nurse-managed federally qualified health centers and was a founding member of what eventually became the National Nursing Centers Consortium (NNCC). Total mission alignment was present from the beginning. In 2001, the board of the Regional Nursing Centers Consortium, and Tine Hansen-Turton, who was CEO, decided to go national and focus on the key policy and programmatic issues of the nurse-managed health center movement. The focus on policy and programs led the group to easily decide that affiliating with an organization with strong infrastructure and back-office support would be key to its success, as well as its need to focus on national and state policies impacting nurse practitioners and nurse-managed health clinics. As with most affiliations, the rubber hit the road when the organizations began to discuss control and ownership. In an affiliate model, the parent organization is the legal owner. However, NNCC and PHMC leadership came to an agreement: There should be an exit clause in the affiliation agreement in case the partnership should not work out. NNCC affiliated in 2002 and has seen tremendous growth for its organization while helping to transform how primary care is delivered in the United States, and it has raised more than $300 million on behalf of its members nationally. The affiliation model was key to its success in focusing on its true mission.

The Joseph J. Peters Institute. Richard Cohen and the PHMC board chair, Judge Renee Hughes, were both on the board of the Joseph J. Peters Institute (JJPI). As Richard Cohen often says, patience pays off: Over a 5-year period of discussing the possibility of becoming an affiliate, both the Office of Mental Health and the Office of Community Behavioral Health were supportive of the affiliation, which took place in 2004.

Metropolitan Career Services/Computer Technology Institute.
Metropolitan Career Services/Computer Technology Institute (MCC), one
of the region's most respected workforce and associate degree programs,
affiliated with PHMC in 2011. The affiliation came about through a relationship between the former executive director and Richard Cohen. The
executive director was very well aware that the organization would need
to close its doors if it could not gain the support of an organization such as
PHMC. At this time, PHMC is in the process of turning the organization
around, adding degrees such as allied health as well as growing the workforce programs.

Turning Points for Children. Turning Points for Children (TPFC) CEO
Michael Vogel and PHMC president Richard Cohen and CSO Tine Hansen-
Turton have known one another for years. With the change in human services
toward a community-based intervention, it became clear to Michael Vogel
that he would need to partner with more diverse nonprofits. Specifically, he
was looking for a leadership team that was entrepreneurial and that had an
eye toward future opportunities (and challenges).

Take-Home Points About the PHMC
Affiliation Model

As is the case with all partnerships, relationships built on trust are critical
to the success of nonprofit partnerships. Some of these relationships take
years to build, making patience key. The affiliation process can be taxing
on the staff of both organizations, so it is important that the leadership be
serious about affiliation. In PHMC's case, its affiliation focus tends to be on
organizations that have annual budgets of $3 million or more. The process
usually starts with the leadership of both organizations connecting and taking a joint leap of faith that a strategic alliance is the right way to go based on
a substantial and thorough due diligence process. Mission alignment is critical, and so is the leadership of the partner organization. As critical as this
mission is, equally important is the belief that a partnership will increase
opportunities to help preserve critical community assets and extend programs offered by both organizations. The enhancing of financial stability
and creation of economies of scale, particularly in administration and infrastructure, are equally critical. Finally, career advancement opportunities are
also relevant to keeping nonprofit organizational talent.

Outside agencies such as local government and foundations can play
an important role in the affiliation process, from encouraging nonprofits
to affiliate or merge to investing critical juncture funding to support the
due diligence and implementation phases of the affiliation. One miscon-
ception is that an affiliation is usually cheaper operationally. However, that
is not necessarily true, although PHMC can demonstrate that to date all of
the affiliate organizations through a PHMC partnership have been able to

drive down overhead costs over time through creating economies of scale. PHMC has been appreciative over the years of the past support of local government agencies in supporting and encouraging affiliations, as well as of funders such as the Philadelphia Foundation, United Way, and the Independence Foundation that provided critical juncture funding. More of this kind of leadership is needed to encourage more of these strategic partnerships.

Affiliate Program Profiles in Order of Year of Affiliation

Interim House. Interim House is a corporation licensed by the Commonwealth of Pennsylvania's Bureau of Drug and Alcohol Programs. Interim House provides a continuum of comprehensive services to women addicted to drugs and alcohol that comprises three levels of care: residential treatment, intensive outpatient treatment, and outpatient counseling. Incorporated in 1971, Interim House was the first such specialized program in the Commonwealth of Pennsylvania and one of the first in the nation. It has served as a model for innovative treatment of substance-abusing women. Interim House utilizes a holistic approach to treating drug and alcohol addiction that is trauma-sensitive, focusing on the physical, mental, emotional, and spiritual issues surrounding addiction. Interim House offers a wide range of therapeutic and support services to clients, with an emphasis on preventing relapse, establishing stability and responsibility, improving life and parenting skills, developing and strengthening a support system, and establishing links to support services.

The Bridge. Since 1971, the Bridge has helped over 10,000 people challenged by addictions. The primary goal of the Bridge is to provide quality, accessible treatment while preparing clients to reenter their communities as drug- and alcohol-free members of society. The Bridge is a subsidiary organization of PHMC. The Bridge understands that individuals who have become dependent on alcohol and/or other drugs usually experience many other problems. Their treatment philosophy stresses a holistic approach; interventions focus on treating the addiction, its underlying causes, and its related dysfunctions.

The Bridge offers a range of services designed to meet the needs of persons of all ages with addiction-related issues. The program serves adolescents from neighborhoods throughout Philadelphia, the suburban counties, and the state of Delaware. The Bridge offers long- and short-term residential programs for up to 38 adolescents as well as outpatient counseling for children, adolescents, and adults. Individualized treatment plans are created to meet clients' needs, and clients have access to the comprehensive addiction, mental health, educational, and life skills services provided at the Bridge.

The Health Promotion Council and Resources for Children's Health.
The HPC is a nonprofit corporation that was organized in 1981. The HPC's mission is to promote health and prevent and manage chronic diseases, especially among vulnerable populations, through community-based outreach, education, and advocacy. Its unique programs advocating positive health behaviors, together with its innovative work with minority groups, have advanced the field of health promotion in southeastern Pennsylvania and across the nation. As part of its mission to promote health and provide outreach and education, the HPC conducts family support and healthy parenting education programs. These include its Health Intervention Program and Focus on Families, formerly available through Resources for Children's Health (RCH). The HPC has a diverse, multicultural, multilingual staff and fulfills its mission through programs in four major areas: chronic disease risk reduction, chronic disease prevention and management, community and capacity building, and professional education and consulting.

The National Nursing Centers Consortium. The NNCC is the leading advocate for nurse-managed health care. The NNCC is a nonprofit corporation with the mission of strengthening the capacity, growth, and development of nurse-managed health centers, providing quality care to vulnerable populations, and eliminating health disparities in underserved communities. Founded in 1996, the NNCC joined PHMC in 2002. The NNCC advocates for accessible health care through using nurses as primary providers of health care. Our nurse-run member health centers provide community-based care that is sensitive to patient needs and concerns. The NNCC works to improve policies for nurse practitioners as primary care providers and also helps member health centers meet the costs of providing care to the uninsured and underinsured by taking the lead in developing and running programs in partnership with its member centers that help people lead healthier and safer lives. These programs help avert future health problems and keep health care costs from rising.

The Joseph J. Peters Institute. The JJPI is a nonprofit mental health agency providing outpatient assessment and treatment services in the area of sexual abuse. The JJPI's mission is to reduce the causes and overall impact and outcomes of sexually abusive behaviors through research, training, prevention, and treatment. The JJPI evaluates and treats survivors of sexual abuse as well as offenders. In addition, the JJPI provides training to organizations throughout the region, holding a national reputation for its work in assessment, treatment, prevention, and education related to sexual abuse. Its research arm has received numerous grants from foundations such as the National Institutes of Health and the National Institute of Justice.

Metropolitan Career Center. The Metropolitan Career Center (MCC) was launched in 1974 as a nonprofit workforce development organization established by the clergy and members of the First United Methodist Church of Germantown to help neighborhood youth and adults gain greater access to resources that could lead to better careers and higher education. Today, the MCC and its nonprofit career school, the Computer Technology Institute (CTI), educate and train individuals who have limited access to resources to connect them to employers and help meet the changing needs of the workforce. The MCC and CTI encourage sustainable careers and economic independence by building a supportive learning environment in which students receive personalized attention. To further that mission, CTI, an approved and accredited training provider through the Department of Education and one of the few nonprofit secondary career schools in Pennsylvania, offers an associate degree in specialized technology and a diploma in health information technology.

Turning Points for Children. TPFC is one of PHMC's recent affiliates. TPFC serves approximately 2,500 families and 5,700 children per year through a range of prevention and intervention programs. TPFC joined PHMC on February 1, 2013, with the intent to operationalize natural synergies between TPFC's prevention and child welfare services and PHMC's medical and behavioral health services. This affiliation enables TPFC to offer more comprehensive and coordinated services for children and families. TPFC was initially created in 2008, when the Children's Aid Society of Pennsylvania (CASPA) merged with the Philadelphia Society for Services to Children (PSSC). CASPA and PSSC—both small organizations similar to each other in size, mission, and programming—chose to merge in order to become one organization with a stronger infrastructure with more sustainable resources. This merger has proven to be a successful venture in that the organization can now operate more efficiently, has a greater ability to attract public and private funding, and has an enhanced portfolio of outcome-based services through which to serve vulnerable children and families. Before the merger, the PSSC and CASPA had nearly 300 years of collective experience in serving youth and families. For many decades, the services were primarily related to placement (foster care, group homes, residential treatment, and adoption). With the beginning of family support strategies in the early 1970s, the agencies began to provide in-home and community-based services. TPFC uses its resources to serve those struggling with the effects of chronic poverty: difficult family relationships, domestic violence, substance abuse, child abuse and neglect, teen pregnancy, poor education and high dropout rates, unemployment, substandard housing, and inadequate health care. The goal is not simply to prevent negative outcomes but to help families recognize and act upon their strengths, helping them reach their greatest potential by identifying and achieving individual and family goals. Throughout TPFC's programming, there is a long history of effectively working with children, youth, and families to enable them to develop the skills they need to set and achieve goals, overcome obstacles, locate and utilize community resources, advocate on their own behalves, and develop stability, healthy lifestyles and productive futures. Turning Points for Children is accredited by the Council on Accreditation (COA) and is a member of the Alliance for Children and Families and the Pennsylvania Council for Children, Youth and Family Services (PCCYFS).

Recognized nationally as an authority in the public health management arena, PHMC's president and CEO Richard J. Cohen has led the organization since 1980. Dr. Cohen leads close to 1,400 employees, over 250 public health programs, and approximately 10 subsidiary organizations. Under his watch, the organization has expanded more than 75-fold and continues to grow, with a current operating budget of approximately $180 million. Dr. Cohen has devoted his professional life to the needs of Philadelphia and the surrounding region while playing a critical role at a national level as well.

Tine Hansen-Turton is the chief strategy officer of PHMC, where she develops and supports PHMC's overall strategy and leads partnership development around new and emerging business opportunities. She works across the organization, but specifically oversees Management Services and the Research and Evaluation Group. She also manages organizational development and learning, regional emergency preparedness services, and mergers and affiliations, as well as the trade associations National Nursing Centers Consortium and Convenient Care Association. She is nationally known for her development and policy systems-change work with nurse-led care as well as for expanding access to care for millions through retail clinics.

A TALE OF TWO CITIES: SELLER AND BUYER—THE HOLY FAMILY INSTITUTE AND PUBLIC HEALTH MANAGEMENT PARTNERSHIP

Partnerships

Partnerships can take many forms. In the late summer of 2012, two Alliance for Children and Families Strategy Counts grantees, the Holy Family Institute (HFI) in Pittsburgh and Public Health Management Corporation (PHMC) in Philadelphia, came together to discuss a partnership through which the HFI could divest itself of a major program—St. Mary's Villa for Children and Families (SMVCF)—in such a manner that both organizations, the youth being served, and the employees would all benefit. The idea of PHMC as likely partner was not an accident. For years, the CEOs of the two agencies had discussed the possibility of this idea should the HFI ever decide to divest itself of SMVCF. What made the project easier was that both leaders had a single point of contact, their chief strategy officers, who could work together and who had the authority and oversight within each of their organizations to get things done as needed and set the stage for a long-term partnership beyond the current initiative.

Making a Mission-Driven Decision:
HFI's $9 Million Question

For many years, the HFI had somewhat insulated itself against cutbacks in government funding by diversifying its programs and revenue streams, and by finding support in the strong and generous philanthropic community that Pittsburgh enjoys. However, the present economic environment has required the HFI to strategically assess its future. In the true spirit of viewing challenges as opportunities, the HFI examined a number of realignment options, including divesting itself of the SMVCF program as a way to improve services and ensure organizational sustainability.

St. Mary's Villa for Children and Families has been providing residential services for children and youth for 100 years and was sponsored by the Sisters of the Holy Family of Nazareth (SHFN). In 2001, SMVCF merged with the Holy Family Institute, another sponsored ministry of the SHFN. Under the HFI's management, SMVCF was able to stabilize its residential program and acquire an outpatient license and a private academic license. However, the program had not diversified or grown enough to be economically self-sufficient. Its mission was clear, but the challenges of managing SMVCF from a distance, including not having the high levels of investor relationships needed to help the programs thrive, along with the current economic challenges across the state, made divesting ourselves of that part of our programs a difficult but necessary decision. It's very tough to think about giving up a legacy program and a $9 million income stream. The HFI worked with its management team in both locations to view the situation not as a failure of the present but as an opportunity for success into the future.

Strategic Choices

The strategic choices were few: Either we (HFI) find a partner with a like mission, proven experience, and a passion for continuing our work into the future (our best case) or we dissolve the corporation (our worst case), which would require closing the program. Our thoughts went first to the people. "So what happens to those we serve?" Because of the trauma that dissolving would have caused to the youth we serve, to our staff, and to the child welfare community, we focused our energy on identifying local, respected, and experienced organizations, with common values and strong local-investor relationships, that were willing to take over all the programs and the staff.

Four potential partners were identified based on mission and value alignment, location, capacity, and commitment to sustaining and growing the SMVCF programs. Many conference calls were conducted to better understand the needs, desires, interest, and motivation of the potential partners. We conducted many site visits and met with senior leadership and operations staff. We also met with our local funders (payers to our programs) to ensure that transferring the programs to another organization would be permitted. All the hard work and diligence paid off. About 4 months into our process, we knew exactly what we could do and how we could do it, even though it would not be easy to give up the program nurtured over the last 100 years.

Of the partners we identified, our clear and easy choice was to work with Public Health Management Corporation of Philadelphia. The hard work to find a trusted partner to take over the program resulted in continued and uninterrupted service to the youth and continued employment for the staff.

Making a Mission-Driven Decision: PHMC's $9 Million Question

A critical point in determining whether a partnership can work between two organizations is the mission alignment. In this case, the missions of both PHMC and the HFI were aligned in their focus on children and youth services. PHMC was already in the business of residential treatment and had a desire to grow the business to serve more children and youth, so there was mission alignment from the get-go from PHMC's perspective, including a respect for the HFI as long-term colleagues.

Due Diligence

Due diligence is the act of evaluating all the possibilities, and the implications of those possibilities, for a particular situation, an activity engaged in by both buyer and seller. It is the part in the process where all information is collected that will have a substantively materially effect on the decision to move forward, or not, on an opportunity.

Due diligence for the seller includes such things as conducting financial analysis of the impact of the divestiture, sale, or transfer of property or programs, identifying the value of and the process for selling off or transferring real and personal property, identifying how leased items (e.g., physical plant, office equipment) and vendor contracts can and will be managed, understanding the issues surrounding all current licenses and permits (transfer, get new, terminate); managing employee termination (meeting state and federal regulations such as the WARN Act), transfers, accrued vacation time (can be huge), benefits, 401(k) plans, and the like; and readying the reports for the buyer, among many other tasks.

Due diligence for the buyers includes such things as ensuring that the new business will meet their mission and align with and strengthen their current business portfolio, taking all the time needed to analyze and understand the business from a financial perspective (this will require many conversations between both parties), conducting multiple site visits, meeting with leadership and staff teams, figuring out staffing needs, identifying licensing requirements, seeking approval from government officials (e.g., the state attorney general and local contractors such as human services departments), vendor management, and so forth.

In addition, committee recommendations and board approvals are required each step of the way. When multiple boards are involved, a clear plan of who needs to do what and when is critical. In addition, both buyer and seller will want and need to have trusted legal counsel who are experienced in business acquisitions and contracts. Throughout the process, the boards' decisions will rely heavily on the recommendations of the attorneys. The attorneys will also be involved in many of the conference calls on which legal matters are discussed. Note that due diligence continues throughout the entire process right down to the day of transfer. As issues emerged during our partnership process, both parties conducted their own investigations into the matter and came back together to compare notes and take action.

Who Needs to Be on the Team?

Deciding who was needed on the team, assembling the team, and ensuring that they gave the transaction high priority and would be available for all calls were critical to the success of the project. Team members were chosen and aligned between both parties. The alignment went to the person or persons responsible for a particular function of the organization. For example, the chief strategy officers worked together as the points of contact for all communications and activities and were responsible for holding others accountable for work plans and deadlines. We also brought the key leadership teams together, including lawyers, CFOs, and COOs, on a regular basis to ensure that the terms of the deals along the way were agreed upon at the highest levels.

Other pairings included having our respective CFOs manage the financials, and having our respective HR directors manage all the HR work. In addition, members of the team on both sides were selected to work together to obtain all the required licenses, transfer or assign leases, manage vendors, transfer phone and data lines, transfer vehicles, manage marketing and communication (to the staff and public), and—one of the most important tasks—coordinate our respective IT teams. IT oversaw the websites, employee data, employee emails, client records, and transfers of all servers, software, hardware, email addresses, and so forth.

Sample Checklist at Transition Point

The following is a list of general issues that need to be addressed and resolved, including those that were specific to the HFI-PHMC partnership.

Agreements

Develop the transfer agreement
Acquire attorney general notice or approval
Transfer licenses or acquire new licenses related to the transfer
Transfer or negotiate new contracts
Transfer or reapply for applicable local or state licenses
Transfer relevant service agreements
Transfer or assign the lease

Vehicles

Reassign, retitle, and notarize vehicles
Cancel and get new vehicle insurance policies

Insurance

End and renew insurance policies
Property
Professional liability
Workers comp
Pay for insurance rider on PHMC/Bridge insurance policy to cover items in event of loss

Human Resources

Continue or obtain new insurance policies
Continue health, dental, and eye policies for all active SMVCF employees as of the transfer date
Notify COBRA administrator in order to deliver COBRA information to employees who had remained on the HFI's medical, dental, vision, and medical flex spending policies
Notify Liberty Mutual to remove employees from life, disability, and FMLA policies at the time of transfer
Notify broker about unemployment and workers comp

Employees

HRIS System
  Terminate HR records
  Terminate payroll records
  Stop benefit deductions and fringe benefits
  Send termination letter to all employees, explaining what will happen to their benefits
  401(k): Send distribution paperwork within a few weeks of transfer to affected employees
  Change date and send personnel action form
  Identify and pay out vacation accruals

Finance

Vendor/Contracts
  Terminate vendor contracts and accounts
Utilities
  Terminate and start new accounts for all utility services, including (but not limited to):

Gas
Electric
Water
Sewer
Fuel
Telephone

IT/Communication

Terminate all communication pathways
    IT T1 lines
    Phone lines
Terminate and renew software

Records

Develop a clear process for transferring records, including
    Active client records (residential, medical, school)
    Inactive records
Transfer records in storage and both active and inactive records on site
Transfer donor lists as spelled out in contract

Public relations

Develop and implement press release about the transfer
Issue private communications to donors
Create general public knowledge
Create government offices
Contact vendors and suppliers

Challenges

Before we describe the challenges of transfer, it needs to be noted that the success of this project stemmed from the continuous communication, clarity of purpose, dedication to mission, and most of all, respect and trust between all parties that kept this project on solid ground throughout the process. For example, although new licenses were required for the outpatient, residential, and education programs—licenses that had to be applied for and submitted by PHMC—that task could only be achieved by working with the HFI because we knew the details of the programs, had the state and local contacts, and had been through the licensing and renewal processes before. It would have been very difficult, and would have led to extended timelines, had good communication and willingness to work together toward a common goal not been in place or had relationships between top key players not been built face-to-face early in the process.

The saying goes that "theory changes in application," and so it goes with transactions such as this. Luckily, the biggest challenges were not between people, but with time. It seemed that no matter how well we planned, everything took longer than expected. Overall, we failed to realize that we were in the middle of the transfer during some of the most popular vacation and holiday times of the year—from Thanksgiving through New Year's Day. We originally thought the transfer could take place by Thanksgiving, then by December 31, then by January 31, and then by February 28—it actually took place on April 1, 2013.

One example of one of our timeline challenges was the one that emerged on February 27. We all thought the property would transfer on February 28, 2013. On February 27th, the state licensing boards sent out the completed and approved outpatient and residential licenses. But at that time, the attorney general had not yet approved the transfer of assets, which stopped us in our tracks and delayed the closing. So at this point, the new organization had a license but no clients and no lease to be on the property (not until transfer), while the current organization had no license to operate. Communication back to the licensing boards quickly resolved the issues—but, again, it took time.

Another example of a time delay centered on getting the Pennsylvania Department of Education's approval for the education licenses. Because two new school licenses were required, applications for each school had to be completed and submitted. As that process started, we found out that the licenses would be approved after a meeting with the Pennsylvania State Board of Education. That board only met four times a year, and the next meeting was toward the end of April, but we were already ready to transfer all employees, assets, leases, and so forth, and the outpatient and residential licenses were awaiting our call. To move forward with the transfer on April 1, and after much investigation, a business services agreement (BSA) was drafted that allowed our schools to remain open using HFI's license and the new owner's staff and assets (to be transferred on April 1). That BSA would be in effect until the two new education licenses were received.

Tips When Partnering

- Keep your eye on your mission.
- Communicate often.
- Don't let things slide—deal with them today.
- Have a clear contact list of who does what—and use it.
- Have a single person from each organization with the knowledge and authority to get things done be responsible for the project.
- Rely heavily on and listen to your legal counsel.
- Figure out your best guess on how long it will take and keep to the plan, but be prepared for the timeline to double. The shorter timeline will generate the productive tension to keep everyone on track.

About the Partners

Public Health Management Corporation is a large, state-recognized, non-profit public health institute with more than 250 programs in diverse areas that include workforce development, primary care, health promotion, behavioral health, human services, and early intervention, serving more than 200,000 people annually. As a public health institute, PHMC improves public health outcomes by fostering innovation, leveraging resources, and building partnerships with governmental agencies, communities, the health care delivery system, media, and academia.

Holy Family Institute is a nonprofit social services organization in the western Pennsylvania region. Our mission is to empower children and families to lead responsible lives and develop healthy and meaningful relationships built on faith, hope, and love. We do this by helping children, youth, adults, and families overcome the challenges of isolation, poverty, trauma, addiction, abuse, and neglect by partnering with them to cocreate a vision for the lives they want to live and doing all we can to transform that vision into a reality. Our current service portfolio contains 18 lines of service, and we currently serve over 13,000 people and families annually.

CHAPTER 11

Responding to Policy Change and Creating Policy Impact and Systems Change Through Strategy

Marilyn Mason-Plunkett, Timothy Johnstone, Barbara Vollmer,
Daniel L. Daly, and Rebecca M. Robuck

CREATING SYSTEMS CHANGE AND POLICY IMPACT THROUGH STRATEGY AT HOPELINK

The ground under nonprofits is shifting quickly and profoundly, especially for organizations with a mission to ameliorate or solve intractable social problems. In the current political and economic environment, the demand for increased and more measurable service impacts is greater than ever before, with agency and program funding increasingly tied to demonstrable success. This is ultimately a positive trend for the nonprofit sector, but it is a sea change in its operational implications for many nonprofits.

The scrutiny and accompanying demands for accountability will become even more intense as government budget woes deepen and performance-based contracting proponents become more common. To thrive during this period of change and uncertainty, savvy organizations are getting out in front of these changes and developing clear and effective long-term strategies to influence positive change in their communities and in their clients' lives.

These high-performing organizations are learning that effective social change must come as a result of a collective effort, not the isolated interventions that have often been the more traditional approach to solving specific social problems. In fact, studies of impact successes have led more and more often to the conclusion that large-scale social change *only* comes with better cross-sector coordination (Kania & Kramer, 2011). This recognition is causing a profound shift in thinking as organizations look beyond their borders, not just to their peers in the nonprofit world but to other sectors as well, to look for solutions and for partners in achieving their missions.

This is much easier said than done, and many early attempts at collaboration met with failure. But the successes, those that resulted in the biggest impacts, had things in common worth noting and replicating. First and foremost, these organizations not only wanted to help people in their communities, but they also had an "unstoppable desire to create *lasting* impact as well" (Crutchfield & Grant, 2008, p. 24). In the most successful cases, this passion has led nonprofit leaders to a crystal-clear statement of mission and guided their thinking about the broad drivers of the impact they sought.

It has also become apparent that lasting impact requires a fundamental change in the way the communities served by these nonprofits approach these problems. Ultimately, *all* sectors of the community—nonprofits, governmental entities, for-profit businesses, and individual citizens—must transform the way they approach and make decisions about policies, programs, the allocation of resources, and, in the end, the way they deliver services to people who need them (Crutchfield & Grant, 2008, p. 6). This can be a daunting task, one that requires all stakeholders to develop and use new skills, learn how to lead and drive the necessary systems changes in their communities, and develop and execute broader strategies to guide them.

The complexity and scope of both the social problems that need to be solved *and* the collaboration necessary to solve them require a fresh approach to strategy development, planning, and execution.

Driving Systems Change Through Strategy

It all starts at home. Nonprofit organizations committed to driving lasting change must first develop a deep understanding of the nature of the broader problem. They must then clearly define what success looks like—including both their role and what others' roles in the process might be. To do that, these organizations must develop a clear view of their target service areas, and they must also know who else in the community is serving the same client base and how those services are being provided.

The first step is developing a clear understanding of the theory (or theories) of change that will yield the desired results. Having strong evidence that the broad approach and collective interventions suggested by the theory of change is important, for purposes of both internal alignment and external communication. To make lasting change for clients and the communities in which they live, theories must predict solid, positive impact on clients and the community—and they *must* deliver.

Many social problems that nonprofits want to affect defy easy measurement. Some are of a more technical nature, with well-defined issues and determinable solutions, so the answer is known in advance; these are social issues for which one organization, or a combination of several, has the ability to implement a solution. However, the more complex, adaptive-style social problems that most organizations face are quite the opposite, with answers not fully known in advance and no single entity having the resources or authority to bring about the necessary change (Kania & Kramer, 2011, p. 39). As a result, successful organizations aren't always able to immediately quantify their results but nevertheless work hard at rigorously assembling the combination of quantitative and qualitative evidence that enables them to track their progress (Collins, 2005, p. 7).

After the theory of change and the related success measures are established, the next step is to identify all the elements of change that must be influenced to yield the desired results for clients and the community, and then to determine the indicators of success for each such element. Logic models can be applied to each element of success to understand the combination of interventions that may yield the best result. Because the theory of change may be quite broad in scope, care must be taken to include the timing and coordination of interventions that best benefit each client.

This thinking drives program changes as well. In the past, nonprofits may have painted clients with broad swaths, using generic, one-size-fits-all services with activity-based outputs and outcomes. The recognition that this approach is not as effective for driving permanent results for clients has triggered the realization for many agencies that their programs may need to be modified. In addition, this new approach may call for a significant shift in organizational culture. However, after these organizations understand the drivers of broader success, they can make much more effective choices about resource allocation.

At the core of program evaluation is the need to develop a deep understanding of the organization's own strengths, weaknesses, and passions, as well as those of other organizations and potential collaborators or partners. Because the adaptive issues that the nonprofit sector is facing today often require collective, cross-sector coalitions and the development of systematic solutions (Kania & Kramer, 2011, p. 39), developing an understanding of the collective competence of the resources in the organization's service area is foundational to successful program development. And these areas of collective strength are where the opportunities for client success—and future funding opportunities—lie. This approach to program analysis can also lead to learning the key drivers of success for more narrowly defined groups of clients. Understanding which program interventions are most effective for clients of a specific age, gender, or cultural heritage can yield striking results.

Internally, the organization's culture may need to evolve as it becomes ever clearer that the time of doing good work in a silo and simply reporting outcomes has passed. Smart agencies are by necessity becoming highly disciplined and determined about leveraging their core strengths, strategically yielding their less effective activities to others having greater core competencies in a particular arena. They also are making good but difficult decisions to shed less efficient and less effective programs in order to create the greatest impact possible with their available resources. At the same time, effective organizations are becoming more aware and adept at engaging in richer collaborations with others, all in the effort to yield greater impact on client outcomes.

This doesn't happen on an ad hoc basis. When an organization understands itself and its role, it must create a strategy that can be shared and that will work to transform the thinking of others. Interventions directed at system improvements are likely to be more practical and realistic in today's resource-constrained environment (Fleming et al., 2010, pp. 1–2). A recent U.S. Justice Department study suggested that to transform a community's systems, all five of the following strategic elements must be created or change simultaneously:

1. Joint governance and shared decision making
2. Cultural competence
3. A unified fiscal strategy
4. Service coordination and integration
5. Supportive public policy (USDOJ, 1999)

As a part of the strategic planning process, successful organizations build in short- and long-term goals for understanding and analyzing their roles in leading change in the broader community. This process may take years of continuing analysis, evaluation, and midcourse corrections, but if it is done deliberately and intentionally, it can yield transformational results.

A Case Lesson

As one example, the Community Action Partnership (CAP) is a collection of more than 1,000 agencies nationally that share a commitment to ending poverty by promoting self-sufficiency and helping clients make lasting change. They also share a commitment to local solutions for local problems, so they work within their local communities to identify and create solutions that are holistic and crafted to the specific needs of their communities. When one of these partner agencies in Washington State examined these commitments more carefully in order to better measure its impact on both the clients served and the local community, it realized that "self-sufficiency" was both an elusive concept and inadequate to describe what its clients needed and wanted. This was further accentuated through recognition of the diverse cultural populations the agency served.

Historically, a key metric for success in moving low-income people out of poverty has been the federal poverty line. This measure was created in the mid-1960s by calculating the amount of money it cost to buy a basic amount of food and then multiplying that amount by three. Each year, the line is updated to account for inflation. However, the causes and solutions of "poverty" are complex and multifaceted and thus require more than a static number that was created more than 50 years ago and that is based on economic circumstances and measures that have changed dramatically since that time. Because that threshold is used to determine eligibility for federal, state, and local assistance, understanding what it takes to move clients out of poverty has vast implications for the clients served by CAP agencies. However, given the well-documented limitations of the federal poverty line measurement, a deeper dive into the dynamics of poverty has taken place in the more recent past.

Working from that view, the agency took a closer look at its community and found that within the broad category of poverty, several key learnings emerged that helped it refine and reshape its core programs to more fully address its mission. The first was a result of recognizing how fragile the platform of stability is for people living in poverty and how prone to crisis they live on a daily basis. Thus people living in poverty experience ongoing stress and often live with a pervasive sense of hopelessness. Clarifying that perspective, the agency recognized that helping people achieve success in creating even short-term stability with the basic needs of food, shelter, warmth, and safety was a highly important foundation from which its clients could then focus on setting and working toward mid- to longer-term goals to build the personal skills and assets they would need to move permanently out of poverty.

A second area of service developed from the recognition that there is a significant group of people who will never achieve full economic self-sufficiency but who nevertheless can achieve a high level of quality of life, independence, well-being, and self-efficacy. These people might have permanent physical or mental barriers or simply live on fixed incomes owing to retirement or other situations. Living on a fixed, relatively restricted income often engenders a sense of permanent anxiety. Understanding this enabled the agency to offer services to that segment of its clients with a menu of targeted assistance, focusing on those services that enable consumers in such circumstances to reduce their reliance on public assistance and also achieve a greater feeling of security, thus realizing an enhanced quality of life in the long term.

A third and critical insight came with the recognition of differences that exist within the broad category of poverty and the resources needed to address these differences. Generational poverty and situational poverty are different, for example. Situational poverty is typically of shorter duration and is caused by circumstance, whereas generational poverty is defined as being in poverty for two or more generations. Where situational poverty can often be addressed in a straightforward manner with various resources, addressing generational poverty is a more complex process (Payne, DeVol, & Smith, 2006, p. 6). Depending on the particular needs of the family, clients living in generational poverty may need access to a variety of resources, which can include financial, emotional, mental, physical, and spiritual resources, as well as support systems and knowledge of middle-class hidden rules and role models (Payne, DeVol, & Smith, 2006, pp. 11–13). Successful poverty-reduction programs have recognized that clients do not need (or want) to be in long-term, highly prescriptive programs with specific steps outlined by agency experts. Agencies recognized that impact occurred when they used more holistic, strengths-based approaches that (a) appreciated the complexity of individuals and family units, (b) holistically supported clients' strengths and resilience and built on both, (c) identified obstacles that clients needed to remove or mitigate, and (d) provided a success platform on which clients were able build the personal skills, assets, and tools they would need to acquire to move successfully—and permanently—out of poverty.

These learnings fundamentally changed the work of the agency. While CAP is a large organization and provides a broad level of services to support clients in their journeys, it quickly recognized that it does not cover all of the life domains in which clients need to be successful. As a result of this work, a burgeoning realization came that in some life domains, service interventions were woefully lacking in the community. "Workarounds" were developed to help clients in the short term, and collaborative community and provider discussions have begun to seek more permanent, systemwide solutions.

Further insight came from a deeper understanding of cultural differences in client groups. While demographic data had long been captured and individual service providers within the agency had always tried to accommodate the individuality of clients, the realization that basic needs and success mean different things in different cultures was profound, especially in a community that has become exponentially more diverse in the past decades.

For the agency, two important changes came out of this analysis. First, the role of the case manager was changed from one of urging prescriptive assignments upon client families to one of joining with the clients as collaborative coaches. A significant investment was made in training and developing these professionals to help them be consistent and more effective with clients while also enabling the clients to develop and own the behaviors and changes they identified as necessary.

Second, a targeted effort was initiated to identify and develop deeper relationships with other organizations and entities that would be critical partners in a holistic approach to working with clients in the key areas in which they needed specific assistance. While these relationships are not formed quickly or easily, the understanding and clearer communication with partners has the long-term potential to improve client outcomes significantly. Thus, focused partnerships and coalitions with community members, government, private businesses, and other nonprofits are increasingly becoming part of the mix to help clients as they make the challenging transition from poverty toward permanent self-sufficiency.

This broad effort was undertaken very intentionally. In its strategic planning process, the agency developed a clear vision of the future that included a goal to improve its effectiveness and the impact of its services on both the clients and the communities served. It also set the stretch goal of dramatically increasing the number of clients it affected while raising the level of success each achieved. To achieve lasting impact, organizational leaders must be able to observe the larger system at work and create a collective intervention that includes the entire value delivery system, not just the components in which they engage (Rainey, 2006). While community partners are not always able to predict the detailed outcomes of their collective efforts, they can make much better judgments about the direction they and their collaborators need to travel when they can see the larger community goal. Even then, things will likely not happen as they expect, so building a strategic process that allows for flexible, rapid, and collective course corrections is important (Burns, 2007, p. 39).

Policy Impact

For many nonprofit organizations, active participation in helping shape public policy may seem daunting and is therefore often prioritized behind internally focused strategy development and execution. This may be because of agencies' perception that they lack experience in the political arena, as well as the ongoing challenge of providing direct services to their clients with increasingly limited resources. Thus, the tendency is to focus strategy development and execution on internal process improvements, adoption of evidence-based programs, and increased client outcomes, not only because these are so important (to clients served and to funders) but also because they seem more controllable. The demands and "strings" placed on organizations by clients, donors, grantors, and others all compete for strategic attention. Many organizations barely have time to just react to everything else, let alone address other issues effectively.

Yet public and social policy changes can be key to true system change; these factors can have the biggest effects on an organization's success and its ability to effectively achieve its mission. Even in the best of times the sands can shift unexpectedly, but in the current highly volatile world of wild swings in public sentiment and tight government budgets, leaving public policy to unnamed others is a mistake. As a U.S. Justice Department (1999) study suggested, public policy changes are critical to overall systems change success. Thus organizations seeking greater impact must learn how to work with government and advocate for policy change in addition to providing services (Crutchfield & Grant, 2008, p. 6).

It is almost impossible for any single organization to sway the broad opinion of a state legislature or Congress in a meaningful way, and there is no amount of money that can't be spent in the attempt. And yet the nonprofit sector has typically operated using an approach that was geared toward finding a solution within a single organization—what has been called looking for "isolated impact" (Crutchfield & Grant, 2008, p. 38). The secret to success lies in how well organizations can mobilize *every* sector of society—government, businesses, nonprofits, and the public—to be forces for good. Large-scale social change requires broad cross-sector coordination, not just the isolated intervention of individual organizations (Kania & Kramer, 2011, p. 38).

There are two truths that, at first, seem to contradict each other but that in fact are complementary. The first: In order to have any impact on public policy and systems change, individual nonprofits must employ a very narrow focus and specific intent. To do that, advocacy goals must become an integral part of agency strategy. However, the second truth is just as important: Nonprofits must be part of a larger, collective effort across sectors, something in which they have not traditionally engaged (Kania & Kramer, 2011, p. 39).

How? As a first step, organizations must develop as much clarity as possible around the opportunities for and threats to them. Areas of funding concentration and short-term, high-dollar government contracts or grants should be key focus areas. As much as possible should be learned about how those decisions are made and are likely to be made in the future, as well as who the influential decision-makers are. Because this is seldom a core competency for nonprofit organizations, determining this may require professional assistance.

Second, the nonprofit must develop a long-term, multipartner strategic initiative to advocate with and for its clients to specifically target the work that will lead to a positive impact on the policies that directly affect the ability to implement successful initiatives. This requires not only broad participation by many of the agency's stakeholders but also the prioritization of funding for this initiative. The effort can begin with small dollars that can increase over time: For example, in the first year, an organization could fund a consultant to advise it, and then commit some dollars toward a modest lobbying effort in the following year.

Third, the nonprofit must identify potential partners with interests that align with its own. One local agency partnered with 30 other agencies in its state that had similar missions and created a statewide impact statement and a communal dashboard. The partners also came together to fund a state-level lobbyist who could follow and collectively inform them about the progress of their agenda in the state legislature; these agencies also helped support a national effort to fund a federal-level lobbyist who would inform them of congressional work, the federal legislative agenda, and the ongoing decision-making process. Both the state and federal lobbyists are able to get key information into the hands of decision makers about the important work being done. Because the agencies shared the expense and data-gathering work, the cost to each was modest.

Fourth, know when to supplement the collective effort with individual action. One of the agencies in the partnership described above decided that not all of its key initiatives were being represented by the collective dashboard and the state lobbyist, so it additionally funded a part-time lobbyist to address the unique and specific interests that were critical to its success. This organization carefully coordinated the efforts of the two to ensure maximum impact and avoid duplication of effort.

Fifth, stay focused and choose battles carefully. Once an organization is identified as being "in the game," it will be called upon to lend support to one side or another of every issue that surfaces. While the sentiment of being a good neighbor is embedded in nonprofit DNA, it is very expensive to lobby on everything, and, more importantly, doing so highly dilutes an organization's influence. Legislators appreciate being approached with a clear and consistent message backed up with data that informs them. Maintain a tight and clearly communicated agenda.

Sixth, use internal resources to augment and optimize the paid lobbyist's work. An agency's strategic public policy initiative should include having its CEO, clients, board members, and subject matter experts dedicate time to the effort, be available to testify on important issues to legislative committees, or call on legislators to help them understand key issues from the agency's perspective and the potential effects of proposed legislation.

Finally, listen to feedback and use it to modify and refine the advocacy strategy and agenda. Many agencies ignore or discount the information they get from their lobbyists because they believe "there's nothing we can do." That is not the case. Learning to read patterns in the shifting sands, and then constantly evaluating how an organization's mission and areas of competence fit into those patterns, can help every entity be more effective in channeling resources and energy into programs that provide the most effective outcomes.

One organization reported having been given information that a late-arising but critical amendment, which could have had a huge negative effect on their agency, had been added to a budget request. The agency was able to inform and educate legislators about the issue, even late in the session, and the budget amendment was defeated—averting potential disaster.

For a relatively modest investment in time and resources, an agency can have a significant impact on key elements of legislative agendas that will positively affect its ability to achieve its mission. Further, the information gained about pending legislation, changes in the way funding decisions are made, and opportunities to add incremental value by taking advantage of legislative priorities can and should influence the ongoing evaluation of strategic plans and agendas.

Expanding the reach of nonprofit organizations beyond those we serve to include all who play a role in shaping our community—from makers of public policy and partners throughout the community to those delivering complementary services—is the path to greater effectiveness for the clients we all serve. Doing so with strategic intent and careful planning can dramatically improve the odds of success while providing the bold organization with an opportunity to step to the front to lead these collaborative efforts.

BOYS TOWN'S ROLE IN THE STRATEGIC EFFORT TO REFORM NEBRASKA'S CHILD WELFARE SYSTEM THROUGH PRIVATIZATION

The following section describes the significant role Boys Town has played in Nebraska's efforts to improve its child welfare system through privatization. As a partner in Nebraska Families Collaborative, the remaining private

Lead Agency the state contracts with, Boys Town has been immersed in the financial, political, programmatic, philosophical, and sometimes emotional debate and negotiations that have punctuated the venture, now in its fourth year.

The Need for Reform

Nebraska's child welfare system was broken. For years, the state had ranked near the bottom nationally in federal Child and Family Services Review (CFSR) measures of safety, permanency, and well-being outcomes for children and near the top in the rate at which it removed children from their homes. In fact, as recently as 2011, Nebraska was removing children from their homes at the second-highest rate in the country (7.9 children per 1,000, more than twice the national average of 3.4 children per 1,000). Caseloads for state caseworkers were above national recommended standards, and families often were forced to navigate an inconsistent, fragmented, and unfamiliar system. And, like many other states, Nebraska was on a federal performance improvement plan for not achieving its desired outcomes.

Nebraska Gov. Dave Heineman and the director of the Department Health and Human Services decided that Nebraska could better serve its children and families. In 2009, as part of an effort to improve and reform the child welfare system, the Nebraska Department of Health and Human Services (DHHS) finalized contracts with five Lead Agencies that would assume service coordination and service provision responsibilities. (In Nebraska's privatization effort, a Lead Agency is defined as a private agency—or a collection of private organizations—that contracts with the Department of Health and Human Services to assume responsibility for managing the care and treatment of children and families that are involved with the child welfare and/or juvenile justice systems.)

One of those five Lead Agencies was the Nebraska Families Collaborative (NFC). The NFC was created through the formation of a partnership of Boys Town and four other respected local organizations, each with many years of experience serving children and families. Boys Town was instrumental in bringing these organizations together to form an entity that would be able to manage care with quality service provision as its main focus. The other partner organizations are the Child Saving Institute (CSI), Heartland Family Services, the Nebraska Family Support Network, and OMNI Behavioral Health. These organizations were selected because they had years of experience working with Nebraska's children and families, could provide a comprehensive network of needed services, and together could provide guidance on services needed in the general eastern Nebraska provider community. Also, the NFC Board comprised representatives of service provider organizations.

Thus, Boys Town entered the world of managing care for children and families, and Nebraska began its often tumultuous journey to improve its child welfare system through a public–private partnership known as privatization. The reasons for Boys Town's direct involvement in Nebraska's reform effort are numerous and varied.

Historically, Boys Town has always been a direct services provider, offering children and families a wide variety of life-changing services and programs through our Integrated Continuum of Care®. The Integrated Continuum enables Boys Town to link four main categories of care in a research-proven approach that is based on the consistent delivery of the Boys Town Model®.

- **Behavioral health care**, which includes psychiatric residential, outpatient mental health, and substance abuse interventions
- **Out-of-home services**, which includes foster care and group care
- **In-home and community-based services**, which include the Boys Town National Hotline®, Common Sense Parenting® classes, and community- and school-based programs
- **Health care**, which includes physical health care and research and treatment of communication disorders in young children

This unique approach enables us to help more children and families in more ways with the same expectations for positive results. For children, this means being successful in school, at home, and on the job while growing into productive citizens. For families, it means having a safe home, being able to solve problems, and staying together. For communities, it means stronger families and neighborhoods and a safer, more productive society.

While Boys Town has taken a leadership role in advocating for change in child care systems, taking on the task of managing care was a big step into uncharted waters. Boys Town had never viewed itself as a manager of services, and had not seen the required business and financial model as something in which we wanted to be involved. However, Boys Town decided to move forward because we saw the state's reform effort as the first window of opportunity in recent times to significantly improve the quality of services for children and families in the child welfare system.

Boys Town felt an obligation to actively participate in system reform, because doing so fit well with our advocacy of finding better ways to help children by keeping more families together. Furthermore, taking a leadership role in managing care matched well with our strategic plan goal of growing more family- and community-based programs. And the experience of partnering with other organizations and individuals in a collaborative reform initiative would serve us well as we worked with community leaders to identify and address the needs of children and families in specific neighborhoods.

Getting Established

In establishing a framework for its privatization venture, the state of Nebraska set the following goals:

- Improved CFSR outcomes in the areas of safety, permanency, and well-being
- Serving more children in their homes rather than through out-of-home care
- Shared ownership in achievement of outcomes through public–private connections
- A streamlined system for families that reduced or eliminated service gaps
- Greater use of best practices and evidence-based models
- Improved continuity of services and stability of placements
- Individualized service plans rather than a limited menu of specific services
- Performance-based contracts with incentives and sanctions
- Aftercare services and support

To prepare for privatization, Boys Town took a number of steps to establish a solid foundation for creating the Nebraska Families Collaborative.

- First, Boys Town sought to manage liability. Making the NFC a separate 501(c)(3) allowed it to purchase separate insurance and mitigate risks.
- Second, Boys Town selected local partner organizations with a shared vision, quality programs, solid management and staff, services Boys Town didn't offer, and a wide-ranging capacity to network with providers, funders, and advocates. All of the organizations were experienced and widely respected.

After decisions were made about the best legal structure and partners, Boys Town and its NFC partners turned to learning more about how to make privatization work in Nebraska.

- Boys Town drew on its extensive experience as a service provider in states such as Florida and New York, as well as still others where reform initiatives had been under way for years.
- Boys Town and its NFC partners visited organizations that served as Lead Agencies and sought advice from experts with national reputations in privatization. We learned about the critical elements of developing a successful structure, as well as about the successes and failures other states had experienced.
- Boys Town and its NFC partners conducted a financial analysis, learning that the state's contract was less than optimal for the following reasons:

o   The effort was clearly underfunded. All five original Lead Agencies cautioned the state that funding was insufficient and that some providers would go under. The state maintained its course. As a result, Boys Town and its NFC partners had to financially subsidize NFC's operations, with Boys Town providing the largest contribution. Boys Town was willing to do this to make sure the window of opportunity for real change stayed open and to advocate for high standards and best practices.

o   For the first 2 years of privatization, the state maintained case management authority, leaving Lead Agencies with little control over children's entry into and exit from the system or over decisions about children moving back home. This created further financial complications, mainly because the state and other stakeholders were making decisions about the budgets of the Lead Agencies with little or no input from those agencies.

The state contract also called for an increased community-based approach to providing alternatives to out-of-home placements. Network development called for a stronger provider base with increased accountability so it could effectively serve more families through preventive programs.

The NFC was designed to promote the concept of providing "the right service at the right time" for children and families. This mirrored the main goal of Boys Town's 5-year strategic plan to implement its Integrated Continuum of Care. The NFC would offer both case management and service coordination services that would help children and families stay together, prevent the removal of children to out-of-home placements, and put a greater emphasis on family-focused needs and outcomes. This would improve the continuity of the physical, emotional, and mental health aspects of youth and family well-being. If children were required to receive out-of-home care, NFC would have services and resources in place to maintain progress and provide support once children returned to their families or entered other permanent placements.

Progress and Achievements

When the NFC began providing services, it initially was responsible for one-third of the child welfare cases in the jurisdiction (Eastern Service Area, or ESA) that comprises Nebraska's two most populous counties. These counties are home to approximately 40% of all of the children and families in the state's child welfare system. By March 2012, the NFC had assumed case management of 100% of the child welfare cases in the jurisdiction, more than tripling the number of families to which it was providing services. With an effective combination of a stable caseworker and support staff, a variety of innovations that promote family-centered practice, frequent family team meetings, and aftercare supports and services, the NFC brought consistency and an outcomes-driven approach to the system in the jurisdiction it served.

A little over a year after NFC assumed full responsibility for all cases in the ESA, there has been significant progress and notable gains in a number of outcome areas. However, we recognize that we have a long way to go. With the support and advocacy of its partner organizations, NFC has stayed the course through numerous challenges and setbacks in order to do what is best for the children and families of Nebraska.

New Approaches

One major accomplishment, thanks to system reform, has been the introduction to the state of new child care philosophies and technologies. For example, there is a more conscious effort to work toward providing more adoptive or relative care for children. This effort is backed by a proliferation of in-home and intensive family preservation services and the implementation of evidence-based assessments. For instance, for more than 2 years, NFC strongly advocated adopting the structured decision-making safety model, because the old system was inadequate and allowed too many children to enter the system unnecessarily. The DHHS has adopted this model and now credits it with helping to lower the number of children in care.

Building on the foundation that was established through their earlier work, the NFC's contributing partners and other community agencies have played a major role in improvements in key areas of child welfare system reform.

Outcome Accomplishments: Reducing State Wards, Increasing Adoptions

In October 2012, the Nebraska DHHS announced a decrease in the number of state wards in Nebraska's child welfare system. Data results showed a 5% drop from July 2012, resulting in a 12-year low.

The NFC provides case management for 40% of the total child welfare cases statewide. The cases the NFC manages now account for

- 68% of the reduction in total cases statewide
- 67% of the reduction in wards in out-of-home care statewide
- 55% of the reduction in the total number of state wards

Data from previous years (2009–2011) showed that between 35% and 38% of all adoptions of children in Nebraska's child welfare system occurred in the Eastern Service Area. Year-end data for 2012 indicate that the ESA accounted for 50% of all the adoptions in the state.

Process Accomplishments: Greater Staff Stability, Increased Family Interaction, Lower Caseload Ratios

In accordance with national standards, the NFC is fully staffed and has had little turnover of its family permanency specialists, who are responsible for case management and service coordination. This means that families are able to work with the same specialist and receive consistent guidance, support, encouragement, and care throughout their involvement in the child welfare system. With a full staff, the number of family team meetings will also continue to increase so that families can be more engaged and involved in the care they receive. Caseload numbers are also improving, with more than 70% of family permanency specialists in the ESA assigned to best-practice caseloads of 17 or fewer cases. All of these factors contribute to building stronger, successful families.

CFSR Accomplishments: Improved Safety, Permanency, and Well-being of Children and Families

NFC has made significant improvements in all federal CFSR measures related to safety, permanency, and well-being. In the Eastern Service Area, the NFC has met four measures with scores that are equal to or higher than the state average; in a fifth area, the ESA scored higher than the federal target score.

Community Accomplishments: Positive Consumer Survey Results

In August 2012, NFC conducted the first of its annual consumer surveys to gather input from youth, parents, and stakeholders in the areas of staff professionalism, the NFC network, community supports and services, barriers, and family-centered practices. The sampling selection included all current NFC-served youth and families and stakeholders.

Parents and youth were asked to rate their satisfaction with services on a 5-point scale, with 1 as "poor" and 5 as "excellent." Overall, parents and youth said they were satisfied that services had helped their family make positive changes. The average parent rating for overall performance was 3.8, and the average youth rating for overall performance was 3.9. The highest rating from both parents (81%) and youth (80%) was for "being treated with respect." Stakeholders' highest rating (97.3%) was for the level of professional skills of NFC staff. (The full consumer survey and executive summary can be viewed at www.nebraskafc.org.)

Important NFC Milestones

A top achievement for NFC in late 2012 was the endorsement of its work as a Lead Agency by an outside evaluator. Legislative action required an external evaluation of both the DHHS and NFC, and the evaluation was conducted by an independent organization, the Center for the Support of Families of Silver Spring, Maryland. The Center, which has extensive experience with outcome measures and organizational assessment of systems, particularly child welfare practices and services, contracted with Hornby Zeller Associates, Inc., to complete the Nebraska review.

Hornby Zeller representatives spent two weeks in Nebraska gathering and reviewing information and interviewing stakeholders, providers, and families. The top recommendation in their report was for the Eastern Service Area (comprising Nebraska's two most populous counties) to remain with the NFC to ensure system stability for children and families. This, they said, would keep the focus on meaningful, family-centered reform and the delivery of quality services.

The main point derived from this recommendation is that Nebraska is following the right course of action to improve care and services for the state's children and families. It also means that a private provider such as the NFC can continue to play a critical role in moving the state's reform efforts forward, and that through a continued collaborative effort involving the DHHS, the legislature, the governor's office, stakeholders and other agencies, and NFC, Nebraska can raise its child welfare system standards and achieve better outcomes.

In December 2012, NFC received national accreditation from the Council on Accreditation. It was the first time in Nebraska history that a child welfare and juvenile justice services case management entity earned national accreditation. Recently, NFC data were transferred from an old information management system to a new system called FamCare, a flexible, customizable, web-based case management system that will provide NFC with improved organizational and provider oversight and foster better communication among employees by way of advanced reporting, notification, and operational workflow controls.

NFC currently contracts directly with nearly 50 qualified Nebraska service providers, capitalizing on their collective excellence in management, best practices, and support systems to help ensure that children and families receive effective services and experience positive results.

Even with all of these significant improvements, system change is very difficult, and as one goal is reached, another obstacle or barrier looms ahead. All is not rosy.

Challenges and Obstacles

The challenges of and obstacles to reforming Nebraska's child welfare system have been numerous, complex, and sometimes self-inflicted. A sustained collaborative and cooperative relationship between the state, its Lead

Agencies, and its private service providers was critical to the success of the reform effort. Unfortunately, such relationships have not always been stable or reliable, and it has been difficult to create and maintain steady momentum toward desired goals. Here are some of the main challenges and obstacles that have hindered progress toward positive changes in the child welfare culture and climate:

- There was a significant lack of education on how reform would occur. Despite receiving advice and recommendations from experts on reform efforts in other states, Nebraska moved quickly toward privatization without preparing stakeholders such as judges, legislators, agencies, and families. As a result, there was insufficient consensus-building among key decision-makers regarding the direction and implications of this plan.
- The privatization effort has consistently been underfunded, and there has been an ongoing struggle to procure funding that can adequately cover the costs of providing quality, effective, and individualized services to children and families. In fact, each of the original five Lead Agencies except the NFC withdrew or terminated its contract because of inadequate funding, leaving the state to take back case management and service provision responsibilities in the four jurisdictions these agencies served. Specifically, one Lead Agency filed for bankruptcy, two gave notice to terminate their roles as Lead Agencies, and the fourth negotiated a settlement to leave. The NFC, with its partnership of Boys Town and the four other local organizations intact, remained as the sole Lead Agency, and continues to negotiate with the state in order to achieve the financial viability and payment system necessary for continuing its Lead Agency role.

    In recommendations from its evaluation report on NFC last year, Hornby Zeller Associates stated, "There is no reasonable expectation that the private sector will pick up some of the costs of what is fundamentally a public function. The implication is that the State has to cover the legitimate costs of NFC's operations, if it is to continue with privatization."
- As other Lead Agencies departed, the NFC assumed responsibility for more cases in the Eastern Service Area. Over a 5-month period, the NFC's responsibility grew from one-third of all cases to 100% of all cases. This necessitated the hiring of 102 additional staff members and the transition of 1,217 families to NFC-managed services, both of which had to occur very quickly in order to maintain stability and consistency. Such swift, dramatic growth challenged both NFC's culture and its systems.
- Approximately 1 year after privatization efforts began, the director of the DHHS left and was replaced by a new director. With turnover in this and other key positions, new people with new ideas, new visions, and new priorities for how reform should proceed were added to an already tumultuous situation.
- Political support for privatization has constantly changed over the past several years, especially as some Lead Agencies departed. Some legislators and political figures who initially supported privatization became

soured over these departures, and the exit of some agencies created significant animosity because they had been delinquent on their payments to providers. Some providers could not keep their doors open without these payments, and provider capacity was lost in some of the most underserved areas of the state. The issue of privatization also has become a major part of legislative activities, with many child welfare system–related bills being introduced during the Nebraska legislature's two most recent sessions.

- State data systems were not in place to support Lead Agencies. They had to be developed so that there could be measures to determine if acceptable standards were being met and whether children and families were receiving quality services in a timely manner.

Lessons From Boys Town's Venture Into System Reform: What We Learned, How We Changed

Boys Town and the NFC have faced many challenges and obstacles since privatization began. But Boys Town and its NFC partner organizations have been unwavering in their support of continuing privatization as a viable reform approach. This support has remained firm because it is based on a commitment to doing what is best for the children and families of Nebraska. System reform created a window of opportunity for providing improved services for children and families that were not previously available in Nebraska. This window needed to be kept open long enough to assess progress and to build on the solid foundation that had been established.

We also have thrived because we were well prepared for the job. With a partnership involving five experienced local organizations, each with a well-qualified workforce and substantial private funding, the NFC was and is today the model of a Lead Agency that can work collaboratively with the state, its local provider network, and other stakeholders for true system reform. Consumers such as families, the judiciary, many legislators, and child advocates acknowledge system improvement.

The overriding purpose of any system reform effort must be to ensure the safety, permanency, and well-being of the children and families being served. Collaboratively finding ways to provide the best services possible in ways that prevent or reduce trauma, instill confidence, and result in positive outcomes should supersede pointless squabbles that are politically, financially, or personality driven.

Lesson 1: Solid strategic planning is critical to the success of any system reform effort. A clear direction and a concrete plan must be developed by those in charge of system reform far in advance of reform rollout and must include input from all involved agencies and stakeholders as well as those who will be indirectly affected by implementation of the plan. Planning should look at every element that will be necessary for success, from organization, staffing, and finances to decision making, vision, and capacity building. Even though contributors bring different ideas and resources to the table, everyone eventually must be on the same page when it comes to goals, processes, outcomes, and responsibilities.

In addition to having a viable plan for system reform, it also must be possible to implement and sustain the plan over time in order to accomplish short- and long-term goals. For the state of Nebraska, 3 years was barely enough time to implement such enormous change, particularly with the failure of Lead Agencies and the subsequent acquisition of more families and territory by Nebraska Families Collaborative, the remaining Lead Agency. There must be an understanding that turning a very large ship in a different direction requires patience and endurance.

Lesson 2: It takes a potent, established organization with a developed infrastructure to take on the task of managing care. The fact that Boys Town had financial stability, IT resources, human resources expertise and experience, and other important strengths such as insurance coverage and national accreditation enabled us to weather the storms of uncertainty, doubt, and outright confusion that plagued Nebraska's reform effort.

Even with all of the essential elements in place, Boys Town encountered challenges, most significantly with financing and budget issues. For example, we learned that if planning needs weren't completed before the state established its fiscal year budget or if changes were necessary during the budget year, no significant revisions could be made until the state's next budget cycle.

Lesson 3: Dealing with the complexities of multiple systems is a major challenge to reform success. As a service provider, Boys Town has always understood our responsibilities to our stakeholders. But our stakeholders had always been children and families—the recipients of our services.

Direct involvement in managing care for thousands of families meant dealing with and assuming new responsibilities with a much larger population of stakeholders—state officials, legislators, judges, county attorneys, other child and family care agencies, child and family advocates, and others—as well as entering the political decision-making arena. Decisions that were being made, sometimes with our input and sometimes without, affected the people of entire communities and counties, and Boys Town had to learn how to build alliances with many diverse participants in the child welfare system.

Even with our experience in working with others in the child and family care field for many years, Boys Town had to learn how to do things much differently and to revamp its negotiation, compromise, and advocacy skills.

One major positive outcome of the NFC partnership and its involvement in multiple systems was that Boys Town and other providers increased their advocacy efforts and political engagement with the state by working closely with legislators, the DHHS, and the governor. Boys Town has much greater access to decision-makers and stakeholders at the top levels of state government and has forged relationships that promote a better understanding of the child welfare challenges Nebraska faces and the best ways to address them. Agencies have worked together like never before and are continually seeking partnership opportunities to create innovation.

Lesson 4: Leadership and hard work do pay off. Despite the struggles and pitfalls, the Nebraska child welfare system is better than it was before reform efforts started, and more children and families are getting the right help in the right way. There has been little financial or political gain, and little media or public fanfare, but consumers are telling us their lives are better because of the services they now receive. Services and care management have improved, and fewer children are experiencing the trauma of being removed from their homes. Falling back on the mission to save children and heal families is never more important than when it appears there are no concrete rewards on which to rely. Solid, determined leadership is essential to keeping staff and organizations on course.

Lesson 5: Many people want to reform the child welfare system for the right reasons, but bureaucratic processes make it difficult to achieve significant progress. Boys Town has developed relationships with many state, agency, and care provider staff members who are committed to making a positive difference in the lives of children and families in need. Their motives are altruistic and they are dedicated to bringing about real change. Unfortunately, Boys Town has learned that its own bureaucracy, along with those of the state and the general provider system, and the restrictions under which they operate, can stymie progress just as easily as it can make it possible. Any organization that gets involved in child welfare system reform must be aware of the gauntlet of obstacles that has to be negotiated in order to accomplish even the simplest goal.

Lesson 6: Discouraging accounts of reform mistakes reported in the research and the experiences of those in other states who trod the same path of reform Nebraska is traveling now are more than warnings—they are replicable realities. Because private providers are state-funded businesses, even the most well-intentioned state leaders can stumble into the pitfalls of underfunding, moving too quickly, inadequate planning, and lack of education for stakeholders. Boys Town was told about these pitfalls, read about them, tried to listen, and tried to educate the state about them. Yet Boys Town, its NFC partners, and the state all fell prey to many of the mistakes of the past. The lesson here is that being aware of the worst things that can happen is no insurance against the worst things happening again. It's best to plan for the worst and to stay focused on the prize: ensuring the safety, permanency, and well-being of children and families in need.

It's no accident that the NFC partnership is the remaining Lead Agency in Nebraska's reform effort. From the start, the NFC had the support, infrastructure, staffing, funding and business models, and committed network of local child care providers with experience and expertise in child and family care necessary to make system reform a success. The NFC's contributions are helping to drive down the number of children in the state's care and provide additional services to meet more of the needs of children and families while actually increasing the number of families that receive services. (In each state where reform has been attempted, an enhanced network of services has been critical to success.)

Lesson 7: Change is the only certainty! Nebraska's effort to privatize the provision and coordination of services for children and families generated changes that rippled through every aspect of the child welfare and juvenile justice systems, and the agencies and organizations that were involved. There were leadership changes, funding changes, changes in the scope of services, changes in how everyone did business, and changes in the dynamics of control and decision making, to name a few. These changes demanded flexibility and open-mindedness on the part of the NFC and its partner organizations. Resisting or not adapting to any of these changes would lead to self-implosion and end the venture.

At the NFC's partner organizations, including Boys Town, senior management had to take a leadership role in convincing their respective boards that privatization could and would work, and that despite the challenges and changes everyone faced, moving forward would result in better care and services for the children and families of Nebraska. For Boys Town, this meant falling back on our mission as the motivation for accepting and implementing the changes that were necessary for success. Without our mission and its focus on the betterment of the child and family care system, the required changes would not have been worth making.

While the NFC's status remains somewhat tenuous in the future big picture of reform and there is still much more to learn, significant improvements have been achieved in services, programs, systems, and management of the needs of Nebraska's children and families.

We don't know what the future holds for privatization and continued efforts to reform Nebraska's child welfare system. But Boys Town and its NFC partners remain committed to advocating in the best interests of children and families, simply because it's the right thing to do.

INNOVATION AT THE PHILADELPHIA DEPARTMENT OF HUMAN SERVICES: IMPROVING OUTCOMES FOR CHILDREN BY INCREASING ACCOUNTABILITY AND STRENGTHENING COMMUNITY PARTNERSHIPS

Summary

The old African proverb "It takes a village to raise a child" is one that the Philadelphia Department of Human Services (DHS) has come to embrace. The latest in a series of reforms at the agency is a new initiative called Improving Outcomes for Children (IOC), which aims to improve service delivery and outcomes for children in care by engaging community partners, streamlining case management, and vigilantly tracking outcomes indicators to measure the initiative's success. With this initiative, the Philadelphia DHS is embracing a new model of child welfare that acknowledges that public agencies cannot singlehandedly combat child abuse and neglect, but rather that communities are in the best position to help protect children and support families during times of need. By engaging these communities more effectively and recognizing their essential, if informal, roles in service delivery, and by using data to measure success, DHS believes it can improve the safety, permanency, and well-being of the children in its care. The Philadelphia DHS is not the first agency to experiment with this hypothesis of change, but given the particular challenges they face, if they are successful, there is enormous potential to influence child welfare agencies nationwide by changing practices and the mindset of child welfare service delivery.

The Issue: The State of Child Welfare in Philadelphia

The federal government charges states and localities with ensuring the "safety, permanency, and well-being" of all children who may be at risk for child abuse or neglect (Adoption and Safe Families Act of 1997). To meet these mandates, child welfare agencies investigate reports of alleged child abuse and neglect, provide services to the families, or, if the child's safety is determined to be at risk, remove children to foster family homes, the homes of screened relatives, or group homes. At any given time, roughly 400,000 children are living in foster care (Department of Health and Human Services, 2012).

Although the federal government sets the national standards for the services states must provide through their child welfare systems, states and local jurisdictions are charged with implementing these services in ways that best meet the needs of their individual communities. Pennsylvania's system is county-based, with all 67 county child welfare agencies in the state overseen by the Pennsylvania Department of Public Welfare. The Philadelphia DHS is the largest child welfare agency in the state and among the largest in the country. Philadelphia handles both dependent and delinquent children as well as families provided with in-home court-ordered or voluntary prevention services. However, unlike most other systems, Philadelphia also places children into the system for truancy, introducing into the system a population of children not normally seen by these agencies.

In FY 2011, on a budget of approximately $600 million, DHS served a total of 11,330 children in dependent and delinquent placement settings as well as 60,000 youth and 20,000 families through nonplacement in-home services, both court-ordered and voluntary (Philadelphia Department of Human Services, 2012). Like so many other agencies, the DHS has also suffered system breakdowns leading to tragedy. In early August 2006, an ambulance was called to the home of the family of a DHS client named Danieal Kelly to find the 14-year-old girl lifeless, weighing only 46 pounds, and with weeks-old bedsores covering her body from gross neglect. Most horrifying was that her family had been receiving services from the DHS for years, and was supposed to be receiving biweekly visits from a caseworker through a private provider with whom DHS was con-tracting. Like other children before her, Danieal fell through the cracks of the system.

In the aftermath of the incident, then-mayor John F. Street appointed a group of national and local child welfare experts to a community over-sight board (COB) to systematically investigate what led to Danieal's death and make reform recommendations. In its first report, in 2007, the COB focused many of its recommendations on safety, which the panel identified as the primary and essential role of child welfare departments. To help ensure safety for children in care, the COB recommended that the DHS implement an appropriate safety assessment tool to more accurately assess a child's safety and risk in different placement settings, increase the num-ber of face-to-face contacts required between caseworkers and children, and implement an intensive team decision-making process for all young children in care.

The COB also recommended that the agency improve its performance monitoring to track the outcomes of children served, measure the impact of policy changes, and identify areas needing improvement. This included enhanced oversight of the provider agencies under contract with the DHS, including linking outcomes to financial incentives for the agencies. Responding to this recommendation, Commissioner Anne Marie Ambrose created the Division for Performance Management and Accountability (PMA). She further emphasized the importance of monitoring by recruiting a deputy commissioner to staff the new division and implement processes for rigorous quality assurance. Although the federal government requires states to report basic statistics related to safety, permanency, and well-being, for the first time the DHS began to use these statistics to describe its own performance.

In creating the new division, the DHS made an important distinction in social sector management between outcomes and indicators. An outcome, as nonprofit consultant David Hunter argues, is "an enduring change in something about which the organization cares deeply." The DHS's primary outcomes are safety, permanency, and well-being. Indicators are "concrete and measurable things that an organization will look at to assess whether it has succeeded in reaching a given outcome" (Hunter, 2006). A decrease in the number of incidents of child abuse and neglect while receiving services, for example, is an indicator of safety; an increase in the number of children exiting foster care to a permanent placement (i.e., adoption or reunification with birth family) is an indicator for permanency; increased rates of school attendance are an indicator for child well-being.

This new focus on outcomes and accountability is also exemplified by the successful, though difficult, implementation of a performance-based contracting (PBC) system in which all provider agencies contracting with the DHS are held to strict performance standards, including permanency indicators and placement stability (City of Philadelphia Department of Human Services, 2011). Initially this system applied to general foster care agencies only, but it has since been expanded to apply to treatment foster care and in-home protective services. In 2009, DHS began publishing annual rankings of these providers, with the expectation that if the agencies did not perform well, the DHS would no longer offer them the contracts. This type of transparency was an enormous step towards increasing accountability within an agency that had operated for years without it. Concrete outcomes are now the norm by which provider agencies in Philadelphia serve. Although it was a difficult reform process for both the agency and its provider partners, PBC has positively affected the quality of care provided to DHS-involved families. By holding itself and provider agencies accountable to continuously monitored outcomes and indicators, the DHS has achieved permanency for thousands more children.

The challenge for all child welfare agencies is to ensure that no child falls through the cracks. The DHS has completed the majority of the reforms the COB recommended, including a host of other reform initiatives not mentioned above, in furtherance of the three-part aim of safety, permanency, and well-being. The agency is committed to seeing through the COB's recommendations and its new policies and initiatives to keep Philadelphia's children safe and protected.

The Problem: The Challenge of Keeping Children Safe

Despite the thousands of children DHS does keep safe every year, and the enormous improvements that have been made since Danieal's death, some children remain at risk. The DHS, of course, wants to ensure that *all* children remain safe under their care, and both agency and city leaders continue to make that a primary goal for the agency. Mayor Michael Nutter has made reforming the DHS a priority during his tenure and, like Mayor Street, has relied heavily on the COB's recommendations as a force for reforming the city's child welfare department. Mayor Nutter also appointed Commissioner Anne Marie Ambrose, a child welfare and juvenile justice systems veteran with a record of reform, to take the reforms at the DHS even further.

Under Commissioner Ambrose's leadership, the agency has made impressive and measurable progress. She has devoted significantly more resources to the newly developed PMA division of the DHS, allowing for a more serious focus on data collection and tracking and giving the division more muscle within the agency to create change. Since her appointment in June 2008, she has also decreased the number of children in foster care by 33%, decreased the number of out-of-state placements by 79% for dependent youth and 91% for delinquent youth, and increased the number of children leaving foster care for permanent placement by 12% (Philadelphia Department of Human Services, 2012). The *Philadelphia Inquirer* editorial board, a harsh critic of the DHS in the past, noted this progress 3 years after Commissioner Ambrose's appointment: "Important reforms have been made within DHS, with more to come. That means better protection for vulnerable children" (Philadelphia Inquirer Editorial Board, 2011).

One of the most difficult of the COB recommendations left for the DHS and Commissioner Ambrose to address was the problem, caused by a dual case-management system, of the lack of clarity regarding the responsibilities of DHS caseworkers versus provider agency caseworkers. To families and foster parents, dual case management can feel like a rotating door: Families don't always know which caseworker will be visiting their home, which one to contact, and who will be with them in court. Importantly, and as illustrated by the Danieal Kelly tragedy, dual case management doesn't allow for clear accountability. The Philadelphia DHS is one of the largest child welfare systems in the nation that gives case management responsibilities to both DHS workers and provider agency caseworkers, and it has become clear that this duplication of roles could be eliminated with more clarity and structure between the agency and providers. With this in mind, the DHS decided on a bold innovation, moving from the current dual case-management system to a more streamlined model to improve the quality of services provided to families. On its face, this recommendation seems like better management through simplification, but within an agency as complex as the DHS, making it happen has proved daunting. The new initiative is appropriately named Improving Outcomes for Children, and the COB will oversee its implementation.

The COB also recommended that the DHS strengthen community partnerships to encourage community participation and input in DHS practices and improve continuity of care. This recommendation is based on a few model programs nationwide that have demonstrated that effectively engaging community partners can greatly improve outcomes for children and families (Center for the Study of Social Policy, 2011). Although the DHS has partnered with more formal organizations providing supports such as legal aid, health care, and social services, they have yet to engage more informal supports such as faith-based organizations and community members in areas that touch the child welfare system the most. By not working alongside such partners, the DHS is often viewed as an enemy by many communities, and fails to tap into networks that could help them stabilize families to keep vulnerable children safe.

To tackle these remaining challenges, the DHS turned to Casey Family Programs (CFP), which has been supporting the agency's reform efforts since 2006. CFP is a highly regarded national foundation established by UPS founder Jim Casey in 1966. Since its inception, CFP has worked with countless child welfare agencies across the country to improve their practices based on the best knowledge in the field.

The Solution: Improving Outcomes for Children

With the help of CFP, the DHS began exploration of the new IOC initiative in November 2008 by visiting New York City, looking at Commissioner John Mattingly's IOC initiative, and conducting a comprehensive review of initiatives around the country that have created a single case-management system and effectively engaged community partners. After studying several individual reform models, the DHS ultimately decided to design its own model based on similar initiatives in Florida and New York City, both of which, like Philadelphia, rely heavily on provider agencies for day-to-day case management. The DHS believes that its new IOC model will be transformative for the agency and will do more to improve outcomes for all children and families in the system than any prior agency initiative. It is indeed the most ambitious of any of the DHS's reform efforts to date.

The research in child welfare is clear that children do best when they remain in families, preferably their own families, whenever possible (Doyle, 2007). Emerging successful initiatives have shown that families, particularly families most at risk of coming to the attention of the child welfare system, need strong communities to support them, and that public child welfare agencies must partner with members of those communities to effectively ensure the safety and well-being of at-risk children. The theory holds that by engaging members of a community, making them aware of how the child welfare system affects their community, and empowering them to intervene with a family who may be struggling, neighborhoods may recapture a sense of responsibility for the welfare of their children. This engagement helps protect vulnerable children by supporting families before child abuse and neglect occur in the first place, in turn thus preventing some families from even coming to the attention of the DHS.

Achieving this new community partnership approach will rely on a streamlined case-management system and on strengthening the level of performance monitoring and accountability at the agency to track in precise terms the outcomes of this initiative:

> If the DHS partners with communities through a streamlined case-management system and clearly defines and tracks relevant outcomes and indicators, holding staff and providers accountable to these indicators, then Philadelphia children will remain safer, find permanent homes, and experience greater well-being.

The DHS will measure the success of its programs, including IOC, based on a number of key child welfare indicators it believes can be substantially improved through the IOC initiative. Though the DHS uses many more indicators to assess its overall performance, the IOC indicators do touch all aspects of the three essential goals of child welfare agencies:

Safety

- Decreased rates of abuse
- Fewer initial placements
- Decreased rates of abuse and neglect occurring in care
- Decreased rates of children returning to care (reentry)

Permanency

- More discharges to reunification (biological or kinship family), adoption, or permanent legal custody
- Decreased length of stay in care
- Fewer movements between placements while in care

Well-being

- Fewer children in group homes and institutional placements

- More sibling placements and connections over the life of a case
- Decreased racial disproportionality

Throughout the design and implementation process, the agency has relied heavily on the voices of the children and families they serve, community residents, stakeholders, provider agencies, and the DHS staff to inform the development of the model. The DHS believes that its formal system of care can be made better by involving informal systems of care as well, including faith-based groups and other community members and stakeholders who may not have otherwise recognized the degree to which they can play a role in supporting the families in their neighborhoods.

The new case-management system model eliminates duplication and clearly delineates roles and responsibilities. Providers, called Community Umbrella Agencies, or CUAs, will be responsible and accountable for ongoing case management and day-to-day service delivery, while the DHS's role will focus on providing guidance and technical support. What makes the CUAs' role unique, as compared with the traditional role of private providers, is their focus on a specific region of the city: according to the DHS, the CUAs "will ensure that local solutions and resources are more accessible to children and families" and "develop connections to formal and informal neighborhood networks that can strengthen and stabilize families" (Philadelphia Department of Human Services, 2013b).

To facilitate this community engagement, the DHS used geographic information systems (GIS) to map the neighborhoods with the highest DHS involvement and met with stakeholders in those areas to explore how the entire community could work alongside the DHS to support the families. The DHS's mapping technology also gave the agency more information about where children go once they are placed in foster care, information that community members would have had no way of knowing before. Taking children out of their homes and neighborhoods entirely can be detrimental for communities. It also does not foster well-being for children in care: Taking youth out of their communities can have the unintended effect of disconnecting children from their neighborhoods entirely, disrupting their schooling and friendships and discouraging reunification with family. Keeping children within their own communities by encouraging community support networks to promote child safety is thus a desirable goal for the children, their families, their communities, and the child welfare system as a whole.

The implementation phase of IOC began in January 2012, with the DHS focusing first on areas with the highest system involvement before moving to other areas of the city. In March 2012, the department released requests for proposals (RFPs) for the two initial CUAs. The proposed rollout of IOC, in order of the CUAs with the highest level of need, is shown in Table 11.1.

TABLE 11.1 Proposed Rollout of IOC

	Planned date for RFP process	Planned date for receiving in-home referrals	Planned date for receiving placement referrals	Planned full implementation
CUA 1	April 2012	January 2013	April 2013	December 2013
CUA 2	April 2012	April 2013	July 2013	March 2014
CUA 3	December 2012	October 2013	January 2014	September 2014
CUA 4	December 2012	April 2014	July 2014	March 2015
CUA 5	July 2013	April 2014	July 2014	March 2015
CUA 6	July 2013	July 2014	October 2014	June 2015
CUA 7	July 2013	July 2014	October 2014	June 2015
CUA 8	July 2013	January 2015	April 2015	December 2015
CUA 9	July 2013	January 2015	April 2015	December 2015
CUA 10	July 2013	January 2015	April 2015	December 2015

Adapted from the DHS IOC Implementation Plan (Philadelphia Department of Human Services, 2013a).

The Innovation: Performance Accountability and Community Partnership

The innovation in the IOC initiative is twofold. First, the data-tracking component of IOC represents the latest, and boldest ever, step towards real and meaningful accountability within the DHS. The initiative is results-oriented, making everyone single-mindedly focused on quality service delivery and improving clients' outcomes. Accountability done well—using outcomes to assess the impact of programs and policies—leads to improved client outcomes. Although accountability is not a new concept in child welfare, and some agencies nationally have embraced it, most still have not. If Philadelphia can make its system more transparent and accountable, it could serve as an important model for similar jurisdictions around the country.

The second true innovation in IOC is the community partnership component. The premise is fairly intuitive: Children belong in families, families operate in a sphere of communities, and most often the reason families enter the child welfare system is that they are isolated from these communities and have nowhere to turn during times of need. If families are well-supported and have access to the resources they need during times of crisis, then children will do better too.

In some ways, enhancing community partnership can be best described as building a continuum of care for at-risk children and families. The model acknowledges that many of the children who touch the child welfare system come from broken communities and are the children of yesterday's at-risk children from similarly broken communities, or even of the child welfare system itself. By working to establish a continuum of care that can catch families when they need support, and acknowledging that the DHS cannot perform this task alone, the DHS may be able to significantly reduce caseloads and improve outcomes for all children at risk of entering the child welfare system in Philadelphia.

These reforms are particularly innovative and meaningful given certain restrictions in federal child welfare financing. A gaping flaw in the federal funding structure is the inflexibility of Title IV-E (Title IV, Subpart E of the Social Security Act) and its limitations in reimbursing certain services. Though the legislation accounts for the majority of the money spent on child welfare services, states may only be reimbursed for foster care services; funding from Title IV-E cannot be used for prevention services or other wraparound services to support families in other ways, which could prevent the need for children to enter foster care in the first place. The IOC approach is twofold: supporting a state request to the federal government for a Title IV-E waiver and leveraging community resources to provide these upfront prevention and wraparound supports in a community context. With no stigma of a DHS worker coming to the family home, the DHS may be able to improve overall service delivery even within the confines of restrictive funding sources.

Barriers to Implementation

There are, of course, a number of potential barriers to successful implementation that the DHS faces in the months to come. Chief among these is stakeholder buy-in. A unique feature of the child welfare system is that it involves multiple decision-makers: a typical child welfare case includes not only the DHS but also Family Court and the presiding judge, parent advocates, child advocates, family advocates, provider agency caseworkers, and the city itself through its policies. All of these constituencies are major stakeholders who must become partners in the IOC initiative, and this type of collaboration can be problematic. For IOC to be successful, the DHS must bring all stakeholders to a place where they can find something to agree on. To the extent that IOC is seen as a threat to key constituencies, the success of the initiative will be difficult.

As is often the case in Philadelphia, unions are a huge DHS stakeholder in IOC. Because changes in job descriptions and responsibilities will be required under the new single case management model, the DHS must continue to work with both caseworker and supervisor unions in order to facilitate a smooth transition to the new system. To be sure, being a child welfare caseworker is one of the most taxing jobs in any child welfare agency, sometimes leading to high turnover rates and poor case management continuity for families. The DHS has therefore made a concerted effort to bring caseworkers to the table, to reassure workers that their jobs are secure and that although their work may change, their workloads will not increase. DHS workers will continue to provide a valuable service under IOC.

Another key stakeholder constituency is the provider community, whose perspective can get lost in discussions about increasing accountability. Under the new single case-management system, provider agencies, in many ways the heart of the Philadelphia child welfare system, will be performing all of the day-to-day casework. Reforms of the magnitude of the IOC initiative will require significant changes to the provider agencies themselves, and must take into account the capacity of the agencies to work through these changes. They are truly partners with the DHS in this reform endeavor.

DHS leadership firmly believes that they have and will continue to overcome these inevitable buy-in challenges. They view all these stakeholders as partners in the process with an important perspective to bring to the table. And, given the headway the agency has made in implementing IOC, it is clear that they have been successful in getting much of the buy-in they need. The collaboration of all stakeholders has been key to the implementation process thus far.

Financial Costs and Potential Savings

For the vast majority of children, simply entering the child welfare system puts them on an unstable path. A major goal of IOC is to reduce the number of children in residential and foster placements and to instead keep them within their own families and kinship supports whenever possible. It also turns out that the most restrictive settings, specifically residential and family foster care, are the most expensive. The average monthly cost of different levels of placement is shown below:

- Approximate monthly cost of family foster care per child = $1,800
- Approximate monthly cost of residential care per child = $3,900
- Approximate monthly cost of kinship care per child = $1,450

If the DHS is successful in reducing the number of children in foster and residential care placements, and if it can prevent the need for children to enter out-of-home care in the first place, it will not only improve child welfare outcomes but also reduce the DHS's costs substantially. It is a true win–win scenario.

The challenge, now and in the future, is working within the current funding structure to make these changes. Because the primary child welfare funding stream will reimburse child welfare dollars only for out-of-home care, the DHS must learn to be creative with the money available—the agency could lose this needed reimbursement money for good if it is too successful at reducing the number of children in out-of-home care, money that neither the state nor the city governments will be able to compensate for in today's budgetary conditions.

On the other hand, involving informal networks of support within communities that may be available to families can help the DHS do a better job taking care of the families it serves without having to pay them to do it. To the extent that the DHS is successful in its goal of connecting families with community supports that already exist, it may be able to make up for the potential lack of resources.

Finally, streamlining case management means decreased duplication and more efficiency in their processes. Though the DHS does not yet have an estimate for the financial savings that could result from this increased efficiency, and though Commissioner Ambrose insists that DHS workers will not lose their jobs as a result of the initiative, eventually savings are likely to be substantial, and could free up resources to be invested in community prevention programs.

Policy and Practice Implications: Will It Work?

In many ways, Philadelphia is acting as a pilot site to test the hypothesis that all components of the IOC initiative—community partnerships, single case management, rigorous data tracking, and system accountability for articulated outcomes—will in fact lead to improved outcomes for children. Commissioner Ambrose envisions the DHS becoming a leading child welfare agency in the nation. If she succeeds in this goal, as she has in many others, Philadelphia will become a model for child welfare system reform in other cities nationwide. This is particularly true given the oversight of the COB and the involvement and strong support of Casey Family Programs in IOC.

Although the changes required to fully implement IOC will happen over several years, and progress may seem slow at times, the DHS believes that through this process people will come to realize that they are sincere when they say will become a more transparent system. Their job in the meantime, and in the near future, is to help people see that there isn't a hidden agenda in this initiative, nor is it just another reform initiative that everyone will forget about in a few years. The Philadelphia DHS believes that IOC, like the PBC system, will stand the tests of time and of leadership change. According to a member of the IOC implementation team, although the initiative is a big challenge, the DHS would not be engaging in this enormous effort if they didn't believe it could achieve concrete and meaningful outcomes for the children they serve.

Clearly, whether these efforts succeed will have enormous implications for the field of child welfare. Any lessons learned from this project will inform other child welfare agencies as they consider future reforms. The child welfare field will surely be watching the Philadelphia DHS with interest.

REFERENCES

Adoption and Safe Families Act of 1997, Pub. L. No. 105–89 (1997).

Burns, D. (2007). *Systemic action research: A strategy for whole system change.* Bristol, UK: The Policy Press.

Center for the Study of Social Policy. (2011). Community partnerships for the protection of children. Retrieved from http://www.cssp.org/reform/child-welfare/community-partnerships-for-the-protection-of-children.

City of Philadelphia Department of Human Services. (2011). Needs-based plan and budget for fiscal year 2012–2013, implementation plan and budget for fiscal year 2011–2012. Retrieved from http://www.phila.gov/dhs/pdfs/NBB00_1112_Narrative_Template_Philadelphia_81310.pdf

Collins, J. (2005). *Good to great and the social sectors*. Boulder, CO: Jim Collins.

Crutchfield, L. & Grant, H. M. (2008). *Forces for good*. San Francisco, CA: Jossey-Bass.

Department of Health and Human Services, Children's Bureau. (2012). *The AFCARS report #20 preliminary FY2011 estimates as of July 2012*.

Doyle, J. J. (2007). Child protection and child outcomes: Measuring the effects of foster care. *The American Economic Review, 97*(5), 1583–1610.

Fleming, D., Koh, H., Roux, A., He, J., Hebert, K., Husten, C., . . . Willett, W. (2010). A population-based policy and systems change approach to prevent and control hypertension. Washington, DC: The National Academies Press.

Hunter, D. E. K. (2006). Using a theory of change approach to build organizational strength, capacity and sustainability with not-for-profit organizations in the human services sector. *Evaluation and Program Planning, 29*(2), 193–200.

Kania, J., & Kramer, M. (2011). Collective impact. *Stanford Social Innovation Review, Winter*, 38.

Payne, R. K., DeVol, P. E., & Smith, T. D. (2006). *Bridges out of poverty: Strategies for professionals and communities* (rev. ed.). Highland, TX: aha! Process, Inc.

Philadelphia Department of Human Services. (2012). *Performance management and accountability report February, 2012*.

Philadelphia Department of Human Services. (2013a). *Implementation plan*. Retrieved from http://dynamicsights.com/dhs/ioc/implement.php

Philadelphia Department of Human Services. (2013b). *Practice model*. Retrieved from http://dynamicsights.com/dhs/ioc/practice.php

Philadelphia Inquirer Editorial Board. (2011, June 20). Inquirer editorial: Keeping children safe. *Philadelphia Inquirer*. Retrieved from http://articles.philly.com/2011-06-20/news/29680117_1_dhs-social-workers-commissioner-anne-marie-ambrose-child-welfare-agency

Rainey, D. L. (2006). *Sustainable business development: Inventing the future through strategy, innovation and leadership*. Cambridge, UK: Cambridge University Press.

U.S. Department of Justice. 1999. What is systems change? In *CCITools for Federal Staff*. Retrieved from http://www.ccitoolsforfeds.org/systems_change.asp

CHAPTER 12

Being Deliberate About Strategy Through Leadership and Governance

Richard Graziano, Vincent Hillyer, and Donald Layden Jr.

THE CEO PERSPECTIVE ON THE ROLE OF STRATEGY AND THE CSO AT THE VILLAGE NETWORK

In the dynamic business environment of today, complex organizations must cope with many diverse challenges. Most chief executive officers (CEOs) have less time than ever to devote to addressing these challenges strategically, and as a result, the CEO needs another executive. Delegating strategy to the chief operating officer (COO) or chief financial officer (CFO) creates risk because those officers may focus on their own strategic needs and lose focus on other possible strategies. Consequently, some CEOs feel the need to appoint chief strategy officers (CSOs) to assist in developing strategies that include all facets of the business and improving the efficiency of the organization.

Although there are many benefits to bringing on a CSO, doing so is not without challenges. Finding someone who is well-rounded and who has the skills and experience needed to develop strategy, translate it for people across departments, influence culture, and drive change, is a tall order. The CSO should generally be given great authority to manage the company and to tackle new challenges. This requires a strong, trusting relationship between the CEO and CSO if the position is to be successful. In addition, it is the CEO's role to clarify how the CSO will function within the team and across departments. If the CSO's role is not well defined, the CSO can be successful in developing strategic initiatives.

CSOs must be multitaskers who have the ability to relay a company's strategy to every department within the organization so that all employees, partners, contractors, customers, and investors understand the organization's strategic plan and how it plugs into the organization's overall goals. They must drive immediate results in support of the long-term strategy, whereas the chief executive officer is normally responsible for driving long-term results and providing vision. They must also drive decision making that creates immediate change within the organization.

Organizations plan for the future for many reasons. Often they do so as a reaction to uncertainty about issues outside of their control, such as health care policy, rapidly changing technology, limited resources, prevailing values including diversity, and local community instability. Unpredictable change is rapidly transforming the way organizations plan for the future. It's becoming more and more difficult for senior executives to survive in such an environment. The turnover rate of executives for large organizations is extremely high, resulting in unmanaged priorities that ultimately lead to incomplete objectives. Chief executive officers fail for a number of reasons, such as financial malpractice, the inability to adapt to changing markets, and mental or physical incapacity; but chiefly they fail because of a lack of leadership skills. CEOs are most often unsuccessful because they fail to put the right people in the right jobs and fail to address people problems quickly enough. Specifically, failed CEOs are often unable to deal with a few key subordinates whose sustained or negligent performances deeply harm the organization. The modern pace of change has put considerable pressure on CEOs, increasing their reliance on their senior executive team to fill the void.

Not all executives can successfully operate strategically. It is lonely at the top, and the pressure can be intense. For this reason, contrary to what many people might believe, even those at the top of the organization find that they need outside sources of insight.

The people you surround yourself with must be skilled at preventing and recovering from mistakes.

The two questions all executives should ask themselves are:

1. "What skills do we need to accomplish our goals?"
2. "Who do I have around me to help us accomplish these goals?"

Don't think you have to do it by yourself. Your executive team is always more powerful than you are in terms of creativity and helping with complex issues. But how do you get the star players on your team? And where do you start? The answer usually lies in looking first to the key positions on the team and ensuring that you have the right talent in the right places.

A key position exerts critical influence on organizational activities both operationally and strategically. Ask yourself which positions, if left vacant or unproductive, will prevent the organization from meeting stakeholder expectations, confront competition successfully, and follow through with long-term strategies.

The Rise of the Chief Strategy Officer (CSO)

There are a number of key players on the executive team whom we must consider. There's a chief operating officer (COO), who is one of the highest-ranking members of an organization and is the person responsible for managing the day-to-day activities of the organization.

Then there is the chief financial officer (CFO), who is primarily responsible for managing the financial planning, record keeping, and potential risks of the organization.

Also, there is the chief strategy officer (CSO). Many publications describe the CSO as an internal consultant, specialist, or coach. In fact, the CSO should be viewed as a change agent who ensures that strategies are enacted with fidelity. A typical chief strategy officer is not a pure strategist who creates long-term planning isolated from the organization's current initiatives. A CSO should have the experience to help influence and advise as well as execute.

From a functional perspective, CSOs are responsible for helping CEOs decide what kind of support will be provided from the corporate office to its departments as regards management information and decision-making systems. They must also give advice about the kind of structure the organization will adopt: a centralized integrated structure that optimizes cross-department synergies, or a portfolio-oriented organization that operates each department as independent from the others?

Chief strategy officers are usually responsible for identifying major changes in the environment, customer base, or competition and defining required adjustments. They are often also responsible for corporate development activities: acquisitions, divestitures, and joint ventures. Although in most organizations the vision is led by the CEO, in many organizations the CSO plays a critical role communicating the vision both internally and externally.

Whether you are currently a CEO or on your way to becoming one, you want to be a good one. To accomplish this, you must realize right now that you can't do it alone. For sustained success, it is important to put the right people in the right positions. The leadership team you develop has the prime responsibility to communicate expectations and shape a successful culture. A successful culture is one in which people help each other achieve greatness by fostering creativity and innovation and consistently striving to exceed the expectations of those your organization serves. For this reason, the chief strategy officer position is becoming important to many organizations, including most of the Fortune 500 companies.

Organizations that have CSOs on their executive teams reveal recurring functions such as

- Overall business strategy as it relates to mission
- Strategic alliances
- Guiding internal and external communications

- Strategic growth initiatives
- Process improvement
- Public relations

From these functions, we can identify the primary roles for the chief strategy officer in shaping organizational strategy:

- Strategic foresight
- Strategic innovation
- Strategic communications
- Knowledge sharing

Despite the challenges of finding an executive who possesses the traits I've described and who also has the necessary range of experience, more and more companies are exploring the CSO option. For those striving for high performance, adding a seasoned, energetic chief strategy officer can be compared to a professional sports organization signing a top veteran player from another team. It simply improves the chances of beating the opposition. As one of my C-level executives put it: "We've added a talent capacity in a place that we didn't have any capability before."

Every company already has a strategy. CEOs are looking for a leader who can help implement it, not just refine it. To fulfill this quest, chief executives are tapping company veterans who have the experience and social and political skills to cross boundaries quickly and effectively while bringing fresh growth perspectives into the C-suite. It's time to recognize the ever-growing value of having a trusted, in-house strategy expert, an executive who will keep the organization focused through both the development and the execution of its strategy, as a member of the top team.

THE CEO PERSPECTIVE ON THE ROLE OF STRATEGY AND THE CSO AT GREAT CIRCLE

Great Circle came to be a multiservice organization over the last 35 years through acquisitions and mergers. We now realize more than $50 million in revenue and we have over 800 staff helping provide a full array of services for children and families—and our growth continues. When I took over as the president and CEO of what was then Boys & Girls Town of Missouri in 1999, we were a three-site organization with a budget of approximately $10 million and 200 employees. This was even significantly different from 10 years earlier, when it was a single-site agency with a budget of approximately $4 million. But as I look back on these years, specifically since 1999, not all of this was driven by strategy. I think that as the CEO in the modern-day sector of the not-for-profit world, I would never do it the way we did it only 15 years ago.

Today, as the CEO of one of the largest nonprofits serving children and families in Missouri and the Midwest, we must have an organizational strategy for how child welfare agencies can achieve long-term social impact. That's one of the reasons we use strategy. It is important to improve organizational capacity and infrastructure in addition to looking at what type of collective impact we can have on the communities in which we work versus impact by ourselves. Yes, the term "collective impact" is newly popular—but it's a concept Great Circle has been using for a long time.

Strategy should be used to create a culture in an organization, and it should be used to create policies that significantly affect and change systems. Strategy is necessary in the nonprofit sector. Strategy takes normal day-to-day activities and turns them into the way to accomplish the task at hand. It takes you from participating in your business to guiding your business.

In those early years, we certainly were not guiding our business. We were chasing revenue. We were chasing contracts. When a new organization came to us and asked if we would like to partner, we often did so without knowing where it would lead. We have been fortunate that the decisions we made, although not strictly on strategic measures, have been beneficial to the organization. In hindsight, strategy would have been much more effective at making those decisions. To my mind, strategy is a way of doing things—a culture, if you will. Every day, every meeting, every person associated with your agency is on the same page as it relates to strategy.

It is not easy. You must create a culture. We are a 180-year-old child welfare agency. It seems to me that we are most often identified as an agency that is 180 years old as opposed to an agency that is having the type of effects we want to have on the communities we serve. If I had a dime for every time we were described as an agency with 180 years of service, I would be a millionaire. But if I had a dime for every time we were introduced as an agency that has been strategically driven for 180 years, I wouldn't be able to buy lunch. As you can see, strategy is important in language and in implementation.

Traditionally we haven't used strategic plans the way we're looking at them today in 2013. The first time I participated in and really heard about strategic plans was in the late 1980s and early 1990s, but back then it was different. It was macro-level planning. It was a plan that looked 3 to 5 years down the road and that often sat on the shelf collecting dust. Yes, anybody who has done strategic plans will use that terminology as well. But it's not just terminology: many, if not most, plans often sit on a shelf after they are adopted. It should be said that the strategic planning process is a journey. The early days were a step along that journey that now has us to where we are today.

You need to be careful not to allow strategy to take over your business. There is a balancing act between tactical operations and strategy, and it's important that one not take from the other. For example, too much tactical energy towards your agency leads to what I call fire engine mentality. This is where you are always chasing the latest problems; you are always reacting to the next crisis. Once that fire is put out and the crisis is solved, you wait for the next crisis, hop on the fire engine, turn on the sirens, and you're off and running.

How do you move strategy into a way of doing business every day, in every meeting, and with every person in your organization?

A CEO's job is to head up this process. Some CEOs want the next "in" program. Or want to be bigger than their competition. But the CEO must take care of the 180-year-old organization. We must take care of our base. We have a moral and social obligation to carry out the mission that was given to us. We must never take our eye off the services we currently offer.

The CEO dilemma can be resolved. The solution came true when they introduced the new position of chief strategy officer along with the already proven position of chief operating officer. Yes, I was hired as the CEO to provide strategy and vision, but I also have responsibility for all aspects of day-to-day operations. The COO is a great tool. This position has as many job descriptions as it does positions, but the truth is that for our sector, the COO is the team member who is mostly focused on the day-to-day, ensuring that the vision is being manifested through quality services and best practices and is data-driven, to ensure that our clients and families are getting the best help possible.

CSOs help produce overarching plans. They drive a strategy from the micro and the macro points of view. They turn a strategy into processes that drive our overarching plan. They take a 1-year, 18-month, or even 3-year strategy plan and turn it into annual plans for every department, every region, and every program and for every staff person in the organization. They work hard to make strategy and day-to-day service delivery the same. The services we used to provide in the sector we provided simply because that's what we had always done. However, with strategy, what we do from day to day drives our strategy.

CSOs transform mission, value, and what we have always done daily into strategy. They work side by side with the CEO, COO, and others. Having a CSO allows the complete transformation of an agency into a strategy-driven system: nothing happens that is not part of the strategic plan. With a CSO, all staff—yes, all staff—are now aligned with management and board in terms of the direction of the agency. All staff play a role in this process and are "players" in the agency. Therefore, everyone not only participates in fulfilling the strategy but also holds everyone else accountable to the plans and, indeed, participates in developing those plans.

CEOs with these tools at their side have the ability to carry out their responsibilities in a much grander way. They must protect and nurture the 180-year-old agency and the customs and traditions they have established (the primary role of the COO). They must also make sure that the services they are providing are mission-driven based on best practices and are provided in ways that are right for clients, for the founders of the organization, and for the board. They need to make sure their work is ethical and complete.

They must also look forward to the future and see what's coming up so that their agency can be nimble enough to make the move and remain a player in the sector. CSOs need to be prepared to meet the needs of the agency and the communities in which they serve and must be able to prepare the agency to be viable in the future.

CEOs have are responsible for fulfilling the vision of making the agencies they lead better for generations to come. One of the responsibilities we take on as CEOs is not only maintaining the agency, not only maintaining the 180 years that we've been given, but also moving the agency in a direction that ensures that it will be around 180 years from now. In addition, to make sure that we've made our agencies better, we have pushed the envelope to ensure that we have had greater collective impacts on the communities we serve and that we have looked in a responsible and strategic manner to find partnerships and to work each day in ways that will make things better for many generations to come.

CEOs now have the tools to be responsible for the vision of their agencies like never before. They can continue to protect the traditions and the services, ensuring that they are in the best interest of each agency's consumers and missions. CEOs now also have the tools to promote their often unspoken core responsibilities, to guarantee that the agencies they've been given the task of leading remain vibrant and nimble.

A BOARD MEMBER'S PERSPECTIVE ON THE ROLE OF GOOD CORPORATE GOVERNANCE IN HIGH-PERFORMING STRATEGIC NONPROFITS

A high-functioning board is the single most important contributor to an organization's success and sustainability. Indeed, an effective board is a leading indicator of an organization's health and its ability to respond to a changing environment, manage risk, and find new ways to deliver services. High-performing organizations understand that the board as a body including each of its individual members is a key strategic asset that effective organizations leverage as they set direction and strategy. Good boards look forward, not back, enabling their organizations to anticipate challenges and avoid pitfalls.

This section begins by setting the stage for the function of corporate governance in an organization, paying particular attention to the specific nuances of governance within a nonprofit corporation. This will be followed by a review of the normative behaviors of nonprofit governance as observed and studied by BoardSource (www.boardsource.org) and the National Association of Corporate Directors (www.nacdonline.org). The section ends with some observations on best practices and emerging trends based on my personal observations and experiences.

I come to this effort as a practitioner, not as an academic, consultant, or theorist. I currently serve on the boards of two public companies—one in the United States and one in India. I serve on a half-dozen private company boards, including as the chair of two of them. I also serve on about a dozen nonprofit boards and have chaired more than my fair share of the boards I have served on, including serving as chair of Families International. So my comments are shaped by my regular engagement in the hard work of serving on boards.

Amazingly, it was only a few years ago that Chait, Holland, and Taylor wrote, "Effective governance by a board of trustees is a relatively rare and unnatural act . . . trustees are little more than high-powered, well-intentioned people engaged in low-level activities" (1996, p. 1). Observers of nonprofits have regularly chronicled that boards, even though they comprise smart people, have a reputation for not behaving smartly. Indeed, Peter Drucker summed it up thus: "There is one thing boards have in common . . . they do not function" (1993, p. 50). Fortunately, most boards have moved beyond these limitations and have transformed to become the voices of their members, their communities, their donors, and their clients.

According to John and Miriam Carver in their formulation of corporate governance, the main role of the board is "to govern in an organized, planned and highly disciplined manner" (Carver & Carver, 2001). As with most things in life, the devil is in the details. Richard Chait summarizes a board's fiduciary obligations as "fidelity to mission, integrity of operations, and conservation of core values" (*Trusteeship*, 2013, para. 6).

But in the nonprofit setting, misconceptions about corporate governance abound.

- Are board members primarily fundraisers? Cheerleaders? A rubber stamp to legitimize the actions and decisions of the executives?
- Do they run the organization to the extent that staff is unable?
- Are they window dressing to spruce up the organization's letterhead?
- If they are prominent or have marquee names or reputations, must they attend board meetings?
- How do they know whether they are doing a good job and when it is time to go?

Good governance starts with the board of directors. The board's role and legal obligation is to oversee the operations and management of the organization and ensure that the organization fulfills its mission. Good board members monitor, guide, and enable good management; they do not do it themselves. The board generally has decision-making powers regarding matters of policy, direction, strategy, and governance of the organization.

The board of a well-governed nonprofit organization, like the board of a well-governed profit-making company, will do the following:

- Formulate key corporate policies and strategic goals, focusing on both near-term and longer-term challenges and opportunities.
- Authorize major transactions or other actions.
- Oversee matters critical to the health of the organization—not decisions or approvals about specific matters, which is management's role, but

instead those involving fundamental matters such as the viability of the organization's business model, the integrity of its internal systems and controls, and the accuracy of its financial statements.

- Monitor, but not perform, operations. Boards accomplish this obligation by hiring CEOs, evaluating their performance, and establishing succession plans. The board also reviews and confirms the organization's personnel philosophy, practices, and policies.
- Monitor the performance of the organization's programs and services.
- Establish the risk appetite of the organization and evaluate and help manage risk.
- Provide proper financial oversight and effectively steward the resources of the organization for the longer run, not just by carefully reviewing annual budgets and evaluating operations but also by encouraging foresight through several budget cycles, considering investments in light of future evolution, and planning for future capital needs.
- Enhance the organization's public standing.
- Mentor senior management; provide resources, advice, and introductions to help facilitate operations.
- Recruit and orient new board members and assess board performance.

In a well-governed organization, whether for profit or not for profit, the board does not permit executives to run and dominate board meetings, set agendas, or determine what information will be provided to board members. Under the leadership of an active and functioning board chair, there is adequate opportunity at board meetings for members to receive and discuss reports not only from the chief executive but also, as appropriate, directly from other executives, in-house and outside professionals, and independent consultants if necessary. Time should be reserved for executive sessions from which management is excluded, so that its performance may be fully and freely discussed.

Mission is what distinguishes nonprofits from their for-profit cousins: Nonprofits have missions instead of owners or shareholders. In for-profit enterprises, directors have a primary obligation to create shareholder value, and although stakeholder theory allows for considerations impacting all stakeholders of an enterprise, including employees, communities, clients, and vendors, in a nonprofit enterprise directors are expected to bring the same rigor to ensuring mission fulfillment and effectiveness.

Now that we have set the stage for the basis of the directors' obligations and the roles they play in governing an organization, let's turn to some of the normative practices found in nonprofits. The latest BoardSource study on nonprofit governance (2012) cites four frequently asked questions, which do not have easy answers and which I assert belie some of the problems in nonprofit governance that require dramatically more radical action than most nonprofits are considering. In other words, if these are the four most frequently asked questions, then the sector may be in trouble.

The four questions are:

1. *What size should our board be?* While citing a preference for smaller boards, BoardSource identifies the sweet spot of size at 15 to 22 directors. They go on to report that community engagement, fundraising, and tradition may all result in larger boards. The notion that governance can be effective with a board of 15, 20, 30, or more directors is ludicrous. But I will come back to this issue of board size and structure in the discussion of emerging and best practices.
2. *How much should board members give?* The minimum expectation on all boards, irrespective of size, is that directors will participate 100% in giving and that all directors will make a gift that is personally significant. Of course, these expectations ignore the conflicts that arise when all board members are donors. The priorities of the institution should be determined strategically and not by the pet interest of a large and influential donor.
3. *What does a diverse board look like?* BoardSource defines diversity by three demographic factors: race or ethnicity, gender, and age. Other important factors, such as background and competencies, are ignored.
4. *How often should we have board meetings?* Not surprisingly, most boards are trying to reduce the time spent in meetings and the number of meetings. Perhaps the better question would be, *Are our board meetings effective?*

Surveys of boards and CEOs find that in assessing their normative performance, CEOs give their boards a C+ while directors evaluate their performance as a solid B. Yet boards rarely remove board members, instead allowing ineffective members to serve on less important committees and reducing expectations. The most often cited reason for failing to replace ineffective board members is the fear of losing financial commitments from those members and others whom they influence.

Across organizations of all sizes, only half of directors are well informed of their legal and governance obligations. The larger the organization, the better-prepared directors tend to be. A bare majority (60%) of nonprofit boards assess their own performance. For most boards that have never done a formal evaluation, the organizations' CEOs rated the boards as ineffective.

A little more than half of boards use a consent agenda to allow more time to be spent on strategic issues and discussion. Similarly, 50% of boards have an annual retreat to review strategy and direction and conduct scenario planning. About 37% of nonprofits use an organizational dashboard to track and report performance against strategic and operational objectives.

Because of the large size of boards, 78% use an executive committee that meets regularly to make decisions about the organization. In my experience, this is where the actual governance takes place in these nonprofits.

Finally, in the board recruitment arena, we see similar results. Forty-four percent of nonprofits find it difficult to recruit board members, with smaller organizations finding it almost twice as difficult as large organizations. In contrast, foundations find it relatively easy to recruit board members. Anecdotally there are probably two reasons for this relative ease in recruitment: Most foundations have no fundraising expectations, and a large number of foundations pay the foundation directors for their service.

Not surprisingly, most board members serve, on average, on two nonprofit boards, confirming the trend of more limited community involvement by most nonprofit board members.

The remainder of this chapter will be a review of three emerging trends in governance for nonprofits:

1. Board structure and size
2. Board recruitment, qualification, and evaluation
3. Risk management

Large boards are ineffective at properly governing an organization. The typical nonprofit board size is almost double the typical size of a for-profit corporate board. Nonprofits have addressed the challenge of large boards through a proliferation of committees; the typical nonprofit board has between seven and eight committees, and an increasing number of nonprofits use an executive committee to do the real governance work of the board. Organizations that wish to be high-performing need to rethink this strategy. Many board members are not fulfilling a governance role today and are probably better moved to advisory or friend groups, or to serving on operating committees where the organization needs community buy-in or support. Governance should be more strategic, and organizations that want to perform better should carefully assess their board agendas and the time spent during board meetings on key strategic issues. If less than 50% of the time is spent on issues of strategic impact and mission fulfillment, the priorities of the board are misaligned.

Boards need to be more creative in how they leverage the skill sets of board members. In large boards, to facilitate discussion, portions of meetings should be set aside for small-group discussion. Directors who rarely speak up in a large group setting will often engage in a smaller group. If a retreat can't be scheduled because of time constraints or attendance issues, the organization should find other creative ways to make time for addressing long-term issues, such as by one or two board meetings by an hour or two. At the end of each board meeting, directors should fill out a standardized instant evaluation form that includes no more than four questions:

1. Was our discussion mission-focused and strategic?
2. What was the most valuable thing the board did today to further the strategy of the organization?

3. What should be on the agenda for the next board meeting?
4. Did we waste time on issues today? If so, what?

You can use a scale or a simple yes/no. The questions will vary by organization, but not much. The important thing is to treat the board as a strategic asset that needs to be engaged to drive performance and to create a simple feedback and communication mechanism.

On each for-profit board on which I serve, the CEO calls me at least once between every meeting to discuss the company's performance, challenges, and opportunities for achieving our objectives. Nonprofit CEOs rarely make these phone calls. Why?

Our second emerging trend is board recruitment, qualification, and evaluation. Most CEOs identify board recruitment as one of the most difficult issues they face, yet few organizations have changed their methods for recruiting board members. Indeed, most boards recruit directors who have been recommended by existing directors. Boards need to be more creative in the ways they recruit. Large organizations should consider using headhunters. Governance committees should seek out candidates from a variety of sources outside the organization and should review job boards and other electronic postings for available directors. Most important, boards need to find ways to be attractive. When I advise my adult children on board service, we discuss the psychic compensation they will receive from serving on a board, the collegiality and effectiveness of the board and its members, and the degree to which they can make a difference and have their voices be heard. Boards need to make themselves attractive as places where younger and more diverse board members want to hang out with the aging demographic that dominates boards today.

Boards also need to be much more cognizant of the skills and competencies of their directors. Audit committees and finance committees need people who are financially literate; investment committees need people who understand market dynamics; risk committees need people with technology and other technical expertise; and so forth. To conduct effective oversight, a certain level of knowledge is required. In for-profit corporations, audit committee members must be financial experts or at least be financially literate. Most people believe that compensation committee members will need to demonstrate expertise in compensation, benefits, and human resource management. Risk committee charters in the for-profit world typically set forth specific competencies committee members must possess. The nonprofit world must follow these advances in the practices of for-profit companies and emulate their behavior.

I was asked to chair the audit committee of a large and well-respected organization. In reviewing the scope of the auditors' work plan, I discovered two significant limitations in the work plan they proposed. I asked the auditors about these limitations and was told that this was how the work had always been done. The other committee members and the CEO said that they were surprised by these limitations and agreed with me that they should be changed. Boards need members who have the competency and confidence to ask questions and challenge long-standing assumptions. We need to find those kinds of directors, not the marquee names that show up when pictures are being taken.

We will end with risk management. Recent initiatives by the IRS have created greater transparency in the operation of most nonprofits. Indeed, today most organizations have clear conflict-of-interest policies, have established whistleblower policies, have boards that are approving executive compensation rather than allowing the board chair to set compensation, and are posting their 990s on their websites.

These are all important steps for nonprofits to take, and those organizations that have been slow to adapt to this new level of accountability and transparency are likely to find themselves in the middle of a tax review or audit, or worse, subject to uncomfortable public scrutiny that can damage their reputations (Bice, 2013). I serve on the board of a large fraternal life insurance company. Because of our fraternal activities and our charitable intent, we are an exempt organization, albeit under a different subpart of section 501(c) than most nonprofits. The IRS is auditing several fraternal organizations nationally to confirm that their fraternal and charitable operations are sufficient to warrant exempt status (Bice, 2013). Not surprisingly, the audited organizations tend to be those that have been the least transparent in their reporting.

Best practices by nonprofits today, however, require organizations to go well beyond the formal requirements of policy adoption and rule compliance. Boards that want to be high-performing need to establish their organizations' appetites for risk and assess the organizational culture to ensure adherence to those standards. Employees throughout the organization need to understand how the organization's tolerance for risk has been defined and how that plays out in day-to-day decisions.

There are lessons to be learned about board governance from Penn State to fully understand the implications of the failure of board leadership that underlines the findings of the Freeh Report and that caused the NCAA and the public to react so negatively and decisively against the institution. The Freeh Report found that the culture that the board allowed to operate at Penn State created some of the conditions that allowed the tragedy of the events that unfolded to go unreported and ultimately ignored for years. The board failed in its oversight and allowed the perpetuation of a culture that sought at all costs to preserve the football program unchecked.

As I review the normative behavior reported by BoardSource, I wonder whether those same conditions of failed oversight have been allowed to fester at most nonprofits. We hear that CEOs of most nonprofits believe that their boards are ineffective, that average attendance by board members is well below 60%, that half of directors are not well informed, and that most boards do not fully and adequately assess their performance or that of individual board members.

In a for-profit corporation, it is superficially easy to determine adequate performance. The profitability of the firm in both absolute and comparative terms can be easily calculated. Some of us have asked nonprofits to set clear, deliverable performance metrics against a typology of results that allows for some test of normative performance. Unfortunately, that measures outcome effectiveness but not mission effectiveness, which is the ultimate role of the nonprofit and, by extension, the role of the board to help assess and achieve.

REFERENCES

Bice, D. (2013, May 19). Summerfest CEO Don Smiley's compensation rises $114,000. *The JournalSentinel Online*. Retrieved from http://www.jsonline.com/watchdog/noquarter/summerfest-ceo-don-smileys-compensation-rises-114000-4oa01nr-208076291.html

BoardSource. (2012). *Nonprofit governance index 2012*. Retrieved from https://www.boardsource.org/eweb/dynamicpage.aspx?webcode=GovernanceIndex

Carver, J., & Carver, M. (2001). Carver's Policy Governance® model in nonprofit organizations. (Reprinted from *Gouvernance—revue internationale, 2*(1), 30–48.) Retrieved from http://www.carvergovernance.com/pg-np.htm

Chait, R. P., Holland, T. P., & Taylor, B. E. (1996). *Improving the performance of governing boards*. Westport, CT: Oryx Press.

Drucker, P. (1993). *Management: Tasks, responsibilities, practices*. New York, NY: HarperBusiness.

Fiduciary behavior: What's the responsible trustee to do (and not do)? (2013). *Trusteeship, 21*(2), para. 6. Retrieved from http://agb.org/trusteeship/2013/3/fiduciary-behavior-whats-responsible-trustee-do-and-not-do

CHAPTER 13

The Health and Human Services Sector Constituent Voice

David Bonbright

CONSTITUENT VOICE

This chapter explores how Constituent Voice (CV) can contribute to effective strategy for human services organizations. The promise of this contribution is nothing less than fundamentally transformative. The present-day reality, however, is anything but. This chapter explains why the great potential of Constituent Voice remains unrealized and offers a clear road map for those ready to begin the journey to more effective strategy informed by Constituent Voice.

After defining CV and situating it in organizational systems, the chapter (1) reviews the state of CV practice today, (2) considers the relationship between CV and civic engagement, (3) describes CV as a tool of performance management, and (4) proposes the development of a field-level strategy tool based on comparative feedback from those served.

How Does Constituent Voice Fit Into Strategy in Human Services?

Constituent Voice is best understood as both an outcome and as a tool. Understood as an outcome, CV is what results when an organization listens and responds effectively to the priorities of those it serves as well as to their assessments of their experiences with the organization. Constituents have a voice when they are heard and responded to by an organization. Constituents who have a voice invest time and effort to make the organization better for themselves and their families. Such constituents are far more likely to realize the benefits that are intended from the organization's work.

Understood as a tool, Constituent Voice measures how those meant to benefit from an organization themselves assess those benefits. It answers four main questions: (1) How important is this organization to me? (2) What changes for me and my family because of this organization? (3) What is the quality of service at this organization? (4) What is the quality of my relationship with this organization? This last relationship quality question is informed by the other questions, but surveys core values such as trust, voice, empowerment, and respectfulness. With respect to voice, for example, a commonly asked survey question is, "On a scale of 0 to 10, how likely are you to engage with this organization to make it serve you and your family better?" Organizations that are scoring 9s and 10s from more than half their clients/participants are realizing outstanding results.

With this definition of Constituent Voice in mind, we turn now to where it sits within organizational systems. CV is an element in performance management. In his excellent how-to guide for performance management in human services organizations, David Hunter draws a distinction between "tactical performance management" and "strategic performance management" (Hunter, 2013, p. 2).

Tactical performance management involves daily monitoring of activities and their observable consequences. Those on the front lines use the resulting information to adjust their work in real time. It focuses on the actual touch points[1] between the organization and those it serves, mapping these for what benefits are or are not being realized.

Strategic performance management "consists of monitoring activities and their results in aggregated ways over extended periods of time (usually quarterly or yearly). It uses large feedback loops to drive learning and identify needed adjustments that, while infrequent, are more substantial in nature than those required by tactical performance management" (Hunter, 2013, p. 5). Strategic performance management enables organizations to (1) maintain program quality, (2) expand programs to new sites, and (3) decide when and how to introduce new programs or cut back on old ones that no longer work well. These quarterly and yearly aggregations of information are vitally important for maintaining the credibility of the organization with external stakeholders such as donors.

Constituent Voice contributes to both tactical and strategic performance management, depending on which questions are asked and how quickly the feedback loop from data collection to corrective action is closed. This chapter concentrates on Constituent Voice and strategy, but to understand CV's contribution to strategy we will see how the strategic level is sometimes reached by an aggregation of data gathered daily and weekly through Constituent Voice.

---

[1]Significant moments in the course of a project at which the organizations seeks to create some value or benefit for those it serves—for example, a training or counseling session, or a meeting or an event.

The State of the Field: A Broken Hallelujah

From late 2007 through early 2009, the Alliance for Children and Families (ACF), the United Neighborhood Centers of America, and Keystone Accountability conducted an action research inquiry into how human services organizations in the United States listened to those they intend to help. In March 2009, we published a white paper that concluded that inquiry (Bonbright, Campbell, & Nguyen, 2009). In it we wrestled with a seeming paradox. There is an enduring and widely held conviction among human services leaders that feedback from primary constituents is of great, and perhaps even paramount, importance in their work, but in practice, human services agencies do not find current formal feedback practices to be helpful. The myriad forms of feedback human service organizations receive from service beneficiaries and other stakeholders (such as satisfaction and outcome surveys) are not realizing their potential for transforming the way human service providers, service beneficiaries, and funders work together to create positive social change. (This could be described as "a broken Hallelujah," a phrase that comes from a 1984 song by Leonard Cohen, "Hallelujah.")

The report produced a set of clear and powerful findings with respect to current practices:

- The quality of feedback practices at organizations was generally poor. Staff were not convinced of the accuracy or evidentiary value of the data they collected. Organizations did not close the loop with their clients by reporting back what they were hearing in the surveys. There was no effort to make corrections based on feedback and then rely on new feedback to assess the effectiveness of those changes. Leaders saw Likert-scale surveys as completely separate from qualitative research. They did not seem to be aware of the common business practice of using written surveys to provide a first-level diagnosis to be deepened through subsequent open-ended interview methods. Nor was there a sense expressed in which the written surveys could provide a reality check with respect to organizational investments made in response to diagnoses from interviews and focus groups. In short, the quality of feedback practices did not reach the threshold for ensuring effectiveness.

    One exception to generally weak feedback practices further illustrates the general rule. The research identified a strong practice of responding to individual grievances, which all organizations reported were recorded and followed up on as a matter of management priority. In most organizations, status reports on outstanding grievances were featured in weekly management reports that reached the CEO. This was true irrespective of how the grievance was expressed, whether at the instigation of the aggrieved party or in the normal course of data collection through some other mechanism. The fact that providers seem to have a zero-tolerance policy for failure to respond to grievances stands in stark contrast to more general formal constituency feedback practices. This also contrasts markedly with the standards of client feedback among, for example, consumer-facing businesses.

- Feedback practices are undertaken more to comply with funder requirements than to improve performance. Funder requirements for service recipient feedback are uncoordinated and betray no discernible intention to utilize recipient feedback for improvement by their grantees or to bring client feedback data into their own funding decisions. There is no agreement between funders and providers about the goals of feedback. The goals that providers seek from feedback differ from the goals implied in funders' reporting requirements.

For example, government funders may seek feedback to demonstrate conformity with contracted activities or as a basis for assessing their funding priorities, whereas providers seek feedback as the basis for shared learning with primary constituents. The different feedback purposes raise difficult management questions because they could imply different questions and methodologies as well as different relationships between stakeholders. Fund accountability-oriented feedback efforts emphasize government funders' roles as contract managers overseeing agencies and ensuring that they meet contractual obligations. That model emphasizes the power that public funders hold over contracted providers and drives feedback mechanisms into tight and narrow channels. This contrasts with the use of Constituent Voice as a way to rebalance power relationships in favor of marginalized stakeholders in order to create conditions under which all stakeholders can work together to address shared public concerns. This approach argues for feedback systems that are more open and deliberative and that aim for ongoing, mutually accountable dialogues.

Funder requirements that grantees conduct client satisfaction surveys amount to unfunded and misunderstood mandates.

- Feedback from clients sits within generally weak performance management systems. Data collection is generally seen more as chore than core. Existing systems to collect, analyze, compare, and act on different kinds of monitoring data (inputs, costs, and activities, as well as feedback) are rarely driving day-to-day decision making for managers. No one's performance appraisal and remuneration turn on the trends in these numbers. There is little accountability in human service organizations for performance management, let alone accountability to the data generated by these systems. This may be the main reason we don't see more leadership from agencies on Constituent Voice.
- Absent effective feedback practices and given the existing structure of rewards and incentives, nonprofit organizations will heed other signals (notably, those of funders, boards, and staff) most readily. As a result, the voice of primary constituents remains grossly underrepresented in organizational decision making.

These several factors seem to "weigh down" investments in feedback: the low utility of data gathered through prescribed customer satisfaction surveys, the failure of donors to appreciate those aspects of feedback other than as ways to provide evidence of follow-through on contractual obligations, and the unfamiliarity of donors and agencies alike of these dimensions of evaluative action. It is a strong human services leader indeed who can heft this weight and go the extra distance to cultivate feedback in order to produce Constituent Voice.

Agency leaders expressed a feeling of being caught between a rock and a hard place. They believe in the potential of taking primary constituency feedback seriously, including the transformative step from feedback to voice. But with austerity-era resource constraints, they feel they must prioritize what they experience as a conflicting imperative to report back to funders about their activities and outcomes. Funder-mandated client surveys currently yield little value for either agencies or funders.

Since there is general agreement about this, however, providers have a leadership opportunity—if not an obligation—to present government funders with enriched approaches to constituency feedback, thereby converting a burden into a catalyst for improvement.

A persuasive precedent for this may be found in the business literature on customer satisfaction. Over 50 years' worth of data derived from diverse companies show a clear correlation between customer loyalty and growth and profits. It is time for human service organizations to marshal the empirical evidence required to map the fine details of the links between outcomes and the quality of agency–service recipient relationships.

Strategy, Civic Engagement, and Constituent Voice

Constituent Voice has a strong affinity with one of the leading trends in human services organizations—civic engagement. Investments in civic engagement flow from a theory of change that says that low-income families will improve their well-being when they organize politically to advance their collective interests in health, education, and community welfare. A growing number of human service agencies find that when they enable their service recipients to become active citizens, their service recipients directly improve their lives while contributing to policy improvements (Pinsoneault, 2006). This is based on the idea of "development as freedom": that where there is freedom, individuals and families are the best agents of their own development (Sen, 1999).

Investments in Constituent Voice flow from a theory of change that says something similar—namely, that service recipients will realize more benefits from organizations when they hold those organizations to account for those benefits.

Put together, there is a theory of change that says that organizations that cultivate CV in their beneficiaries are creating the values and habits of democracy that underpin effective civic engagement. In this context, feedback

EXHIBIT 13.1   Constituent Voice and Ugandan Public Health Services

An important recent study has illustrated how civic engagement can improve community health. In this case, a government-supported social accountability project in Uganda involved citizens in a rural district organizing to monitor, assess, and report on the quality of the local clinics' care.

The study established that the citizen report cards on the clinics caused several significant benefits. Waiting times decreased. Doctor and nurse absenteeism plummeted. Clinics became cleaner, and fewer drugs were stolen. Clinics were used more; 40% to 50% more children were vaccinated.

Most important, one-third fewer children died under the age of five. In the region served by the clinics, an area of 55,000 households, an estimated 550 lives were saved.

None of these improvements were realized at a number of control clinics where citizen report cards were not implemented (Björkman & Svensson, 2010).

is focused on advancing the collective thinking and action among service recipients for civic improvement. It is particularly useful for gauging the extent to which organizations are enabling the agency of their constituents.

If we apply this perspective directly to human services organizations, we would think of the organizations as polities, and the service recipients as constituents whose voice in the organization needs to be cultivated and listened to. This is not an unqualified argument for formal governance rights (although in some cases that is appropriate). From this perspective, data derived from feedback take a backseat to the ongoing relationships between organizations and their primary constituents. Civic engagement promoters value feedback as a way of engaging with constituents that puts beneficiaries first (Keystone, 2006b).

This approach emphasizes transparency and responsiveness to service recipients; it uses feedback activities to address inherent power imbalances in the relationships between organizations and their constituents (Bonbright, 2007; Kiryttopoulou, 2008). Feedback from this perspective is the means for establishing terms of partnership between an organization and its primary constituents; it legitimizes organizations with their primary constituents (Oxfam, 2008), builds trust, and ensures mutual concern and respect. Some argue that offering citizens the opportunity to define what feedback is important and to participate in evaluation efforts increases trust in public institutions in general (Yang & Holzer, 2006).

In this context, the learning that comes from getting and analyzing feedback is defined in terms of its value to primary constituents. This approach emphasizes that those most affected by the problems organizations seek to address are most likely to know what works well and what does not (Kiryttopoulou, 2008). It also hypothesizes that the quality of the relationship with primary constituents is the best predictor of impact (Keystone, 2006a). This is important for a field in which impacts (defined as sustainable positive changes in well-being by service recipients) are often unknowable in the short term. This perspective is similar to the emphasis in the for-profit sector on getting feedback from customers to enable businesses to develop products that meet customer needs. One recent article describes how the San Francisco Opera used this kind of feedback. The opera made changes in its operation based on surveys of what patrons "want to see, how they want to see it, how much they are willing to pay or donate, and what they expect in return. . . . The changes led to increased attendance and renewed energy in the organization" (Snibbe, 2007, p. 1).

CONSTITUENT VOICE: A TOOL OF PERFORMANCE MANAGEMENT

Constituent Voice is an empirically rigorous and systematic way of listening to and learning from our most important constituents—those in whose name we do our work—and then using this knowledge in dialogue with constituents to improve the relationships and the effectiveness of programs.

Constituent Voice does not replace traditional monitoring of a program's operations, nor does it do away with the need for formal evaluation. But it does assert that systematically listening to our primary constituents provides an important—and too often neglected—source of real-time knowledge and insight that we can use to manage performance, strengthen relationships, and improve outcomes.

Feedback data are an early indicator of the health of an intervention and of the changes taking place, planned or unplanned. Data can be triangulated with other evidence of results (including outcome measures and operational monitoring information) to enrich understanding of what is happening now. Dialogue about findings generates correction action and innovation. Feedback is a reliable predictor of future outcomes. And, over time, the accumulated evidence can reveal patterns—the ebb and flow of an intervention's results—that help understand the nature and process of change.

There are many different ways of generating Constituent Voice, but over the last 2 years Keystone has worked with many different partners and arrived at a core methodology that consists of five linked elements or stages:

1. Designing
2. Collecting information

3. Analyzing
4. Sense-making: closing the loop and reporting
5. Learning and improving

This chapter will discuss each of the elements in the operational cycle of CV in turn. Keystone Accountability has named this cycle the Hirschman Voice Cycle (see Figure 13.1), after the economist Albert O. Hirschman, whose seminal work on how people engage with organizations is central to the Constituent Voice. (For a blog post on the Hirschman cycle that acknowledges his contributions, see feedbacklabs.org/voice-as-both-means-and-end.)

Constituent Voice measures and the accompanying practice of public reporting and dialogue are powerful ways of enabling real citizen engagement in the programs and interventions that claim to serve citizens at a local level. CV is light-touch and cost-effective, making it practical, replicable, and scalable. We believe that by quantifying and aggregating qualitative

FIGURE 13.1   Hirschman Voice Cycle.

Source: Keystone Accountability (2013b).

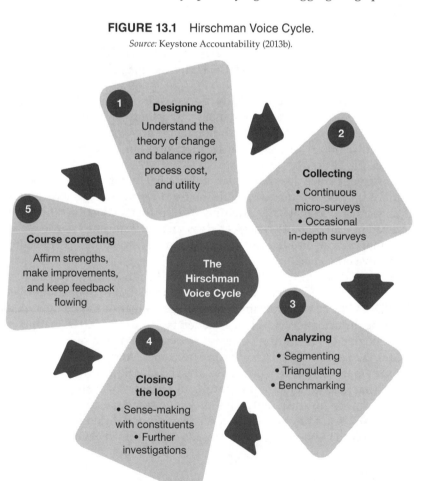

feedback data, it is possible to establish credible performance benchmarks across organizations providing similar services. Constituent Voice enables real-time local, regional, and national comparison and learning about what interventions are working well, what lessons can be learned, and where management interventions are required before problems become too serious. Most important, it turns subjects into actors.

Step 1: Designing

Design is critical. Constituent Voice seeks to **balance** the four central principles of good developmental performance measurement practice:

- *Rigor*
  Performance management data must be accurate and reliable and provide credible evidence of what we need to know. Good social research and evaluation practices apply to sampling, ensuring data quality, conducting statistical analysis, and reporting findings.
- *Sensitivity to process*
  An important part of all human services work involves building people's capacity to discover solutions and take control of their lives. It is a living, generative process, and this means we need to measure and nurture those things that give life to an intervention: attitudes, relationships, capabilities, and agency as well as changes in material conditions. Constituents must feel that they belong and contribute. The questions we ask and the way we ask them must be empowering and respectful: They must be meaningful to constituents, must enable them to say what they want to say, must generate knowledge and insights that they can use, and must build their capacity to use it.
- *Cost and burden*
  For data collection to be sustainable, its costs must be modest and the burden on respondents light.
- *Utility*
  Performance measurement must generate data and data management systems that are used by key constituents for ongoing learning and improving through the life of the program—these are not ex post facto assessments.

This is not an easy balance to achieve. In recent times, one approach, experimental studies with statistically significant proofs of causality, has been elevated above others as the gold standard. Gradually, a more sophisticated consensus is emerging that sees utility as the real gold standard (for a blog piece making the case for use, see Twersky, 2007). More practical materials are being produced to support the use of evaluative findings. (See, for example, a recent guidance note on use of impact evaluation results written by this author for InterAction, www.interaction.org/document/guidance-note-4-use-impact-evaluation-results.)

Constituent Voice surveys emerge out of a deep inquiry into the organization's context and theory of change. Grounded in clear "if, then" statements that tell us what we want to learn from respondents, survey instruments are tempered through input from key stakeholders. Questions are pretested to make sure they are understood as they were meant to be understood by the drafters.

This does take time, but Keystone is making this easy by building a trove of questions that work well and can be applied across diverse contexts. These questions fall into four categories introduced and elaborated on in Step 2.

Step 2: Collecting Data

CV metrics make use of innovative survey techniques and information technologies to generate accurate, timely, and actionable performance data at all levels of management.

Keystone has made a careful study of customer satisfaction measurement in the business world and combined its insights with our own deep experience of participatory learning to develop a new and effective mix of data-gathering methods. Keystone's core hypothesis is that just as customer satisfaction has proven to be a reliable predictor of business success, so can CV—and even more so when properly measured—be the best available predictor of development outcomes.

Periodic comprehensive and anonymous feedback surveys by an independent agency. At the level of specific interventions (where most of the data are generated), carefully planned independent and anonymous surveys of a representative sample of constituents provide robust perceptual data on the relevance and quality of services, the self-confidence of constituents, and the quality of relationships, as well as the perceived progress towards outcomes.

The importance of independently collected anonymous feedback was demonstrated in a recent experiment in Tanzania, where Keystone was surveying households in the villages affected by a sustainable forestry project. We created two research teams, one clearly identifying itself as representing the forestry company and the other presenting itself as an independent research firm contracted by the company. The feedback collected by the company researchers was consistently around 30% more positive than the feedback collected by the independent team.

These surveys should ideally take place every 1 to 2 years. They ask a number of questions derived from the intervention's theory of change and can provide empirically valid data on four main dimensions of an intervention's performance (see Figure 13.2):

- *Importance of the organization and its services to constituents*
  Questions here explore the overarching questions, "How important is this organization to me and my family? Which of these services are most important to me?"

FIGURE 13.2   Four types of constituent feedback.
Source: Keystone Accountability (2013a).

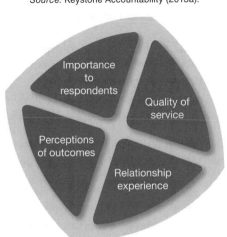

- *Quality of services*
  Questions here explore the quality of services with a focus on a specific touch point of one or more services. They can be more or less objective, depending on what the organization is working on improving. A more objective question might ask about waiting times or service punctuality. More subjective questions might look to overall ratings.
- *Quality of relationships*
  Separate questions cover different relationship dimensions such as confidence (in the knowledge and capabilities of organization staff), integrity (perceptions of honesty, commitment, and fairness), voice (do service recipients feel respected, that their voice is encouraged and heard, and that they belong and play a meaningful role in the intervention?), empowerment (do service recipients feel the intervention is helping them stand on their own feet with less outside help), readiness (service recipients' levels of confidence and commitment to investing their own time and energy), and overall satisfaction (how strongly would recipients recommend the program and/or its activities to others like them?).
- *Outcomes*
  The changes that constituents themselves see and value, and that they attribute to the organization.

The comprehensive surveys include both quantifiable rating questions (using Likert scales) and open-ended questions that allow respondents to say what they like.

Quantification enables comparisons of program performance over time and across interventions or across regions to help identify which are working better from the beneficiary perspective, and why. The open questions enable unstructured insights to emerge and can also be analyzed and quantified using standard statistical techniques.

Selected demographic questions enable disaggregation and comparison of responses by age, sex, location, level of education, employment, and/or any other category relevant to the intervention.

Ongoing independent or self-collected microsurveys at key program touch points. Continuous microsurveys complement the annual or biannual comprehensive surveys. Microsurveys tell you what is happening as you implement a program or make changes as a result of the feedback you have received. They give a picture of the ebb and flow of the intervention. They can act as an early warning system, and they allow you to respond to challenges before they become threats.

Microsurveys are very short surveys ranging from a single question to five or six questions. They are conducted at significant moments in the course of a project that are known as touch points—for example, after a training session, at a meeting or an event. They provide a light-touch, continual "finger on the pulse" of constituents' experience and perceptions of the project or program. The data can be fed into and compared with data from the comprehensive surveys.

When it is appropriate to collect feedback independently, doing so does not have to be expensive. Community volunteers, students, and other local data collectors can be trained to impart rigor to data collection by following clear data collection protocols and guaranteeing respondents anonymity and confidentiality.

Microsurvey questions can ask for a "single button" response or contain one or two demographic questions and closed and open questions. For example, a question such as "On a scale of 0 to 10, how strongly would you recommend this training workshop to a friend or neighbor?" could be followed by a request to please give reasons for the rating or mention any things the respondent liked or disliked about the training.

Microsurveys are ideally suited to data-gathering technologies such as text messages on simple cell phones and handheld devices that have the potential to significantly reduce costs, improve timeliness, and automate data analysis and reporting. Microsurveys create a continuous stream of real-time performance data on the constituent experience of activities and outputs, relationship quality, and the impacts of the intervention on livelihoods, all of which allow organizations to track progress against outcomes, monitor relationships, and triangulate with self-reported data on activities and outputs.

In other words—to use a health check analogy—whereas comprehensive surveys provide periodic complete checkups, continuous feedback allows you to monitor your blood pressure every day.

Survey methods vary according to budget and context and can include the following:

- E-mail surveys using low-bandwidth interactive PDF questionnaires. It is advisable to avoid web-based surveys unless connectivity is not an issue at all.

- Focus group discussions after which participants score privately on their own questionnaires.
- Individual interviews and household surveys.

Where appropriate, CV can utilize simple but widely recognized participatory methods for rating and scoring.

Step 3: Analyzing

Quantified perceptual data can be analyzed using standard statistical methods to give reliable insights into the perceptions of different groups of constituents. One method now extremely popular in customer satisfaction bears special mention.

Net promoter analysis. The customer satisfaction industry has found a simple technique known as net promoter analysis (NPA) to be accurate and convenient (Net Promoter, n.d.). NPA classifies respondents into promoters, passives, and detractors and calculates a single net promoter score (NP score).

NPA is disarmingly simple, but hundreds of the world's leading corporations use it. It has proven to be a reliable measure of customer loyalty and a powerful lever for positive organizational motivation and change. A score of 9 or 10 classifies the respondent as a promoter, a 7 or 8 as passive, and a 6 or below as a detractor. Figure 13.3 presents an NPA for two questions. The NP score is derived by subtracting the percentage of detractors from the percentage of promoters. The most storied customer service

FIGURE 13.3   Net promoter analysis of two questions.
Source: Keystone Accountability (2012a).

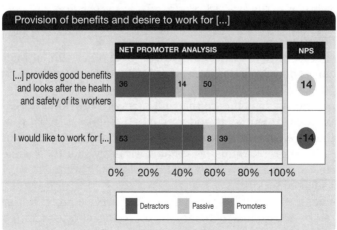

FIGURE 13.4 Using comparison to motivate change.

Source: Kaufman (2009).

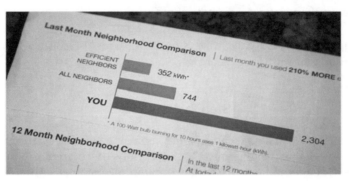

companies in the world achieve NP scores in the 70s and 80s. Some entire industries—you can guess which they are—struggle to achieve NP scores in positive numbers.

This way of presenting data has the advantage of focusing analysis on developing strategies appropriate to each group. "What do we need to do to turn our detractors into passives or promoters?"

Scores for a number of related questions on a particular area of performance (such as the importance and utility of services), or from a number of short touch point surveys over a year, can be aggregated into performance indexes for comparative analysis.

Benchmarking. Quantification of qualitative feedback data enables us to create performance benchmarks not on the basis of technical ratings by external inspectors but on internal feedback using common questions.

Comparison is a proven way to get people and organizations to act on metrics. The approach to presenting bills to customers of a public utility in California shown in Figure 13.4 produced a first-ever dramatic reduction in energy use. Figure 13.5 shows an example of one of Keystone's comparative data visualizations.

Published benchmarks and comparison with other, similar interventions enable organizations to better understand what defines "good" for the work they do.

Organizations can compare their ratings with how other organizations are rated by their constituents and gain a better sense of what is achievable and how they are performing relative to similar organizations. Benchmarks drive the utilization of evaluative data—a strategy that the business world has perfected to a fine art. We can put this proven technique to work to solve important societal problems.

In business, customer ratings of goods and services are now very public, and are used by consumers in making their product choices. Companies cannot ignore what their customers are saying, and they put in a great deal of

FIGURE 13.5 Example of comparative data visualizations used by Keystone.
Source: Keystone Accountability (2012).

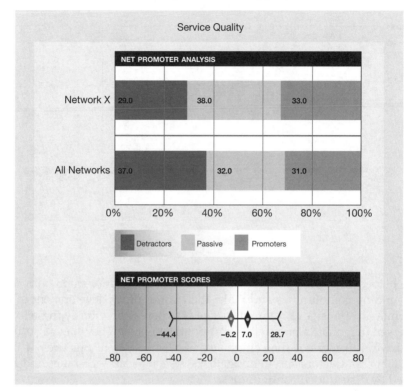

effort to gain positive reviews. Imagine what would happen if human service organizations knew that their potential funders were able to review independently collected constituent feedback on their work as well as on the work of other organizations like them. Public benchmarking could become a powerful driver of performance and of greater accountability to constituents. Some moves in this direction are discussed further in the discussion "Benchmark data sets—a strategy tool" hereafter.

Triangulation. In the customer satisfaction industry, it is universally recognized that customer loyalty scores correlate to company growth and profits. Similar correlations are now being discovered by organizations seeking to create social value. In high schools in the United States, we know that student feedback collected early in the school year correlates to their measurable performance later in the year (this and related cases are catalogued in Twersky, Buchanan, & Threlfall, 2013).

A good illustration of this comes from two sustainable forestry companies in Tanzania and Swaziland that used Constituent Voice to better understand their effects on their surrounding communities. The findings

FIGURE 13.6   Correlation of community impacts on company forests with community perceptions of the company.

Source: Keystone Accountability (2012b).

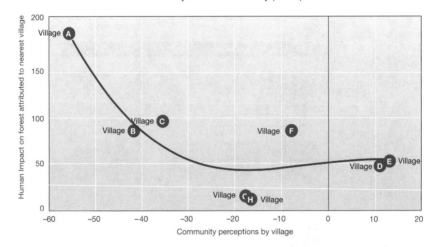

have helped them understand the nature of their relationships with their surrounding communities and make their community development initiatives more responsive to community needs (whereas previously these initiatives were negotiated only with local political elites). They have also used the surveys to monitor the compliance and employment practices of their local labor contractors and to mitigate risks such as labor disputes and fires started by disgruntled communities.

Figure 13.6 is based on actual data from one of the company surveys. The data showed that poor perceptions of the company were closely related to destructive behaviors such as burning and poaching. The company is now using CV feedback as an early warning signal to guide relationship-building efforts.

Step 4: Sense-Making—Closing the Loop with Constituents and Reporting

Information transforms into shared understanding and voice when it is reported back to and discussed with constituents. This deliberative approach to sense-making fosters an improvement-oriented shared inquiry between organization staff and those who are meant to benefit from its work (see Figure 13.7). It creates the kind of transparency and accountability that builds confidence and trust and enhances the credibility of the program among key constituents.

When organizations engage in this kind of sense-making, they routinely discover insights for program improvement, form new mutual commitments, identify new activities, and, above all, strengthen the bonds of connection with those they serve.

FIGURE 13.7   Sense-making in action.
Source: Andre Proctor, Founder of Keystone Accountability, used with permission.

There are many different ways of reporting back and discussing feedback. Some organizations prefer independently facilitated meetings, others favor running a series of internal dialogues themselves. Where constituents are local, face-to-face meetings are possible. Where they are widely dispersed, a mix of print and other interactive media can be used.

The significance of deliberative sense-making with constituents is increased when it is extended into public reporting. As described in the 2009 ACF Constituent Voice report, sense-making yields the feedback principle of public reporting. This principle holds that when reporting its results to funders and the public at large, an organization should also publish what those who are meant to enjoy those reported results have to say about them (for a discussion of the feedback principle of public reporting in the U.S. nonprofit sector context, see Bonbright, Campbell, & Nguyen, 2009).

The charity rating agency Charity Navigator incorporated this deliberative element of Constituent Voice in its January 2013 revisions to its rating model. That new rating model suggests that donors to human service organizations should ask the following questions:

1. Does the charity publish feedback data from its primary constituents?
2. Do the published feedback data include an explanation of how likely they are to be representative of all primary constituents?
3. Do the data include an explanation of why the organization believes the feedback is frank and honest?
4. Are those data presented in a way that shows changes over time going back at least 1 year?
5. Do the data include questions that speak to the organization's effectiveness?
6. Does the organization report back to its primary constituents what it heard from them?

Question 6 directly raises the all-important deliberative sense-making with primary constituents. At least when it comes to information that relates to effectiveness, performance, and outcomes, the meaning of information in an ecosystem is best found through deliberation of the issue being addressed across different constituents.

Since the beneficiaries are not the payers, their voice counts for more when donors hear it directly. When donors pay attention to their views, then charities will pay attention to them. By requiring charities to answer these six questions, Charity Navigator has taken the largest step ever taken to date by any development agency to cultivate beneficiary voices. (It may soon be eclipsed by the World Bank, however, which is looking at how to build Constituent Voice into its government lending for health and human services.)

Benchmark data sets: A strategy tool. The move to shared information for strategic performance management has already begun among ACF members. Twenty-eight percent of ACF members responding to a 2008 survey indicated that they were participating in benchmarking studies (Bonbright, Campbell, & Ngyuen, 2009). Presumably many of these were part of the Alliance for Children and Families' Benchmarking Initiative, which is run by Behavioral Pathway Systems. That effort provides cohort, state, and national comparative data for participating Alliance members on over 50 performance indicators across a range of administrative, financial, operational, and clinical data. It does not include feedback. Behavioral Pathway Systems CEO Paul Lefkovitz indicates that this initiative has already, in its first year, enabled participants to work through the initial resistance to being compared against others, to learn from each other, and to begin to focus in on areas for improvement. The participants in this project, though still only a minority of Alliance members, represent a leading trend toward creating a stronger, evidence-based decision-making culture among human services organizations.

The opportunity now is for human service organizations to share feedback data to create a new and powerful strategy development tool for the field.

REFERENCES

Björkman, M., & Svensson, J. (2010). When is community-based monitoring effective? Evidence from a randomized experiment in primary health in Uganda. *Journal of the European Economic Association, 8*, 571–581.

Bonbright, D. (2007). What do we need to know? *Alliance Magazine, 12*(4), 29–33.

Bonbright, D., Campbell, D., & Nguyen, L. (2009). *The 21st century potential of constituent voice: Opportunities for reform in the United States human services sector.* Milwaukee, WI: Alliance for Children and Families.

Hunter, D. E. K. (2013). *Working hard and working well: A practical guide to performance management.* Hamden, CT: Hunter Consulting LLC.

Kaufman, L. (2009, January 30). Utilities turn their customers green, with envy. *The New York Times.* Retrieved from http://www.nytimes.com/2009/01/31/science/earth/31compete.html

Keystone. (2006a). Keystone Capabilities Profiler. Retrieved from http://www. keystoneaccountability.org/sites/default/files/Keystone capabilities profiler _4.1_ Aug 2006_0.pdf

Keystone. (2006b). *A BOND approach to quality in non-governmental organisations: Putting beneficiaries first.* Retrieved from http://www.bond.org.uk/data/files/Effectiveness_ Programme/research/A_bond_approach_to_quality_2006.pdf

Keystone Accountability. (2012a). *Net promoter analysis.* London, UK: Author.

Keystone Accountability. (2012b). *Constituent voice and community impacts.* London, UK: Author.

Keystone Accountability (2013a). *Four types of constituent feedback.* London, UK: Author.

Keystone Accountability (2013b). *Hirschman voice cycle.* London, UK: Author. Retrieved from http://feedbacklabs.org/voice-as-both-means-and-end

Kiryttopoulou, N. (2008). *Strengthening civil society's accountability for results: The opportunity of comparative constituency feedback.* Paper presented at the 8th International Society for Third Sector Research Conference, Barcelona, Spain.

Net Promoter. (n.d.). Retrieved from http://www.netpromotersystem.com

Oxfam. (2008). *How Oxfam monitors and evaluates its work.* Retrieved from http://www .oxfam.org.uk/resources/evaluations

Pinsoneault, L. (2006). *New voices at the civic table: How six human service organizations are supporting the civic engagement of community members.* Milwaukee, WI: Alliance for Children and Families.

Sen, A. (1999). *Development as freedom.* Cambridge, UK: Oxford University Press.

Snibbe, A. C. (2007). Listening is lucrative: The most successful nonprofits pay close heed to their markets. *Stanford Social Innovation Review*, Winter 2007, 1.

Twersky, F. (2012, February 27). *Time for a gold standard of use.* Retrieved from http://www .effectivephilanthropy.org/blog/2012/02/time-for-a-gold-standard-of-use/?utm_ source=feedburner&utm_medium=email&utm_campaign=Feed%3A+effectivephilant hropy+%28The+CEP+Blog%29

Twersky, F., Buchanan, P., & Threlfall, V. (2013). Listening to those who matter most, the beneficiaries. *Stanford Social Innovation Review*, Spring 2013.

Yang, K., & Holzer, M. (2006). The performance-trust link: Implications for performance management. *Public Administration Review*, 66(1), 114–126.

CHAPTER 14

Initial Reflections on the Strategy Counts Initiative

Laura T. Pinsoneault

Human services organizations have mastered the art of responsive tactics—at the individual level and in their day-to-day operations, they benefit the many individuals and families they serve. On a larger, more strategic level, however, organizations struggle to be truly proactive and transformative in producing wider, systems-level change. Although the number of individuals who benefit from the programs and services of human services organizations is great, the perceived value of the organizations themselves by the public has all but disappeared. This is because evaluation and monitoring are focused on the transactional outcomes of programs and services and not on the strategy.

Take, for example, a fictional organization, Family & Children's Programs and Services. They have been in their community for 60 years. With an annual operating budget of more than $20 million and approximately 400 staff, they serve 12,000 children and families in the greater metropolis through behavioral health services, basic needs, after-school and Head Start programming, and ESL and language learning. Each year they grow about 1% to 2% based on available funding and programming. They have a solid reputation, competitively bid on contracts for services they know they can provide, and obtain good outcomes. They benchmark their performance each year and adjust programs accordingly.

In contrast, fictional organization Youth Futures is the result of a recent reorganization of a residential care provider. They have an operating budget of about $30 million and serve about 1,500 children and families annually through their residential programs and services and an additional 5,000 through site-based community centers in three neighborhoods, offering basic needs services, parenting programs, and workforce development and job placement opportunities. About 5 years ago, the residential provider was unable to meet the types of outcomes the leadership desired. They embarked on a strategic planning process, refined their mission and values, focused on outcomes reflecting this mission, and reviewed research, data, and needs assessments to address policy and practice gaps. In those 5 years, Youth Futures has tripled the number of children it serves and touched the lives of many more families than they intended through their site-based work.

Both organizations are stable in the short term, but they are engaged in very different strategies and business models. Strategy Counts would take the position that even though Family & Children's demonstrates positive outcomes and short-term impacts and appears sustainable on paper, because of the lack of a grand strategy or any examination of the values and theories that drive their work forward, they are placing themselves and in turn the communities they work with at greater risk. This risk is not readily apparent by examining performance and results alone, but if an organization is also evaluating the underlying strategy of its work opportunities, risks become more apparent and the organization is more likely to execute and sustain broader, long-term outcomes.

This chapter sets out a framework put forth by Michael Quinn Patton and Patricia Patrizi (2010) for evaluating strategy to challenge nonprofit organizations to think beyond doing what gets measured and get to what needs to be done. The Alliance also shares its strategy for evaluating the Strategy Counts initiative and its preliminary findings to date.

FROM STRATEGIC EVALUATION TO EVALUATING STRATEGY

Evaluating strategy is a difficult transition for nonprofit human services organizations that are just starting to grasp what it means to monitor outputs and manage outcomes. As a sector, nonprofits are only now engaging in regular processes to produce strategic plans, create program logic models, and identify indicators and measures to determine the effectiveness of what they do in the short term. All of these tools are critical for creating the capacity to evaluate programs and services and eventually engage in strategic evaluation.

Strategic evaluation is about using data to drive decision making and ultimately expand the benefits and sustainability of valuable programs and services. There are many models of strategic evaluation (balanced scorecards, SWOT analysis, management matrices, etc.). These tools are designed to help us examine the results of our strategies given the target outcomes. *Evaluating strategy*, on the other hand, is about understanding how and why we obtained the outcomes that we did—what was intended, what was actually done, and whether it was of any value.

The language of logic models and measurement is not easily transferable to evaluating strategy, because these tools start from the assumption that the tactics chosen were indeed the best options. For example, looking at increases in the number of foster families as an indicator of capacity to serve children in foster care begins with the premise that the strategy for care is in having more families to place children with. An effort to reduce poverty by measuring growth in job skills as an indicator of success assumes that it is a lack of job skills that is causing poverty. In both cases, measurable outcomes may indicate success, but children in foster care may not benefit in terms of well-being and the communities may not move out of poverty because of a strategic misunderstanding of the root cause and best policies and practices to address that need.

For strategy to actually drive an organization forward on its mission, it cannot focus solely on the outcomes of its programs and services but needs to engage in evaluating the process of strategy itself, which is qualitative in nature. And, for a sector that is often dismissed for being too "anecdotal," this can be an issue. Evaluating strategy can be done both quantitatively and qualitatively. And process evaluation, which is somewhat qualitative by design, can be systematic.

A Framework for Evaluating Strategy

Patrizi (2010) puts forth a process for evaluating strategy that begins with the critical elements of strategy itself. The strategic plan is one of the most critical pieces of data an organization has at its fingertips. According to Patrizi, "[strategic] plans provide a useful window into how strategic actors view the world in terms of cause and effect, as well as what they value and believe, and how they treat information to formulate a case" (p. 95). Essentially, our tactics often speak to our assumptions about cause and effect. To understand strategy, it is necessary to look not only at what is written and intended but at what gets done and how. Patrizi identifies a framework in which strategy can be understood through (a) perspective, (b) position, and (c) pattern.

Perspective

Patrizi's (2010) idea of perspective is essentially about *how* strategy takes place. In the nonprofit human services sector, organizational perspective is often reflected in a theory of change. Whether explicit or implicit, acknowledged or unacknowledged, dominant or marginalized, an organization's operations are rooted in assumptions, beliefs, and cultures about how they will best meet their goals. In evaluating strategy, there needs to be an examination of commonality of perspective from within the organization and of how perspectives align across business lines, funding institutions and opportunities, and organizational policies and practices. A place to start when strategy is weakened is to look at whether or not perspective is aligned, and, if it is not, where, how, and by whom it should be addressed.

Assessing perspective necessitates constant probing to understand assumptions that drive beliefs, what is actually meant, and how that perspective is being perceived. The perspective of the Strategy Counts initiative is that children, adults, families, and communities impacted by poverty would benefit by strengthening the strategic capacity of the organizations that operate within them. The Alliance defined strategic learning and development as the pathway for this change to occur. Strategy Counts charged funded organizations with setting a strategy that would positively affect people living in poverty, but did not define a singular pathway for change.

As we move through the first year of the Strategy Counts grants, a multiplicity of perspectives on the poverty charge has emerged. It is increasingly clear that there is no common measurement of impact on poverty within Strategy Counts, but that does not mean that we cannot look at the different values of strategic perspective on poverty. At this point in time, inherent in the strategy of Strategy Counts is critical discussion about how private human services providers as a sector should approach our strategic work on poverty.

Position

Strategic position, in contrast to perspective, is not how but where an organization sees the change or effect taking place (Patrizi, 2010, p. 96). Position informs where to measure change and who the informants of change may be. Questions of position are business questions:

- How much and where will we invest?
- Does the strategy actually get at the position determined?
- Is the strategy workable given this position?
- Does the position require reexamining perspective?
- Did the intended outcome occur? How, and why?

The intended position of Strategy Counts is to initiate change at an organizational level through a strategy leader within an organization. Resource investment should align with these sources of impact or change. Our evaluation of the Strategy Counts initiative will need to ask whether or not the strategy leader and the organization are appropriate for investment. Patrizi (2010) importantly cautions strategists that position can become so diffuse or so narrow that achievement is impossible. This is often a point of risk for nonprofits that focus too broadly and draw down on necessary resources for mission attainment.

Pattern

Patrizi (2010) identifies pattern as a central tool in evaluating strategy. The examination of the patterns of how strategy moves from intention to execution helps refine and understand whether positions and perspectives are relevant to the results being sought. Examination of pattern is the nuts and bolts of process evaluation—tracking behaviors and drawing connections between people and actions, structures, and processes.

Some of the evaluation questions of pattern are as follow:

- What is actually being done? By who, and when?
- How are decisions being made?
- How do perspective and position come together to inform each other?
- How are people being connected to the meaning behind the strategy?
- Who is influencing what is getting done?
- What are the roles of those involved? How do they change over time? What precipitates this change?

Cohort learning as a component of Strategy Counts exemplifies a way to look at pattern as a framework for strategy. The Strategy Counts perspective is that strategic learning, to be effective, needs to occur through a network of peer support in which ideas can be explored, exchanged, and refined. The position is that by gathering strategy leaders, we will see a growing comfort and confidence in the capacity to implement and share strategy throughout an organization. As the Alliance evaluates Strategy Counts, our evaluation includes ways in which organizations spread strategic learning through their strategy leaders but also looks at how the Alliance moves its focus on strategy within the sector.

Strategy Counts? Evaluating Strategy

The goal of the Alliance in evaluating strategy was not to look at the strategy itself to determine its utility but rather to understand (1) how strategy looks in nonprofit human services organizations and (2) how the capacity to develop and focus on strategy creates transformational shifts in systems, organizations, and the outcomes of missions.

Our perspective on strategy at the Alliance was that when strategy is refined, monitored, and aligned, a number of critical benefits may be realized:

- Expansion of successful core services
- Elimination of nonaligned, "off-mission" programs and initiatives
- Reconfiguration of existing services and greater program efficiencies
- Development of new value-added services through innovation
- Greater resilience in the face of economic downturns and therefore enhanced sustainability of highly effective programs
- Enhancement of revenues available for service delivery
- Successful reorientation of board energies, efforts, and attention to issues more central to the responsibilities of governance
- Greater social impact on the communities that organizations serve

TABLE 14.1 Alliance Tools for Evaluating Strategy and Strategy Counts

Tools	Perspective	Position	Pattern	Results	Purpose
Request for Proposal	✓				To reflect the change perspective of Strategy Counts
Responses to RFP (round 1) (funded and nonfunded)	✓	✓			To reflect the intended and initial approach to strategy; the theory of how strategy will move the organization forward; how well Strategy Counts has aligned position and perspective
Responses to RFP (round 2) (funded and nonfunded)			✓		To provide reflection on how Strategy Counts has realigned perspective and position
Lightning Rounds (2–3 times a year shared across cohorts)			✓		To allow strategy leaders to reflect on progress, plans, and open issues moving forward
Learning Opportunity Evaluations		✓	✓	✓	To reflect the investments of the Strategy Count initiatives in moving strategic thinking and learning forward
Grant Reports		✓	✓		To provide updates every 6 months on the execution of intended strategy and any realignments and financials related to each strategy site's grant
Pulse and Critical Moments Survey			✓		To allow strategy leaders to reflect on momentum and critical moments in strategic learning
Common Measures (annually administered)		✓		✓	To measure culture change in organization resulting from strategic focus and
Institutional Case Studies	✓	✓	✓	✓	To inform the full understanding of the strategy process in the context of being the "most successful"

Tools for Evaluating Strategy

Because the Alliance desires not only to understand what effective strategy looks like within organizations but also to begin to understand how focusing efforts on strategic thinking and learning might strengthen an organization's sustainability and performance, multiple tools and methods are necessary to capture all of the dynamics of strategy. Based on the iterative nature of strategy, the Alliance does not expect the initiative's effects to follow a typical linear logic model but rather expects that each action, asset, or activity of Strategy Counts will have evolving ripple effects that will ultimately place organizations in a strong position with respect to their own missions and outcomes (Coyne & Cox, 2008).

For Strategy Counts, then, the Alliance did not establish a set of outputs matched to outcomes, but rather generated a set of research questions and hypotheses and the indicators that would help us understand these better. From these research questions, the Alliance looked at the tools that would be available to us through the grant process—tools we could create in collaboration with the funded sites given their strategies—and existing data we could draw from to help us situate Strategy Counts within the broader sector. The tools we are using to gather information about the role of strategy, although not isolated across perspective, position, and pattern, offer unique vantage points to each of these elements of strategy (see Table 14.1).

EVALUATING STRATEGY COUNTS TODAY

Strategy evaluation is no less challenging for us as a national organization or grant intermediary than it is for any organization providing programs and services within a community. The Alliance is just beginning to understand how to work with our evaluation process to understand both the value of strategy in organizations and the value of our strategy as an intermediary in Strategy Counts. The perspective that a focus on strategy, both for its design and its execution, is critical to the private, nonprofit human services sector has not shifted. Activity-focused evaluations provide data and insight into how we may be affecting in the short term the thinking and development of strategy leaders. For example, at the second in-person cohort gathering of Strategy Counts, we asked strategy leaders before and after the gathering about their comfort levels with understanding strategy, executing strategy, and sharing strategy with others. What we found was that immediately after the gathering itself, strategy leaders grew very little in their comfort levels but that in looking at patterns over the course of the first year of the grant, those strategy leaders showed significant increases in their comfort levels in understanding, applying, and communicating strategy (Pinsoneault & Dahlquist, 2013).

While the cohort evaluation tools support our strategy approach, the pulse survey administered every 8 to 12 weeks is showing very little variation in momentum and in strategy design and execution. These data pose two strategic questions. The first is about the validity and purposefulness of the tool itself: Are we measuring what our strategy is intending? The second is about position: Is the perception of the strategy leader where we intend to have impact? Examining this pattern over time will help us both understand our perspective and position and shape the strategy of cohort learning as a tool for creating transformational shifts in an organization.

As the Alliance moves forward with the evaluation and the strategy of Strategy Counts, we continue to engage in the process of reflection with the evaluation tools and the project sites and to grapple with questions of strategy evaluation. We are experimenting with what is a both new yet natural frame of evaluation in which examining process systematically in real time, rather than reporting, is where the most valuable data sit. That level of evaluation is what is driving ahead the strategy of Strategy Counts and the continued sense of the project that is being experienced and realized. That being said, the Alliance is also looking to the results of Strategy Counts to understand the role of strategy.

Organizational Results of Strategy

Although the Alliance did not dictate a specific strategy model or outcome focus, the Strategy Counts project team, the evaluation team, and the 14 initial project sites agreed upon a common measures tool for exploring potential indicators of organizational change. The common measures tool is collected each year by the strategy leader at each of the program sites as part of the Strategy Counts initiative. The indicators selected include the following:

- Financial health
- Growth in the organization's use of data
- Change in organizational learning culture

At the time of publication, 14 pilot sites had completed the common measures both at the beginning of, and 1 year into, their strategy initiatives.

Financial Health

Fiscal health and stability are not only relevant to the larger financial sustainability of the organization but also to the capacity of an organization to focus strategically. First, organizations tend to pull back on strategy in complex, fiscally unstable periods, because strategy is perceived as discretionary spending and is often not clearly connected to day-to-day operations (Alliance for Families and Children, 2010; Top-Consultant.com, 2010). Second, fiscal stability allows for greater agility in executing strategic options.

It is increasingly clear in the human services nonprofit sector that an organization's size and budget are not signs of its fiscal health and sustainability; large organizations can and do fail. The capacity of an organization to access capital and continue daily operations can be critical to long-term health and to experimentation and innovation. Through the common measures tool, all of the pilot sites provide the data and calculate a working capital ratio (assets to liabilities) as an indicator of their ability to pay short-term obligations by accessing cash; higher ratios indicate greater access to cash. Organizations also calculate the debt/equity ratio (liabilities to net assets) each year. A higher debt/asset ratio indicates that the organization is financing its growth with debt. In the evaluation of Strategy Counts, we look to each of these ratios to improve or maintain stability as an indication that the organization is effective in managing fiscal resources. These indicators are short-term measures that show the investment potential of the organization. Within the first year, there were swings in both directions. The next step in the evaluative process is to ask more questions of the data tools that may help us understand movement in fiscal indicators and to engage the Strategy Counts pilot sites in helping us understand the processes that may have influenced these shifts.

Strategy Counts shared this perspective and looked toward organizations that were in a financial position to focus on strategy. This does not necessarily mean all Strategy Counts sites were "fiscally healthy" according to our measures, but all were prepared to make their strategy initiative investment sustainable.

Data Usage

How do we know what we are doing really works? Are the decisions we are making grounded in what we know? Moving the nonprofit sector toward more strategic thinking and the integration of science to produce greater positive impact in their work with individuals, families, and communities requires that organizations not only collect and review data but understand and participate in the development of evidence as an asset. Many organizations already utilize, and consider adequate, data monitoring (the tracking of basic outputs) for substantiating their existence. However, the Strategy Counts initiative believes that truly strategic and transformative organizations need to move from monitoring to using assessment, management, evaluation, and even research as tools to grow programming, document outcomes, and use evidence to establish a more beneficial experience across systems of care.

The pilot sites through their strategy development are each on their own journey of experimentation and data usage. Each of the profiled organizations can talk about how data can make the organization better and have myriad examples. Our assessment through the common measures was to determine whether a focus on strategy improved the way data would be used with the assumption that this reflected a greater understanding of data and how they can be utilized to develop and execute strategy (Top-Consultant.com, 2010).

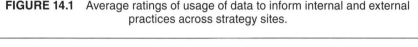

FIGURE 14.1   Average ratings of usage of data to inform internal and external practices across strategy sites.

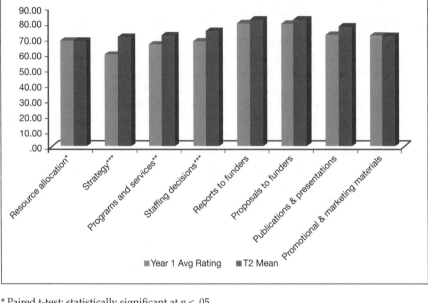

* Paired t-test: statistically significant at *p* < .05
** Paired t-test: statistically significant at *p* < .01
*** Paired t-test statistically significant at *p* < .001

The common measures tools ask strategy leaders to reflect upon and grade their organizations' data usage on a 100-point scale to inform internal practices (resource allocation, strategy, programs and services, and staffing decisions) and external decision-makers (funders and the public) through reports, presentations, and promotional materials. When the first 14 pilot sites started their strategy initiative, the use of data for external audiences was effective, at 70% or higher, whereas its use in informing internal practices was ineffective, at less than 70%. Within 1 year of focusing on a strategy initiative, real gains were evidenced in the average use of data to inform internal practices (see Figure 14.1).

Culture of Learning

The third area of common measurement across strategy pilot sites is in organizational culture. Several of the strategy sites are measuring culture change as part of their strategy initiative. Our purpose in evaluation was to understand how strategy leaders assessed the culture of their organizations. Gill (2010) defines a culture of learning as one that "supports and encourages collective discovery, sharing and application knowledge" (p. 4). To develop

FIGURE 14.2 Ratings of learning culture across strategy sites.

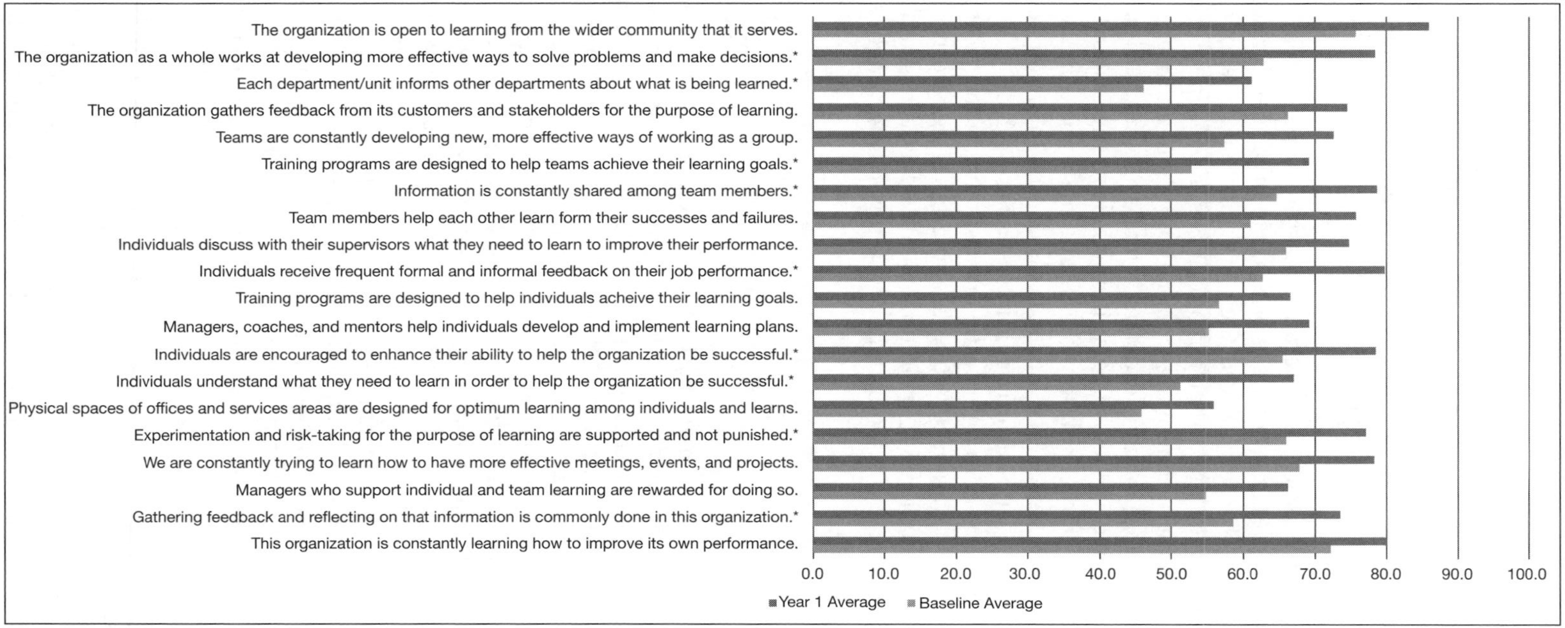

The organization is open to learning from the wider community that it serves.
The organization as a whole works at developing more effective ways to solve problems and make decisions.*
Each department/unit informs other departments about what is being learned.*
The organization gathers feedback from its customers and stakeholders for the purpose of learning.
Teams are constantly developing new, more effective ways of working as a group.
Training programs are designed to help teams achieve their learning goals.*
Information is constantly shared among team members.*
Team members help each other learn form their successes and failures.
Individuals discuss with their supervisors what they need to learn to improve their performance.
Individuals receive frequent formal and informal feedback on their job performance.*
Training programs are designed to help individuals achieve their learning goals.
Managers, coaches, and mentors help individuals develop and implement learning plans.
Individuals are encouraged to enhance their ability to help the organization be successful.*
Individuals understand what they need to learn in order to help the organization be successful.*
Physical spaces of offices and services areas are designed for optimum learning among individuals and learns.
Experimentation and risk-taking for the purpose of learning are supported and not punished.*
We are constantly trying to learn how to have more effective meetings, events, and projects.
Managers who support individual and team learning are rewarded for doing so.
Gathering feedback and reflecting on that information is commonly done in this organization.*
This organization is constantly learning how to improve its own performance.

0.0 10.0 20.0 30.0 40.0 50.0 60.0 70.0 80.0 90.0 100.0

■ Year 1 Average ■ Baseline Average

285

a learning culture, learning must extend beyond individuals and be developed at the team and organizational levels. To measure culture change in the Strategy Counts organizations, we adapted Gill's a culture of learning audit using the same 100-point scale to assess the organization's culture of learning.

For this discussion, we examined each item individually and looked at a total culture score across the original 14 pilot sites. Strategy leaders at the beginning of year 1 placed their organizations at about 60%. Within another year, they rated their organizations at 73% ($p < .05$). Those who are scoring higher are moving from talking about culture as being solely about performance to more leadership and development. Figure 14.2 shows how strategy leaders viewed organizational learning culture as they began their strategy efforts, and how the needle has moved in the first year of their strategy initiative. The largest areas of growth are on items related to individual and team learning cultures (see Figure 14.2). Culture change is slow and intentional. In light of the intentionality of the strategies to create learning and innovation cultures, this progress is significant. The next step in strategy evaluation will be to understand what tactics and activities led to this change and to understand how culture change might alter perspective and position.

CONCLUSIONS

As an evaluator, I no longer have to convince organizations of the value of measurable short-term and broader outcomes (although arguably there are still a great number of organizations challenged with "the how" of how to measure). The many chapters of this book highlight the innovations in strategy that occur when an organization invests critical resources (time, capital, creativity) in the development and, preferably, the execution of strategy. And strategic evaluation has a role in every one of these projects.

However, the greater challenge may be in how organizations strategize to evaluate strategy in and of itself. There is an excess of resources on how to develop strategy. There is also an abundance of resources on how to develop and measure the anticipated outcomes of strategy. However, there is next to nothing to help strategy leaders and strategic organizations understand how to evaluate and assess strategy in and of itself. Patton and Patrizi (2010) argue that in examining strategy, organizations are better equipped to separate rhetoric from the reality of their work (p. 26) and realize strategy rather than get stuck before a strategy can be fully realized and its effects fully understood. For strategy to be effective, its creators must reflect upon the process and the results. In doing so, we move from strategy as intended to strategy as executed.

There was virtually no framework to position and evaluate the strategy of Strategy Counts as the Alliance began this project. As is a condition of strategy, we, too, are learning alongside the Strategy Counts sites how to look at and develop a strategy of moving the human services sector forward on its mission. This chapter covers only the beginning of a longitudinal initiative to inform not only the development of strategy but also the development of an evaluation for strategy.

REFERENCES

Alliance for Children and Families (2010). *Research findings. Augmenting leadership and management planning projects* [unpublished report]. Milwaukee, WI: Kohls Consulting.

Cox, Kozak, Griep, & Moffat. (2008). *Splash and ripple: Using outcomes to design and manage community activities.* Calgary, AB: PLAN:NET LIMITED. Retrieved from http://www.hc-sc.gc.ca/ahc-asc/alt_formats/pacrb-dgapcr/pdf/finance/contribution/splash-ricochet-eng.pdf

Coyne, K., & Cox, P. (2008). Splash and ripple: Using outcomes to design and manage community activities. Calgary: Plan: Net Limited. Retrieved from http://www.hc-sc.gc.ca/ahc-asc/alt_formats/pacrb-dgapcr/pdf/finance/contribution/splash-ricochet-eng.pdf

Gill, S. J. (2010). *Developing a learning culture in nonprofit organizations.* Thousand Oaks, CA: Sage Publications.

Patrizi, P. A. (2010). Strategy evaluation: Emerging processes and methods. *New Directions for Evaluation, Winter* (128), 87–102.

Patton, M. Q., & Patrizi, P. A. (2010). Strategy as the focus for evaluation. *New Directions for Evaluation, Winter* (128), 5–28.

Pinsoneault, L. T., & Dahlquist, A. (2013). *Interim Strategy Counts cohort learning group evaluation* [unpublished report]. Milwaukee, WI: Alliance for Children and Families.

Top-Consultant.com. *Management consulting recruitment channel report 2010.* Retrieved from http://www.top-consultant.com/Top-Consultant_2010_Recruitment_Channel_Report.pdf

APPENDIX

Strategy Counts Pilot Sites and Map

BEECH BROOK, CLEVELAND, OH

Debra Rex, Chief Executive Officer
Jean Solomon, Vice President of Campus Programs

Description of Organization

Founded in 1852, Beech Brook is now a nationally recognized center for the treatment of emotionally disturbed and at-risk children, youth, and their families. Over the years, services have evolved to meet the changing needs of young children and youth, including those who have been affected by abuse and neglect, violence, and substance abuse. Many of our clients have suffered some kind of trauma, and consequently many of our services are trauma-informed and evidence-based.

Summary of Transformational Project

As changes are coming nationwide in the health and human services arena, Ohio has been adopting changes ahead of many other states. This transformational initiative at Beech Brook will retool operations to pilot the health home model by creating an integrated physical and behavioral health care service line for specific high-risk, high-need populations, leading to improved health.

FAMILIES INTERNATIONAL, MILWAUKEE, WI

Susan N. Dreyfus, President and Chief Executive Officer
John R. Schmidt, Chief Operating Officer and Chief Financial Officer

Description of Organization

Families International is the parent organization/nonprofit holding company for the nonprofit organizations Alliance for Children and Families, United Neighborhood Centers of America (UNCA), and Ways to Work. Together, the Alliance and UNCA networks number more than 500 nonprofit member organizations throughout North America. FEI Behavioral Health, a for-profit company and social enterprise, is also under the FI umbrella. Families International is an impact-generating vehicle created by the Alliance to strengthen its efforts to realize the shared vision of a healthy society and strong communities for all children, adults, and families. Families International leverages the unique strengths of its affiliates by promoting collaboration, synergy, growth, creativity, and innovation.

Summary of Project

Families International is engaged in a significant transformation driven by current and future opportunities and demands for Families International to more closely connect its five companies. Families International is conducting intensive evaluation of its organizational and governance structure in order to create synergies and increase innovation, influence and impact. Families International and the Alliance also are reorganizing internally to drive the transformational strategy. The COO role at Families International was expanded to lead strategy efforts across all FI companies. Based on a series of discussions with key stakeholders, a new mission, vision, and set of goals and guiding principles were created that position Families International, its companies, and their national network as transformational agents within communities, strategically aligned around the larger purposes of poverty reduction, health improvement, and educational and employment success. The Alliance for Children and Families founded Families International as an integrated network of companies with one vision. The transformation work is focused on how to leverage their strategic competencies and amplify impact.

GREAT CIRCLE, ST. LOUIS, MO

Vincent Hillyer, President
Kathy O'Brien, Vice President, Chief Strategy Officer

Description of Organization

Great Circle's mission is to reshape vulnerable lives through a community of partners, teachers, and leaders, giving children and families the confidence to create bright futures. It is one of the largest behavioral health agencies in Missouri and touches the lives of 11,000 children and family members annually. Their community-based services include Day Treatment/Special Education, Family Reunification Services, Foster Care Case Management, Life Skills, Occupational Speech, Art and Music Therapies, Residential Program for Children with Autism, Residential Treatment, Respite Care, Self-Injury Treatment, and Therapeutic Recreation. All services are provided by Great Circle in one or more of the organization's four campuses across the state.

Summary of Transformational Project

Great Circle will incorporate the Baldrige Model of Performance Excellence to align and focus the entire organization, from the board of directors, to the nearly 900 staff on a single strategic vision that defines and implements institutionwide outcomes measurement, evidence-based practices, stakeholder feedback, and decision making. This transformational project will enhance Great Circle's effectiveness in fundamentally altering the life trajectory of children, youth and families served, enabling them to secure stable employment, maintain financial security, and effectively break cycles of poverty by fostering academic progress, developing skills for independent living, and improving interpersonal and long-term resilience skills.

HATHAWAY-SYCAMORES CHILD & FAMILY SERVICES, PASADENA, CA

William P. Martone, President and Chief Executive Officer
Rob Myers, Executive Vice President of Fund Development

Description of Organization

Founded in 1902, Hathaway-Sycamores offers children and families a variety of clinical, social, and mental health services, including residential treatment, in-home family support, outpatient mental health, foster care and adoptions, transitional independent living services for former foster youth, early childhood school readiness, psychological assessments, and grief and loss counseling.

Summary of Transformational Project

In the midst of real-time strategic planning and with the assistance of a consulting firm, members of management were trained in Six Sigma concepts and Baldrige criteria, which were then implemented and monitored by a transformation leadership team. The organization is now ready for the structure to address broader strategic initiatives with continued assistance from a consultant in completing the organizational strategic plan.

HEARTLAND FAMILY SERVICE, OMAHA, NE

John H. Jeanetta, President and Chief Executive Officer
Greg Ryan, Chief Strategy Officer

Description of Organization

Established in 1875, Heartland Family Service operates from 16 locations in east-central Nebraska and southwest Iowa. By integrating counseling, education, and support services through over 40 high-impact programs, the agency successfully addresses the wide array of issues that threaten the well-being of children, adults, and families.

Summary of Chief Strategy Officer Project

Heartland Family Service will build on their successes in strategic planning by adding a Chief Strategy Officer who will work with the Strategic Planning Task Force of the board to conduct an in-depth analysis of progress made against the agency's existing strategic plan, implement biannual environmental scanning, and better evaluate and plan for strategic threats and opportunities that emerge outside of the strategic plan. Customized reports and data visualization strategies will be implemented to leverage the information generated by these expanded strategic planning efforts and to further refine the agency's Balanced Scorecard performance management system.

HOLY FAMILY INSTITUTE, PITTSBURGH, PA

Sister Linda Yankoski, Chief Executive Officer
Glenn Wilson, Chief Strategy and Innovation Officer

Description of Organization

For more than 110 years, Holy Family Institute has provided a continuum of programs serving at-risk children, youth, and families, including residential treatment, mental health services, substance abuse, and education programs.

Summary of Chief Strategy Officer Project

Currently, Holy Family Institute is experiencing a shift in focus and funding from residential care to community-based services. Holy Family Institute will align knowledge management and strategy by utilizing the Human-Centered Design process to drive innovation. Human-Centered Design is a holistic system of addressing challenges and opportunities beginning with techniques to form a deep understanding of the needs and desires of all stakeholders, constituencies, and communities. The chief strategy officer will receive training to apply HCD and align the organization in support of the vision, strategies and plans that result from the implementation of this approach.

HOPELINK, REDMOND, WA

Marilyn Mason-Plunkett, President and Chief Executive Officer
Tim Johnstone, Chief Strategy Officer

Description of Organization

Hopelink serves homeless and low-income families, children, older adults and people with disabilities, providing critical basic needs such as food, emergency financial assistance, and shelter, as well as a number of transportation services. Hopelink also provides housing and asset-building services, including case management, adult education, financial literacy skills, and employment services to help its clients move toward permanent self-sufficiency.

Summary of Chief Strategy Officer Project

Hopelink is committed to create a chief strategy officer position to build capacity to coordinate and drive organizational change on a continuing basis. As with many nonprofits, senior leaders struggle to balance the demands of day-to-day operations with creating the capacity required to maintain a focus on mid- to long-term impact. The CSO will enable a change in the culture toward one that combines a business focus on results with the social service ethos of compassion for clients and community needs.

JEWISH FAMILY AND CHILDREN'S SERVICE, SARASOTA, FL

Rose Chapman, President Chief Executive Officer
Denise Roberts, Director of Special Projects

Description of Organization

Jewish Family and Children's Service (JFCS) serves low-income persons of all ages with school-based programs, parenting education, homelessness prevention, senior outreach, veterans' services, and counseling. In the past 7 years, services offered have increased by 300%, and the number of staff by 177%.

Summary of Transformational Project

With unprecedented growth, JFCS views this opportunity to build stronger teams and transform the current culture into one of shared ownership and responsibility. Forming a Strategy Team and utilizing a process of shared inquiry will build an understanding and a sense of ownership of mission and strategy. With the assistance of a consultant to implement the Denison Organizational Culture Survey, the agency will identify the culture, values, and strategies necessary to increase adaptability and to create a more widely shared mission, shared decision making, and increased consistency by committed employees.

JEWISH FAMILY AND CHILDREN'S SERVICE OF MINNEAPOLIS, MINNETONKA, MN

Judy Halper, Chief Executive Officer
Mari Forbush, Chief Operating Officer

Description of Organization

Jewish Family and Children's Service of Minneapolis (JFSC) is organized into three service areas: aging and disability services, career and community services, and clinical services. The core programming provides (a) an umbrella of services to seniors that help them to remain healthy and independent in their own homes, (b) career-related counseling, training, assistance, and support, and (c) counseling, mental health case management, and early childhood literacy.

Summary of Transformational Project

Jewish Family and Children's Service of Minneapolis (JFCS) has been responding to increasing needs in the community and the reality of decreasing resources. For continued success, the organization recognizes the need to create a new framework that continuously supports an organic, ground-up strategic perspective. Through a whole-scale change approach, JFCS will engage stakeholders at all levels to build staff capacity, increase organizational alignment, and incorporate a process for continuous quality improvement with the intent of having individuals and families prepared to succeed in life and able to lead vibrant and independent lives free from violence, poverty, and isolation.

KIDS CENTRAL, OCALA, FL

John Cooper, Chief Executive Officer
David DeStefano, Chief Strategy Officer

Description of Organization

Kids Central, Inc., is the private nonprofit selected by the Florida Department of Children and Families (DCF) as the lead agency responsible for the privatization of child protection services in Circuit 5. Kids Central's mission is to develop and manage a child-centered community-based system of care for abused, neglected, and abandoned children and their families in order to strengthen families and prevent them from entering the child welfare system. Kids Central firmly believes in its core values including that all children have the inalienable right to grow up safe, healthy, and fulfilled in families that love and nurture them. Services are provided with the vision of maintaining and strengthening the ties between children, families, and communities, while causing as little disruption as possible in their lives.

Summary of Transformational Project

A recent change in leadership at Kids Central has presented an opportunity to assess the organization and reevaluate strategic objectives, execution, and performance. The Florida Sterling Challenge, based on the nationally acclaimed Baldrige criteria, is an excellent approach for transitioning to a mature organization with the capacity to administer programs in a manner providing the greatest impact to our communities. Participation in the Challenge is expected to result in a strategically aligned organization with the capacity to provide enhanced services with greater impact and measurable results.

LEAKE AND WATTS SERVICES, YONKERS, NY

Alan Mucatel, Executive Director
Belinda Conway, Associate Executive Director and Chief Strategy Officer

Description of Organization

Founded in the 1830s, Leake and Watts is dedicated to impacting the lives of children, adults, and families through their child welfare programs, special education schools, early childhood education centers, and developmental disabilities services.

Summary of Chief Strategy Officer Project

With the completion of a 3-year strategic plan in October 2011, the addition of a CSO will provide a lead person for overseeing the implementation process, and thus increase the organization's capacity to test the current strategic plan, its initiatives, action, and performance against their mission and goals, as well as concurrently plan for future growth and sustainability.

NEIGHBORHOOD CENTERS, HOUSTON, TX

Angela Blanchard, President and Chief Executive Officer
Ray Chung, Chief Strategy Officer

Description of Organization

Neighborhood Centers, Inc., works directly with residents in emerging neighborhoods to discover their individual strengths, understand their ideas for improvement, and work in partnership to develop resources to benefit their community. Their work can be seen in six community centers, 22 senior locations, and numerous tax centers; at monthly citizenship forums, annual health fairs, and education rallies; and in a range of additional programming where they invest resources.

Summary of Chief Strategy Officer Project

Having recently undergone a comprehensive internal evaluation, Neighborhood Centers has identified six key characteristics—education, economic opportunity, health services, housing, community connectivity, and infrastructure—that are always present in strong, vibrant communities. A chief strategy officer will drive the implementation of these characteristics as strategic priorities for the agency.

PUBLIC HEALTH MANAGEMENT CORPORATION, PHILADELPHIA, PA

Richard J. Cohen, President and Chief Executive Officer
Tine Hansen-Turton, Chief Strategy Officer

Description of Organization

Public Health Management Corporation is a nonprofit public health institute that creates and sustains healthier communities. PHMC uses best practices to improve community health through direct service, partnership, innovation, policy, research, technical assistance, and a prepared workforce. PHMC has served its region since 1972.

Summary of Chief Strategy Officer Project

PHMC recently completed an 18-month strategic repositioning process that encompassed organizational realignment, restructuring of top-line management, and development of a new strategic plan. The new chief strategy officer position, held by Tine Hansen-Turton, is critical to this transformation, integrally contributing to its implementation, the achievement of strategic plan results, and facilitation of ongoing strategy development across the organization with a focus on smart, mission-led growth.

STARR COMMONWEALTH, ALBION, MI

Martin Mitchell, President and Chief Executive Officer
Elizabeth Carey, Executive Vice President and Chief Strategy and Administrative Services Officer

Description of Organization

For almost 100 years, Starr Commonwealth has served troubled children and their families, offering intervention and prevention, community-based, specialized residential programs and professional training and consultation services. Starr is poised to share its vast accumulation of knowledge and expertise with every community worldwide.

Summary of Transformational Project

Starr Commonwealth has invested in creating a chief strategy officer position and completed the planning phase for a new strategic direction that focuses heavily on growth and increased impact on children and families. As implementation begins, this project will help better define and deploy the role of the current CSO while organizing strategic implementation throughout the entire organization.

THE CHILDREN'S HOME OF CINCINNATI, CINCINNATI, OH

Ellen Katz, President and Chief Executive Officer
Shannon Starkey, Vice President of Strategy Development

Description of Organization

The Children's Home of Cincinnati operates over 20 educational and/or mental health treatment programs for children and youth of all ages through a wide array of intensive day programs and community-based services. Throughout its history, the Children's Home has responded to the needs of the community with flexibility and innovation, while maintaining a commitment to the welfare of children and their families—especially low-income children and youth. Their breadth of educational programming includes early childhood care; therapeutic elementary and high schools; educational evaluations for children, teens, and young adults; mental health treatment programs, including counseling and case management; early childhood mental health consultations; and therapeutic programming for youth having co-occurring substance abuse and mental health diagnoses.

Summary of Transformational Project

The Children's Home of Cincinnati's transformational project will strengthen its capacity to ensure that 90% of the children and youth served are annually on track for school success. This goal will be achieved in several ways: by increasing staff's sense of shared contribution, vision and purpose; strengthening continuous quality improvement practices, including developing a customized data system; and increasing the number of children who achieve improved behavior and social and emotional wellness, thus strengthening their academic opportunities. As a rigorous and accountable process, our strategic implementation includes quarterly audits of key benchmarks that will build our capacity to serve more children and empower them with the necessary skills to achieve age-appropriate success in school.

THE CHILDREN'S VILLAGE, DOBBS FERRY, NY

Jeremy C. Kohomban, President and Chief Executive Officer
Deborah Finley-Troup, Vice President for Human Resources

Description of Organization

For 160 years The Children's Village has served at-risk youth by providing short-term residential care, runaway and homeless shelters, street outreach, adoptive and foster homes, and immigration services.

Summary of Transformational Project

Experiencing the shift from residential programs to a continuum of community-based services, The Children's Village will develop and implement a strategic plan to align their image, culture, and practices with their current focus, and engage all levels of the organization to contribute to this transformation.

THE OPPORTUNITY ALLIANCE, SOUTH PORTLAND, ME

Michael J. Tarpinian, President and Chief Executive Officer
Elizabeth Banwell, Chief Strategy Officer

Description of Organization

In November of 2011, PROP (People's Regional Opportunity Program), a Community Action agency, and Youth Alternatives Ingraham unified their missions to form the Opportunity Alliance. The new organization has integrated its programs to serve children, youth, adults, and seniors, as well as individuals, families, and communities, throughout Maine. The merger will allow The Opportunity Alliance to deliver maximum mission impact with lower administrative costs by efficiently partnering with state and federal government agencies, other nonprofit entities, community groups, individuals, and consumers and their families.

Summary of Chief Strategy Officer Project

By means of the merger, the Opportunity Alliance has been able to harness the missions, values, and service components of both PROP and Youth Alternatives Ingraham. Programming has thus become more varied and complex, and senior staff members have taken on expanded job responsibilities and are now occupied with day-to-day operations. With the hiring of a chief strategy officer, the agency will be able to take a comprehensive, long-term look at challenges and opportunities in the larger community that the current structure only allows to be added piecemeal.

THE VILLAGE NETWORK, SMITHVILLE, OH

Richard Graziano, President and Chief Executive Officer
Dave Paxton, Chief Strategy Officer

Description of Organization

The Village Network partners with 50 Ohio counties and has locations in 14 cities. The agency provides services for abused and neglected boys and girls who have behavioral and mental health concerns. It operates under a Continuum of Care model, providing residential treatment, day treatment, treatment foster care, community-based juvenile court intervention, respite care, and alternative school programs. The Village Network's Sexually Reactive and Juvenile Sex Offender programs were the first programs certified by the Ohio Department of Youth Services (ODYS).

Summary of Chief Strategy Officer Project

In spring 2011, stimulated by the Alliance's webinars and research, the Village Network made a decision to hire a chief strategy officer to enhance the organization's capacity and community impact. The CSO would secure commitment to the current strategic plan, assess the current environment, facilitate ongoing strategy development, and provide greater integration of services and activities with clients and community partners. Actions planned are community forums and initiating a measurement system of community impact.

VILLA OF HOPE, ROCHESTER, NY

Christina Gullo, President and Chief Executive Officer

Description of Organization

Villa of Hope programs offer a range of services to youth and families through mental health counseling, addiction services, life skills development, and a specialized eating disorders program. Services are provided through at-home and in-school community-based and residential service programs.

Summary of Transformational Project

Villa of Hope envisions being driven by the needs of the youth and families they serve and is currently realigning program services to meet those needs. A local consultant, in tandem with the strategy team, will help create a balanced scorecard and strategic direction. This strategic plan will be implemented and executed at all levels of the organization. Leadership staff will be trained in crucial conversations and executive coaching tools to be innovative leaders.

VOLUNTEERS OF AMERICA OF MINNESOTA, MINNEAPOLIS, MN

Paula Hart, President and Chief Executive Officer
Jim Bettendorf, Chief Strategy Officer

Description of Organization

Serving the state since 1896, Volunteers of America-Minnesota helps people gain self-reliance, dignity, and hope through a wide variety of health and human services. Each year, Volunteers of America serves more than 26,500 Minnesotans in three impact areas: (a) children, youth, families, (b) seniors and people who have special needs, and (c) adults in community reentry.

Summary of Chief Strategy Officer Project

While the agency has grown significantly over the previous decade, attention was not focused on creating a collective vision of impact, a comprehensive strategy, or a common approach to data-driven decision making. The organization's first organizational assessment of quality using the Baldrige framework provided feedback, focus, and guidance on building strength through a comprehensive approach to strategy development. This groundwork has readied the agency for a chief strategy officer position.

FIGURE A.1 Alliance Strategy Counts pilot site map.

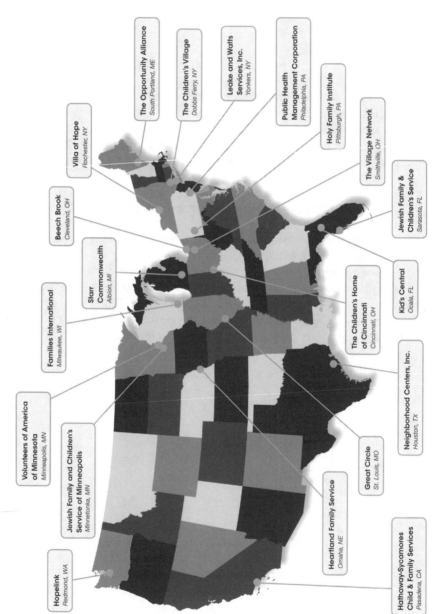

Index